W9-DBA-503

Does It Pay
to Advertise?

Does It Pay to Advertise?

Cases Illustrating Successful Brand Advertising

John Philip Jones
Newhouse School of Public
Communications,
Syracuse University

Foreword by
Sir David Orr

LEXINGTON BOOKS
An Imprint of Macmillan, Inc.
NEW YORK

Maxwell Macmillan Canada
TORONTO

Maxwell Macmillan International
NEW YORK   OXFORD   SINGAPORE   SYDNEY

Lexington Books
An Imprint of Macmillan, Inc.
866 Third Avenue, New York, N.Y. 10022

Maxwell Macmillan Canada, Inc.
1200 Eglinton Avenue East
Suite 200
Don Mills, Ontario M3C 3N1

Macmillan, Inc. is part of the Maxwell Communication
Group of Companies.

Printed in the United States of America

printing number
4   5   6   7   8   9   10

Library of Congress Cataloging-in-Publication Data

Jones, John Philip.
    Does it pay to advertise? : cases illustrating successful brand advertising / John Philip
Jones : foreword by Sir David Orr.
        p.   cm.
    Includes index.
    ISBN 0–669–15897–6 (alk. paper)
    1. Advertising—Brand name products—United States—Case studies.
I. Title.
HF5823.J717   1989
659.1—dc19
                                                                                        86–46382
                                                                                              CIP

It has been our experience here that advertising that produced results and increased sales, regardless of its expense, is inexpensive. On the other hand, advertising that does not increase sales, no matter how cheap it may be, is a drag on the business.

—George Washington Hill, quoted by Martin Mayer in *Madison Avenue, U.S.A.*

To Harold F. Clark, Jr.

Contents

Figures and Tables

Preface

People have been writing books about advertising for almost a century, and the rate at which such books are published has increased during the past few decades at a high, if not quite spectacular, rate. This suggests that there is much public interest in advertising. Indeed, one suspects that there is a good deal more interest in books about advertising than in advertisements themselves—an emphasis that to some extent is wrongheaded, because, as has been pointed out by many knowledgeable observers, the best way to study advertising is to study specific advertising campaigns. (As the reader will soon discover, this book *is* about specific advertising campaigns.)

Of the many books written about advertising, some edge our knowledge of the subject forward, others do not, and still others move us backward as they continue to propagate myths and half-truths. Although advertising is an intrinsically interesting subject and has some economic importance to the working of the capitalist economy, many people greatly exaggerate its social influence. Nevertheless, enormous amounts of money are spent on advertising. In 1987, advertising in the main media, excluding expenditure on promotions, accounted for $67 billion in the United States, or 1.5 percent of the gross national product. In view of such a massive—and continuous—level of investment, it is in the public interest that everyone connected with advertising should use it with maximum efficiency, or at least with as little inefficiency as possible.

As an important part of this endeavor, many people, the author included, believe that it is the task of everyone who studies the subject seriously, for pleasure or for professional benefit, to make an effort to increase our understanding of it. This means pursuing inquiries rigorously and with an open mind, and it means weaning ourselves as far away as possible from the many preconceptions we all hold.

Advertising as a subject of study is characterized by an extraordinary diversity: in the variety of problems to be solved and the creative solutions to those problems; in the variations in the force we apply and the combinations of media in which we deploy that force; and in the large number of (sometimes misleading) methods of evaluating advertising's effectiveness.

These subjects are the day-to-day occupations and preoccupations—indeed, the dominant forces in the lives—of tens of thousands of talented men and women in the United States and other countries. In view of the amount of imagination, analytical horsepower, and energy deployed in the advertising business, it is not surprising that we have acquired a reasonably extensive knowledge of parts of it. We know with fair certainty perhaps a third of everything we would need to know in a perfect world. A prominent surgeon in a teaching hospital once told the author that humankind's knowledge of medical science is of an approximately similar order. Yet the difference between the two subjects—setting aside the obvious disparity in their relative importance—is that in medical research, the scientific method employed has substantially eliminated myth and folklore, whereas in advertising, a significant proportion of the things many academicians and practitioners believe to be true are in fact wrong.

In many scientific disciplines, knowledge has for centuries been advanced by the inductive process. Facts—sometimes important ones but sometimes very small ones indeed—have been assembled laboriously until any underlying patterns that existed were gradually encouraged to emerge. The author's efforts to understand advertising, which have taken place in both a professional and an academic environment, have convinced him that the only way that we can dispel errors and increase our reliable knowledge of the subject is to operate in a similar way: to study the particular and to tease general patterns out of a multiplicity of specifics.

This book is a small step toward that goal. Although other collections of case studies have been published in the past, this book differs in two respects. First, an effort is made here to draw specific *and general* lessons from the sample of nineteen brands whose campaigns are described and evaluated. Second, all the work reviewed in the cases was carried out by a single advertising agency, J. Walter Thompson (JWT). This extraordinary organization, which has operated for 124 years, has, not surprisingly, built an enviable corpus of experience and acquired much worthwhile knowledge on its own account, some of which it has synthesized and today uses in its planning systems.

Between 1953 and 1980 (with a two-year gap), the author worked for JWT. During that long period, it is inevitable that some of the things that the agency knows about the advertising field would rub off on him. This knowledge has enabled him not only to write about a small sample of nineteen cases but also to generalize about the advertising business from a wider empirical base than that offered by the data in these cases alone. In fact, the cases serve to represent, illustrate, and highlight the substantial body of knowledge that JWT possesses.

The first purpose of this book is to make some of that knowledge available to students of marketing and advertising—students who may be in universities but who are equally likely to be earning their living as advertising men and women. The second purpose is to try to make these people understand that we need to know much more about the subject. If a good number of them were to accept the point that theories must be subjected to empirical validation, they could use their talents and energies to sweep away the detritus. And if each of these searchers for truth were also to add a few grains of corn to our partly-filled granary of knowledge, advertising would rapidly become a much more intellectually respectable subject than it is today.

Prologue

By Burt Manning
Chairman and Chief Executive Officer, J. Walter Thompson Company

This book is a serious empirical study of real brands. The author has benefited from the insights provided by many present (and past) clients of J. Walter Thompson. Substantial numbers of my colleagues in the agency have also helped—creative people, account managers, and researchers. All have been deeply and continuously involved with the advertising for the brands described in these pages. As the author states, the book could not have been possible without the unstinting help of these busy people, who between them provided the basic materials with which the author worked. With these materials, Professor Jones has constructed an impressive edifice.

The author's hypothesis was that a detailed and informed study of a cross section of brands would probably yield what he calls general patterns. As the work progressed, the evidence started to accumulate that such patterns were indeed beginning to emerge.

Many of them are described in this book. And while they are not necessarily supported by data that statisticians would call robust, very many of them certainly strike a chord with people who have spent time in the marketing and advertising of consumer goods. As the author says when describing such patterns, they are both impressionistic and thought-provoking. This also suggests that there is need for an even broader study of cases than can be carried out realistically in a single book like this.

It should be clear that although many executives at the various client firms and at the agency provided the basic working data, the analysis and interpretation are entirely Professor Jones's. He is well known to JWT, because of the twenty-five years he spent working for the agency. But he is now an independent academic. He has always had views of his own, and he has always been prepared to be conjectural, even provocative.

JWT shares many of his opinions, including a number of those expressed in this book. But the author would not be a successful academic, nor would this work be a worthwhile study of brands in the marketplace, if the book were merely a reflection of the agency's opinions and feelings. JWT does not, therefore, see eye to eye with Professor Jones over everything he says.

We do, however, recommend that readers give the opinions appearing here a fair evaluation. Readers can then weigh these opinions and make up their own minds about the sometimes complex and controversial—but also generally very important—matters discussed in this book.

Foreword

By Sir David Orr
Chairman, Unilever Ltd., 1974–1982

I am pleased to write the foreword to this book because it is about brands. It is primarily about the contribution of advertising in building and sustaining brands. For Unilever (the company I served for thirty-five years), brands are the company's major asset, the visible embodiment of all its strengths. As a former brand manager for Lux Toilet Soap in the United Kingdom, I am familiar with the requirement that John Philip Jones describes of keeping an established brand up-to-date. Unilever as a group is itself familiar mainly to the business and investor communities, but its consumer brands are household names throughout the world. Lux and Timotei are two examples of Unilever's international brands that are discussed in this book, but there are others, such as Lipton Yellow Label Tea and Blue Band margarine. Unilever also has many local brands, particularly in food, such as Oxo in the United Kingdom (an example also discussed in this book).

A brand thrives only by being different. It is always a mixture of what in this book is described as "rational" and "nonrational" benefits. It is an assurance of consistent quality to consumers and to retailers. A brand's only justification is that it provides what the customer wants better than the competition does. In a market economy, the purchaser will decide what benefits he or she values most highly and will vote with his or her dollars. As this book points out, at least half of all new product introductions are failures (and in some product fields, the rate of failure is much higher). Objective assessment of the relative merits of products that fail is neither possible nor relevant; market success and profit are the criteria in a competitive economy.

The mid-1980s have seen a resurgence of faith in and commitment to brands. This is in contrast to the late 1970s, when higher inflation and other economic difficulties led to a greater cost consciousness on the part of producers and consumers. The late 1970s were also a period of relatively strong retail competition, based on price. There was a greater concentration on cost cutting, exemplified by the emergence in the United States of generics and some loss of commitment to sustaining the major brands. Now, following a period of at times painful adjustment, manufacturers have recovered their confidence in themselves and in their brands. The major manufacturers are leaner, more flexible, and committed to value and excellence in their areas of strength.

Branding is possible in virtually all product categories, as this book shows. The categories include services as well as goods, for businesses as well as for personal customers. There is no essential difference between manufacturer brands and private brands. Manufacturer brands are specialist, focusing on a narrow range of products but covering the distribution spectrum. Private-label brands are focused on a set of outlets but are spread across product categories.

Just as major brands collectively have shown that they can survive and prosper, so have individual brands, as this book demonstrates, refuted the concept of life cycles for products. The decline, or "milking," phase of the life cycle exists only as a self-fulfilling prophecy. A brand is a wasting asset, one that must be replaced and rejuvenated if it is to thrive. Provided that it is kept up-to-date as a product, by technical innovation and updating, and that its communication is kept relevant, it can be sustained for decades or more.

Yet while a brand can, if nurtured, evolve and prosper over large time periods, the transfer over geographic borders is more problematical. As noted, a multinational corporation like Unilever will have a mixture of international and national brands. The transfer of products and associated know-how between countries is a key source of economies for a multinational marketing company. There is a whole spectrum of degree of feasibility of transfer. At one extreme, the product, its positioning, and its presentation, including its name, can all be used in a number of countries—Colgate Toothpaste is an example. In most cases, there will be a degree of tailoring, so that it might be the product concept—for example, instant soup or low-fat spreads—that is transferred and presented with a variety of names. At the other end of the spectrum, there are relatively few products for which there is no scope to learn from experience elsewhere.

A brand is a result of the combination of the familiar elements in the marketing mix. Of those elements, advertising, on which this book focuses, is the most visible. It is, however, merely the tip of an iceberg of activity. It is nonetheless a key feature of the Western way of life, both reflecting and influencing our culture.

A successful product, a strong, profitable brand, is a complex mixture of art and science, of organization and creativity. In this mixture the roles of company and advertising agency are closely intertwined. Nonetheless, a key contribution from the producer company is organization to deliver the product, embodying, for instance, R&D, manufacturing technology, packaging, sales, and distribution. The advertising agency's particular input is its creative flair. Its role is to enable the company to communicate to the customer the distinctive difference of its brand. It translates the difference into terms that the customer can understand.

In principle, advertising could be an in-house function, and for a long time Unilever owned an advertising agency. There are, however, a number of advantages to the advertising agency's being independent. The agency will accumulate a breadth of vision across a number of product fields. It can provide a pool of creativity, and it runs less risk of becoming stale or blinkered. It also, frankly, thrives on a very different culture, as John Philip Jones implies; the product company, whether in goods or services, is always more structured and hierarchical than the advertising agency should be. The producer will also be steeped in its product, whereas the agency is more sensitive to wider trends in the market. Both the producer and the advertising agent gain from being separate and specialized.

In the 1980s, producer companies have drawn the boundaries of their activities much more tightly. This focus applies both to their target market and to the functions they choose to perform in-house. There is a clearer recognition that a number of functions can be carried out more effectively by a specialist third party.

This book focuses on the role of advertising and of the agency that creates it. Advertising is a major element of costs, equaling or exceeding the profit margin on many products. We have known (ever since Lord Leverhulme's famous statement) that much of what is spent on advertising is wasted. Only by analyzing the contribution of advertising in different circumstances can we hope to make our advertising spending more productive. I welcome this book as a step along that path.

Acknowledgments

The author is extremely grateful for the cooperation and help of all the advertisers whose brands are featured in this book. In the majority of cases, executives working on those brands have scrutinized the manuscript carefully, checked the facts, and given the author their invariably wise suggestions for improving the interpretation and argument.

He has also received considerable cooperation and patient assistance from more than fifty present and past members of J. Walter Thompson. Without their help, there would not have been a book, and the author is wholeheartedly in their debt.

He would also like to thank Dr. Simon Broadbent, Dr. Arthur Ecker (a member of the medical profession and a connoisseur of the English language, who suggested the title), Professor Andrew Ehrenberg, and Mr. William M. Weilbacher.

The author's wife, Wendy, despite her active professional and personal life, made time to type every single draft of this book, a task she undertook with punctilious accuracy. She also gave the author continuous advice about the book's content and writing style: detailed suggestions that in every instance pointed the way to a better manuscript.

1
Signposts

> You can get far more lost in a maze of tracks than you will ever get traveling cross-country (that is, always provided you have a map and a compass.)
> —Bernard Fergusson[1]

Two Books In One

We have set ourselves two separate tasks in putting this book together. First, we have examined a number of brands—nineteen in all—and concentrated on trying to demonstrate the contribution of their advertising during at least a short period of their history. These studies are all freestanding and independent of one another, and we have drawn a number of specific advertising lessons from each. We hope that these cases will be helpful to people who are interested in the specific product fields covered and who can therefore use the book selectively if they wish to.

The second task is more ambitious. In the way we have selected and written these cases, we have tried to demonstrate a number of general principles about marketing and advertising, principles that have themselves emerged from a broader and deeper body of empirical knowledge than that provided by the advertising history of the nineteen brands described here. These principles have come out of J. Walter Thompson's general experience of the marketing and advertising fields, an experience that to some extent has been shared by the author as a result of the twenty-five years he spent working for the agency, managing the advertising for a variety of different brands and products.

It is obviously unwise to generalize from a sample of nineteen brands on their own, even though they may cover a reasonably representative range of markets. Nevertheless, we believe that these cases are strong enough individually to highlight and illustrate JWT's much wider, deeper, and more longitudinal professional experience.

The reader will note the overlap and duplication between the various lessons from the individual cases; this is fragmentary evidence of the emergence of general patterns. In joining us in the search for such patterns, readers are encouraged, in the words of Bernard Fergusson, to travel "cross-country." In this introductory chapter, we shall try to provide the necessary "map and compass," or, as we prefer to say, set of signposts that point toward some of the more important lessons emerging from the cases.

Our nineteen brands cover eighteen product categories and are dealt with in eighteen chapters (chapters 2 through 19). They include eleven brands of packaged goods in ten different product fields. Going through them in the order of the chapters, our packaged goods are wines and spirits (two separate brands), cheese, mouthwash, toilet soap, coffee, bouillon cubes, pet food, soft drinks, confectionery, and shampoo. We also cover one product category not normally classified as packaged goods but sharing many of their characteristics: cameras and film; this we shall call a quasi-packaged-goods field. We deal with two automotive categories, cars and tires (plus a number of spin-offs); two financial markets, credit cards and banking; and three other wide-ranging but interesting fields, gemstones, pest protection, and military recruitment. Each of the eighteen chapters is devoted to a product category, or, to be more precise, one brand in each category (although one of the chapters covers more than one brand).

The reader should be aware that our coverage of markets is not comprehensive.[2] (We review some of the larger omissions in the last section of this chapter.) Nevertheless, those we do cover are reasonably representative of the product fields in which advertising is considered an important part of the marketing mix. And in particular, our selection of eleven packaged goods or quasi-packaged goods out of our total of eighteen product fields is approximately in line with the types of business handled by major agencies, although JWT's clients tend to be weighted rather above the average toward packaged goods (a matter discussed in chapter 20).

As another representation of JWT's business, our cases have a fairly wide geographical spread. Nine chapters describe U.S. experience and are the work of five separate offices of the agency; one case is based in Canada; five are based in Europe (three in the United Kingdom, one in Germany, and one in Spain); and the remaining three—gemstones (DeBeers), toilet soap (Lux), and shampoo (Timotei)—are fully international in scope. There is, incidentally, an interesting contrast between these last three cases and Kraft P'tit Québec, which is market-specific; we discuss the reasons for that specificity in the text of the latter case.

It may surprise some readers that there could be anything at all in common among the elements of this seemingly heterogeneous collection of categories, brands, and countries. We have, however, found that as our work progressed, a surprisingly large number of commonalities emerged, some of them in themselves rather surprising.

In order to prime the reader with what to look for, we shall now list twenty points. These are essentially independent from one another, although there are many interconnections. Readers familiar with the work of J. Walter

Thompson will be aware of many of these points. Some are simple descriptions that most readers will not dispute too much. But others will be regarded by some readers outside JWT as contentious. We ask such readers to suspend their disbelief temporarily and to treat these more difficult and controversial points as hypotheses. They will be described here with minimal detail, but readers will find that, if they keep them in the back of their minds while studying the individual cases, the cases will yield repeated examples to confirm the hypotheses, perhaps not comprehensively, but at least in a broad, suggestive way that will stimulate thought. Some of our hypotheses are discussed more fully in chapters 20, 21, and 22, which follow the cases.

Our twenty points are collected into five groups—generalizations about markets, brands, advertising, budgets and media, and research—and numbered in a single series.

Generalizations About Markets

1. Maturity Equals Flatness. The concept of stationary market conditions recurs frequently in this book. It applies extremely widely to packaged goods, at least in the medium (three to five year) term; small growth overall is characteristic of most of the packaged goods markets in this collection, with the major exception of soft drinks (the Slice case). Advertising—either the efforts of individual brands or the combined effort of all the brands in a market—seems to be able to do little to stimulate total market expansion. (Again, there are limited exceptions—Oxo and Smarties, or, rather, relatively new competitors to these brands that acted as temporary stimuli to their markets.) Marketing and advertising activities are in most circumstances a market share game. Many markets other than packaged goods are, however, still growing, although such growth is often accompanied by volatility. The growth in different types of markets is illustrated in chapter 20.

The lack of buoyancy of packaged goods leads to an increase in the importance of discriminating arguments in all advertising for such products (see point 10). The relative rarity of expanding markets is also important in its influence on the direction of agencies' new business efforts: the best long-term potential is obviously in fields other than packaged goods.

2. A Growing Heterogeneity. In contradiction to the received wisdom of microeconomics, markets as they develop over time do not become more homogeneous; they grow more heterogeneous. This is the result of the operation of oligopolistic competition, the most common market organization for consumer goods, an organization in which manufacturers constantly try to steal a march on one another by searching for unexploited market segments. Once a brand has established a new segment, it is followed almost immediately by competitive brands from other manufacturers. (Active awareness of and response to the competition are among the most salient characteristics of oligopoly.)

This process means that as markets mature, the often huge market shares of pioneer brands become rapidly eroded, although many of those leaders settle down in a highly profitable and stable 15 percent to 25 percent bracket (rather less, in larger countries). In many cases, however, the franchise is in turn fragmented as a result of the introduction of product varieties, and this situation can lead to a dangerous splitting of advertising budgets. (A dominant brand is in any event somewhat vulnerable; witness Nescafé in Spain.) The growth in the heterogeneity of markets is influenced by a secular tendency toward a relative increase in the amount of trade and consumer promotions and a countervailing relative decline in consumer advertising. This increase in promotions has been caused in the main by another manifestation of oligopoly, that in the retail field, with an accompanying increase in the size and bargaining power of individual retail chains, which in turn forces the increase in trade rebates etc.

This tendency (like that described in point 1) leads to an increasing emphasis on discriminating advertising arguments.

Generalizations About Brands

Although we shall avoid elementary descriptions of the most important characteristics of brands, a few points are especially germane to the cases in this book.[3]

3. Few New Brands Succeed. This book describes nineteen successful brands, most of which are household names in the countries in which they are marketed. Looking at such a list, it is difficult to comprehend that the names represent a tiny minority, perhaps only 5 percent of new brands that end up as long-term successes. We mean not successes in achieving absolute market leadership but more often a lower order of success in seizing and holding respectably large (5 percent to 10 percent), stable, and profitable brand shares. Such odds against success are daunting. And as markets become more heterogeneous, these odds do not get any better, except in one special and limiting circumstance. If an innovative market segment is exploited by a new brand, competitors that follow the pioneer—if they in turn are functionally effective and differentiated—can often secure a franchise, but they do so with a market share less than half that of the original brand. (The Smarties case, which describes the test-market experience of M & Ms in Britain, provides something of an exception to the normal share achieved by a second brand.)

We believe that the success of a new brand stems from the concatenation of a large number of factors—well planned and imaginative marketing inputs plus certain favorable exogenous circumstances. These points are well illustrated by the Slice case.

Research has its uses in helping us to develop new brands, but it provides us with virtually no help in forecasting whether or not they will succeed.

4. An Indefinitely Long Life. This book contains many examples of large and very long-lived brands that today hold buoyant (or better) shares of stationary total markets. (*Kodak,* Listerine, Lux, and Oxo are but four striking examples, and there are many others outside the brands cited in this book.) Such successes have been the result of a continuous process of nurturing by both manufacturers and advertising agencies, particularly in matters of product and packaging improvements and of advertising and promotions.

Marketing history nevertheless contains numerous examples of once-strong brands that have dwindled and died, a matter that warrants brief explanation here. The reason in many cases is that such brands have become functionally outmoded or else have not been transformed in the radical direction that the market may have demanded. On other occasions, the demise has been the result of simple inattention and underinvestment that, not infrequently, have been influenced by manufacturers' and agencies' belief in life-cycle theory, a model taught widely in universities and believed almost as widely in marketing circles. This pessimistic and counterproductive doctrine of inevitable decline is self-fulfilling, because it generally leads to the kind of inattention and lack of investment in brands that will indeed eventually bring about their collapse.

This is all a matter of first importance, for the good reason that successful brands are in all events rare and should therefore be protected to maximize the value of the manufacturer's investment in developing them (including compensation for the wasted investment in failures). Successful brands are also the source of important scale economies (see points 6 and 18).

5. Branding in Every Market. The brand concept has a relevance far beyond the realm of repeat-purchase packaged goods with which we most commonly associate it. In this book readers will make the acquaintance of brands in markets as disparate as credit cards and pest-protection systems. The requirements for branding are (a) the ability to differentiate a product or service in functional terms, (b) reasonably wide public availability (that is, by an effective distributional system), and (c) the capacity to build added values through consumer advertising.

6. Scale Economies. There are manufacturing economies in production and packaging resulting from bulk purchasing and long production runs; there are also distributional and sales-force economies, as well as quantity rebates in buying advertising media. These are all rather obvious points. But there are equally important and more subtle economies, including those connected with the capacity of large brands to stimulate progressively greater frequency of purchase and repurchase. This is a function of such brands' size, and it is related to the strength of the added values built by past consumer advertising. There is also a second major scale economy related to the advertising alone (see point 18). One of the results—but not the only one—of all these economies is the ability of large brands to justify premium prices in the marketplace.

The existence of such scale economies means quite simply that large brands are, per unit of weight or volume, significantly more profitable than small brands are. This is the best possible reason for manufacturers to make great efforts to preserve such brands' market shares and to avoid succumbing to the allure of new ventures, if the opportunity cost of doing so is to neglect the established brand properties that are the source of the scale economies described here.

7. Added Values. The concept of added values is a familiar one. The notion of psychological values being added on top of functional values as the main difference between a brand and an unbranded product has been described in the work of James Webb Young and other analysts.[4]

Young, a JWT copywriter of great distinction and one of the agency's founding fathers, first introduced the idea of added values as one of the five ways in which he believed advertising to work. The other ways are spreading news, familiarizing, reminding, and overcoming inertia, all clearly and engagingly described in one of the simplest (and in some respects the best) books ever written about advertising, *How to Become an Advertising Man,* based on Young's teaching at the University of Chicago.[5]

Young implies (though he does not make the point comprehensively) that the five roles of advertising vary in importance according to the stage of a brand's growth (for example, spreading news has an obvious relevance for launches and restages). For ongoing and stable brands, advertising-created added values resemble a capital investment in that they repay their cost on a continuous basis. Acting in conjunction with consumer satisfaction with a brand's functional properties, they confirm and increase repeat purchase, which is the key to its long-term profitability, and in this process they enable the advertising to operate with an ever-increasing productivity. We strongly suggest that creating added values is the single most important function that advertising performs. And it does so on a much wider scale than solely in the field of fast-moving consumer goods. In fact, added values are as ubiquitous as brands themselves (which is not surprising, since added values are essentially what create brands).

Generalizations About Advertising

8. The Creative Content is the Heart. The effectiveness of advertising depends on three variables: the creative content of the campaign, the budget deployed, and the choice and phasing of the media. As noted, we believe emphatically that building added values is the prime creative task, and advertising's major contribution to brands. Hence the overall supremacy of the creative role.

It cannot, however, be denied that a creatively effective campaign can be emasculated if the budget and media are deficient, though in the real world, budgetary and media weaknesses are less common than creative weaknesses. Clients and agencies employ fairly well tested pragmatic guidelines in budgetary and media planning, which are anyway more systematized procedures than the actual writing of advertisements. Moreover, even if the budget and media plans are less than optimal, a campaign with a cutting edge can often have a limited effect, whereas, if the campaign itself is deficient, everything is lost, despite the strength of budget and media.

An advertising campaign can work only if it brings about some intellectual or emotional engagement with its audience. Cognitive experiments have demonstrated persuasively that selective perception exists and that people notice advertisements but subconsciously screen most of them from their fuller attention. An advertisement can therefore work only if it operates at a sometimes subtle level, to lure and to seduce. And the number of people upon whom an individual advertisement will have an effect is likely to be rather small in most circumstances. (But it is the repeat business from such people that builds the manufacturer's sales and profits.)

The major reason that individual advertisements influence only relatively small numbers of consumers is the reluctance of most people to waste their time with advertising, which they regard as a matter of low priority. The problem with television is not so much physical zapping as mental zapping, that is, switching off attention. The problem with print media is the instinctive urge to turn the page.

There are, however, three important circumstances in which advertising will get looked at. The first is when people are shopping around, mostly but not always for goods or services with a high ticket price, and are prepared to use advertising to help them compare the alternatives. Second is the relatively rare circumstance in which an advertisement is looked upon as good entertainment. Such entertainment must be relevant to the brand if the advertisement is to be successful and must not stale with repetition.

The third circumstance, however, is the most common of the three. One of the things we know with fair certainty about advertising is that users of a brand will pay more attention to advertisements for it than nonusers will—a result again of selective perception. This may be the reason that advertising for large brands (those with high consumer penetration—more users—to provide a wider scope in which advertising can have an effect) is generally more productive than is advertising for small brands.[6]

Paradoxically, although the creative content is the single most important element in any advertising, it is the variable about which we know the least. By a change of viewpoint, however, we can make a strong, albeit negative, hypothesis about it. This book contains examples of a wide range of different creative styles, all of which have been effective in the marketplace. It is therefore evident that no single creative formula has a monopoly in generating sales, despite the fact that important agencies have in the past associated themselves with such formulas. By *creative formula* we refer, for instance, to the techniques of the "Unique Selling Proposition," "Slice of Life," "Brand Image," "Reason-Why," "Long-Copy," Photo Animation and Computer Graphics, Humor, Emotion, and other fashionable devices that the advertising business has promulgated, with predictable regularity, over many decades.

We do not deny that certain techniques may be more widely successful for certain types of products and services than for others. But it would need a very extensive empirical study to demonstrate this point, and we are not sure that the findings would have much practical use. Creative ideas are not generated by a study of predictable patterns; the creative genius lies in its ability to create unpredictable patterns.

We must also make it clear that research (as with the launch of new products) is of little help to us in forecasting which campaigns will succeed. Equally disheartening, empirical study has shown us that the judgment of advertising experts about the selling power of campaigns is also rather inadequate, except in determining which advertisements will be noticed.[7] But we know, again with virtual certainty, that noticeability and selling power are uncorrelated.[8]

9. The Connection Between the Creative Process and the Research Process. Although market research is treated later in this discussion (point 19), we think it is important to raise now the endemic difficulty of using research fruitfully in connection with the creative process: to stimulate advertising ideas. There is the constant danger that the rigidity and deadening weight of many research methods will discourage creative endeavor and extinguish originality.

The Planning Cycle, an analytical device originated by Stephen King of JWT London and used in many offices of the agency for almost two decades, is a way of separating the five phases involved in writing and running advertising campaigns. Its most important feature is the way in which it helps us to describe the roles of the creative and research processes during each of these five phases. This in turn leads us to consider the best types of research to use in each phase thereby avoiding a reliance on any single, inflexible technique.

As figure 1–1 shows, the Planning Cycle comprises five simple (sometimes deceptively simple) questions intended to guide a brand through the process of planning, exposing, and evaluating a new advertising campaign.

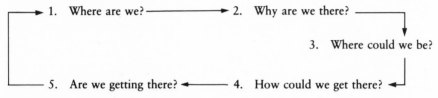

Figure 1–1. The Planning Cycle

The first two questions, "Where are we?" and "Why are we there?" call for a barrage of longitudinal data describing the position of the brand in the market and the reasons for this position. The information needed is quantitative and qualitative, mostly the former. The purpose of the data collection and analysis is to enable us to draw up the brand's advertising strategy.

The third and fourth questions, "Where could we be?" and "How could we get there?" are concerned with generating, refining, and evaluating creative ideas. Various qualitative techniques are helpful (for example, focus groups to stimulate ideas and to rank-order alternatives, and individual "depth" interviews to evaluate their communication). The main use of the research at these stages is to help the creative process in a "green thumb" way, encouraging us to move in promising directions and turning us away from alternatives that seem to have obvious or potential problems. (In the United States, the fourth stage often calls for the use of quantitative copytesting, a device generally rejected in Europe because of the skepticism of European research practitioners on methodological grounds).[9]

The fifth question, "Are we getting there?" concentrates attention on evaluating the campaign in the marketplace, with the object of improving its effectiveness in the future. This stage encompasses the use of various types of tracking studies.

An important feature of the Planning Cycle is that the questions follow a sequence and are in a loop, which tells us that when we get to question five, it is time to start with question one again. This is an admirable reminder that an agency's relationship with the brands it handles is continuous and does not stop when the advertising has been exposed to the public.

10. Types of Advertising Arguments. A *motivating* argument in an advertisement concerns general product benefits; it is not very brand-specific. A *discriminating* argument is concerned with the reasons for buying one brand rather than another. When a market is growing, pioneer brands use mainly motivating arguments. This also holds to a considerable degree for large brands, because they have the most to gain from stimulating people to come into and remain in the product category (*Kodak,* Orkin). Smaller brands tend to employ discriminating arguments, since in stationary markets their business can only come out of the "hide" of the larger brands (the Discover Card, Slice.) As noted, the tendency toward heterogeneity in markets encourages the growth in the relative importance of discriminating arguments.

An *intrinsic* argument in an advertisement is mainly concerned with the product features of a brand, particularly its relative functional advantages. An *extrinsic* argument is concerned with the brand's added values and is perhaps better described as a nonrational communication. There are two types of extrinsic arguments. The first features the users of the brand. A brand has been described as a necktie or a club because the very act of using it says something about its users; they are likely to have something in common, perhaps some degree of demographic or psychographic similarity in addition to their brand choice. The second type of extrinsic argument, which is extremely widespread, is concerned with exogenous linkages between the brand and features of the outside world that in normal circumstances are unconnected with it. This type of argument is harmonious with the notion of "bisociative fusion," one of the few theories that go some way toward helping us to understand the shadowy but fascinating process of idea generation.[10]

11. The Different Roles of Advertising. For more than a decade, JWT has employed a simple but useful device to help plan advertising strategy: a range of steps that measure how directly an advertisement is planned to work. In this book we shall refer to these steps as the King Continuum, a name borrowed from Stephen King of JWT London, who originated this device as well as the Planning Cycle.[11]

Most direct	Direct action
C	
O	Seek information
N	
T	Relate to needs/wants/desires
I	
N	Recall satisfactions/reorder/short list
U	
U	Modify attitudes
M	
Most indirect	Reinforce attitudes

Figure 1–2. The King Continuum

As shown in Figure 1–2, the King Continuum comprises six steps. Its value in planning strategy lies in its specific focus on the job to be done by the campaign. It does not dictate the means by which that job should be fulfilled. This distinction is important, because dictation of means rather than ends almost invariably inhibits the creative process.

The different steps on the continuum apply with above-average importance to certain product fields, for instance:

- *Direct action,* which is planned to achieve an immediate behavioral effect, applies to direct-response and retail advertising, as well as to promotional advertising in the packaged goods field.

- *Seek information* applies mostly to those products which have a high ticket price and for which advertising plays an important part in getting the brand on the list for the buyer to consider. When the brand is on the buyer's list of alternatives, advertising plays a different part (sometimes of smaller but occasionally of larger importance) in the actual purchase decision. (Good examples in this book are in the cases describing Orkin and the U.S. Marine Corps; see point 15.)

- *Relate to needs/wants/desires* applies in general to products like proprietary drugs, which are used widely but only occasionally, and to brands of cosmetics and toiletries that come in a broad range of varieties and appeal to different people.

- *Recall satisfactions/reorder/short list* pertains mainly to brands that are in competitive markets and bought repeatedly.

- *Modify attitudes* applies frequently to brand restages and new advertising campaigns (mainly in packaged goods markets).

- *Reinforce attitudes* applies to continuous advertising in large markets (again, mainly packaged goods).

It will be seen that the last three categories apply substantially to the field of fast-moving consumer goods, where advertising is commonly seen in its most pervasive role. In this field advertising does not necessarily represent a high proportion of the sales value of the individual unit sold; it is almost always calculated on the basis of a massive total sales volume. Such markets tend to be mature and stationary, with large consumer franchises for individual brands. Even larger numbers of people know about these brands, thus providing a broad canvas upon which advertising can work to modify or reinforce attitudes. The advertising is directed mostly toward frequent or infrequent users of a brand, with the object of maintaining the buying habits of the former and increasing the frequency of usage of the latter. Most of the work of JWT is in such markets.

A further point, important enough to be treated separately, needs to be made about the King Continuum. The model in fact contains a paradox that needs some explanation; see point 12, following.

12. Advertising that Works Does so Immediately. Not all advertising has a demonstrable effect. Many campaigns—perhaps the majority of them—have creative, budgetary, or media weaknesses that make them ineffective in the marketplace. Evaluative techniques, too, are often not good enough to enable advertising's contribution to be separated from those of the other marketing inputs.

These criticisms do not apply to the cases in this book, nor do they apply to numbers of additional cases that could be written to describe the work of other sophisticated manufacturers and advertising agencies, both in the product fields covered here and in others. All such examples of effective advertising share a key characteristic: the advertising has an immediate effect. This factor holds for every case in this book, with the exception of Oxo, to which special circumstances (discussed in chapter 8) have applied.

Since immediacy characterizes all effective advertising, how can this point be reconciled with the supposed indirect end of the King Continuum? The answer is to be found by introducing the notion of a double (short-term and long-term) effect. At the direct end of the continuum, the advertising achieves an immediate effect and also a *lagged effect*. This is another way of saying that it builds added values, which, as we have noted, operate in conjunction with consumer satisfaction with a brand's functional properties to ensure repeat purchase of the brand in a competitive marketplace.

This lagged effect of advertising is a feature of most of the cases in this book. And it is compatible with a long-term and gradual strategic change away from penetration growth and toward usage growth, which is a feature of many of the cases, among them Campari, the Discover Card, Listerine, and Quaker Kibbles 'n Bits. Long-term should be interpreted literally. The slow but continuous influence of advertising on users of a brand is one of the reasons that campaigns can have long lives.

Modification of attitudes does not mean a reversal of what people feel about a brand at the moment; it means a process of modest adaptation or fine-tuning, if possible by building on strengths and correcting weaknesses. In this book, two major cases describe such a modification of attitudes: With the Trustee Savings Banks, success was achieved, but it took almost a decade of consistent effort to bring it about; with Goodyear, progress has been made with a campaign that has run for four years, but the path yet to be traveled is greater than the distance already covered.

13. Campaigns Can also Have a Long Life. Both manufacturing companies and advertising agencies often have an inbuilt restlessness about their existing advertising campaigns. This, abetted by the relentless volatility of advertising styles and techniques in the major world centers where innovation is both demanded and supplied, often causes campaigns to be changed before they have reached the point of exhaustion. But despite such pressures, there are numerous examples—including a few in this book (for example, De Beers, *Kodak,* Lux, and Oxo)—in which a single campaign has been exposed successfully for a decade at least and sometimes for much longer. Is there any rule about when to change? Is there any research technique that will guide judgment reliably? The potential longevity of campaigns is one of the most important conclusions to be drawn from the case studies in this book. But an even more important one is that discussed in point 14, below.

14. The "Point of Maximum Sensitivity." One of the most delicate stages in the life of a brand occurs when an advertising campaign needs to be changed. Such a change is sometimes necessitated by some strategic adjustment caused by the forces of the market, but more often it is prompted by the exhaustion of the present campaign—or sometimes because there are strong opinions at the client firm and/or the agency that it will shortly become exhausted. This all involves a very nice exercise in judgment, not least because the problems with existing campaigns often lie below the surface (as in the cases of Goodyear and Oxo). The difficulty is compounded by the hard job of evaluating newly developed alternatives—the same problems that exist when any new campaign is written and brought out for inspection.

The situation is best described as a mine field, although for once there are some directly useful research techniques, in particular, tracking studies (see point 19).

The first problem encountered is timing. When do we change campaigns? When we have hit serious long-term diminishing returns, it is too late. Yet to change prematurely carries a large opportunity cost.

The concept of the "point of maximum sensitivity" will recur in this book, and we shall describe a number of cases in which brands have passed it with demonstrable success—Campari, Mumm, Goodyear, Listerine, Lux (in this case, with a return to an earlier campaign), Oxo, and Smarties. But in the cases of the Discover Card and Slice, the JWT advertising did not manage to pass this nodal point, and in both cases the agency lost the business. This holds a substantial lesson in itself. We are not suggesting that an inability to pass the point of maximum sensitivity is the sole reason that agencies lose clients.[12] We hypothesize, however, that it is one of the most important reasons and possibly the leading one.

15. How Important is Advertising? In none of the cases in this book does advertising act as the sole stimulus to purchase a brand. Rather obviously, advertising is of greatest relative importance in the fields where the ratio of advertising to sales is highest: in direct response (where advertising does represent the sole sales stimulus) and in certain cosmetic, toiletry, and pharmaceutical fields (where added values are spectacularly important).

In certain cases in this book, we see advertising as having a polarized importance. We refer to high ticket items (like Orkin and the U.S. Marine Corps), for which purchase or action is a two-stage process: seeking information and giving rational consideration. In the former, advertising is of critical short-term importance, but in the latter, it plays a background role in solidifying attitudes. Since favorable attitudes often close the sale, the advertising's role here is in some circumstances considered even more important than its first role in generating inquiries.

With most packaged goods, the greatest contribution of advertising comes, as noted, from its lagged effect in building added values. Because the effect is delayed, there is a cushion between the action of reducing advertising investment and the resultant reduction in sales (although this factor does not operate in the opposite circumstances: when a successful campaign stimulates sales, the effect is instantaneous). This cushion often acts as an encouragement to "milk" brands (as happened during a short but disastrous period in the life of Listerine).

Generalizations About Budgets and Media

16. Pragmatic Budgeting. The practice of budgeting is essentially practical, the most common procedures being to match the expenditures of competitive brands of approximately equal size and (in the case of launches and restages) to plan for a share of voice well in excess of share of market. The first of these approaches is harmonious with the all but universal system of budgeting advertising as a share of sales or on a "case rate" basis.

The fact that advertising is a residual expense, often of an order of magnitude similar to a brand's earnings, means that marginal changes in advertising can have a significant influence on profits. Increases in advertising reduce profits significantly and vice versa, although the situation is, of course, distorted by the effects of changes in advertising pressure on sales.

Since this close reciprocal relationship between advertising expenditure and profits does exist, it is surprising that there is so little scientific experimentation with judging the effects of differences in advertising pressure. Econometric techniques exist to help such experimentation, although they are often treated with an unjustified skepticism. A number of published cases illustrate these techniques, including some based on the work of JWT.[13]

The numbers of advertisers who carry out work of this type—something at the cutting edge of marketing—is probably larger in Europe than in the United States, although the confidentiality that generally surrounds the activities of many American advertisers gives this activity a lower profile than is actually merited.

The important and controversial topic of determining the optimum advertising budget is discussed in chapter 22.

17. "Flighting" and a Hidden Assumption. Media budgets are normally concentrated into "flights" or "bursts" comprising a minimal number of Gross Rating Points. There is an assumption behind such a policy that is perhaps too often taken for granted. It is that advertising does not work properly if it is dispersed, despite the fact that dispersion provides the considerable countervailing benefit of eking out budgets over the maximum number of months and geographical regions. Dispersion tends to be resisted because of an instinctive belief in an advertising threshold—that some level of pressure is necessary to overcome consumer resistance and inertia. The implication of this belief is that there is thought to be a buildup that turns an ineffective schedule into an effective one. And if such incremental pressure does transform an ineffective schedule, there must be a situation of short-term increasing returns.

This is a complex matter, but there is evidence that very low levels of pressure—unexpectedly—often do work and that boosting those levels does not lead to short-term increasing returns. Advertising in fact most commonly yields either immediate diminishing returns or brief increasing returns followed by diminishing ones. This reality makes the universal use of "flighting" a questionable procedure, and it is sensible for the policy to be scrutinized on a case-by-case basis.[14] One circumstance in which increasing returns do appear to operate is when progressive amounts of advertising are accompanied by extensions in a brand's distribution, a phenomenon first described by the economist Robert Steiner; in this book, that situation will be referred to as the Steiner Paradox, and it is illustrated by the experience of Mumm in Germany.[15]

We emphasize that the patterns of incremental pressure referred to here are strictly short-term: day-by-day increments if the brand advertised is a weekly purchase. And although the normal pattern for such short-term responses is, as noted, one of diminishing returns (or of brief increasing returns followed by diminishing returns), this short-term pattern is not incompatible with a different pattern of returns when they are examined from a long-term point of view. This hypothesis is discussed next, in point 18.

18. Advertising Scale Economies. There is a consistent inverse relationship between a brand's market share and its share of voice. With smaller brands, the share of voice tends to be larger than the share of the market; with larger brands, the opposite holds. The progressive movement toward a reduction in share of voice as a brand increases in market share is indicative of a real increase in advertising productivity.

Yet another way of making this point is to say that if a brand increases its market share over a period of time, then the increase in its advertising will tend not to be as great as its increase in market share. This represents a significant scale economy for a large brand, which can easily be quantified by calculating the amount by which its advertising budget (measured by share of voice) falls short of its share of market (a proportion that can be looked upon, with refinements, as a normal level of expenditure). Many of the cases in this book illustrate this hypothesis, which is also examined empirically in chapter 20.

Generalizations about Research

19. A Useful Aid to Judgment. Appearing in the pages of this book are a number of research techniques that have been found useful over a long period in developing and monitoring advertising. The six most important are listed below; they will be familiar to most readers.

a. Quantitative and qualitative research to help develop a brand's advertising strategy (in the first two stages of the Planning Cycle). The reader will be impressed by the notable contribution made by the study of simple demographics in the Smarties and Trustee Savings Banks cases and by the elegant and creative demographic/psychographic model in the Ford case.

b. Focus groups to stimulate and refine creative hypotheses (in the third stage of the Planning Cycle).

c. Individual qualitative interviews to evaluate how well creative ideas actually communicate (in the third and fourth stages of the Planning Cycle).

d. Tracking studies on brand awareness, image attributes, and brand usage during the exposure of advertising campaigns (in the fifth stage of the Planning Cycle).

e. Econometric analyses of the sales effects of campaigns (in the fifth stage of the Planning Cycle). These analyses, which are often complex, involve establishing the statistical relationship between data series and estimating the relative importance of the variables measured in stimulating sales. The techniques are not widely applied, although in recent years there has been a dramatic increase in the amount of information that can be used. We are thinking in particular of "single source" data that relate consumers' brand purchasing to their exposure to media.

f. Standardized measures of sales and market shares—retail audits, consumer panels, and so forth (in the fifth, first, and second stages of the Planning Cycle).

None will deny the value of these techniques, yet there are problems surrounding all of them. Generally, the first three are much *less* comprehensive and reliable than the last three. In fact, *a, b,* and *c* go only a very short way to help us judge before the event whether or not a campaign will work.

As mentioned, most new brands fail. In addition, a substantial number of campaigns for ongoing brands have little perceptible effect in the marketplace. Yet if these are the efforts of serious and experienced advertisers, the planning for the campaigns for the unsuccessful new brands and the ineffective campaigns for the existing brands will all have embraced research procedures *a, b,* and *c.* And that it was decided to expose the eventually unsuccessful advertising is presumptive evidence that *a, b,* and *c* produced encouraging signals before the advertising was run.

The central difficulty is how to avoid the temptation to rely on these techniques *on their own* as reliable discriminators or predictors. The findings of such research are invariably a balance of positive and negative signals, and it is an artistic as much as a scientific endeavor to interpret but not overinterpret them and also—rather importantly—to avoid the powerful inclination to use the findings selectively to support our own personal prejudices.

In the last analysis, the decision whether or not to expose a campaign is a matter of personal judgment. But it can at least be said about *a, b,* and *c* that our personal judgment will inevitably be better with them than without them. The decision to go with a new campaign means, of course, that a decision has been made to spend money on advertising production and media.

When we come to consider prolonging our investment, the campaign will have established some track record, and help is at hand from research techniques *d, e,* and *f* which can be both reliable and enlightening if used knowledgeably. As readers will discover, technique *d* was of considerable help to Oxo in passing the point of maximum sensitivity; this was a major contribution made by research to the success of the brand.

20. A Disastrous Substitute for Judgment. For decades the research industry has been aware that there is a large gap between what we need to know about forecasting the effects of advertising to reduce some of the risks and what we actually do know. The industry has responded conscientiously, by inventing and promoting a rich flow of innovative techniques, nearly all of them quantitative and standardized and all of them flawed. These techniques provided what have seemed to be plausible answers to difficult questions, thus apparently simplifying the decision about whether or not to run the tested advertising.

As we have said, none of these techniques has proved reliable, although the search for truth still proceeds with energy and optimism. One of the interesting lessons from the cases in this book—which, it should be remembered, all describe successful brands—is that they include so few examples of the use of these standardized techniques, either separately or (as is popular today) jointly. (As an aside, it is difficult to see how multiple use of inadequate procedures can eliminate their deficiencies.) But much of the advertising industry refuses to accept too much criticism of the techniques. Simple actionable answers are attractive even if they are wrong. Personal decisions based on judgment are perplexing and uncertain, despite the fact that they are almost synonymous with entrepreneurship, the feature of modern business so widely admired in the 1980s.

Lacunae and a Tone of Voice

Earlier in this chapter we regretted that our coverage of cases is less than comprehensive. We are particularly conscious of three things missing: We have no direct-response case, nor do we have one in the fast-food or retail categories. Our coverage of packaged goods is good but not perfect, with gaps in beer, detergents, perfumes and cosmetics, proprietary drugs, and tobacco products. Although we searched for cases in these fields and examined candidates, we were defeated not by an absolute scarcity of material but rather by a lack of cases that offered relevant and contemporary advertising lessons.

We have asked ourselves honestly whether these lacunae represent a decisive handicap. We believe not. Our existing range of eighteen categories is broad enough to illustrate general patterns, and we are reasonably confident that readers will agree when they have read the cases. Further product fields would certainly have enriched the book; they would have added an extra course or two to the meal. But we believe that the meal, as it is, is substantial and well balanced already.

This book has been written with the cooperation of J. Walter Thompson. Harold F. Clark, Jr., to whom the book is dedicated, provided the main stimulus for the enterprise. He has been its godfather since its inception, and he has scrutinized the whole manuscript and made many wise improvements. In addition to his other contributions, he has written a significant afterword: an independent chapter devoted to a number of important qualitative aspects of advertising campaigns. With Harry Clark's active encouragement, the various JWT account groups gave their wholehearted help to the author's analysis of the history of the brands reviewed (although they did not, of course, discuss any confidential plans for the future). It must be made clear, however, that despite such cooperation, this book has been written with as much objectivity as the author can muster. It is not a work of hagiography, special pleading, or promotion for the agency.

The reader will nevertheless note in these pages many words of praise for the work of J. Walter Thompson. Major advertising agencies operate in an acutely and cruelly combative world. Quite simply, if their work is not demonstrably excellent—if it is not judged effective in a fiercely competitive marketplace—agencies will progressively lose their clients. At the same time, if the clients sell their brands successfully at least partly because of excellent advertising, it would be both misleading and unfair to deny an agency the accolade for its excellence. As something of a corrective, however, this book includes cases about two valuable and important clients whose business JWT has lost: the Discover Card and Slice. These have been chosen because it is just as likely—perhaps more likely—that lessons will emerge from situations of difficulty as from continuous successes. For much of its time on these accounts, JWT produced highly effective work. But, as noted earlier, with both accounts the JWT advertising did not succeed in passing the point of maximum sensitivity. This is arguably the most valuable lesson this book contains.

In conclusion, readers will readily understand that all the expressions of opinion in this book are the author's, except where explicitly indicated otherwise. And the author also takes responsibility for all errors of fact and interpretation. At the end of the book are a substantial number of notes for each chapter. Many of the sources listed are published materials in the public domain. But in some instances they are not. If readers wish to consult these normally inaccessible sources, they should approach the clients for permission to see them.

2
Campari and Mumm in Germany

> Remains of Roman drinking cups and vessels have been found in
> great quantities in many parts of the Rhineland, proving beyond doubt
> that wine was in common use during the first century of the Christian
> era.
>
> —Fritz Hallgarten[1]

A Distinctive Aperitif and a Sparkling Wine

The preceding quotation, written by a celebrated contemporary German wine-
expert and wine-lover, reminds us that because Germans first learned about
wine from the Romans, the tradition of German viticulture is among the
oldest in the world. This Italian heritage, even more than the influence of
the European Economic Community in the international spreading of brands
and products once narrowly confined within national frontiers, provides an
excuse to bracket together in this chapter two disparate brands of alcoholic
drinks. First is Campari, an aperitif made to a secret formula based on spirits
flavored with bitter herbs and orange peel; it is an Italian invention and,
more than a hundred years after its discovery, still exported exclusively by
the Campari Company of Milan.[2] Second is Mumm, a *sekt* made in Hoch-
heim, Germany; it is a sparkling wine, comparable in quality if not in character to the champagne produced by the Mumm company of Reims. (There
is, as we shall see, a historical connection between the German and French
Mumm organizations.)

Campari has a clear and unique reddish color and is sometimes (though
not always) diluted with unflavored sparkling club soda. Mumm *sekt* has
the limpid light amber color of the best Riesling wine and in the glass produces bubbles that rise from what seems to be the heart of the liquid. It is
not too fanciful to describe the natural clarity and effervescence of Mumm
as the qualities that give it a "star-bright" appearance. This point is important, because it is universally acknowledged that the quality of any drink
depends on its appeal to the eye and the nose almost as much as to the
palate. The way in which these three sensory appeals work closely together
is relevant to the advertising we shall be discussing in this chapter.

In Germany, grapes are grown mainly in the river valleys in the West;
in the East there are only two small wine-producing areas. The climate al-

lows Germany to make relatively little wine, although the native production is of high quality. And despite importing twenty times as much wine as it exports, Germany consumes relatively little wine. The average annual consumption (more than 20 liters per capita) is a fraction of that in France and Italy (more than 100 liters per capita in each case), although far ahead of the United States (9 liters per capita). By no means does everyone in Germany drink wine, and although for the vast majority of wine drinkers the consumption of wine is a common habit, it is not an everyday one, as it is in France, Italy, Portugal, Argentina, and Spain.[3]

In Germany as in a number of economically developed countries, there is no growth in the total market for alcoholic drinks. There are, by contrast, a modest expansion in the consumption of coffee, tea, and milk and a more pronounced upward trend for waters, soft drinks, and fruit juice, as shown in table 2–1.

The overall consumption of alcoholic drinks is 178 liters per capita, broken down as follows:

Beer	146 liters	(82% of the total)
Still wine	21 liters	(12% of the total)
Sparkling wine	4 liters	(2% of the total)
Spirits	7 liters	(4% of the total)

Consumption of beer, still wine, and spirits is stagnating. Sparkling wine, the category in which Mumm is positioned, shows a degree of buoyancy, with a small but consistent annual increase between 1976 and 1981, although since then it has made no further progress.[4] There is a significant internal movement—an upgrading—within the sparkling wine category, a point we shall later consider in more detail. This upgrading is important to Mumm, despite the fact that the brand is in a very small market category overall.

Campari competes most directly with spirits, although to classify it in the spirits category is slightly uncomfortable, because it also competes

Table 2–1
Index of Per Capita Consumption of Various Drinks in Germany
(1976 = 100)

	1985
Alcoholic drinks	97
Coffee/tea/milk	114
Waters/soft drinks/fruit juice	137

obliquely with other types of alcoholic beverages. The spirits market can be described at best as stationary, although there is also an internal movement, which we shall describe later, that tends to favor Campari.

"A Conspiracy of Silence. You Will Never Know What Is in It"[5]

The secrecy of the Campari formula, guarded as jealously as those for Coca-Cola and Pepsi-Cola, provides a clear commercial benefit in protecting the brand from direct competition. But from this secrecy grows something else—a mystique, an exclusivity, which offers an additional advantage of no less importance. The air of mystery makes it easier to build added values: those nonfunctional benefits that transform Campari from being simply an agreeable drink to sharpen the appetite to being a signal of the drinker's sophistication and savoir faire and something that can transform the drinking of Campari into an activity with romantic, even faintly erotic overtones. The main role of the advertising has been to build these added values, and in this chapter we will attempt to describe what we know about the progress it has made.

Before doing so, however, we must look at Campari's competitive position. As noted, Campari and other aperitifs compete indirectly with spirits, which in general are in a stagnant position. Like all other forms of alcoholic drinks in Germany, they are distributed mainly in food stores, the most important spirits sold being *korn* (clear schnapps distilled from grain and potatoes), brandy, liqueurs, and cordials, rum, whiskey, and (of lower but increasing importance) the "soft" spirits that contain less alcohol.

Aperitifs compete with spirits when the latter are mixed into long drinks, such as rum and Coca-Cola, and gin and tonic, and it is these spirits used as mixers that are making some progress in an otherwise rather depressed total market. (This is the internal movement in the spirits market to which we referred earlier—effectively, a move toward drinks with a lighter alcohol content.) This market for aperitifs is not very clearly defined, but it is much smaller than that for spirits (one estimate puts aperitif consumption at less than 5 percent of that of spirits). The markets for aperitifs, sherry, and long drinks made with spirits (such as gin and tonic) are increasing rapidly, all at the expense of spirits consumed undiluted.

Although reasons for the move toward aperitifs have not been explored in depth, they are connected with a universal increase in people's interest in their physical well-being, leading to a growth in more active and health-conscious life-styles. The move toward aperitifs is also the result of foreign travel, which has introduced many people—the young in particular—to new products and brands. Advertising, too, has played a part, by capturing—

rather than attempting to create—the life-styles of the trend-setters in the market.

Campari is the dominant aperitif, with a consistent share of two-thirds of all sales in the rather ambiguously defined aperitif category. Its nearest rival is Pernod, and there is a tail of smaller, although internationally familiar brands—Ricard, Cynar, Suze, Cinzano Bitter, Solaris, and Aperol—plus many small brands that copy their larger competitors and whose proliferation has contributed to the growth of the category.

Although the sales volume of Campari is much smaller than that of the spirits with which it competes indirectly, the brand has a remarkable overall penetration level. Campari has succeeded in attracting large numbers of new users (much of this because of advertising), but many have not yet begun to drink it with much regularity. The reason, of course, is that Campari's distinctive bitterness is very much an acquired taste, and the slowness with which people take to it has an obvious implication for the brand's long-term marketing strategy. Great care, for instance, is taken not to emphasize the natural bitterness. And a rapid increase is currently taking place in the consumption of Campari mixed with orange juice and other fruit juices, which modify and sweeten the taste. Once Campari drinkers have sampled it often enough to acquire the taste, they drink a substantial amount; in fact, regular drinkers of Campari have a higher per capita consumption than have drinkers of other aperitifs.

Campari is drunk as much by women as by men, and its usage is reasonably evenly spread over all age-groups; these data apply to both numbers of drinkers and volume of consumption. The relatively small numbers of *regular* Campari drinkers are evenly spread over the age-groups. There are, of course, more infrequent drinkers, who might be regarded as people who have been baptized but await full conversion.

Although Campari is seen (particularly by older drinkers) as an aperitif, there is no rigidity about when it is drunk; many people, especially the young, drink it at parties and indeed whenever they fancy it. The brand still has a strong seasonality, being drunk much more frequently and/or by more people during the summer, not only because it is thirst-quenching but also as a legacy of earlier days, when Campari was seen as something associated with vacations at the popular Mediterranean resorts.[6]

This study is mostly concerned with the decade of the 1980s, the beginning of which represented something of a watershed in Campari's fortunes. Before 1980, although the brand had been sold for decades and was widely known, it had an undefined personality and was mainly associated, as noted, with summer drinking in the mass-market holiday resorts. The brand was familiar enough but had a low and unclear profile.

In 1980, the German Campari company and the advertising agency JWT, Frankfurt took a hard look at the brand. Marketing support was stepped up

Campari advertisement first run in color magazines in West Germany in January, 1986. The headline reads, "Campari. What else."

and retail distribution was taken over by the company (agents had formerly been used). This meant that extra attention was devoted to boosting retail deliveries and to increasing sales pressure in-store. Most importantly, a new advertising campaign was developed, with the objective of broadening the appeal of Campari beyond summer drinking. In planning the advertising, it was decided to look at the psychographics of the population and to target people who were cosmopolitan and above average in self-assurance and sophistication. The intention of the campaign was for Campari eventually to become a symbol for such trend-setters or, rather, for the larger numbers of people, particularly the young, who aspired to be cosmopolitan, self-assured, and sophisticated. As such a strategy might be described in U.S. marketing circles, it was intended to make Campari a "necktie" brand, telling as much about the user as a man's necktie says about the personality of its wearer.

Modifying perceptions of a brand in this fashion normally takes some time to accomplish. But from what we know of the actual effect of the Campari campaign on existing and potential consumers, public perceptions of the brand began to change significantly in the first year. Moreover, there was an effect on Campari sales. Mainly as a result of the increased marketing effort but also partly because of the new advertising campaign, sales of the brand responded significantly and quickly, with a 20 percent volume uplift in 1980.[7]

The campaign has an arresting quality. Its most striking characteristic is its abstraction, both literal and figurative. Featured in each of the many different advertisements are a man and a woman dressed for dinner and an evening's festivity. They are handsome rather than beautiful, with the poise, confidence, and class that bring to mind such names as Porsche, Cartier, and the Tour d'Argent. They are perfectly—and expensively—dressed. In their relationship to each other—in their body language—there is a hint of latent eroticism. The couple are shown in spare, stripped-down settings, an ambience that is not a realistic portrayal of any particular place yet unmistakably suggests a life-style of unobtrusive luxury. The most important artifact is a bare, polished bar, its shape similarly abstract, always photographed from an unusual angle to make it visually striking. The bar is magenta, a color that complements the color of Campari itself. The couple have glasses of Campari, but they are not shown drinking it.

There is very little copy: another dimension of the abstraction of the advertising. There is a three-word headline: "Campari. What else." In the press advertising, the two glasses of Campari on the bar are accompanied by a straightforward description of the glasses' contents: the specific ingredients mixed with Campari to make the drinks that we see. In the television advertisements, there are sumptuous close-ups of the Campari being poured, in some cases into Lalique glasses. (On television, appetite appeal is best communicated visually.) The music is atmospheric and works synergistically with the pictures.

The campaign says little rationally about Campari (only the description of the contents of the glasses in the press advertisements). But it says a good deal in both sensory and emotional terms. The Campari itself looks delicious and immediately appealing to the taste buds. But even more importantly, the advertising says a great deal about the style and glamour of the Campari drinker, thereby making a powerful aspirational appeal to the many people who would like some of those attributes to rub off onto their own more mundane lives.

The campaign is conceptually distinctive and has retained its unique identity among the welter of competitive liquor advertising in the market. It is also enriched with extraordinary production values, notably in the lighting and camera work in both press and television executions. That two of the films have won national awards given by the advertising industry furnishes yet another example demonstrating that the recognition of a campaign by the advertising community can be accompanied by marketplace effectiveness.

The advertising has been exposed at a moderately high level by the standards of the market, approximately $2 million per year. Campari is the dominant advertiser in the aperitif field, although it is outspent by a number of its indirect competitors, the larger brands of spirits. The Campari budget has been divided more or less equally between color magazines and television, with outdoor billboards and bus-stop posters more recently included in the media mix. Despite the spectacular quality of the television commercials, the fact that television is used for only half the budget can be explained by the peculiarities of the media market in Germany. The amount of television airtime is severely restricted; however, it has been found that television, used at a level of frequency that would be considered subthreshold in markets where television time is more plentiful, is nevertheless effective. Since the total volume of television advertising in Germany is low, advertisers with a relatively small level of exposure can have a high share of voice. This is evidence of an important characteristic of media effectiveness—that the determinant of the quantitative effect of advertising exposure is its share of voice and not the absolute expenditure.[8]

There is some evidence that the advertising has penetrated the public consciousness, although in interpreting this factor we need to bear in mind the problems associated with the measurement of advertising recall.[9] A number of the individual components of the advertising have become familiar to consumers. Their uniqueness is noticed and there is no evidence that they are seen as either silly or irrelevant.

The progress of the brand's sales has been very positive. The 20 percent volume increase in 1980 was followed by an 8 percent growth in 1982 and the same in 1983. In an increased competitive climate in 1984, 1985, and

1986, sales continued to move ahead, with Campari holding its dominant share of the growing market for aperitifs. Sales of spirits continued in general to be under pressure.

The facts of the market have for some time pointed to the need to increase the average consumer's frequency of drinking Campari. One way of doing so would be to broaden the ways in which the brand is viewed— as something over and beyond an aperitif, narrowly defined. This means that it is important to bring more young people to the brand and to extend the ways in which Campari is drunk. At the moment in Germany, more people drink Campari with orange juice than in the traditional aperitif mixture of Campari with unflavored club soda. Increasingly, they also drink it with grapefruit and other fruit juices and with various sparkling soft drinks. The Campari-orange mixture has been specifically featured in the advertising. Interestingly enough, the idea of introducing new mixers—first orange juice, and later and more importantly lemon soda—gave a major impetus to the sales of Campari in the United Kingdom during the late 1970s.[10]

The Campari campaign has been exposed in Germany since 1980, and it has evolved during this period without eroding either its strategic essentials or its absolute distinctiveness. It has successfully contributed to implementing an evolving marketing strategy. But the basic role of the campaign remains, as always, the building of added values. What we know of its impact on the consumer—and even more importantly, what we know of its direct effectiveness in generating sales in the marketplace—suggests that this task is being accomplished. Judgment also tells us that the campaign has the long-term staying power to carry out the large amount of additional brand-building that will be needed in the future if the present impetus is to be maintained.

Most significantly, in building the added values, the creative flair of the campaign has been not in creating artificial symbols and imagery but in recognizing the psychographic forces already at work and stemming from this, in being able to mirror an evolving society and in some ways even to capture its aspirations.

"Sending Up Bubbles with the Fermentation"[11]

In the past, some wine experts —even some well-known figures who should have known better[12]—have taken a somewhat disparaging view of *sekt*. This is partly because so much sparkling wine is produced in Germany—more than 200 million liters per year (there are at least forty advertised brands)— and partly because the wine is extremely variable in quality: much wine at the lower end of the market is a blend of cheap imports that are of lower quality than German-produced wine.[13] (In the 1930s, apple juice was also sometimes used.)[14]

All sparkling wine is made in one of three ways[15] Two of these production methods are natural processes; the third is artificial. With the two natural processes, the sparkle is produced by the wine itself, the bubbles of carbon dioxide being a by-product of the fermentation (the natural yeast working on the sugar to produce alcohol and gas). The traditional method of trapping these bubbles in the wine is to cause the last stage of fermentation to take place in the bottle itself. This is the essence of the *méthode champenoise,* which, as the name implies, is universally used for champagne, a name that by French law and European Economic Community regulations can be used only to describe certain selected wines produced in the Champagne region of France. This or a similar method is also used for certain other sparkling wines from France and for sparkling wine produced in a handful of other countries, including parts of the United States; however, it is used hardly at all for German *sekt.* The *méthode champenoise* is in fact a rather complex five-step process, but the most striking point that distinguishes it from the other methods is the fermentation inside the bottle. It is, incidentally, the same Mumm family that makes its *sekt* in Germany that in 1827 founded the celebrated Mumm champagne house in Reims. The associations with Mumm champagne have a favorable, although unquantifiable, ruboff onto Mumm *sekt.* Mumm is by no means the only German name associated with champagne—witness Bollinger, Heidsieck, Krug, and Roederer.

The second method of making sparkling wine is to trap the last stages of fermentation while the wine is in a tank; when this is complete, the wine is then bottled. This method is less complicated and is the one used for the best German *sekt.* And although it is different from the *méthode champenoise,* the wines fermented in the tank deserve to be discussed alongside those fermented in the bottle. The tank method is in fact better than bottle fermentation in one respect—the yeast can work better on a larger quantity of wine, thus maintaining a high quality over a long period of time.

The third method of making sparkling wine is much inferior and will not concern us much here, because it cannot by law be used for German *sekt.* A well-known reference book on wine has said that it "may be good enough when cheapness is the first consideration"; it involves pumping "just the right amount of carbonic gas into a bottle of still—and always sweet—wine to make it effervescent."[16] The process resembles the manufacture of carbonated soft drinks.

It is important to remember, however, that Mumm and other brands of *sekt* are made by the superior method of tank fermentation. The expense of this production method is the main reason for the price of *sekt,* and it is the differences in the quality of the grapes and in the length of time the different brands are allowed to ferment that cause the price variability in the market.

There are four standard grades of *sekt,* with the following consumer prices and approximate 1986 market shares:[17]

$2.00 to $4.00	45%
$4.00 to $5.00	18%
$5.00 to $6.50	29%
$6.50 and up	8%

As we have seen, the total market for *sekt* has been growing over the past decade. Per capita consumption rose from 2.7 liters in 1976 to a high point of 4.4 liters in 1981 and then varied rather erratically, returning to the same level of 4.4 liters in 1986. But the 1986 level still represents an increase of 63 percent over 1976.

Most importantly, clear upgrading is taking place within the total market, as the two least expensive segments are continuously losing ground and the top two gaining. In particular, the top segment, where Mumm is located, increased in share from 4.5 percent in 1981 to 8 percent in 1986. Aggregate volume sales of the three main brands in the segment, Fuerst von Metternich, Mumm, and Deinhard Lila, rose by 63 percent, an average annual compound growth rate of more than 10 percent over the five-year period.

This upgrading in the market has taken place against a background of general economic growth (despite relatively high levels of unemployment). It is possibly also connected with the growing popularity of active and health-conscious life-styles that were mentioned earlier explaining the stagnation in the demand for distilled spirits. It is possible that the indirect competition between spirits and *sekt* has led gradually to a shift from one to the other, particularly for aperitif drinking. Demographically, the drinkers of Mumm tend to be the younger and better-educated segments of the population. All in all, the same market trends that have encouraged the growth of Campari seem also to have favored Mumm.

There is something important concerning the volume of consumption, and to introduce this point we should examine the relationship between *sekt* and its most direct competitor, still table wine. The ratio between the volume consumption of wine and *sekt* in 1986 was 18.9 liters to 4.4 liters per capita (or 100 to 23.)

There are, however, a very large number of *sekt* drinkers. In 1986, 26 percent of people had drunk it during the previous two weeks. The comparable figures for still table wine were 25 percent for dry white wine, 19 percent for other white wine, and 24 percent for red wine. With *sekt* being drunk by such large numbers of people, it is inevitable that there is a low per capita volume of consumption. The reader will note the obvious implication for the future marketing strategy of *sekt* brands.

We have seen so far that overall *sekt* consumption is increasing and that top-quality *sekt* is growing even faster. Most importantly for our purposes, Mumm is growing faster still. If we index the 1981 sales volume as 100, by 1987 it had climbed to 490. We shall shortly be looking at this progression in more detail.

First, though, we must point out that this rate of growth is quite outside the norm for established brands in packaged goods markets. The market trend that Mumm has been riding—the growth in *sekt* in general and in the premium brands in particular—goes some way toward helping us to understand this growth. But the greater contribution must be from forces we have not yet examined. Four in particular seem important, and we shall attempt to assess their contributions.

The Product

The product is of consistently high quality. As explained, Mumm is made exclusively by the superior method of tank fermentation. The Brut and Extra Dry varieties are made from single harvestings of the Riesling grape grown in the Rheingau, Germany's finest wine-growing region. The Riesling is the best of the grape varieties used for German wine, with an average yield only half that of the lower quality Sylvaner. This obviously makes it more expensive to produce wine from the Riesling.[18] Mumm Dry is made from a mixture of high-quality grape musts.

The three varieties of Mumm have different degrees of sweetness. Brut is the driest; Extra Dry comes from the middle; and Dry is actually the least dry (although with less sweetness than certain other brands of *sekt*). It is this third variety that has grown most rapidly and currently accounts for more than 80 percent of all Mumm sales. As is obvious from this enormous share, Mumm Dry must be extraordinarily well attuned to the German palate. Another important point is that the product quality of Mumm, like that of most good German *sekt*, is consistent. In quality, Mumm is generally considered on a par with Fuerst von Metternich, although the former is almost a dollar a bottle less expensive.

Retail Distribution

In 1981, more than half the sales of Mumm were in traditional wine and liquor stores and in hotels and bars. It was at this time that a concerted effort was made to boost the distribution in grocery stores, mainly as a strategy to capture a share of the rapidly expanding market for *sekt* bought for in-home consumption. This strategy meant a major financial commitment in reinforcing the sales force, but it was phenomenally successful. The retail distribution, which was at a weighted level of only 11 percent in 1981, was forced up progressively to 70 percent in 1987. Mumm's two most direct competitors both had a higher distribution in 1981. Fuerst von Metternich gradually built its 1981 weighted level of 68 to 80 percent in 1986; the distribution of Deinhard Lila, by contrast, eroded from 55 percent to 45 percent over the same period. The enormous increase in Mumm distribution is arguably the single most important factor in stimulating the brand's large sales increase, although not the only one. And the extension of the distribution was, of course, facilitated indirectly but to a major degree by the advertising.

The Advertising: Quantitative Considerations

Since 1981, there has been a major increase in the advertising investment behind Mumm. Expenditure measured in deutsch marks rose from an index of 100 in 1981 to 392 in 1986, representing an expenditure on the order of $3 million. It was slightly reduced in 1987. Taking into account media inflation, however, the investment per liter was marginally less in 1986 and 1987 than it had been in 1981. In most years, Mumm's advertising investment is greater than that of the brand leader, Fuerst von Metternich. Mumm's share of voice of the aggregate advertising of the three leading premium brands, which had been 42 percent in 1981, made a large jump to 62 percent in 1986 (it was cut back in 1987). Mumm is outspent, however, by some of the big brands in the cheaper market segments with which it competes indirectly.

The Mumm advertising is exposed in color magazines, television (with twenty second spots), and the trade press: an important medium in view of the drive to extend the brand's distribution.

The Advertising: Qualitative Considerations

The Mumm advertising campaign is characterized by simplicity, but a rather sophisticated simplicity. It is based on the simple principle that in advertising the most telling way of communicating appetite appeal is by visual means. The magazine and television advertisements are composed of close-ups of Mumm in tall glasses with the bubbles ascending and blinking n the most enticing way. There is a bottle, a label, and a brief piece of copy. Much of the quality of the photography comes from the lighting; much also from juxtaposition of the elements—in particular, the unusual angles between them. In the television films, a surrealist effect is introduced: through tilting the camera, the Mumm is shown being poured sideways into a horizontal glass, making a striking visual impression. The campaign is far from the conventions of normal liquor advertising, which almost invariably shows the advertised brand being drunk in a social milieu. An interesting feature of the campaign is that all the consumer advertising features Mumm Extra Dry,

Magazine advertisement first run in Germany in 1988. The copy reads:
   Sometimes it just has to be Mumm
   Mumm Extra Dry
   The German with the dry accent

although that is not the widest-selling variety. It is, however, believed—with some justification—that the drier wine carries the more prestigious associations, and people can quite easily opt for Mumm Dry (the less dry wine) at the point of purchase.

The label design appropriately enough echoes those brand values which the advertising strives to build. It is modern, yet it echoes the simplicity of the classical style.

What can be said about the relative contributions of these four factors to the success of the brand? The first of them—product quality—is, of course, fundamental and has been unchanged since Mumm was first marketed. Nothing new happened during the 1980s, when there was such a large sales improvement. We should therefore look for *changes* in the marketing mix for clues to this success.

Table 2–2
Index of Mumm Marketing Variables

	Sales	Distribution	Advertising	Sales per Store
1981	100	100	100	100
1982	123	173	143	71
1983	178	264	156	68
1984	235	327	209	72
1985	316	391	293	81
1986	410	482	392	85
1987	490	636	363	78

Source: Derived from A. C. Nielsen data. (This information does not, of course, cover the hotel and catering trades.)

Table 2–2 is (for reasons of confidentiality) presented in index numbers. Starting in 1981 as the base year, we track the movement of four variables: sales of Mumm in volume, weighted distribution in the food trade, advertising expenditure, and sales per store (computed as sales per percentage point of weighted distribution).

The first two columns follow a similar trend, although there is a steeper rise in distribution than in sales. The third column shows growth in advertising, but that growth is less than in sales and distribution. Distribution and advertising together are obviously strongly associated with the sales increase; there is a synergistic effect. And it must not be forgotten that a strong and successful consumer advertising campaign nearly always has a stimulating and positive effect on the attitude of store owners and store buyers, making them much more receptive to stocking the brand if they do not carry it already. (This is the rationale for the expensive, but not uncommon and generally effective, strategy of using consumer advertising to force retail distribution.)

There is little doubt that the increased distribution had a major effect, but do we know for sure that the advertising also made a significant contribution to the growth of the brand? Beyond a strong feeling based on judgment that the campaign worked, evidence is to be found in the fourth column of table 2–2. There it will be seen that after a two-year shakedown in sales per store as the distribution drive got under way (initially picking up new outlets that made relatively low sales), 1983 saw the start of an increase in average sales per store, that continued in 1984, 1985, and 1986. Only in 1987 did the figure fall back slightly, reflecting the large increase in weighted distribution that took place in 1987 (70 percent, up from 53 percent), which brought in some low-volume outlets. It is obvious from the increase in sales per store that a dynamic was at work, almost certainly advertising working in conjunction with the quality of the product to build repeat business. Mumm was benefiting from more stores carrying the brand, plus an increased rate of sale in all the stores, old and new. It is difficult not to conclude that advertising, both quantitatively and qualitatively, played an important role in both these processes. In 1987, Mumm became the leading brand in the premium segment, with a 60 percent market share.

There is one final point of interest in this case. If we take the first column in table 2–2 and track the increase in the sales index year by year, what emerges are the results shown in table 2–3. As can be seen, from 1982 through 1986 there was an *increasing* progression, pointing to a situation of increasing returns to incremental advertising pressure—an exceptional circumstance in the real world.[19] The explanation for it can be found in the work of the economist Robert Steiner, who has demonstrated in theoretical terms that this phenomenon is likely to be caused by the very factor we have been examining in this study: increased distribution applied on top of the dynamic of increased advertising pressure.[20] As the reader will remember from chapter 1, we call this phenomenon the Steiner Paradox.

Table 2–3
Mumm Sales Index, Year-by-Year Change

	Percentage Points
1981	—
1982	+23
1983	+55
1984	+57
1985	+81
1986	+94
1987	+80

Six Lessons from the Experience of Campari and Mumm

1. Small Dynamic Market Segments Can Occasionally be Discovered in Mature Total Markets. Both Campari and Mumm compete in an overall market for distilled spirits and wine that exhibits classic symptoms of stationary conditions. Despite this, there are important internal movements within the market, movements that almost certainly are connected with changing life-styles of the German population. Campari managed to tap into a growth in the drinking of aperitifs and managed to continue to dominate this small market segment, whose growth has been essentially at the expense of spirits. Mumm rode, indeed led, the vigorous growth of the premium subsegment of the sparkling wine market (a growth that was probably also connected with changing life-styles of the population). Both Campari and Mumm increased in sales as a result of a disciplined narrowing of their field of competition, following a search for a growing subsegment within overall markets that appeared prima facie highly unpromising.

2. The Success of Campari Was Largely Based on a Study of Psychographics. The growing market for aperitifs attracted a drinker with recognizable characteristics—elitist, stylish, cosmopolitan, above all aspirational. These characteristics are subtle, and the definition (as opposed to recognition) of them was an artistic as well as scientific endeavor. Following its definition of target consumers, the agency managed to capture them in psychographic terms in the Campari campaign, using flair and skills of an exceptional order. The life-style characteristics existed already with groups of the population; the advertising tapped into them but did not create them. The campaign has been exposed for more than six years, and although it has evolved both to maintain its freshness and to respond to an evolving marketing strategy, it has been consistent in the way it mirrors the brand's target consumers. The campaign has succeeded in avoiding the stereotypes of liquor advertising—conventional social situations. It is therefore unique.

3. The Mumm Campaign has Preempted the Appetite Appeal for Sekt. An essential guideline covering all advertising for food and drink is that appetite appeal—an advertising argument of the highest importance—is best communicated by visual means. The Mumm advertising has concentrated single-mindedly on appetite appeal and has not deviated from that approach. This concentration has required resolution and discipline and has involved the deliberate exclusion from consideration of a number of other seemingly attractive advertising arguments. The result has been a unique campaign, far removed from the stereotypes of advertising in the liquor field. Although the

Campari and Mumm campaigns are quite different from each other, each of them is "one of a kind" in a highly competitive marketplace.

4. The Expansion in Mumm Sales Was Mainly Caused by Distribution Growth and Advertising Working in Cooperation. The considerable investment in sales-force time necessary to raise the food store distribution of Mumm yielded impressive sales results. As is normally the case in such circumstances, however, the promise of a strong and effective advertising campaign made the task of the sales force easier. Moreover, the evidence of a progressive increase between 1982 and 1986 in the rate of sale per store shows fairly clearly the positive effect of the campaign—an effect unrelated to the distribution drive. The increasing returns to incremental advertising pressure that characterized the advertising response were the effect of the added impact of the expanding distribution. (This is a good example of the added effect of distribution growth in bringing about increasing returns to incremental advertising pressure, the phenomenon we call the Steiner Paradox.)

5. The need for Increasing Consumption Per Consumer. In the case of both Campari and Mumm, the advertising and marketing efforts have clearly had a positive influence on levels of consumer trial. These efforts have not yet worked their way through to build levels of repeat purchase compatible with the extent of the consumer franchises. An obvious objective for the future must be to direct attention to increasing both purchase frequency and volume of consumption; in this, advertising above-the-line and (perhaps even more importantly) promotions below-the-line have important roles.

6. Advertising Investment Levels. Both Campari and Mumm have been supported consistently by advertising budgets set at competitive levels dictated by the advertising levels in the marketplace. Campari has maintained its dominant level of expenditure among the various brands of aperitifs, which has worked very effectively despite the fact that a number of the brand's indirect competitors—the larger brands of distilled spirits—outspend it by a wide margin. We judge that, during the years covered by this study, the Campari advertising budget has been a significant, albeit carefully evaluated, business expense but set some way below the sort of investment that might have endangered the brand's profitability. Mumm, in a rather dynamic market situation, has increased its advertising more or less in line with the expansion of its distribution and sales. But note that the former has grown not quite so fast as the latter. This means that there has been a small but progressive reduction in the advertising expenditure per liter, a reduction that is entirely harmonious with the increasing returns to incremental advertising pressure that have characterized the sales progress of the brand.

3
Kodak Cameras and Film

> The letter K had been a favorite with me—it seemed a strong, incisive sort of letter. Therefore, the word I wanted had to start with K. Then it became a question of trying out a great number of combinations of letters that made words starting and ending with K. The word Kodak is the result.
>
> —George Eastman[1]

An American Legend

The technology of the roll-film camera, the dramatic rise of the snapshot as the most universal as well as the most vivid (and on occasion the most poignant) record of personal history, indeed the entire worldwide phenomenon of amateur photography—all these were the creation of George Eastman, founder of Eastman *Kodak* Company.

The *Kodak* name had at the beginning no intrinsic meaning. Admittedly, it had distinctiveness, and its onomatopoeia conjured up the most characteristic sound in photography, the click of the camera shutter. But by the end of George Eastman's life in 1932, the word had become impregnated with a very special meaning. It was synonymous with photography and communicated much to photographers, or at any rate their most widespread species, the amateur snapshooter. If the word *great* can be associated with a brand name, *Kodak* was and is indeed a great brand. And it is impossible to deny that advertising has played a role in building it. *Kodak* has always been a large advertiser when measured in absolute terms. Eastman *Kodak* Company is not, however, an advertising-intensive operation—a paradox that will be discussed later in this chapter.

Although George Eastman was not a trained artisan, he had manual skills that remained with him to the end of his days. His respect for good craftsmanship had a powerful influence on his company's products, which from the beginning were (and have remained) robustly constructed, easy to operate, based on sound but simple design, and inexpensive enough to appeal to the widest mass market.

This does not mean that there has ever been a lack of technological innovation in *Kodak* product development, merely that great pains have been taken always to translate innovation into the simplest consumer terms.

By contrast, the early innovative designers in companies that made cameras for mainly professional use (Leica, Contax, Rolleiflex, and others) took a different approach. Their cameras were for a small, sophisticated market, meaning that, within limits, expense and complexity of design and operation imposed no restriction on a designer's work. What resulted was a series of cameras that were marvels of miniature precision-engineering. The leadership in the design of cameras of this type was initially in German hands, but the baton was taken over by the Japanese in the 1960s (some experts say earlier). From the time of the Japanese assuming leadership, there occurred a substantial expansion in the use of such cameras outside the professional realm and into the amateur field, so that without exaggeration we can say today that the 35-mm camera (both the single-lens reflex and the automated "lens shutter" type) has reached a huge and still-expanding market in most developed Western countries.

The expansion of the market for precision 35-mm cameras during and after the 1960s was not therefore a movement led by *Kodak* (although *Kodak* was represented in this market by the relatively inexpensive Retina cameras). This lack of leadership role was an unusual (and, some would say, uncomfortable) situation for the company and is a not-unimportant feature of our study. But it needs detailed consideration, and we shall return to it.

The development of photographic film is an entirely different matter. In this, *Kodak* has always led the way. This was true of the development of monochrome film with increasing speed and improved resolution; in the original pioneering and growth of transparency color film (the leading brands today remain *Kodachrome* and *Ektachrome*); in the invention and rapid development of color negative film, with progressively increasing speed, definition, and color quality (*Kodacolor* is today the leading brand); and in the development and expansion of the vast majority of innovative means of delivering the film to the camera shutter to produce the picture, means that ranged from the paper-roll film of the 1880s to the film disc of the 1980s.

It is obvious from these facts that *Kodak* today is a company of massive and even towering strength. And if our study discusses the company's relatively slow growth during the decade of the 1980s, such growth must be seen in comparison with the past, when the growth in *Kodak's* business (from a smaller base) was on occasion dramatic. But with an organization the size of *Kodak* in the 1980s, where is future growth going to come from? The company has for years been pursuing, with varying degrees of success, a strategy of diversification, and *Kodak* is today an important force in videotaping, computing, electronic publishing, batteries, and chemicals. Those activities are not, however, the concern of this chapter, which will concentrate on what the company calls imaging (the production of mainly photograhic products), a division of the business that accounts for at least 80 percent of its worldwide sales and the lion's share of its net earnings.[2]

Amateur Photographers and Their Cameras

The proportion of adults in the United States who own one or more cameras has grown relatively steadily from 54.5 percent in 1976 to 69.2 percent in 1985. Although there are some discontinuities in the progression of these figures, their total thrust is clear. The growth does, however, show different patterns when looked at from the angles of the owners of different numbers of cameras. Those who possess only one camera have increased hardly at all (from 36.2 percent in 1976 to 37.8 percent in 1985), whereas the ownership of two cameras has climbed from 14.2 to 22.4 percent and ownership of three or more cameras has gone up from 4.1 to 8.9 percent. What we see, then, is a market in which virtually all the growth in camera ownership during the past decade has gone to build multicamera ownership.[3] This factor has had an influence both on the total number of active photographers and on the amount of film used, matters of great importance that we will discuss in the next section.

Buying a new camera is quite a common practice; the proportion of adults who do so in any given year has varied between a low of 14.2 percent and a high of 22.3 percent over the course of the past six years. In most years, twice as many people buy a camera for their own use as buy one as a gift for someone else. (The number of people who give cameras as gifts has varied over the past decade between a low of 5.6 percent and to a high of 8.5 percent of the of the adult population.)[4]

Among cameras bought in any one year, 35-mm equipment has now grown to assume first place position. The proportion of adults who bought a 35-mm camera in 1980 was only 3.7 percent; that figure is now 6.3 percent. The 35-mm cameras include all three main types—manual single-lens reflexes, automatic single-lens reflexes, and the simple-to-operate "lens shutter" types, the latter being the fastest growing.

The total number of adults buying a new camera in 1985 were as follows:[5]

Any type of camera	22.3%
35 mm	6.3%
Disc	3.7%
"Instant developing"	3.0%
Cartridge 110	2.4%
Cartridge 126	1.2%

Three important points concern *Kodak's* position in this market. First, *Kodak* has returned to the 35-mm camera market after an absence of well over a decade but is not yet well established there. Second, following prolonged litigation, the company has been forced out of the instant-developing camera market. Third, manufacturers in Japan, Taiwan, and Hong Kong now sell in the United States disc and cartridge cameras that accept both *Kodak* film and their own reloads. Because of these facts, *Kodak* cameras currently account for probably well below half of all new camera sales.[6] Although such a share would be impressively high for any other manufacturer in any other market, *Kodak* is a company accustomed to a much higher share in its main business, film.

Kodak's dominance of the film market remains great, with a share of approximately 80 percent of total sales, although an erosion of a few percentage points has occurred over recent years.[7] *Kodak* film is currently used extremely widely, but to an already-large and probably increasing degree it is used by people who do not possess *Kodak* cameras, a fact that is inevitable in view of *Kodak's* importance in the film market. For a brand with a very high market share, it is normally more fruitful to increase the size of the total market than to strive to increase market share, and *Kodak's* share of total sales of film strongly underlines the importance of maintaining (or reviving) overall market growth, which would bring sales and profits not only from *Kodak* cameras and film but also from processing, photographic paper, and chemicals.

Picture Taking: Some Quantitative Aspects

To someone unacquainted with the photographic market, there are two surprising facts about it that pertain to the amount of picture taking by the average camera owner: (a) he or she takes very few pictures in the course of a year and (b) the amount of picture taking has not increased very much over the recent past.

The average picture taker makes a mere seventy exposures per year, a remarkably low figure, although it is even lower in other countries. Users of 35-mm cameras—the sophisticated upper end of the photographic market— use larger amounts of film than the average, although such usage is still small in absolute terms; a third of 35-mm camera owners use only one roll per month.[8]

By the standards of most repeat purchase markets (packaged foods, fast foods, beverages, tobacco, gasoline) this usage frequency is very low. There is no obvious reason, but it is, of course, not impossible that advertising has played some part.

There is a strong upward trend for 35-mm film, enough to compensate for declining usage of other types. Such a decline has indeed been true of 35-mm color transparency film—from 11.2 percent in 1980 to 5.5 percent in 1985—but usage of color negative film has increased substantially, from 11.2 percent in 1980 to 20.9 percent in 1985. Moreover, high frequency of use also shows strong growth.[9] Judgment suggests that this buoyancy has been the result of progressive increases in the quality of color negative film, and the growth is strong enough to suggest that color negative film is taking over the photographic market.

We have already mentioned the increased usage of 35-mm equipment and the resultant increasing demand for *Kodak* 35-mm film, which in turn has meant that *Kodak* film is being used by a substantial and increasing majority of people who do not use *Kodak* equipment. It can be argued that the move toward precision 35-mm photography, with the consequent re-shaping of the demand for *Kodak* film products, is by a large margin the most important trend in the photographic market during the past decade. The future of the *Kodak* photographic business depends on how well the company is able to adapt itself to this changing marketplace, and *Kodak's* product strategy is already evolving in the appropriate direction, notably with the launch of Kodacolor VR Film (1982) and the Kodak VR 35 camera (1986).

We have looked at frequency-of-purchase patterns of individual photographic systems. When we examine data on picture taking in total, we also find evidence of overall stasis, or at best very moderate growth. Estimates of the proportion of adults who have used photographic film during the past year progressed from 56.2 percent in 1975 to 59.6 percent in 1985 (with some discontinuities in the data).[10] This increase of 3.4 percentage points translates into what seems to be a large net increase in the number of film users, taking population growth into account. But viewed year by year, the increase is modest: an annual average over the decade of a little over 2 percent compound, on a base of 78.5 million adult film buyers in 1975. Further, much of the increase took place in 1985 and could have been either an erratic statistical artifact or the result of special marketing activity during that year. Estimates from a trade-press source suggest that the average annual increase in the number of pictures taken had been 8 percent over the course of the 1970s but that this figure decreased to 4 percent during the 1980s.[11] This is not a flat market; indeed, that kind of annual increase would be considered very reasonable for normal packaged goods. But it was the reduction in the rate of growth that was the worrying feature.

We have, then, a relatively modest increase in recent years in the total amount of picture taking. This makes an instructive comparison with the growth in camera ownership, a matter discussed in the last section. Table 3–1 shows some comparative figures. The table has two striking features, both of which are more or less similar aspects of the same point. First, the relatively healthy growth in camera ownership over the decade has *not* been accompanied by a similar growth in camera use. Second, while there was not much difference in the mid-1970s between levels of camera ownership and camera usage, a gap had opened up by the mid-1980s, meaning that as many as 14 percent of owners at the present time never use their cameras.

Table 3–1
Growth in Camera Ownership and Film Purchasing

Proportion of the Adult Population:	In the Mid-1970s	In the Mid-1980s
Owning a camera	54.5%	69.2%
Buying a film	56.2%	59.6%

Source: Annual reports on the photographic market by the Target Group Index (Axiom Market Research Bureau) and Simmons Market Research Bureau.

This evidence, together with the data reviewed earlier indicating that the growth in camera ownership has in reality been a growth in multicamera ownership, suggests that what has been happening over the past decade has been a progressive purchase of new equipment, the use of which has dwindled.

This change has resulted in a situation in which people still tend to use a single camera, although they may own more than one. And their overall level of picture taking, despite various vicissitudes, remains not much above what it was ten years ago. It is possible to think of some reasons for this situation—the relatively low birth rate (providing fewer babies and children to be photographed), fluctuations in the amount of overseas travel, *Kodak's* greater strength with older rather than young photographers, and that numbers of people could be perceiving photography as rather "square" and old-fashioned. These are all long-term problems, susceptible only to long-term solutions.

The growing 35-mm market has been an exception to this overall stasis, but it will be remembered that this market to date has not been of considerable importance to *Kodak* as a camera marketer, although it has always been of vast importance to *Kodak* as a film supplier. Judgment suggests that 35-mm photography is a rather more "trendy" activity than photography with more obviously "amateur" cameras. The significant improvement in the sales of color film that took place in late 1987 was a result of the growing use of 35-mm equipment.[12]

The Roles of Advertising

There is a technical definition that is important to any discussion of the strategy and creative execution of *Kodak* advertising. This was a matter discussed in chapter 1—the distinction between motivating and discriminating advertising arguments. As the reader will remember, we described motivating arguments as those concerned with what is needed to persuade the consumer to use the product field as a whole; they embrace overall benefits that are not heavily related to specific brands. Discriminating arguments, by contrast, are concerned with persuading the consumer that one specific brand is better than others. Large brands in any market normally rely on motivating arguments, since such brands tend to have more to gain from stimulating total market growth than from mopping up their smaller competitors. Motivating arguments can (from the point of view of the large advertiser) be criticized on the grounds that they can generate business for competitors. Yet, since the large brand, by definition, has more to gain than small brands do from total market growth, most large advertisers who employ motivating arguments are prepared to accept the cost that they might be bringing some succor to their smaller rivals.

Over the past two decades, *Kodak* advertising has been characterized by the strength of its motivating arguments and also by the skills with which they have been expressed: advertisements that have relied (and still rely, although to a diminishing degree) on motivators of an essentially nonrational variety. In particular, they have depended on the powerful argument, which has virtually universal appeal, that photographs are a record of people's lives. And if such an argument can be applied with skill and subtlety to advertisements featuring those aspects of life which are close to the hearts of most ordinary people—babyhood, childhood, engagement, creating a family, long marriage, and old age—then such advertising is capable of taking great hold on the sensibilities of those to whom it is addressed.

This describes much of the *Kodak* advertising that has been developed and run over the years. Some of the techniques of the filmmaking repay study, and generalization is possible. The films make effective use of extreme lengths: as long as 120 seconds in many cases. Their other characteristics— the generally slow pace of the action, the use of dissolves (a subtle means of communicating the passage of time), the employment of slow motion for emotional impact, the fastidious use of music and the artfully contrived use of sound effects, the softness of focus, and the unobtrusive commentaries— are all evidence that the craft skills that have gone into the making of *Kodak* commercials have approached close to an art form.

Above all, the strategy, which has concentrated so strongly on motivating appeals, has been well judged for the brand and the market. Even when developments such as the launch of *Kodacolor VR* film in 1982 forced *Kodak* advertising toward greater use of functional discriminators, these have with some artifice been grafted, as it were, onto the trunk of the *Kodak* advertising tree. (*Kodacolor VR* film has been successful, and the partial reliance on discriminating arguments in its advertising is discussed in the last section of this chapter.)

Kodak film advertising has represented a proportion, varying between 29 and 66 percent during each of the past five years, of the overall *Kodak* advertising effort. Most of the remaining advertising has been devoted to the launch and exploitation of a series of innovative cameras. Over the past two or three decades, these cameras have been the 126 cartridge *Kodak* Instamatic® camera (1963), the 110 cartridge *Kodak* Pocket Instamatic camera (1972), the development of the latter into the series of *Kodak* Ektra cameras (1978), the *Kodak* disc camera (1982), and the *Kodak* VR 35 camera (1986). These launches were all news oriented. Certain of them featured well-known sponsors and gained impact thereby. Most importantly, all had a recognizably *Kodak* quality about them: an indelible fingerprint, a ruboff from the film advertising, a reminder of the emotional rewards of picture taking.

The *Kodak* advertising campaign, or rather the series of campaigns for *Kodak* film and for a progression of separate camera introductions, has been noted for the qualities of planning and execution that have already been described. It is tempting to attribute much of *Kodak's* past success to the quality of the advertising, to the consistency of its tone of voice, and in particular to how these have built an enviable battery of nonfunctional added values for the brand. With the slowing in the growth of the total market that occurred in the 1980s, however, it becomes much more difficult for us to evaluate what role consumer advertising is playing at the moment—or, perhaps more importantly, what role it *should* be playing—in the *Kodak* marketing operation.

Two things are fairly evident from the facts we have looked at so far. First, the new camera systems launched during the past two decades have generally been a success in the short and medium terms. Large numbers of all models have been sold, in many cases to slightly different consumer groups (the evidence for which comes from the net expansion in total camera penetration that we have already noted). Even the disc camera, about which some disappointment has been expressed, managed to achieve an 8.3 percent adult usage level (mostly with *Kodak* equipment) within three years. And twenty-five million *Kodak* disc cameras were sold before manufacture of the line was halted.[13] Advertising has been an important element in the launch of each of these products, and insofar as consumer penetration has been achieved (as it was in all cases), then advertising is entitled to take some of the credit. The cartridge and instant-developing systems, however, have been unable to maintain their early usage levels. It is difficult to deny that all too often the cameras have been put away in a closet and forgotten. The task of the advertising was to help sell cameras in the first place, a job it generally succeeded in performing efficiently. But as budgets were cut back, sales inevitably lost their drive.

The second point, which is fairly evident, is that the film business was sluggish for a number of years preceding 1987. The advertising—in its quantity and quality—had not succeeded in injecting any impetus into the film market, although judgment suggests strongly that advertising must have contributed to the maintenance of existing levels of *Kodak* film sales, despite the emergence of competitive brands that have been marketed with varying degrees of aggressiveness—in many cases, deep price-cutting. Price-cutting is, of course, a tactical device aimed at increasing market share; it could not be expected to increase in any strategic fashion the total amount of film used.

Things, however, began to look up in 1987. The increased demand for 35-mm film was the result of the boom in 35-mm autofocus cameras—again an equipment-related phenomenon, although the advertising campaign for *Kodacolor VR-G* film played its part.[14] In the past, however, equipment-related sales increases have tended not to be long lasting, suggesting that the major impetus for growth must still come from the advertising, especially from advertising in its motivating, market-expanding role. The question we need to address is what sort of pressure is going to be needed in the future to bring about a revival of significant advertising-led growth. This, of course, is not an easy question to answer.

Some Thoughts on Budgetary Policy

Kodak has pursued in tandem two strategies to nurture and develop the film market. Such an emphasis is entirely understandable in view of the likelihood (although there are no published data to demonstrate this) that film is relatively and absolutely a more profitable part of the *Kodak* business than camera manufacture is.[15] The first strategy has been to spend substantial funds on the advertising and promotion of *Kodak* film. As we have seen, these have been devoted in the main to exploiting motivating arguments to encourage picture taking, although the recent advertising for the *Kodacolor VR* color film has differed to some extent. The second strategy has been to develop and launch a series of innovative cameras with unique film-loading systems. As we have seen, the success of this latter strategy has been impaired both by the falling frequency of usage of the new types of cameras and by some loss of market share caused by the inevitable introduction of cameras and film manufactured in the Far East with reloading methods compatible with *Kodak* cameras.

It would seem, therefore, that the first of the two strategies—the advertising and promotion of *Kodak* film—offers the greater potential in the long term. The problem is that this strategy has not provided, for most of the 1980s, much evidence of an ability to increase film usage (as opposed to maintaining relatively stable levels).

Although photographic film is not commonly perceived as a species of packaged goods, it can in fact be approximately classified as such. Readers will remember from chapter 1 that we classified it as a quasi-packaged-goods market. It is useful to do this, because a great deal is known about packaged goods and some of the lessons may be relevant to *Kodak* film. Photographic film shares the following characteristics of most packaged goods:

1. There is repeat purchase and (within the limits imposed by the existence of a single 80 percent brand) a degree of multibrand buying. Different film types offer the consumer a wide range of choice in his or her purchases.

2. The brands in the market offer both functional and nonfunctional rewards to the consumer. There is, in other words, strong branding.

3. The market is mature. Despite spurts of short-term growth, there is a tendency for this to slow in the long term. Consumer purchasing probably follows uniform (even predictable) patterns.

In such markets, advertising investments are incurred mainly to protect the market positions of individual brands. And there is general reluctance to reduce advertising and promotional investments even temporarily, because of the perceived danger of loss of business to competitive assault.

A positive payout for advertising in such markets is that branded goods are normally sold at a price premium over unbranded competition. This higher price is a specific recognition by consumers of the nonfunctional added values that have been created in the main by past consumer advertising.[16] Such a situation of premium price and added values is most certainly true of *Kodak* film.

Such, then, are the similarities between the markets for photographic film and those for most packaged goods. But there are also two differences, both of them germane to this study.

First, in most packaged goods markets, it is unusual indeed for a single manufacturer to account for 80 percent of total sales. Such a high share may be pleasing to the manufacturer, especially since it has been the result of a broad consumer franchise, as well as the general consumer satisfaction with the brand that provides repeat purchase. There is, however, an endemic disadvantage in such a situation, in that a dominant single manufacturer is a phenomenon that can inhibit the market from increasing. It is not a uniform tendency, but cases do exist.[17]

Second, the photographic market is a good deal less advertising-intensive than that for most packaged goods. This difference can be measured by a simple yardstick of the percentage of a manufacturer's sales that are accounted for by advertising. Table 3–2 presents the figures for Eastman *Kodak* Company for the five years 1981 through 1985. The figures represent *Kodak* advertising expenditures in measured media (that is, excluding promotions), expressed as a share of the total value of the company's U.S. sales. The two statistical series are based on different published estimates, which differ in detail, although they paint an essentially similar picture.

To anyone well acquainted with packaged goods advertising, these are remarkably low figures. The vast majority of major advertisers of packaged

Table 3–2
Kodak Advertising-to-Sales Ratios

	According to Advertising Age *Data*	*According to Advertising Information Services Data*
1981	1.0%	0.8%
1982	1.3%	1.2%
1983	1.1%	1.3%
1984	1.5%	1.2%
1985	1.1%	0.9%

goods spend larger above-the-line ratios—accounting for shares of their value in the range of 3 to 8 percent, and often more. We do not wish to make facile comparisons between dissimilar markets, but it is a fact that in most packaged goods markets (although not in the photographic market) there is a group of reasonably evenly balanced oligopolistic competitors, a situation that tends to elevate advertising expenditures.[18] High brand advertising has been known to bring growth to markets, although the maturity of most packaged goods categories, expressed in high levels of product usage, often inhibits such growth. But as we have seen, the usage of photographic film is low.

Table 3–3
Comparison of *Kodak* Advertising and Promotional Expenditures

	Total Kodak *Advertising Plus Promotions ($ millions)*	*Advertising Share*	*Promotional Share*
1981	101	64%	36%
1982	143	64%	36%
1983	273	28%	72%
1984	329	33%	67%
1985	247	33%	67%

Of course, on top of the expenditures on measured media advertising, we must add heavy and increasing below-the-line promotional expenditures. Here increases taking place are related to certain well-established changes in most markets, notably the increase in the strength of the retail sector.[19] It is interesting to note that *Kodak* is following to a very pronounced degree this changing pattern of expenditure.[20] (See table 3–3.)

As can be seen quite clearly, *Kodak* has vastly increased its total advertising and promotional budgets during the years since 1981, but this increase has been accompanied by a radical movement of funds below-the-line. This policy has presumably been undertaken to protect *Kodak's* market share in a film market that has not shown dynamic growth, and it has been reasonably successful, although the brand share has not been increased and, more seriously, the size of the total market has not been expanded, except on a short-term basis. The cost has been very high. From the data presented in table 3–4, showing a degree of similarity in *Kodak's* shares of total market advertising year by year, we can infer that other manufacturers have also increased their advertising (and possibly promotional) investments. This is to be expected: Increased advertising and promotional expenditures are normally connected with (either as a response to or a cause of) similar competitive activity.

It can also be seen from table 3–4 that *Kodak's* share of total advertising above-the-line in the photographic market has been kept at levels far below *Kodak's* market share (which, it will be remembered, is 80 percent in the film market). There are advertising-related economies of scale accruing to the large brands in most markets, and these can be expressed by those brands' ability to maintain sales with advertising expenditures lower than what might be thought necessary by size of the brand's market shares.[21] Even taking into account the probability that this force is working for *Kodak*, however, the figures for *Kodak's* share of advertising as shown in the table are unusually low, and in fact relatively lower than those for virtually any other major brand of packaged goods in any major market.

The question naturally raised by such a fact is whether a significant increase in advertising weight is capable of injecting adrenaline into the total market. Possibilities of this kind normally lead to a consideration of pressure-testing programs: marketplace experimentation that has produced clear cut results in the past in many product categories. This experimentation means area testing, which involves a heavy research cost, especially if it includes the use of econometric evaluation. But the cost is normally worth paying, and econometric modeling is a technique that we believe could be applied fruitfully to *Kodak* budgetary planning.

Kodacolor Gold Film

As a footnote to this study, the present campaign for *Kodacolor Gold* film deserves a brief discussion. *Kodacolor VR* film was introduced in 1982 and

Table 3–4
Kodak Share of Advertising in the Photographic Market

1981	31%
1982	44%
1983	47%
1984	45%
1985	39%

Source: Advertising Information Services.

represented a clear improvement over *Kodacolor II* film, in particular because it came in four instead of two film speeds. In 1986, *Kodacolor VR-G* film entered the market. It represented yet a further advance, an improvement in the color saturation, something that consumers wanted, although the preference was not always easily verbalized by the public. In 1988, VR-G film was renamed *Kodacolor Gold* film; it is now available in almost forty world markets.

There are common elements between the campaign used in the United States and that used in other markets, although they differ from each other in important strategic respects. In overseas markets, the advertising is younger, more technically oriented, and more aggressive than in the United States, reflecting differences between the markets, the United States in particular being more conservative.

The advertising overseas has an unusual feature: The campaign devotes a separate commercial to each color, and each advertisement demonstrates its own color with extraordinary style and humorous intrusiveness. The advertisements synthesize the motivating values of traditional *Kodak* advertising and the discriminating qualities of the *Kodacolor Gold* film colors. In so doing, they could be pointing the way to significant future developments in *Kodak* advertising.

The international campaign was developed as an international *Kodak* property by J. Walter Thompson and was written by a project team from a number of different offices of the agency. The campaign has been used successfully in Japan, Latin America, Canada, parts of Europe, and certain oriental countries. Perhaps most importantly, the U.S. campaign has worked well and contributed to the welcome revival in *Kodak* film sales in 1987.[22]

Five Lessons From the History of *Kodak*

1. The *Kodak* Brand Is a Long Term Phenomenon. The *Kodak* brand name has had greater longevity than almost any other brand in any market in the United States. It was given clear and distinct identity by its creator, and its vast strength can easily be evaluated by establishing how many people perceive brands of film as different from one another, how well *Kodak* is regarded in both general and specific terms, and —in the last analysis—how well *Kodak* film manages to command a premium price. *Kodak's* strength is clear to the most superficial observer of the photographic market, as is the company's ability to maintain its hold on the mind of the consumer despite the aggressive promotion of cheaper competitive brands. There is no doubt that *Kodak* advertising has contributed significantly to building the brand.

2. *Kodak* Advertising Has Always Possessed a Unique Tone of Voice. *Tone of voice* is a portmanteau phrase used to describe those qualities of planning, construction, and craftsmanship which have always added a particular distinctiveness to advertising. These qualities are the stock-in-trade of the creative groups in JWT New York that work on the *Kodak* account, and they are passed on, as if by osmosis, from old to new generations of creative people in these groups. This expertise is an asset of incalculable value to Eastman *Kodak* Company. The various elements involved in such planning, construction, and craftsmanship were analyzed earlier in this chapter; in brief, the skills are concerned with the distillation and persuasive communication of nonrational motivating arguments bearing on the proposition that picture taking is a record of human lives.

3. Advertising Has Had an Important Role in the Launch of New Types of Cameras. Each of the major new cameras launched by *Kodak* during the past two decades has been successful in achieving mass-market usage levels. These levels have, however, tended to weaken over time. It is inconceivable that such successful launches could have taken place without successful launch advertising. Because of subsequent budgetary reductions, the advertising cannot be blamed for the eventual erosion of the initial usage levels.

4. *Kodak* Is Not an Advertising-Intensive Brand. In this chapter we have examined information bearing on the relatively low level of advertising investments in the *Kodak* brand. Past investments have been determined pragmatically, and the evidence seems to suggest that *Kodak* advertising has contributed, and still contributes, to the maintenance of relatively flat market conditions. The business is holding, but it is not expanding much, except in short-term spurts. Picture taking is not increasing significantly over time, and expanding ownership of cameras does not stimulate it as much as might have been hoped.

There is not much evidence that the recent extremely generous increases in below-the-line promotional expenditures by *Kodak* and its competitors have managed to encourage any real growth in the total market. But could above-the-line advertising do any better? We cannot forecast reliably whether higher levels of advertising could even begin to stimulate total market growth. We should, however, remember that *Kodak's* share of voice in the photographic market is, relative to its market share, significantly lower than that of major brands in other product categories, and greater expenditures would mean a *Kodak* advertising dominance to match its market dominance.

5. There Is a Need to Know More Reliably and Precisely What Can Be Accomplished by Varying *Kodak* Advertising in Different Ways. This point embraces both the qualitative, creative elements in the campaign and variations in advertising pressure. For a brand whose budget on measured media has ranged from $55 million to $90 million during each of the past five years, the rewards in sales and profits that are likely to follow from reliable *knowledge* of the marketplace consequences of actions in deploying the main marketing variables are too great to warrant further emphasis. The United States is an excellent and economical country for test-market experiments, and econometric techniques have been developed and tested that could enable us to learn dramatically more than we do at present about the effect on sales of varying amounts of advertising pressure.

4
Kraft P'tit Québec

> There is so much difference of taste that cheese, almost alone of all
> foods, is tasted by the customer before purchasing.
>
> —Mrs. Beeton[1]

"Separate Marketing Programs Targeted Toward Language-Based Segments"[2]

It is rather rare today (although less so in Europe than in North America), that a cheese buyer is offered a sample in a grocery store or delicatessen before making a purchase. Nevertheless, Mrs. Beeton's observation that different cheeses vary vastly in taste is as true today—perhaps even more true—as it was in the middle of the nineteenth century when she wrote her classic guide to family cookery and household management.

Although the total number of different cheeses in the world is unknown, the sum is in the thousands rather than hundreds, and nowhere is the variety greater than in francophone countries. France alone produces more than four hundred different cheeses,[3] such a dramatic manifestation of national idiosyncrasies that Charles de Gaulle is said to have made the despairing remark that it is impossible to bring together a country that makes so many. And not only does France produce four hundred different cheeses, but it cherishes both this enormous range and the distinctions among the individual varieties.

This chapter is concerned with a French-speaking country, or, rather, with a province of Canada whose special identity, language, and national characteristics are deeply rooted in the past. Indeed, they have been stubbornly maintained for the more than 220 years during which French Canada has been an integral part of a largely English-speaking colony and (later) self-governing dominion. This francophone region, the province of Quebec, has a population of more than six million, or 27 percent of the total population of Canada. It contains the two great cities of Montreal and Quebec, the former the second-largest French-speaking city in the world.

Much has been written about the individual characteristics of French- and English-speaking Canada. The underlying differences are, of course, racial and religious, as well as linguistic. The province used to be significantly poorer than the rest of Canada, its people less well educated and its birthrate comparatively higher. It never used to be known for creativity and innovation, especially in the sphere of consumer goods. But things began to change during the 1960s—to such a degree that what became known as the "quiet revolution" resulted in nothing less than a cultural, political, and economic renaissance: a stirring of national identity and a positive regeneration of leadership and new ideas. This transformation was particularly strongly marked in the field of communications,[4] one of the smaller manifestations of which was the emergence of strong, locally generated advertising campaigns in place of translations of English originals.[5]

Despite these changes, however, many old attitudes and habits have been too deeply entrenched to alter. These are not a matter of casual observation; the field is well researched. Differences in customs as they relate to the nutrition, cuisine, and domestic and buying habits of French-speaking Canada include such things as the following, all of which have been studied empirically:

> Both studies found French Canadians to be more concerned with cooking, baking, household cleanliness, personal appearance, value consciousness, immediate gratification, and security needs than English-speaking families.[6]

> French families, followed by bilingual families, tended to be heavier consumers of staples (butter, shortening, homemade soup, noodles, hamburger, steak), indicative of more original cooking.[7]

> French housewives did not appear to be more sale, special, price, or coupon sensitive than English-speaking housewives.[8]

> Research has now established beyond any doubt that French-speaking Quebecers are more sensitive to national brand names and far less attracted by private brands.[9]

What this amounts to is a refreshingly traditional attitude on the part of many people in the province: a willingness by housewives to take the trouble to provide the best for their families, a reluctance to be lured by the contemporary idol of convenience products, and a strong inclination to eschew price-cutting in return for the security and elimination of risk that are provided by familiar brand names.

Researchers are clear about the origins of the differences in attitude between French-and English-speaking Canadians: "Generally these differences appear to be due to culture rather than to income or social class, and in some cases are actually strengthened by removal of social class or income effects."[10] This clear mosaic of attitudes and beliefs has an actionable meaning to the marketer of consumer goods. There is indeed an opportunity for brand differentiation in French-speaking Canada, but such differentiation must be an element in the cultural bloodstream of the region. It is not enough to rely on superficial differences based, for instance, on income, occupation, or the French language, in isolation. If a brand is to be successful in French-speaking Canada, it must express the rather special cultural and psychographic characteristics of the people in that region.

"Many Local Cheeses Have a Deservedly High Reputation"[11]

It is not known for certain how long the name P'tit Québec has been used in French Canada. The name is a traditional one and is a more or less generic description of a small wheel of extra mild cheddar that has long been eaten there. Cheddar sold in the United States and in English-speaking Canada normally comes in three strengths, or degrees of maturity: mild, sharp, and extrasharp. P'tit Québec, being more mild than the normal mild cheddar, appeals far more to French Canadians than to English Canadians, because what French-speaking Canadians always look for in their cheese is moistness, firmness, and a freshness not devoid of sharpness but with no richness, maturity, or strength of flavor. (There are good objective data to confirm this generalization.)[12]

In the early 1970s, Kraft was farsighted enough to register the name as its trademark for an extramild natural (unprocessed) cheddar that it hoped to sell in French-speaking Canada. The company was fortunate in being able to register this name and block out competitors, since it is often legally difficult for a manufacturer to take as a proprietary name anything approaching what is used generically.[13]

P'tit Québec cheddar came originally in a single variety, shrink-wrapped in two uniform weights. The package design communicated very distinctively certain well-known symbols of French Canada—the fleur-de-lis emblem, the old City Gate of Quebec, and the red, white, and blue of the Tricolor, besides, of course, the name P'tit Québec and the all-important description *très doux* ("very mild"). This packaging has remained essentially unchanged during the fifteen or so years that the brand has been on the market.

It was introduced without much fanfare into a small number of stores in Montreal and Quebec in the early 1970s. There was some instore promotional support and a modest amount of consumer advertising. The company hoped that the brand would grow but was content in the short term for P'tit Québec to establish its natural level of sales without major advertising and promotional investment.

After a period of time, the signals from the market began to look promising, and with the active encouragement of JWT Montreal, Kraft decided to start advertising P'tit Québec in French-speaking Canada in 1975. When

1. *Mr. Emile:* Florent, I'm hungry! I want some P'tit Québec.

2. *Florent:* Mr. Emile! (he corrects him) . . . P'tit Québec please!

3. *Mr. Emile:* . . . please . . . now can I have it?

4. *Florent:* You'll be happy. I've got something new for you.

Thirty-second television commercial first run in French Canada in 1987. The English copy is a translation of the French original.

5. *Florent:* There's not only your cheddar, now there's new mozzarella and new brick P'tit Québec. Here, taste . . .

6. *Mr. Emile:* Mmmm . . . That's mild to my taste!

7. *Anncr:* Like P'tit Québec cheddar, new brick and mozzarella mild cheeses have that special taste that we love. New P'tit Québec cheeses are . . .

8. *Mr. Emile:* Just for me!

9. *Florent and Customers (correcting him):* Just for us!

this decision was made, total sales were much less than those of Cracker Barrel, which in Canada—as in other countries—represented Kraft's leading entry into the market for natural (as opposed to processed) cheese.

Sales of P'tit Québec before the beginning of the advertising campaign gave no hint of what they were to become as a result of the advertising stimulus. What P'tit Québec offered consumers in the French-speaking region, however, was a cheese perfectly suited to their palates; a single-minded communication on packaging and display material of the symbols of French Canada; and, not least, a *brand*, underpinned by the Kraft name. (Remember the above-average importance of brands to French Canadian consumers.) When these values of product, national symbolism, and branding were supported and reinforced by consumer advertising, there was a synergistic effect that resulted, within a relatively short span of years, in P'tit Québec's becoming by a substantial margin the largest selling natural cheese in French Canada, with a large and loyal consumer franchise and more than one envious competitor in the marketplace.

"Juste Pour Nous Autres"

The consumer advertising campaign, which has been exposed consistently on television and to a lesser degree in magazines that circulate in the French-speaking region, has proceeded through a number of phases since it was first run in 1975.[14] It has, however, remained true to its basic strategy of concentration on the symbols, values, and life styles of French Canada. The family feeling, the proprietary quality, and the exclusivity of the French community are encapsulated in the slogan *"Juste pour Nous Autres"* ("Just for Us"), which has been used consistently. The slogan can be, and indeed is, used as a strategic positioning statement for the brand. It represents (although only as the tip of an iceberg) the essential distinctiveness of P'tit Québec, a distinctiveness that has not been eroded in any way since the brand has been on the market. We shall shortly review the evidence of how this quality comes right through to the consumer, to whom P'tit Québec has an unusual salience.

The introductory commercials (run in 1975–1976) were based on the notion of discovery: Two women in a supermarket discover P'tit Québec and talk about how special it is, while their husbands are at home supposedly preparing a barbecue. When the women get home, they discover that their husbands have been spending the time also talking about, and nibbling, a block of P'tit Québec. The language, the settings, and the casting of the commercials are all typically French Canadian, and the pace and tone are relaxed, friendly, and involving.

The commercials have another important feature: Nowhere is it mentioned that P'tit Québec is new. The implication throughout the commercials is that the brand has been around for some time; it is hinted that the brand is a small but real part of the heritage of the French Canadian consumer. P'tit Québec had, of course, been on sale for some years when the commercials were first exposed, and the regulations of the television industry in Canada would have precluded any explicit claims of newness. But even if that restriction had not applied, client and agency would have been reluctant to state that the brand was new. Its newness was judged a less valuable attribute than the tradition surrounding it.

Qualitative research carried out in 1987 confirmed that "P'tit Québec is a brand believed to possess a long history of distribution and a consistency of quality sufficient to ensure its reputation as a great Québécois brand: trustworthy, credible and responsible. . . . 'P'tit Québec is ours.' "[15] A strategy that does not say or even imply newness is unusual, but it is not entirely unknown; a European marketing man with a sense of humor once named it the "creation of retrospective lead time."

The second series of commercials, run in 1977–1978, moved the brand further into a social setting. P'tit Québec was shown as part of the enjoyment and fun of a traditional square-dance party. The *ambience* of the commercials was (again) very recognizably French Canadian, the singer at one of the parties a well-known personality in the French-speaking community.

The third phase of the campaign—and in some ways the most interesting and successful one—carried the advertising through the first half of the 1980s. A number of attractive commercials built up the association between the brand and the rich, appetizing, and unmistakably French Canadian produce of the region, including the blueberries of Lac St. Jean, maple syrup, and Rougemont apples. Those symbols were used not only to reinforce the association of P'tit Québec with French Canada but also so that some of the appetite appeal of the blueberries, maple syrup, and apples could carry over by association to P'tit Québec. In the maple syrup film, the growers of the produce were named and appeared in the commercial: another identifiable association with the cultural values of P'tit Québec. A subsidiary advantage of this campaign was that because it featured other widely distributed foods, it pleased the grocery trade and was extensively used for instore merchandising.

The most recent advertising, used to launch two new varieties of P'tit Québec (which we will discuss shortly), is based on a popular television series in French-speaking Canada, *Le Matou (The Alley Cat)*, based on a book of the same name. The television series is viewed extremely widely; television viewing is anyway slightly more extensive in French than in English Canada. The central character in the series is a young boy, Monsieur Emile, who is adopted by a restaurateur, and a series of rich, human, and humorous television episodes has given the character an everyday familiarity.

Not unexpectedly, Monsieur Emile's association with P'tit Québec has made a notable impact, which we shall also discuss.

We should emphasize that although there have been four different creative expressions of the brand's advertising strategy over the course of the twelve years it has been advertised, the underlying strategy itself has remained unchanged. P'tit Québec has been embedded in the cultural values of French Canada. All the signals about the brand—from its taste, its packaging, its promotions, and its advertising—have been integrated and been mutually supporting. This single-minded concentration has been a major reason for the brand's success.

The Brand and The Consumer

P'tit Québec has grown from very small beginnings in the early 1970s to become the leading brand of natural cheese in French Canada.[16] More than ninety-five percent of its sales volume is in the French province, the overspill into English Canada being a reflection of the small overspill of Kraft's own sales regions. Both client and agency are convinced that its great success would not be able to carry over into the English-speaking regions, where the taste for cheese is different and where the added values connected with P'tit Québec's French Canadian heritage have less meaning and importance.

The total market for natural cheddar in French Canada is virtually flat. Although there was a degree of buoyancy in 1979, 1980, and 1981, when P'tit Québec was making notable headway, total cheese sales subsequently fell back a little and were only six percent higher in 1985 than they had been in 1978.

The market is highly fragmented. There are at least twenty-five different manufacturers' brands, plus five store brands. These thirty brands (together with a few other tiny and localized ones) account for between 90 and 95 percent of all sales. The remainder of the market goes to unbranded cheddar sold mainly in delicatessens and deli departments of stores (places where the customer is occasionally allowed to taste the cheese before buying, as Mrs. Beeton recommends). The only brands with a significant market share are P'tit Québec (with approximately 20 percent) and Cracker Barrel and Etchemin (each with approximately 10 percent). The long tail of other brands is composed of those holding 1 to 3 percent of the market and therefore of small individual significance.

There is little change over time in the shape of the market. As noted, little overall growth occurred between 1980 and 1986, and individual market shares have more or less stabilized at their current levels over the past two years. The market exhibits, in other words, the classic symptoms of stationary conditions, conditions that are very common if not quite universal in the field of repeat-purchase packaged goods.[17] The particular value of P'tit Québec to Kraft lies in its ability to generate profits rather than growth. The mild taste of the cheese comes from its relatively short maturity, which is less expensive for the manufacturer than a long period of maturity. This means that P'tit Québec is an attractively profitable brand.

That the major growth in the sales of P'tit Québec took place after the beginning of consumer advertising is presumptive evidence of that advertising's effectiveness, with a direct "pull" effect on the consumer, together with an indirect "push" effect on the retail trade (persuading store managers to stock the brand and put in on display). The most dramatic recent period of growth was between 1978 and 1981, when P'tit Québec climbed from 14 percent to its current market share of 20 percent. This growth coincided with that most interesting phase of the advertising campaign which built P'tit Québec's associations with the various types of fresh produce grown in French Canada.

From Kraft's overall point of view, however, the success of P'tit Québec has had a downside. Between 1978 and 1981, Cracker Barrel lost 3 percentage points of market share and became second to P'tit Québec in the market. Nevertheless, the latter's growth did not take place entirely by cannibalization, and Kraft's aggregate share grew from 31 to 35 percent during this period, a generally satisfactory outcome despite the gains and losses in individual brand shares.

P'tit Québec has been a demonstrable sales success. Sales data are, however, never quite sufficient to demonstrate decisively the contribution of consumer advertising, because of the possible intervention of other variables in the marketing mix. To evaluate the results of the campaign with greater rigor and precision, we must examine its effect on consumer awareness and attitudes. Fortunately, reasonably good data are available to help us.

As far as brand awareness is concerned, P'tit Québec holds the highest levels for any brands of natural cheddar in French-speaking Canada. The following percentages refer to June 1987 but show no major changes from the figures collected in September 1986 (another manifestation of stationary market conditions).

Total brand awareness	98%
"Top of mind" awareness	61%
"Share of mind" awareness	38%

In total brand awareness, P'tit Québec is followed reasonably closely by Cracker Barrel with 94 percent, Black Diamond with 72 percent, and Scheider's with 63 percent. Other brands score much lower. As far as "top of mind" and "share of mind" are concerned, however, all other brands trail well behind P'tit Québec, which effectively proves that the latter has a much higher salience in consumers' consciousness.

Total awareness of P'tit Québec advertising is 48 percent (with a spontaneous level of 16 percent). These are the highest figures for any brand of natural cheese, although we consider the information of smaller value than that for brand awareness, because of the proven imperfections of advertising recall as a predictive technique.[19]

When consumer beliefs in individual attributes of cheese are explored, P'tit Québec scores higher than any other Kraft cheese, natural or processed. Since these Kraft brands include Cracker Barrel, the second-ranking natural cheddar in brand awareness, we can reasonably extrapolate the data to conclude that P'tit Québec scores more strongly in consumer attributes than any other natural cheddar on the market does. The individual aspects of consumer beliefs in which P'tit Québec scores highest include the following:

- a Canadian cheese
- wholesome
- reliable
- natural
- active
- attractive
- outdoorsy
- open-minded
- no-nonsense

What this consumer research amounts to is a confirmation that P'tit Québec is better known than any of its competitors; it has a much higher salience in consumers' minds; and its image associations are well rounded and favorable.

Of a lower order of reliability and importance are the data showing that the advertising is also well remembered. To achieve P'tit Québec's high degree of brand and advertising recognition has, however, meant a significant investment for Kraft. The period of strong sales growth in 1978–1981 was accompanied by an increasing advertising investment, although the direction of causality cannot be established for certain, the higher sales probably influencing the increased advertising investment as well as being stimulated by it. The trend in sales and advertising can be seen in table 4–1.

During the majority of more recent years, the annual advertising investment measured by externally audited data has exceeded CDN $300,000— twice the budget spent in 1978 (uncorrected for media inflation). In judging this figure, we should, of course, appreciate that the money was spent in

Table 4–1
Kraft P'tit Québec Sales and Advertising
(Index 1978 = 100)

	Sales	*Advertising*
1978	100	100
1979	114	93
1980	143	145
1981	150	185

Source: Data derived from audited sales estimates and advertising expenditures.

only 27 percent of Canada. The current national equivalent expenditure would be more than CDN $1.2 million, a sizable (though not overwhelming) national budget for a single brand.

Advertising expenditure on P'tit Québec has been maintained, although not significantly augmented, in the stationary conditions of the market. Measured by the rather important criterion of share of voice, the P'tit Québec percentage contribution has varied; in 1983 it fell to 16 percent, well below the brand's share of market, and remained below it for 1984 and 1985. This is a normal manifestation of the advertising-related scale economy of large brands and is the appropriate and normal budgetary policy for a well-established entry with a 20 percent market share.[20] In 1986, because of a reduction in the activity level of competitive advertising in French Canada, P'tit Québec's share of voice increased significantly.

In the fall of 1986, an important competitor arrived on the market—a restaged version of Fleur de Lys from McCain, with a rate of advertising investment in 1987 approaching that for P'tit Québec. McCain's brand is clearly modeled on P'tit Québec in its mildness and French Canadian orientation; in particular its name brings to mind the emblem on the P'tit Québec packaging. An important feature is that the cheese is marketed in three varieties—cheddar, mozzarella, and brick. Cheddar and brick are mostly eaten raw, the latter being slightly harder and less mild than the former; mozzarella is generally eaten in cooked dishes.

The emergence of a serious competitor called for a response from Kraft, although the normal experience in packaged goods markets is that second brands achieve a stable brand share level no higher than half that of the innovator.[21] Nevertheless, the introduction by McCain of two new extramild types of cheese, mozzarella and brick, under the Fleur de Lys name pointed to a market opportunity so far unexploited by Kraft.

Kraft therefore decided to introduce without delay mozzarella and brick varieties of P'tit Québec. Despite the time pressure, Kraft's plans were developed with care. Initial qualitative research among buyers of P'tit Québec and competitive brands gave a green light to the range extension, so long as it could be carried out cautiously, avoiding the danger of any erosion of the brand values that had been successfully built up for the cheddar variety.[22]

JWT Montreal developed four alternative and distinctly different advertising ideas for the launch of the new varieties. The Monsieur Emile campaign (described earlier) was selected as the strongest and most appropriate, and the first commercial was subjected to two separate pretests. The pretests demonstrated that the campaign generates high recall and favorable attitudes; Monsieur Emile is recognized, is obviously popular, and is considered entirely compatible with the personality of P'tit Québec.

Pretesting, no matter how carefully carried out, suffers from technical imperfections.[23] Nonetheless, the initial signals from the marketplace regarding the P'tit Québec range extensions seem prima facie to be favorable. The instore distribution is satisfactory, and the speedy response by Kraft appears to have saved the brand from being preempted by McCain's potentially dangerous entry into the market.

Five Lessons from the History of P'tit Québec

1. The Success of Food Brands Can Depend on National Idiosyncrasies. The main functional characteristic contributing to the success of P'tit Québec is that it possesses the type of mild taste particularly suited to the French Canadian palate. The world is full of strong national differences in people's tastes for food (some, but by no means all, of which reflect differences in per capita income and local agricultural specialization). Examples selected at random are the high consumption of ready-to-eat breakfast cereals in the United States but the low consumption in Latin America, the high usage of butter in France but of margarine in the Netherlands, the popularity of instant coffee in the United Kingdom but its unpopularity in Scandinavia, the high volume of beer drunk in Belgium but of wine drunk in Italy, and the lamb eaten by the Spaniards but not by the Germans.

Such differences make it much more difficult to achieve success with international advertising campaigns in the food field than in many other fields—witness the common and successful use of international campaigns for toiletries, detergents, gasoline, and airlines but their rarity for edible fats, frozen foods, beer, and coffee.

2. P'tit Québec is Embedded in French Canadian Cultural Values. Over and beyond the taste of the cheese, all other signals about the brand—from the packaging and most of all from the consumer advertising—are manifestations of French Canadian cultural identity. Although the campaign has progressed through four phases, the basic strategy has been unchanged, and each campaign has concentrated in its own different way on aspects of French Canadian life. This concentration has extended to the casting and settings of the commercials as well as to the use of the characteristic *argot,* not least the slogan *"Juste pour Nous Autres,"* that has played such a central role in the advertising, and expresses so well the French Canadian national identity.

Integration is a characteristic of all successful brands. Harmony among the different elements that communicate the brand to the consumer leads to a synergism that contributes to its success. There is an additional payoff when it comes to range extension, such as with the two new varieties introduced by P'tit Québec in 1987. Although such range extension requires advertising support at least in the short term, the synergism of the brand will be increased even further in the long term, as P'tit Québec takes a larger and increasingly stable share of not only the supermarket display shelf but also the consumer's mind.

3. A Gradual Approach. The soundness of P'tit Québec as a long-term brand property stems in part from the circumspect way in which it was launched and subsequently developed. The level and stability of consumer interest were measured by allowing the brand to exist virtually unsupported for some years. The basic consumer interest, together with an advertising campaign that has concentrated on traditional values rather than bold flashiness, has led to P'tit Québec's becoming—originally imperceptibly but now to a pronounced degree—a natural part of the cuisine of French-speaking Canada and, just as importantly, a small part of the cultural heritage of the region.

4. The Effective Use of Tracking Studies. Since the major success of P'tit Québec dated from the beginning of the consumer campaign in the mid-1970s, there is little doubt that the advertising was decisively important as a sales-generating activity. We also know, however, that the campaign communicated effectively those brand attributes considered most important for P'tit Québec (a Canadian cheese, wholesome, reliable, natural, and so on), with no major deficiencies or weaknesses. We have information of diagnostic value, which can be used, if necessary, to guide future changes in what is claimed in the consumer advertising. We have such useful insights because tracking data on brand awareness and brand attitudes have been collected and sensibly interpreted. We know that the advertising works. The tracking data help us to understand *how* it works.

5. A Carefully Evaluated Budgetary Policy. In 1987, twelve years after the beginning of the consumer advertising campaign, P'tit Québec was still the brand with the largest advertising budget in French-speaking Canada. Without major advertised competition (until the emergence of McCain's Fleur de Lys in 1987), the success of P'tit Québec might have tempted many other manufacturers to cut back advertising expenditure in the interest of boosting short-term profit. Kraft turned its back on such a strategy, although the brand was admittedly able to maintain its sales leadership with a share of voice below its share of market. The budget was carefully planned to maintain high sales while employing economy of force. With the arrival of serious competition in 1987, Kraft's budgetary strategy could almost certainly be shown also to have done an important protective job for P'tit Québec.

5

Listerine Antiseptic

. . . even your closest friends won't tell you.
—Listerine advertisement, circa 1928

Where the Brand Is

Listerine is a household name in the United States; it is difficult for people in other countries to appreciate fully its importance and ubiquity.

Sixty-three percent of the American adult population use antiseptic mouthwash—a personal habit that was virtually created by Listerine. The brand has been used at one time or another by 90 percent of mouthwash users and in any given month is currently used by 23 percent of all American adults, a statistic that translates to 40 million people.[1] Few brands in any category are as large in terms of user penetration combined with heavy per capita consumption. Listerine is part of the morning routine of its users, who gargle with it an average of 6.5 times per week, week in and month out.[2] And the 22 percent of heaviest users (those who use it 8 or more times per week) account for 43 percent of the total volume of consumption.[3] Not all brands with high penetration also have high sales volumes; many product categories (such as mustard, sticky parcel tape, some toiletries, and many pharmaceuticals) have few or no large volume brands despite their very high penetration levels. One of the main strengths of Listerine is its per captia consumption, a theme that will run throughout this chapter.

The brand's high penetration and large-volume usage have made it a source of considerable sales and profit to Warner-Lambert. A. C. Nielsen estimates Listerine's sales to exceed $114 million annually at consumer prices in food and drug stores alone, a total that can probably be inflated to at least $200 million to take into account the other types of retail outlets in which the brand is distributed.[4] This works out to a mean annual expenditure on the brand of more than $2.40 for every household in the country, an average embracing both the substantial numbers who buy the brand and all those who do not.

With a brand of such size, the demographic skew among its users is less important than the brand's universality. Listerine is used by all sorts of people, although rather above the average by the following:[5]

- fifty-year-olds and older
- the less well educated
- the black and Hispanic populations
- people who live in the South
- people with lower incomes

Because Listerine has been used in the past by most mouthwash users, its attributes are widely familiar, although attitudes toward the brand are polarized, which is what gives them their distinctiveness. While 70 percent of users commend its effectiveness in killing germs and freshening the mouth, there are more users who dislike rather than like the taste (43 percent compared with 32 percent). Judgment suggests that high effectiveness and antiseptic taste are like the two sides of a single coin: inseparable from each other and indeed the first a complementary feature of and reinforcement to the second.[6] JWT creative groups have seen an affinity between this notion and that part of the American cultural ethos which is referred to as the Protestant ethic. Whether or not this idea is fanciful, the harmony (despite the apparent disharmony) between high effectiveness and unappealing flavor is important to the brand, a point that also recurs in this chapter.

Since Listerine is no longer sold for colds and chills, there is barely any seasonal rise in sales in the winter.[7] The reason for the abandonment of advertising for colds and chills forms a significant part of this study.

How Listerine Got There

Listerine was invented in 1879 by Jordan Wheat Lambert, an American chemist of patrician origins. It was originally used as an antiseptic following surgery, because, unlike crude carbolic acid, it does not damage tissue. It was appreciated by Lord Lister, the pioneer of antiseptics, who was persuaded to allow his name to be used for the new product. During the rest of the inventor's lifetime, however, the brand slept and for years remained an "ethical" pharmaceutical, sold only to the medical profession.[8] The present Listerine package, which is a heavy glass bottle with a clinical-looking descriptive label, inserted in a brown cardboard outer tube with a low-key surface design, is a lineal descendant of the Listerine package of the nineteenth century and continues the emphasis on medical association and recommendation that has always been so valuable to the brand.

In 1922, the business was effectively taken over by the inventor's younger son, Gerard B. Lambert, a young man accustomed to luxury but who was facing a personal situation not far short of financial desperation. This situation lent urgency and drive to his endeavors, which soon gave dramatic evidence of something else altogether—a most remarkable flair and sureness of touch, particularly in marketing activities. Indeed, Listerine responded to his carrot and stick in a way that can only be described as magical.

It is the advertising that deserves the closest scrutiny. Three of its features can be isolated as the central causes of Listerine's sudden and dramatic growth.

First was the discovery of a selling appeal. This appeal was for the treatment of bad breath, a condition for which Lambert used the technical expression *halitosis,* a word his advertising caused to enter the American popular vocabulary.

The second device Lambert pioneered was experimentation in the marketplace with different selling appeals: evaluating their effects by *sales* measures, compared with sales in suitable control areas. In the early days he employed crude mechanisms based on direct response. But he later tested different selling appeals while the brand was sold via the normal retail trade, by running different copy in different cities and by ensuring that his sales force eliminated special merchandising efforts that might have obscured the "pull" effect of the campaigns on the consumer. Throughout his career, although he achieved complete retail distribution by offering Listerine inventory on a "sale or return" basis, Lambert always put more emphasis on the sales-generating effects of advertising than on forcing sales by display, competitive discounts, and other merchandising activity at the retail level (below-the -line activity, in modern marketing jargon). This point is directly related to the third feature of Lambert's advertising program.

Against the direct, albeit temporary, opposition of his partners, Lambert began a dramatic series of advertising pressure tests. He persuaded his partners to allow him to lift their advertising expenditure progressively, at the rate of $5,000 increase per month, on the stipulation that profit could be shown to increase at a faster rate than the advertising investment. Today this procedure would be described as an exercise in econometrics: the construction and use of a medium-term advertising response function to decide the point of diminishing returns, when pressure should be cut off (that is, when the incremental advertising cost exceeded the incremental profit by the smallest measurable margin).

Lambert preferred to call this exercise a gamble. But in 1928 this econometric gamble pushed his expenditure on advertising to beyond $5 million, which, by his evaluation procedures, was an entirely profitable investment. Two years previously, Lambert had been making a personal income of $500,000 a year, a not insignificant sum in 1926.

His direct involvement in the advertising operation caused him to found a house agency called Lambert and Feasley. One of the reasons for his doing so was to obtain the exclusive talents of two spectacularly successful copywriters, Milton Feasley and, after Feasley's death, Gordon Seagrove (the author of the words that preface this chapter).

The early advertisements have an elegance of presentation and distinctive tone of voice that almost make one forget their dated visual presentation. But the important thing to remember about these campaigns is the continuous use of marketplace experimentation to evaluate the sales effects of copy changes. This procedure was as much the result of Lambert's brilliant concentration on marketing essentials as of the relatively simple and controllable nature of retailing during the 1920s and 1930s. When, by the 1960s, the retail trade had become a much more complex structure, Warner-Lambert and J. Walter Thompson (like most other advertisers and agencies) elected to use day-after-recall measures as a surrogate for sales effects, a practice that moved the evaluation of advertising a good step away from the marketplace, with results that remain controversial even today.

It was as a result of successful market experimentation that the company began, in the late 1920s, to use the brand's suitability to treat and prevent colds and sore throats as a supplement to the first advertising story based on the treatment of bad breath. Listerine was therefore supported during its long years of growth by two selling appeals, halitosis and colds. Chronologically, the former led the way. It also remained the more important claim. This was serendipitous, because when colds advertising had to be discontinued, the brand received a serious shock, but the effects of abandoning colds claims turned out to be well short of fatal.

Listerine progressed steadily, its growth coming from its solid and expanding user base and from its success in achieving volume usage. Competitors entered the market. But Listerine was virtually unassailable, and no competitor had much success until the market began to plateau and until there arrived, in the late 1960s, a more serious competitor than any of its predecessors—because it came from the most practiced of all the training stables.

But in the 1930s, 1940s, and 1950s, the total market continued its expansion. Indeed, with a dominant share of an increasing market, Listerine's future looked continuously optimistic during the whole of this long period.

J. Walter Thompson won the Listerine account in 1963. Following what was then the most common practice of the largest agencies handling fast-moving consumer goods, the agency produced and exposed a long series of Slice-of-Life commercials. These were sixty seconds, a more common length twenty years ago than today. Some commercials concentrated on bad breath and others (run during the winter) on colds and sore throats. Most were tested for day-after-recall before national exposure, and the recall levels of the commercials (certainly those run on air) compared well with norms in the product field.[9]

Looking at the market as a whole in this period, annual sales in ounces, measured by the Nielsen food and drug indexes, quintupled during the years 1953 through 1967. This average annual increase was at a compound rate of 12 percent, a healthy pace indeed by the standards of most consumer goods markets. And during the whole of this period, Listerine remained the dominant brand, although its annual shares, which had exceeded 50 percent on occasions before 1960, were down to the 44 to 46 percent range during the mid-1960s.[10]

It is difficult, even with the benefit of hindsight, to judge whether the slice-of-life advertising campaign—qualitatively or quantitatively—contributed decisively to the weakening of Listerine's market share. The kind of slice-of-life advertising exposed in the 1960s was used in many cases as a device to achieve high recall scores.[11] It therefore laid stress on factual copy claims, which are of greater importance to nonusers than to users of a brand, because the latter are already familiar with a brand's functional attributes. It could therefore be argued that such advertising was best aimed at increasing the numbers of users—at penetration rather than at consumption per user. This was the agreed strategy at the time, although the importance of increasing volume consumption was also recognized. (The slice-of-life technique is, of course, adaptable to the objective of increasing volume consumption as well as penetration growth, but it seems to have been used more for the latter during the 1960s.)

At that time, the market had grown very large and mouthwash was used by two-thirds of all adults, a penetration level that was possibly capable of a little further increase, although recent annual increases had been slow. Accordingly, it was more than likely that Listerine would have gained more from a strategy directed more strongly at per capita usage growth. For this, the type of slice-of-life advertising then used may have been less appropriate than emotionally oriented advertising that reinforced Listerine's added values and reemphasized the importance of regular usage. It should also be remembered that in the 1960s and 1970s, the slice-of-life advertising technique was strongly associated with Procter and Gamble, who had the skills and experience to use it with maximum proficiency, giving that company a degree of advantage when Scope was launched with a slice-of-life campaign.[12]

The debate is hypothetical, however, because changes now suddenly took place in the market as a whole, demanding an urgent reconsideration of the role of Listerine's advertising.

Competition in a Stationary Total Market

The year 1971 was the last year of high total market growth. Although market sales had reached a plateau in food and drug stores in 1967, in 1971 the business in mass merchandisers also stopped increasing. What caused the cessation of an extremely well-established growth trend is not entirely clear, but it was quite decisive. The probable cause was market saturation related to the high level of per capita consumption, allied to the siphoning of growth to newly introduced toothpastes sold for their mouthwash benefits. Mouthwash itself therefore joined the majority of mature markets for repeat-purchase packaged goods as the first symptom of stationary market conditions set in: a halt to overall market expansion. In fact, total volume sales of mouthwash, measured by the Nielsen food and drug indexes, slowed to a mean compound increase of well below 2 percent during the entire period 1967 through 1985, a rate that barely kept up with the growth in population.[13]

The second characteristic of stationary market conditions—a stabilization of market shares—did not, however, occur. Indeed, by the end of the 1960s the introduction of Scope had heralded an increase in new brand activity of an energy and effectiveness unprecedented by the previous standards of the mouthwash market.

Scope was launched in 1966. The launch program was characterized by the normal Procter and Gamble combination of a product with functional distinctiveness, single-minded advertising, heavy investments above- and below-the-line, weight at point of sale, and the whole preceded by carefully evaluated market experimentation. A volume brand share of 13 percent in 1968 grew to 23 percent in 1976, where it has more or less stabilized but done so in a position to yield substantial profits to its manufacturer. It was, and is, also able to pose a continuous threat to Listerine, which nevertheless remained the clear market leader. Indeed, Listerine's share showed an astonishing series of increases during Scope's early years. Listerine was up to 50 percent in 1972 and thereafter declined only slowly until the late 1970s, when it weakened (for reasons we shall consider shortly) to a level bracketing 30 percent, where the brand has remained ever since.[14]

Three factors were associated with Scope's establishment and early growth:

1. The launch caused an immediate increase in advertising investment levels. Total market advertising expenditure (above-the-line) doubled from less than $20 million in 1965 to more than $40 million in 1967. And they remained at these levels until the 1970s, when advertising went into retreat as the second factor came into prominence.

2. For a number of reasons—not the least of them inflation, the removal of price controls, and the growing strength of the retail trade—the mouthwash market (like many others) became increasingly oriented toward retail promotions.[15] As an example of this trend, the estimated volume of sales of Listerine accounted for by promotional packs moved up from 16 percent in 1975 to a peak of 43 percent in 1978, followed by a descent; for Scope, this

share rose from 17 percent in 1975 to a peak of 34 percent also in 1978, again followed by a descent.

3. Additional new competitors then entered the market: Warner-Lambert's Listermint in 1976 and Unilever's Signal in 1977. These competitors in turn caused a renewal of advertising activity above-the-line and a lifting of total market expenditures to levels in excess of $50 million during the 1980s. This is more or less the situation today.

Enter the Federal Trade Commission

It was during the 1970s that Listerine was assaulted from yet another direction. The long-established winter campaign in which the brand had been sold as a treatment for colds and sore throats came under the hostile scrutiny of the Washington bureaucracy. Although the campaign had gone through a number of evolutions, the main copy claim had remained more or less intact over a long period of time. The Federal Trade Commission had unsuccessfully challenged Listerine's advertising in 1932 and 1944, in the latter year over the colds story. Renewed interest in this issue was now being taken, in the elevated climate of consumerism of the early 1970s[16]

Warner-Lambert's support for their claim that "along with proper rest and diet, Listerine would result in fewer colds, milder colds, and milder symptoms thereof and less severe colds and sore throats" was a long series of clinically supervised tests. These tests employed large samples of men, women, and children, some being Listerine users and others nonusers, for whom the incidence of colds and chills was less for the users than for the nonusers.

The findings of these tests demonstrated to the satisfaction of Warner-Lambert statisticians who reviewed the data (not to speak of the FTC, which accepted the evidence in 1944) that the use of Listerine had a small but statistically significant beneficial effect on people's susceptibility to colds and sore throats.

Nevertheless, after a prolonged series of hearings that took place between 1972 and 1975, the advertising claims were finally and irrevocably rejected, on the grounds that the tests were now thought not to have been carried out with complete scientific rigor and, in particular, because of doubts about whether the identity of the brand used by the Listerine users was well enough concealed from the researchers who supervised the tests.

In addition to the resultant ban on the use of advertising claims based on colds, Warner-Lambert was compelled to insert into advertisements, to the total value of $10 million, the statement "Listerine will not help prevent colds and sore throats, or lessen their severity." This painful mea culpa ran between September 1978 and February 1980. Tracking studies examining consumer attitudes between 1971 and 1979 noted declines in Listerine's rating on a number of attributes. And in particular, the 56 percent of people who rated Listerine "one of the best" for effectiveness in treating colds and sore throats had dropped to 26 percent in 1979.[17]

As noted, this was about the time when Listerine's market share was dropping, and then stabilizing around 30 percent.

Listerine Advertising: Quantitative Elements

The change in the shape of the total market from a steep curve to a plateau and the emergence of Scope as a serious and increasingly successful competitor caused a shock to Listerine that had profound but delayed effects.

For as long as five years, the brand continued to grow in terms of volume, reaching a peak of 50 percent in market share in food and drug outlets in 1972. There were three interrelated reasons for this extraordinary resilience, the third of which concerns the content of the Listerine advertising and is important enough to be evaluated in a separate section of this chapter. But first let us examine the two other factors, which, if not necessarily more important, are more easily disposed of.

First, there is the fundamental and innate strength of the brand, with its positive combination of high penetration and large-volume usage. The impetus of repetitive consumer purchase stemming from established patterns of buying behavior continued to carry Listerine forward with an inbuilt momentum. Judgment suggests that the brand had (and probably still possesses) the ability to generate extra consumer purchase and repurchase simply because of its large size: a scale economy shared by most large brands and thought to be connected with their high level of consumer penetration. The phrase *penetration supercharge* has been used to describe this phenomenon.[18]

Second, the frame of mind of both client and agency did not allow Scope to make headway if this could at any cost be prevented. Warner-Lambert dug deep into its pockets and continued to have Listerine outspend Scope in consumer advertising investments above-the-line every year from 1966 through 1975. These basic data can be viewed in more than one fashion, and it is worthwhile to pause and consider in a more extended (though by no means exhaustive) way the advertising investment policy at this time.

JWT pointed out in a brand review in 1981 that Listerine's share of voice had fallen below its share of market for almost the whole of the decade of the 1970s.[19] Although these facts are not in dispute, it should also be remembered that there is an almost universal tendency for larger brands to operate effectively in the marketplace with a share of voice below the norm suggested by the brand's market share. As we discuss in more detail in chapter 20, this tendency is a major source of the scale economies of such brands, a scale economy that can be quantified by the difference between a brand's hypothetical advertising expenditure in a parity relationship (that is, if its share of market equaled its share of voice) and what the brand actually does spend. This difference can amount to *millions of dollars.*[20]

It can therefore be strongly argued on generalized empirical grounds that the very fact of a reduction of Listerine's share of voice below the norm suggested by its market share is insufficient to cause a collapse in the latter. But this statement needs qualification. A second and more drastic reduction in expenditures above-the-line in the late 1970s (almost certainly associated with the increased promotional investments committed at this time and discussed earlier) seems to have caused decisive damage to the brand's market share, exacerbating the ill effects of the coincident "corrective" advertising required by the FTC.

Listerine is an advertising-intensive brand. By extrapolating recent Nielsen estimates of dollar sales and advertising, the bracket into which we would estimate Listerine's above-the-line advertising is 12 to 15 percent of net sales value. This is high by the standards of packaged goods as a whole but is not high for the toiletries, cosmetics, and pharmaceutical categories.

Advertising-to-sales ratios estimated by *Advertising Age* and computed on a company, not a brand, basis show Warner-Lambert to have spent more than 25 percent in 1966 (the year Scope was launched), ratios in the 15 percent bracket every year from 1967 through 1976, and a precipitous decline for six full years thereafter, to the 7 to 9 percent level, until a sharp recovery in 1983–1984.[21] These data jibe with the estimates discussed in the preceding paragraphs and suggest that the weakening of Listerine's market share coincided in time, and was almost certainly connected causally, with a drastic siphoning of funds from above- to below-the-line. This in turn was probably triggered by competitive activity—mutual sensitivity and reaction between Scope and Listerine. Had it continued, it could very well have led eventually to a disastrous run on profit, and—not to put too fine a point on it—to a gradual but inexorable erosion of brand values in the market as a whole.

During these years of diversion of funds below-the-line, especially 1976 through 1979, Listerine's food and drug share fell progressively from 40 to 32 percent, while Scope maintained its 23 percent. Listermint and Signal were becoming established at this time, and it is clear that they managed to eat into Listerine's share of market much more than into Scope's.

Listerine and Scope were both being promoted heavily, but Scope consistently outspent Listerine above-the-line, both in absolute terms and a fortiori on a per ounce basis. The Warner-Lambert strategy was influenced by the need to release funds for the launch of Listermint. Nevertheless, from the point of view of Listerine, there is little doubt that Procter and Gamble's ability to boost advertising investments for Scope significantly higher than those for Listerine compounded the latter's problems, and caused seriously deleterious effects on it in the medium and long terms.

Listerine Advertising: Qualitative Elements

During the years under review, seven campaigns were exposed nationally for Listerine. We have omitted from consideration those additional campaigns which were tested in various ways before widespread exposure and as a result were not used nationally. The chronology of the campaigns that were used is as follows:[22]

Slice of Life	1963–1969
Hate/Love	1969–1973, West Coast for fifteen months, nationally for eight months
Two-Times Longer	1974–1975
Skeptics	1975–1980
Uh-Uh-Uh	1980–1981
Twice a Day	1981–1983
Antiplaque	1983–1986

The only one of these campaigns that was used for colds advertising was Slice of Life, but even that campaign was used most often for bad breath.

During these years, Listerine performed in the marketplace as follows:

- It was a losing share in an expanding market during the period prior to 1967. During most of this time, slice-of-life advertising was being exposed. This campaign went through some evolution—for instance, to incorporate progressively emotional appeals and arguments to encourage Listerine volume consumption as well as brand penetration. It was also during this time, of course, that Scope was launched.

- The brand then gained share in a gradually plateauing market during each year from 1968 through 1972.

- There then began a progressive decline in Listerine's market share, which slid down to 40 percent in 1976 and then lower, a movement that more or less coincided with serious shifts of budgets from above-to below-the-line.

- Brand share stabilized in the 30 percent range from 1979 onward, following a period of reductions in promotional investments and increasing advertising investments by all brands in the market, including Listerine.

- The decade 1976 through 1985 also showed a weakening of Listerine's (four-week) consumer penetration, from 39 to 23 percent.[23] Although this overall reduction is partly a statistical artifact, the loss of sole users was very serious; it declined from 24 to 11 percent, evidence that Listerine users were increasingly using second and third brands. This situation reemphasized the need to concentrate attention on increasing volume per user—a recurrent theme in this study.

Without attempting to draw robust conclusions about the sales effectiveness of the seven campaigns that ran during this period, we can note certain points that are worthy of fuller consideration.

First, between the discontinuation of the Hate/Love campaign in 1973 and the beginning of the Anti-Plaque advertising in 1983, the length of exposure of each of the four campaigns used was restricted to a relatively short period. (The Skeptics campaign, which had an apparently longer life, had very limited exposure because it was run during the years when Listerine's annual budgets sank drastically; even uncorrected for inflation, they were only about two-thirds of what they had been during the years of Slice of Life and Hate/Love.) These short spans of exposure seem to be evidence of short-term thinking and even uncertainty about where the Listerine advertising was going. Although this is not surprising in view of the enormous uncertainties caused by the competitive and inflationary pressures of the time, not to speak of the problems with the FTC, the number of different Listerine campaigns run between the early 1970s and the early 1980s is worthy of comment.

The second point is the one already discussed, in which it has been hypothesized that the weakening of the brand during the late 1960s may have been influenced by the emphasis in the type of Slice of Life advertising run at the time on the more difficult objective of penetration growth, rather than on the less difficult and more important objective of volume usage growth.

The third point concerns the Hate/Love campaign. Although the only evidence from creative research comes from day-after-recall tests, which tell us nothing about the campaign's selling power, marketplace data do demonstrate that, at least in its early stages (when the campaign was market-tested on the West Coast), the campaign caused significant upward shifts not only in consumer awareness, recall, and frequency of use but also in audited sales via the retail trade.[24] The campaign was based on the thought that although Listerine has a taste that people hate, they use it twice a day because the brand is effective. Judgment of this claim suggests that this campaign, more than any other exposed during those years, managed to capitalize on that combination of brand features—the harmony (despite the apparent disharmony) between high effectiveness and unappealing flavor—

which is absolutely unique to Listerine and which has already been discussed in this chapter. Judgment also reminds us of the old advertising adage that to admit brand weaknesses increases the credibility of the claims we make for our brand strengths.

There was extended discussion at the time about the possibility of wear-out of the Hate/Love campaign, but the campaign was abandoned after a very short national exposure for reasons unconnected with wear-out. The opinion was reached that it was essential to *respond* to the Scope campaign, in particular to react publicly to the Scope advertising's attack on mouthwashes that give "medicine breath."[25] This tactical shift leads naturally to our next point.

The fourth point relates to the various campaigns that were used during the period of Listerine's deepest troubles, when there were heavy movements of funds from above-to below-the-line and when there was litigation with the FTC. Each of the three campaigns exposed between 1974 and 1981 made major use of advertising arguments concerned with brand discriminators. Virtually all the commercials show an explicit consciousness of Scope, referring to "soda-pop tasting mouthwash," and "number two mouthwash," and in some cases even showing the Scope bottle. It is easy to understand the reasons for this policy, but it is relatively unorthodox behavior for a brand leader to employ it, because of the danger that such a defensive stance will actually publicize the competition and divert attention from the primary objective of increasing volume usage: a matter for motivating rather than discriminating arguments. Indeed, there is no evidence that such advertising did much good for the brand, although it is possible that Listerine might have done worse without it.

The fifth point concerns the current Antiplaque campaign, which resulted from a number of years of creative development, seems to have taken the brand beyond the point of maximum sensitivity, and appears to be set for a long run. Not only is there an important educational job to be done in view of the imperfect though increasing consumer awareness of plaque, mouthwash advertising based on plaque, and the association of Listerine with plaque, but also there is a strong feeling, based on judgment and research, that the Antiplaque story, which has already contributed to stabilizing the brand, may have the long-term staying power needed gradually to rebuild it.[26] But the campaign needs to evolve slowly, in order to appeal to younger people. And although volume growth is the main marketing objective, steps must also be taken to arrest any weakening of consumer penetration.

The sixth point is more general and attempts to consider Listerine's position today and how advertising, especially that during the past twenty years, has contributed to bringing the brand to where it is. By no stretch of the imagination can Listerine be considered a failure or even a partial failure.

With its 30 percent brand share, 23 percent consumer penetration in any four-week period, and high-volume usage, the brand is an extremely valuable property and the source of considerable present and future sales and profits to Warner-Lambert. In view of the problems the brand has faced during the past two decades—the cessation of growth in the total market; the increasing competition, notably the establishment of a powerful number-two brand; the increase in retail power vis-à-vis the manufacturing sector; the inflationary pressures of the 1970s; and the potentially disastrous dispute with the FTC—the wonder is that Listerine has survived so well, and not only survived but stabilized, and may indeed be creating the opportunity for the gradual recovery of lost ground.

Nevertheless, it is difficult to deny that certain strategies have been more successful than others. The last section of this chapter will dwell briefly on the main lessons we can draw from our study of Listerine, especially if we employ that faculty so widely (and on occasion irritatingly) deployed in the business and academic worlds, twenty-twenty hindsight.

Five Lessons from the History of Listerine

1. What Matters Most is the Endogenous Characteristics of the Brand. Listerine is an intensely distinctive, polarized brand. The functional performance, the added values (notably the belief in effectiveness that has been built by both the product and the previous advertising), the name, the packaging—are all coherent: They are individually and in combination unique. Other manufacturers, facing the competitive threat of Scope, might have been tempted (suicidally) to change the taste of Listerine. There is little doubt that the campaign that was the most successful in echoing the endogenous characteristics of Listerine—Hate/Love—was individually the most successful campaign in the marketplace over the past twenty years.

2. Volume Consumption. As has been reiterated in this study, one of the secrets of the success of Listerine is that its high penetration has always been accompanied by a high volume of consumption. A consistent theme running through all the advertising has been the encouragement of regular daily, even twice-daily, usage. There is support for the view that the most successful campaigns have been those which place the greatest stress on this element. As a general, if not quite axiomatic, rule, all markets will eventually reach a plateau in overall consumption. When this happens, it is almost impossible to increase penetration, and competing brands, particularly leading ones, are forced by default to encourage usage as the prime marketing strategy. Long-term advertising planning should be carried out with this in mind.

3. Advertising Intensity. Listerine has traditionally been, and continues to be, an advertising-intensive brand, and competitive pressure in the market-place has, if anything, increased this characteristic. It is significant that the time when Listerine suffered its greatest weakening in the market was that period when funds were being siphoned from above- to below-the-line. It is not difficult to appreciate the pressures that caused such a diversion, but the client and agency were clearly more successful in resisting such pressures in the late 1960s than they were ten years later. There are lessons here for the future.

4. Brand Leadership. The psychology of brand leadership makes for an interesting empirical study. The most telling practical example of successful brand leadership in the history of Listerine is Warner-Lambert's aggressive and effective response to the early danger posed by Scope between 1966 and 1971. Some manufacturers might have been intimidated by the threat of competition from Procter and Gamble (as indeed, in its turn, was Warner-Lambert, Canada).[27] Other manufacturers would have believed the essentially self-fulfilling theory of cyclical decline and taken steps, by action or inaction, or both, that inevitably would have caused the eventual extinction of the brand to have followed its maturity, following the classical life cycle model. (Listerine is not the only brand in this book that has been protected by its manufacturer from the supposedly inevitable decline phase of the life cycle; Lux and Oxo are two other excellent cases in point.) And still other manufacturers might have responded prematurely to competitor's copy claims and thus neglected constant reinforcement of their own strengths, in particular the importance of the motivating task of expanding per capita usage. Warner-Lambert and J. Walter Thompson did many, if not most, things right. But this does not mean that they did everything right.

5. The Need For Better Market Research. Listerine was to all intents and purposes created in the 1920s by an imaginative entrepreneur who devised reliable methods of testing experimentally different selling appeals. Always an advertising-intensive brand, Listerine has traditionally responded strongly to copy changes. The increasing complexity of retail distribution during the past thirty years makes it no longer easy to use Lambert's methods, a situation that has encouraged widespread use of psychological measures of campaign effects (such as day-after-recall measures) as surrogates for sales measures. But the fact that it is difficult to make sales measures does not automatically validate the psychological ones, which indeed can be shown in most circumstances to be not only unreliable but actively misleading.[28]

The suspicion remains that inadequate research has had a deleterious effect on Listerine advertising; for example, it may have encouraged the decision to use the slice-of-life advertising for too long. Inadequate research may also have contributed to the premature rejection of advertising ideas before marketplace exposure—among the many tubs of bathwater, how many contained babies? The development of reliable marketplace mechanisms to evaluate the sales effects of campaign changes is being actively pursued at the moment, although with little visible progress. A reminder of Gerard Lambert's seminal work in the 1920s and its contribution to the success of Listerine should spur our efforts to find better research than that available to marketing and advertising practitioners in the 1980s. The first thing for us to do with our research—as with most other things—is not to settle for second best.

6
Lux Toilet Soap

> Ninety-six percent of the lovely complexions you see on the screen
> are cared for by Lux Toilet Soap.
> —Lux Advertisement, 1928

"When Products Can Be Significantly Differentiated, Advertising is Likely to Be Effective"[1]

Toilet soap was one of the very first product categories in which advertising was able to demonstrate its effectiveness in building brands. As early as the 1880s, two soaps were among the four largest advertised brands in the United States.[2] One of those soaps was Procter and Gamble's Ivory, launched in 1879 and quickly established as market leader, as brands began to carve shares out of what had been, and for some decades was to remain, a commodity market. Ivory in the 1980s is still the market leader, after a century of absolute consistency in its positioning. Ivory remains an extremely powerful brand and a living refutation of the cherished academic theory of the product life cycle.

All the brands of toilet soap launched in the United States after 1879 have to some extent remained in the shadow of Ivory. Its strength has come partly from the simplicity and power of its main consumer benefit of purity (and lack of perfume), a primarily functional characteristic; partly from the effectiveness of its advertising, which builds on the concept of purity; and partly from the extent of its distribution and display in food and drug stores, a result of the overall power and influence of Procter and Gamble. In the early days of Ivory, there was no rigid distinction between uses of the soap—it was used equally widely for fabrics, kitchen dishes, and the skin. The first Ivory advertisements talked about all three uses quite freely. (Incidentally, it is refreshing to learn, in these days of supposedly scientific marketing, that both Ivory's name and its property of floating on water were serendipitous discoveries.)[3]

Perfumed beauty bars eventually became available in considerable numbers to compete with Ivory for skin washing and especially face washing, but they were mainly hard-milled formulations (neither aerated nor easy lathering, as was Ivory—qualities that emphasized its purity in the minds of its users). The new beauty bars were each sold in relatively small quantities and distributed primarily in drugstores. Their growth, however, represented the primitive development of a functional market segmentation. Indeed, some strong brands of beauty bars eventually emerged: Palmolive and Woodbury's before the First World War, and Cashmere Bouquet, Camay, and Lux in the 1920s. What was remarkable about these brands was the way in which they succeeded in extending the total consumer appeal of beauty soaps, with a parallel expansion into food stores. Advertising played a part in stimulating both consumer demand and, by its indirect "pull" effect, the broadening of retail distribution.

Camay was a brand of great importance, not only in its own right but also and incidentally for the contribution it made to the development of marketing techniques. Since it was produced by Procter and Gamble, Camay when it was launched in 1923, carried (in the judgment of its manufacturer) the agonizing danger of cannibalizing Ivory. But Procter and Gamble, by its ability to separate Ivory and Camay strategically (which meant separating both the product formulations and the advertising propositions), invented and first practiced the concept of segmentation of markets and the separate positioning of brands within different segments. This device, which was star-tlingly unorthodox at the time, was implemented organizationally by the invention of the brand management system. This combination of segmen-tation strategy and brand management organization was probably chief among the numerous contributions that Procter and Gamble has made to the techniques of consumer goods marketing, and the early history of these developments therefore deserves to be remembered.[4]

Yet, although Camay has been a considerable, though not epoch-mak-ing, long-term success in the market and today is sold in twenty or more countries throughout the world, it has been outsold by a brand that followed it to the marketplace and is today available in more than three times as many countries as Camay. It also leads Camay in almost all of those coun-tries. This more successful soap is Unilever's Lux, a brand of astonishing longevity and ubiquity and today (as we shall soon see in detail), by a con-siderable margin, the largest selling toilet soap in the world. It is also, to-gether with a handful of brands of soft drinks and gasoline, in that select group which are in the first league of penetration and familiarity throughout the whole of the non-Communist world.

How is it that Lux climbed to this remarkable position, which, according to good presumptive evidence, is the envy of competitive manufacturers? This chapter is devoted to trying to answer that question.

"Helen Lansdowne Resor Gets a Large Share of the Credit"[5]

In the minds of its users, not to mention of students of the history and practice of marketing, it is unusually difficult to disentangle Lux the brand—

its combination of functionality and added values—from Lux the legatee and user of a very special advertising campaign. With Lux as with most successful brands, the advertising has substantially created the added values. Toilet soaps have always been an advertising-intensive product category and the Lux campaign, which has had a longer continuously successful life than that of any other make of soap or even of any other brand of packaged goods, is especially important.

The Lux campaign, based on the endorsement of Hollywood movie stars, was supposedly the creation of Helen Lansdowne Resor, wife of Stanley Resor, the man who in all major respects created the J. Walter Thompson Company. She was a remarkable woman: a first-class creative writer and a strong personality. Her impact on the agency was notable not only for the campaigns she wrote (David Ogilvy called her the greatest copywriter of her generation) but also for the influence she exercised on her studious, powerfully intellectual, but rather retiring husband. Even today, extremely funny stories are occasionally told about her views and actions during her long association with the agency. The investigative journalist Martin Mayer, who in 1958 published what some people consider one of the three most perceptive and authoritative books ever written on advertising, wrote (quoting an insider), "You cannot begin to understand the J. Walter Thompson Company until you realize that it is basically an extension of Mr. and Mrs. Resor's living room."[6]

The notion of the movie-star endorsement for Lux can be seen in retrospect to be both powerful and exceptionally relevant, and even our long familiarity with the campaign cannot weaken our appreciation of its special quality. Testimonial endorsement was by no means unknown in the 1920s, but, of course, it was then a much less hackneyed advertising device than it has become in the 1980s.[7] Yet the Lux campaign keeps its freshness even today. Three characteristics of its use of movie-star endorsement make the campaign—deservedly—of first-rate importance not only to toilet soap advertising but to consumer goods advertising in general.

First, movie stars in the 1920s were a means of lending high attention value to any advertising campaign employing them. To be noticed is, after all, the first task of any advertisement.[8] During the 1920s, 1930s, and 1940s, movies were the most important medium of entertainment for the majority of people living outside what we today call the Third World. This was especially true of young women in the United States, who were originally the prime market for Lux, and to whom movie stars were symbols of enormous interest and aspirational appeal. The power of the movies as an entertainment medium was in the way they encouraged audiences to identify with the stars and to hope for a life far different from their present one, which was all too commonly filled with unrelenting poverty and boredom. Moreover, as Lux was extended internationally, it was entirely appropriate that it should keep its connection with Hollywood, which was almost as popular outside the United States as within it; this was especially true of the English-speaking world.

Second, movie-star endorsement held a striking relevance for a facial complexion soap. When the star's face was projected onto the large cinema screen, any imperfections in her complexion were likely to be mercilessly exposed. It follows that movie stars were not only extremely motivated to maintain a flawless complexion but also seen as knowledgeable and authoritative in matters concerning facial beauty. A movie star recommending a facial soap would be more likely to carry weight with women, all of whom want a good complexion, than a movie star recommending, say, a car or a holiday resort would, for the simple reason that the star is less an expert on these things than on the complexion.

The third—and absolutely decisive—advantage of the movie-star recommendation concerned the studio system: the contractual arrangement by which stars were tied exclusively to specific studios in return for a substantial guaranteed income. This meant that actors and actresses, no matter how well known, had little choice in the matter of their roles. Moreover, publicity to build their names and reputations was entirely in the hands of the studios. The heads of these studios, the legendary moguls of the industry, quickly recognized the value of the Lux advertising campaign: It was an excellent device, involving no cost to them, that could generate large amounts of extra publicity for their stars. The studios therefore became partners in the Lux campaign. They provided the stars, and Lever Brothers in the United States provided the publicity. This arrangement had a reciprocal effect, by which the studios' publicity for the stars also began to rub off favorably onto Lux.

To facilitate these cooperative endeavors, J. Walter Thompson opened an operation in Hollywood devoted exclusively to signing up stars, initially for Lux but later also for other clients who sponsored radio programs, such as the Kraft Music Hall. The company's Hollywood representative was Danny Danker, a man still in his twenties and relatively fresh from the walls of Harvard. Danker had notable energy, charm, and contacts, all of which he deployed with skill on behalf of the agency's clients. Although the Lux movie-star campaign began only in 1927, one year later a *Ladies' Home Journal* advertisement for Lux stated that there were 433 "important actresses" in Hollywood, 417 of whom used Lux. Lever Brothers provided supplies of Lux to the studios and the stars to ensure that the stars actually used the brand regularly, in addition (of course) to stating publicly that they used it. This practice provided substantiation for the claim that "96 percent of movie stars use Lux," a claim that was soon simplified to "the beauty soap of nine out of ten movie stars," the slogan that was subsequently used for almost forty years. (It was eventually abandoned, as a result of disputes with various advertising regulatory authorities over the definition of a movie star. Since, in the opinion of these authorities, it was impossible to define a movie star unambiguously, they could not accept the agency's substantiation for any claim as specific as "nine out of ten stars use Lux.")

The Lux campaign was exposed during the 1920s in the United States exclusively in magazines. Some of the advertisements were a feast for the movie fans and featured as many as twenty-one different actresses. Radio was added in 1930, and in 1934 the Lux Radio Theater was born, representing a milestone in the development of radio advertising. Television was used for the first time in 1950.[9]

Lux grew during this time to become a brand large enough to challenge Ivory for leadership of the market and to become a source of significant profits for Lever Brothers. Lux became an established brand in the buying repertoire of large numbers of American women, for whom purchasing a bar of the soap became a habit, one that has persisted in a remarkable fashion.

To digress for a moment and move forward to a much later period, it is sad to note that Lux suffered from great competitive pressures in the United States in the 1950s and 1960s, both from the new deodorant soaps and also from other new brands. As a result of these pressures, Lever Brothers decided in 1967 to stop advertising Lux but to maintain just enough below-the-line promotional support to keep the brand in distribution.

Remarkably, Lux tonnage sales have not dropped very much over the intervening twenty years, and the brand maintains a small but profitable market share. Such is the deeply entrenched nature of housewives' habit of buying Lux that is is bought on at least one occasion by more than 5 million American households every four weeks, a total that increases significantly over the course of a year, as more and more irregular users are added to the net total.[10] The buyer of Lux tends to be older and less affluent than the average homemaker. Lux has in effect become a "price" brand, yet how many other brands could have maintained such a high level of consumer penetration when unsupported by advertising for two decades?

"People Are Very Much Alike The World Over"[11]

Almost as soon as Lux was establishing a successful position in the United States, it was introduced in other countries: first the United Kingdom (where it eventually became market leader), then into other developed markets, and finally (and more gradually) into most undeveloped markets in the Western and oriental worlds. Today there is an extensive local manufacture, although certain smaller markets are still supplied by imports. Constant improvements have taken place over the years in the functional performance of the Lux formula—improvements in lathering, notably "superfatting" (which provides lather of a creamy appearance and feel, a perceptible improvement, especially in hard water); in the perfume; and in the introduction of colors—plus many packaging improvements. The brand has been regularly restaged, and to its users in many countries it tends to be seen simply as a better soap than others on the market.

The formulation used in certain countries differs to some extent from that used in others. In at least three important markets—Brazil, India, and Japan—Lux is available in more than one variety and packaging, with special formulations directed respectively at the mass market and at the top end.

Most importantly, the advertising campaign featuring movie stars has been used in every country in which Lux is advertised. In the majority of places where Hollywood is the major source of entertainment films for movie theaters (and increasingly for television), commercials employing Hollywood movie and television stars are still used to advertise Lux. But in countries that have a strong local film industry (countries as far apart geographically and culturally as France, Germany, India, and the Philippines), Lux films are made employing local stars prominent in their own markets, and these films are in most countries used alongside international films. The Lux campaign will shortly be described and evaluated in more detail.

Today, Lux is manufactured in almost forty countries and sold in more than seventy. It is almost certainly the most ubiquitous brand of grocery goods in the world. From this, as well as from certain other points of view to be discussed in this chapter, it can be said that Lux is a remarkable marketing phenomenon.

How a Big Brand Can Grow in a Mature Market

As we evaluate Lux's total position in the world, the brand can be seen to have two striking features. First, it is by a sizable margin the largest selling brand of toilet soap, with an estimated aggregate volume share of more than 13 percent of the soap market in the non-Communist world—a share twice as large as that of the second brand, Palmolive. Despite its enormous size, Lux is actually increasing in sales year by year, as is demonstrated by the following index of total tonnage sales.[12]

1977	100
1978	108
1979	123
1980	127
1981	127

1982	126
1983	129

That a brand of such size could increase its sales by almost 30 percent over a six-year span requires explanation. To understand the increase it is helpful to look at the aggregate total of toilet soap sales in two separate ways, dividing countries by their state of development and according to the functional segmentation in the market.

For the analysis of markets by their state of development, the simplest grouping puts together first Europe and North America and then the rest of the world. The toilet soap market in Europe and North America demonstrates the first classic symptom of stationary market conditions: stabilization of overall market size. This is not true of the rest of the world. An examination of the toilet soap market by its functional segmentation adds a further dimension, showing that the market is conventionally divided into three main segments (with a more detailed subsegmentation, which will not be a concern of this study), covering soaps with a "skin orientation" (such as Lux); those with an orientation toward "bodily freshness," which include all deodorant soaps; and "price" brands.

In Europe, where Lux is strong, the skin orientation segment accounts for about 40 percent of the market. In North America, where Lux is weak, the skin orientation segment is holding a steady 33 percent of the total market. In North America and most European countries, the bodily freshness segment is large and buoyant. The bodily freshness segment is important only in some countries in the rest of the world.

Lux's weakness in the United States has already been discussed. In Europe, despite the extent of the competition, especially from the bodily freshness sector, not to mention the maturity of the markets, Lux sales are showing a slow but steady—and quite remarkable—improvement. Lux's overall brand share in Europe is above 11 percent.

There has been a similar aggregate rate of growth in Lux sales in the rest of the world, a grouping that includes not only many Third World countries but also some sophisticated markets like Australasia and Japan. But the difference between Lux's situation in these countries and in Europe is that the brand is in a stronger position overall in the rest of the world (with an aggregate market share of 18 percent). These markets also account for a larger quantity of tonnage sales for Lux than occur in Europe, which means that the annual increases in them represent much larger sales volumes in absolute terms.

With the major exception of the United States, the overall situation of the brand both in the mature markets of Europe and in the large and in many cases still-growing markets of the rest of the world is strong and optimistic. Lux could never be in such a position without an advertising campaign that deploys effectively both motivating and discriminating arguments. The Lux campaign that was written by J. Walter Thompson in 1927 is still successful in doing this, and its continuing effectiveness today would surely be a matter of astonishment to those who were originally associated with it in New York sixty years ago.

Movie Stars and Lux Advertising in the 1980s

Lux movie star commercials have a long history. They have been made for cinema and television, in large countries and small. There is also a long history of the use of centrally produced commercials across a wide range of markets, with cost sharing—a process that has generally (though not invariably) meant adapting films from large countries for use in smaller ones. This approach has been taken to make maximum economic use of high-quality film material, rather than to save money per se. Although there have been savings in film production budgets, such economies have not been the main motivation. Indeed, the managerial emphasis of the operation has always been to aim for the best possible commercials that money could buy—always an expensive process—and then to make the widest possible use of such commercials. This has meant that individual markets have had to pay substantial sums, although of course not as great as they would have been had each market gone its own way.

A reasonably large individual market might be expected to pay a significant share of the generally high basic production cost of a Lux commercial produced for international use. To this must be added the expenses of local sound tracks, special packshots, optical work on subtitles, and so on, plus show copies, which means that the basic production contribution could well be doubled. A market paying this sum could conceivably make a local film featuring a local star for an equal amount. But the general feeling on the part of the client and agency is that the local film would not have the magic of the big star's name, nor would the production values of a local film always match those of the commercials featuring international stars. The general validity of these arguments is demonstrated by most countries' willingness to buy into the international productions (except where local legal restrictions impede doing so).

The situation has been thus for decades. Great Britain became the source of many major-star commercials after the Lux advertising had been allowed to dwindle in the United States. But a substantial problem emerged when the British Lux advertising moved away from movie stars (for reasons we shall examine) during the late 1960s and early 1970s. When this change in the British campaign took place, Unilever decided to continue the production of Lux commercials for international use, with the films planned and supervised by the International Unilever Unit located at JWT London. This unit works with Unilever Detergents Coordination as its operating client, although there is a close and regular dialogue with local JWT offices in individual markets, a process paralleled by a similar dialogue between Detergents Coordination and the local Unilever Operating Companies. The total cooperation is very effective, but it has, of course, taken many years to build and strengthen the various interconnecting lines of communication.

We have referred to the abandonment of the movie-star campaign in the United Kingdom. There were two substantial reasons for this event. The first stemmed from the breakdown of the old studio system in Hollywood. It was being found increasingly difficult to sign up top movie stars for the Lux campaign. The stars' agents had become a critical factor in the negotiation, and the agents were in general less receptive than the studios had been to the argument that the Lux campaign provides valuable publicity for the stars. The second reason concerned the evolution of movie stars themselves, who were being cast in roles increasingly far removed from the goddesses of the 1930s. It was thought that this trend would make them less aspirational figures and therefore less valuable to Lux.

It was decided, therefore, that Britain should act as a "precursor market" for a new generation of Lux advertising in which the stars were to play no part. After a prolonged and rigorous development of new creative ideas, it was decided eventually to test in the market an entirely new campaign, the genesis of which lay in Lux's worldwide market leadership. The specific idea on which the campaign was based was that more beautiful women in the world used Lux than any other complexion soap. Lux was therefore the soap of the world's most beautiful women.

A series of commercials was completed, and these were enriched by stunning production values. They were exposed first in a controlled test market in the United Kingdom and slightly later in a few relatively small countries overseas. To shorten a complex story, it was eventually found, however, that this new campaign did not have the depth—the long-term staying power—of the movie-star campaign. It did not have the endemic substance of the movie-star story or its relevance to Lux's preeminent complexion care benefit. The new campaign was consequently abandoned. The experience redirected the attention of both Unilever and JWT toward moviestars, and a serious, prolonged effort was made to tackle the difficulties that had been encountered with the campaign, notably the problem of signing up major stars. Lux therefore passed its point of maximum sensitivity in an unorthodox fashion—by moving from an experimental campaign back to a rejuvenated version of an earlier one.

The experience of the next decade demonstrated that an agency that has a more than superficial understanding of a brand—a situation that comes from decades of working in close cooperation with a supportive client—was

1. *MVO:* for the new breed of star

2. *MVO:* like Nastassja Kinski

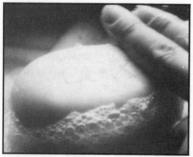

3. *MVO:* there's a new quality to Lux, a new firmness. New firmer Lux

4. *MVO:* Still with that special lather, creamy and rich, but now packed tightly into a firmer bar.

5. *Kinski:* I want softness for my skin and no soap gives me that better than New Lux.

6. *MVO:* New, firmer Lux

Thirty-second television commercial made for international use and first screened in October, 1985.

able to perform an unlikely task: It learned how to bring a real new life back into the movie-star campaign. The agency was able to produce a long series of commercials of distinction that had a demonstrable effect in the marketplace, as evidenced by the persuasive sales data presented earlier in this chapter.

Two problems had to be continuously overcome in making, with no loss of quality, such a long run of Lux commercials: (a) signing up the best stars in the world on satisfactory financial terms and (b) making powerful films that did not become stereotyped. The star must never be allowed to become what Rosser Reeves called a Video Vampire, sucking the viewer's attention away from the brand.

The process of star production begins with the individual markets giving their own ideas about which stars should be selected. Regular investigations are made into the popularity of individual stars, and this process is used for a regular shortlisting of appropriate names. Besides signing up leading stars, a contract is occasionally drawn up with a little-known younger star considered on the way up. Contractual arrangements with the individual stars are carried out by the agency's specialist in this field, the manager of JWT's Hollywood office. The rather complex negotiations must cover such details as the dates, times, locations of the film and still photography; the detailed endorsement of the brand by the star (copy claims, extent of face-washing sequences, and so on); the countries covered; and the time limits of the agreement, which vary country by country. The negotiation is normally difficult and is not becoming any easier.

During the most recent decade, films have been made with (among others) Brigitte Bardot, Natalie Wood, Jacqueline Bisset, Elke Sommer, Raquel Welch, Sophia Loren, Ali McGraw, and Victoria Principal (heroine of *Dallas*). The use of this last actress demonstrates the way the campaign is reaching out of the cinema and into the field of television films. The majority of Lux films are used in fifteen or more countries, many in more than twenty.[13] Such a consistent and extensive use of the campaign is a practical confirmation of the degree to which it is considered (generally on the basis of attitudinal and sales evidence) to have a demonstrable effect in the marketplace.

Many details of the films repay study. They all have a Lux "fingerprint" and are unmistakably directed to complexion care. The star is the prime attention-getter, and she is also the device that ensures the campaign does not become stereotyped. When a film is planned, the JWT creative group learns as much as possible about the star at first hand and endeavors to embody some of her life-style—a matter of great interest to the Lux buyer—into the series of vignettes from which the film is constructed.

The films are cut to sixty- and thirty-second lengths (they are used most commonly in the shorter format.) Recommended versions of the films are used with minimal adaptation in the majority of markets. During the production, however, certain copy claims and also certain specially shot vignettes of the star's life are prepared for specific countries, to provide for local idiosyncrasies. In Arab countries, for example, the only skin that can be shown is the star's hands and face; in Japan, stars are not allowed to say that they use a brand, only that they recommend it; in Australia, most women do not put soap on their face, so that face-washing sequences are normally avoided there; and in certain oriental markets, the stars often need to be presented in a special way. There is relatively sparing use of the star's spoken endorsement, a practice followed not only to enhance the credibility of the star's words but also to avoid the need for excessive subtitling or dubbing in the many countries that do not use the language (usually, although not invariably, English) spoken by the star in the film.

Each film production is planned to take place over five days of location shooting (this includes still photography for Lux press advertising featuring the star). The production is logistically extremely complex. A principal difficulty is that duplicate film crews have to be employed to make special versions of the film for those countries which have legal or trade embargoes on using film material shot by foreign technicians. The budgets for the films are, as noted, invariably high, because the films are enriched with the highest production values available anywhere in the world (a number of directors of Lux commercials have won Oscars for their feature films). The decision to buy the best production talent is made deliberately, and the film shooting is always planned punctiliously to minimize the risk of error. The agency— as it does with its filmmaking for so many other clients—bears a heavy responsibility to deliver films of consistently high quality and with no hint of stereotyping. The final films are evaluated by exacting criteria, both in the center of the Unilever world and in the markets where they will be used. They are also researched in many countries.

It should be emphasized that although the strategy for the campaign is clearly laid down and widely understood, the making of the films is essentially an artistic endeavor. The skills are transferred within JWT partly by a process resembling osmosis, but this is reinforced by more formal procedures. The intention throughout is that some of the qualities of the international productions should be shared by the local ones.

Some Observations on the Lux Media Budget

As can be expected from the fact that Lux is the largest selling toilet soap in the world and also the most ubiquitous brand, Lux's aggregate budgets for both above-the-line advertising and below-the-line promotions are also larger than for any other brand of toilet soap.

There is, however, an important point to be made about the size of these budgets. As we discuss in more detail in chapter 20, brands of the size of Lux normally benefit from economies of scale in their advertising, which can be quantified by such brands' ability to be supported by a slightly lower than expected level of advertising. In specific terms, the brand's share of total advertising (share of voice) can often be a few percentage points below the brand's share of the market. It has been suggested that the share of voice can be reduced slightly because a large brand's share of the consumer's mind is probably high; this is a plausible explanation. This marginal saving in advertising can often make a significant difference to a brand's residual earnings in a large market.[14]

This scale economy is strikingly illustrated in the case of Lux. In 1983, the most recent year for which the cumbrous calculations have been made, Lux sales and Lux advertising were analyzed in thirty leading markets, and it was found that Lux's aggregate market share in them was 17 percent, while its comparable share of voice was 14 percent. The difference is therefore 3 percentage points. We find it interesting that this is the very figure that we demonstrate in chapter 20 to be a generally acceptable level of underinvestment to maintain a large brand's market share. But Lux's sales are of course growing in some markets, which means that the underinvestment the brand can stand is greater than average—a manifestation of Lux's exceptional strength in the marketplace.

The difference between Lux's 17 percent share of market and 14 percent share of voice represents marginal extra profits accruing to the brand measurable by 3 percent of the total advertising by all brands in these thirty markets—a sum equivalent to many millions of dollars.

When similar analyses are made for previous years, the picture is closely similar. The scale economy that benefits Lux is also, as might be expected, greater than that for the brand's closest competitors, Palmolive and Camay, which are, of course, both smaller selling brands.

Over the years, Unilever has acquired extensive experience in manipulating Lux's advertising budgets and is successful in this endeavor, as demonstrated by the generally optimistic progression of the brand's sales. From studying the relationship between Lux's share of voice and share of market in a number of specific countries, there is tentative evidence that Lux's market share is endangered if the brand's share of voice is reduced below an average level of 12 percent. (This figure also shows that a slightly greater degree of underinvestment is possible for Lux than for the average brand described in chapter 20.) It is important to continue studying these productive relationships continuously, and much help can be provided by econometric modeling techniques.[15] This proposal takes us, however, into the realm of future possibilities, and it is now more important to stand back and review the lessons from the long history of this rich and noteworthy brand.

Six Lessons from the History of Lux

1. The Importance of Brand Positioning. Lux is a perfumed beauty soap for complexion care—a soap with a single-minded female orientation. The brand started with this positioning in the 1920s and has not changed in strategic essentials, despite changes in the structure of the market, such as the growth of the bodily freshness segment, which tempted certain manufacturers (examples are Palmolive and Phase Three in the United States) to suicidally unsuccessful attempts to straddle the skin and bodily freshness sectors.

Lux was not the first mass-market beauty soap. It was the third brand (at least) to be introduced into this segment. It was, however, the brand that, more successfully than any of its competitors, succeeded in promoting and developing the concept of a beauty soap. As a result, Lux has managed to maintain a high and buoyant market share in the majority of countries in which it is marketed.

2. The General Coherence of the Brand. Lux is a classic example of a brand from which the consumer receives complementary and coherent signals, no matter from which angle the brand is viewed. The brand's functionality (skin-care properties, lathering ability, perfume, colors, tablet shape), its packaging, above all its advertising, and many (although not all) of its promotions show a unity and have a clearly synergistic effect. In almost all markets, Lux is an evolving entity. The direction and all details of its evolution are in the hands of a client and an agency that have decades of experience with it. An ethos and working procedure have been developed, many of the subtlest details of which not only are passed verbally but are consistently described and illustrated in documents and videotapes.

We can appreciate most strikingly the coherence of Lux by examining the total presentation of the brand in those markets where it is being nurtured to maintain and augment its high sales and earnings, in contrast to the very small minority of markets where Lux is being milked for profit (and where, it must be said, it manages to survive astonishingly well). In the first case, Lux speaks unmistakably in terms of class and quality, even exclusivity; in the second case, it speaks of low price, partially redeemed by a distant and dwindling heritage of better days.

Lux also makes a striking comparison with Ivory. In the many markets where Lux has been continuously successful, the positioning and the advertising have been congruent. Ivory has always been consistent in its positioning, but its advertising has never been uniformly and continuously harmonious with that positioning, although there has been greater congruence in the United States—where Ivory remains so strong—than in other countries in which the brand has been launched.

3. An Advertising Campaign Should be Planned to Last Forever. The Lux campaign must surely be the longest lived in the history of advertising. This does not mean that it has been extended and developed in an unimaginative and stereotyped way. Indeed, the most enormous pains have been taken to reflect the evolution of movie-stars and the film industry itself (as is happening at present, as Hollywood moves so strongly into television film production).

There was even value in the unsuccessful experiment of the late 1960s and early 1970s that led to the partial and temporary abandonment of the movie-star campaign. This experience resulted in a vigorous reappraisal of movie stars as an advertising vehicle and the generally successful attempts to find ways of showing modern stars in a modern way by capitalizing on those features of the star's life which are often of considerable interest to Lux buyers. The commercials that resulted brought an extraordinary new lease on life to a campaign that had been showing real symptoms of tiredness.

4. The International Nature of the Campaign has Brought Significant Advantages and Economies. The international success of the movie-star campaign was attributable to three factors. First was its underlying power and relevance as an advertising vehicle. Second was the way in which the brand and the campaign developed together; Lux has always been intimately connected with movie stars, and the international success of the campaign has paralleled the international success of Hollywood. Third is that the campaign has been executed and evolved with enormous skill and sensibility and has unquestionably made a broadscale contribution to the brand's sales and earnings.

The international syndication of centrally produced advertising material has also brought financial economies. But paradoxically, the main managerial focus has never been merely to save costs. Rather, it has been to encourage the economic use of high quality—and invariably expensive—film productions. These productions would not, however, have been financially feasible without international syndication.

We believe that the economies of Lux's syndication of advertising material—economies relating to extending the usage of high-quality and expensive films—are rather typical of the campaigns for major global brands. There is another example in this book—De Beers.

5. Lux Benefits from Quantifiable Advertising-Related Scale Economies. Although the aggregate advertising budget invested in Lux is higher than that for any other toilet soap, it is nonetheless smaller than the brand's aggregate market share suggests it might be. The marginal earnings expressed in the difference between the expected and actual advertising ratios can be computed as millions of dollars of extra profit, a result essentially of Lux's commanding strength in the market. This scale advantage is larger than that for any other toilet soap in the world. The relationship between share of voice and share of market that has been described in this study should be evaluated continuously to ensure that future advertising investments for Lux be manipulated as precisely as in the past—perhaps increasingly so. The object of this procedure is, of course, an optimization—to maximize the brand's profit and to obviate the latent danger of reducing advertising investments to a level that might result in an erosion of sales.

6. The Lux Campaign is the Product of a Client as Well as an Agency. Lux has provided an example of sixty years of more or less continuous upward progress in a hard and competitive marketplace. It follows that the vast majority of decisions concerning the brand have been correct ones. This is unusual enough in the real world. This study has focused rather more attention on the contribution of J. Walter Thompson to Lux's success than on those of countless Unilever executives in more than seventy markets. It would be seriously misleading for us to neglect to emphasize that success has stemmed from a cooperative endeavor on the part of Unilever and JWT.

Lux represents a brand that has benefited from an exceptional complementarity of effort between client and agency. Both parties share a common ethos, one that has been developed by the joint growth in both parties' experience of the brand. The essentially decentralized organization of Unilever is reflected in that of the agency. But both also benefit from strong and parallel central inputs. Lux has never been run on the oversimplified system of the client just providing the brief and the agency just providing the advertising. By the experience, understanding, support, guidance, and empathy of numerous individuals, Unilever has truly made it possible for the agency to develop in such a fertile fashion and to expose over such a prolonged period an advertising campaign as distinguished and successful as that for Lux.

7

Nescafé in Spain

> Roasting is an operation of the greatest nicety, and one, moreover, of a crucial nature, for equally by insufficient and by excessive roasting much of the aroma of the coffee is lost; and its infusion is neither agreeable to the palate nor exhilarating in its influence.
> —Alfred Barton Rendle and William George Freeman, *Encyclopedia Britiannica*, 1910.[1]

The Emergence of Branded Coffee

In most countries, apart from the United States, coffee was essentially a commodity market until World War II. Housewives bought their roasted beans unbranded in the grocery store and either had them ground on the spot or did it themselves at home. The aroma and taste of coffee depend on two things: (a) the beans themselves, those from different countries yielding pronounced differences to the nose and the palate, and, as noted in the quotation above, (b) the roasting process. Making coffee from beans involves some time and trouble.

Before the introduction of instant (soluble) coffee, there had been attempts for decades to market easily prepared varieties, such as crystals and liquid extracts. But these products had never been very successful, partly because of difficulties of dissolving and, perhaps more importantly, because they could not compete realistically against bean coffee in aroma and taste.[2] The poor product quality of the early crystals and liquid extracts had made people suspicious of "processed" coffee. When instant coffee was introduced, people experienced a product manufactured in such a way that it was greatly superior to the early crystals and liquids (although some experts did not agree that instant coffee had quite as good a taste as bean coffee). Because of its superiority over the earlier types of convenience products, however, instant coffee has always claimed in its advertising that it has a taste and rich smell similar to those of pure coffee, a claim that is not surprising, inasmuch as instant coffee is made from pure coffee and nothing else. This theme has been consistent over the five decades during which instant coffee has been marketed and has generally been true of advertising claims in all countries. The point is an important one, to which we shall return.

The market for instant coffee was essentially created by Nestlé, the company that invented the method of manufacturing an easily dissolving powder through evaporation, by the use of spray dryers (and later freeze-dryers), processes that managed to retain a good deal of the rich pungency of the bean coffee. For this new product, the company coined the name Nescafé: a name destined to be one of the most significant and ubiquitous brands in all categories and in all countries. To some extent the successful branding of Nescafé led to a growth of branding in the market as a whole, and bean coffee began increasingly to be sold ready-ground in airtight cans (more recently in airtight shrunk foil packs). In some more developed markets (like the United States), the branding of bean coffee had been established before the arrival of Nescafé, but the latter provided a major impetus. In other countries, such as Spain—the setting for this study—it was a commodity market before Nescafé, and the branding of bean coffee came late, not taking place until the 1980s.

The Nestlé company was founded in Switzerland in 1866, when Henri Nestlé's milk-food company and the Anglo-Swiss Condensed Milk Company were established. The two organizations were fierce rivals for forty yeas but amalgamated in 1905. From the earliest days, exporting had been a highly important activity for both. (Anglo-Swiss was named in recognition of the country in which most of its sales were made.[3]) This inclination to look outward from its small home country, which led it to establish manufacturing and marketing operations overseas, has characterized Nestlé to this day; English is spoken as widely as French both at company headquarters in Vevey and throughout the Nestlé world.

The early and aggressive penetration of overseas markets is the main reason that Nestlé has become the world's largest food-processing company.[4] But its product range was originally quite limited: For its first seventy years, its business was tied exclusively to milk. It was only in 1938—an inauspicious year in the history of the twentieth century—that Nestlé made the first major broadening of its business, with the invention and marketing of Nescafé in Switzerland, and true to the company's form, the brand had, within a couple of years, also been launched successfully in France, Great Britain, and the United States.[5] (In the United States especially, an important new market was created.)

It is unnecessary to emphasize the extremely damaging effect of the Second World War on the business of a large international marketer of branded foods like Nestlé. Among the ill effects suffered by the company was a loss of dominance in the instant coffee market in the United States, because wartime conditions led to a relaxation in the patent protection given to Nestlé's original invention of the production process. Although the United

States was the market in which Nescafé made its first major mass-market breakthrough, the brand was soon assaulted by locally based competitors with strong resources, notably General Foods, and Nestlé was powerless to prevent this action by recourse to litigation.[6] By 1986, total sales of General Foods brands of instant coffee in the United States had become two-thirds greater than Nestlé's.[7] This situation was the long-term result of the loss of the wartime years, when Nescafé might have become the continuously dominant brand as well as the pioneer.

But despite the loss of such opportunities during the war years, Nestlé resumed its strong growth after 1945. This growth was led by the company's overseas expansion and, most importantly, was substantially brought about by diversification into food businesses other than milk. Today the company is a major force in dairy products (Carnation), frozen foods (Findus/Stouffers), pet foods (Friskies), sauces and culinary products (Maggi), chocolate-malt drinks (Milo), milk products and breakfast cereals (Nestlé), and last but not least, coffee. The Nescafé brand name is used for the most widely sold instant coffee in the world and also for ground coffee in the important markets of the United Kingdom and Japan.[8]

"The Spaniards Have, for Better or for Worse, Now Plumped for Materialism"[9]

Nestlé had established a Spanish operation before the Civil War (which broke out in 1936), and this operation had maintained an uneasy existence until the mid-1940s. During the two decades that followed, however, Nestlé renewed its policy of overseas expansion and opened new manufacturing plants in Spain, among the nearly forty such operations the company established worldwide.[10]

The manufacture and marketing of Nescafé began in 1955. It was, of course, the first instant coffee in Spain, and its competition was unbranded bean coffee. The brand was functionally very acceptable to consumers and was marketed with the help of the most advanced techniques; as a result, it grew rapidly and was soon an established success.

The establishment in Spain of a large clutch of familiar brands of consumer goods, in a wide range of markets—and among which Nescafé is not the least important—reflects the rapid growth in living standards that occurred in the last years of the Franco regime and (from 1975) the era of the "new" popular monarchy. These were years during which Spain, as a rapidly expanding tourist destination, developed its commercial connections with the rest of Europe and indeed the world, and during which the millions of tourists who came to Spain every year soon became accustomed to seeing in

Spanish stores, bars, and filling stations the same brands they were accustomed to buying at home.

Overall consumption of coffee in Spain is approximately 3 pounds per capita per year. (This is a good deal less than in the United States, but American consumption has been declining rapidly for more than two decades, a phenomenon attributed to indirect competition from cold carbonated soft drinks.)[11] The share of total coffee tonnage in Spain accounted for by instant coffee grew steadily from zero in 1958 to 19 percent in 1981. And because instant coffee goes about twice as far as bean coffee in the brewing process, the instant coffee share of the total number of cups of coffee drunk is a good deal higher than this figure.

In 1981, 59 percent of Spanish homes bought bean coffee in any 13-week period, compared with 47 percent who bought instant coffee. But the average volume purchased was four times as high for beans as for instant coffee. This statistic is partly a reflection of the point already made that instant coffee goes further in the brewing, but even taking that factor into account, it provides clear evidence of an overall lower consumption level for instant coffee. It also suggests a degree of dual purchasing: Many buyers of bean coffee are likely to be occasional buyers of instant coffee.[12] Much of the thrust of the advertising and promotion of the latter has been toward the young consumer, reflecting the general feeling in the market that the less traditional consumer can be more easily persuaded to buy the more innovative and convenient product.

The Spanish consumer of instant coffee has one important and unusual drinking habit. In the vast majority of countries in which instant coffee is drunk, the granules are mixed with hot water and either drunk black or made into café au lait by the addition of milk or cream. In Spain, however (as in the United Kingdom), the Nescafé granules are frequently mixed with hot milk to make an exceedingly creamy drink that is appropriate for breakfast but much less so as a *digestif* after meals. It is not clear how this method of preparation developed in Spain, but judgment suggests that advertising played a role, since this method of making the drink has been demonstrated in virtually all the Nescafé advertising. (Nescafé has always been the dominant advertiser, because it has been much the largest selling brand in the market.)

As noted, instant coffee grew steadily in share of the total market during the decades of the 1960s and 1970s. After 1982, however, a major change took place: The market for instant coffee reached a plateau, those stationary conditions so common in mature consumer goods markets.[13] In this case, though, the reason was rather unusual. During the 1980s (later than in most countries), branding techniques began to be applied rapidly to bean coffees in Spain, and this event was accompanied by the widespread introduction of brands of bean coffee in ready-ground form. This meant that Nescafé, which has always been preeminent in the Spanish instant coffee market, was for the first time in its existence confronted with significant branded competition. This development is extremely important, but before considering it in detail we must first evaluate the role of advertising in building the Nescafé brand into its position of great strength (although a market share of such size—at one time 80 percent of the instant coffee market—also meant that the brand would inevitably become vulnerable to competitive assault).

Nescafé Advertising: Qualitative Considerations

The Spanish advertising for Nescafé has always been written and produced in Spain, a result of Nestlé's belief that advertising should, subject to certain guidelines, be originated in local markets.[14]

In the advertising strategy for all brands of instant coffee, there is one element of great significance that has influenced Nestlé and indeed all marketers of the product: Instant coffee appears prima facie to offer a major discriminating advantage over bean coffee in its convenience and ease of preparation. Advertising based on this argument was indeed exposed for General Foods' Maxwell House shortly after the brand was launched in the United States. It was startlingly unsuccessful. To find out why, General Foods employed a University of California researcher, Mason Haire, who constructed an experiment based on a primitive version of what qualitative researchers now call a projective technique.

Two shopping lists were drawn up—they were identical, except that Maxwell House Instant Coffee was listed on one and not the other—and a sample of housewives was asked to describe the housewife who had drawn up each list. It was immediately clear from the respondents' views of the housewife who bought Maxwell House Instant Coffee that she was seen as lazy and self-indulgent. The user associations of the product were therefore intrinsically unfavorable, and the latent problems associated with them had to be defused if the product was to succeed.[15]

This story became something of an advertising legend and caused an immediate shift in the emphasis of all instant coffee advertising—that for Nescafé and other brands as well as Maxwell House—toward a story based on purity, good taste, and rich aroma.[16] This was all intended to overcome the inbuilt negative associations. Generally speaking, instant coffee advertising has succeeded in doing so, and the pitfall of emphasizing convenience and ease of preparation has entered the folklore of instant coffee advertising.

The various campaigns for Nescafé in Spain can best be evaluated in groups exposed during chronological periods. Since the advertising began by introducing consumers to the concept of instant coffee and since for all the rest of the period Nescafé remained the dominant brand in the market, the emphasis of the advertising argument throughout has been on the qualities of instant coffee as a product. The advertising has been based, in other words, on arguments of a character that is motivating rather than discriminating—on generic product-related arguments rather than on narrow brand-based advantages. This approach was logical and correct.

The various phases of the Nescafé advertising were as follows:

1955–1970	Brand establishment
1971–1981	Brand growth and consolidation
1981–1987	Response to competitive assault

During the period when Nescafé was being established on the market and when Spanish people were being educated into an understanding and acceptance of instant coffee, the Nescafé advertising was consistently based on the themes that the product is 100 percent real coffee and that it has all the taste and rich smell of coffee made from ground beans. The advertising stimulated awareness and began to build emotional values. It featured family scenes and stressed that a cup of Nescafé is a quick and happy way to start the day. The campaigns during this period laid an effective foundation for later growth.

The long period of the brand's expansion and consolidation—the decade of the seventies—saw a single campaign that was used more or less continuously—and successfully. This campaign deserves description and comment. Its basic concept was to show real people, with all the sympathy and credibility that high-quality film production was able to evoke, relishing their "Nescafé moment." The cup of Nescafé was seen as something special, to be relished: a reward, a small high point in the routine of the day.

This bare description does not communicate the emotional appeal of the long series of commercials. That appeal was partly the result of first-class casting of the characters whom we see during their daily round: the letter carrier, the lighthouse keeper, the farmer, the ship's pilot, the boat builder, the guitar maker, the potter, the sailor home on leave, the pastry cook, the miner bicycling home and picking a wildflower. It was also the result of the techniques of the filmmaking, notably the slow pace of the action, which makes the films both evocative and particularly easy on the eye. (The film lengths are forty-five and thirty seconds, but because of the slow dissolves they give the impression of being longer.) The musical theme, used consistently although in different arrangements over the whole period, has a Latin American beat but nonetheless is essentially placid and makes a subtle contribution to the overall atmosphere of relaxation. All the signals in the commercials emphasize the message of the "Nescafé moment," and judgment suggests that they work synergistically.

During this long period, sales of all instant coffee were climbing to their

1. (Musical theme)

2. *MVO:* The lighthouse keeper watching out all night through and every daybreak.

3. *MVO:* Someone who loves him prepares his breakfast with Nescafé.

4. (Special sound effect of wave breaking against rocks).

5. *MVO:* These are the good moments of . . . (Super runs up to end commercial).

6. *MVO:* NESCAFE.

Forty-five-second television commercial first run in Spain in the fall of 1973. The English copy is a translation of the Spanish original.

high point of 19 percent by weight of all coffee sales in 1981. And Nescafé retained its lead in market share, registering an extraordinary 80 percent of the instant coffee market during that year. But the downside of such a massive market share is that the introduction of new brands—inevitable in this as in most markets—took sales predominantly from Nescafé, which was therefore bound to suffer erosion at the margin. This competitive pressure took place at both the retail and the consumer levels. Store brands of instant coffee began to make their presence felt, although this factor represented the smaller of two competitive assaults on Nescafé.

The signs of competition were evident in Spain during the early 1980s, and the stronger attack came from an unexpected source. There took place a rapid growth of branding in the bean/ground coffee market, which led to a rapid siphoning of growth out of the instant sector and into the bean sector of the market. This development can be clearly seen from the indexed data in table 7–1. (Remember that the bean coffee sector had started at a much higher base level.)

Table 7–1
Coffee Sales Index, Spain
(tonnage basis)

	Bean Coffee	Instant Coffee
1981	100	100
1982	109	102
1983	107	95
1984	112	93
1985	114	93
1986	116	91
1987 (provisional)	119	90

Source: J. Walter Thompson, Madrid, May 1, 1987.

It is possible that the growth in ground coffee was partly influenced by the likelihood that some people preferred its taste to that of instant coffee. At the same time, it offered an advantage in convenience over unground bean coffee. (This shift in the market was also accompanied by a significant increase in the advertising noise level, a point we shall shortly examine in more detail.)

Nestlé responded to the new market situation in two ways. First, it introduced new product varieties with the objective of protecting corporate market share. It brought onto the market two new versions of Nescafé, one extremely light (Puro Colombia) and the other extremely strong (Alta Rica). Even more significantly, Nestlé, which had for some time marketed a brand of bean coffee—Bonka—acquired three additional brands and in 1979 began to advertise Bonka and two of the new ones.

Nestlé's second response was to experiment with variations and alternatives to the Nescafé advertising campaign. Five of these deserve comment.

1. In 1980, the main Nescafé campaign was changed by the introduction into commercials of heroes who had trendier, more aspirational jobs, such as photojournalist and architect, this change being accompanied by a faster pace of movement in the commercials themselves. This change in the campaign was not welcomed by consumers, and Nestlé concluded that one of the main strengths of the original campaign had been the way in which it captured, in an involving fashion, the lives of everyday people. The main advertising therefore returned in 1981 to the traditional, more relaxed campaign, with more ordinary people and warmer, family-centered commercials, although with rather more emphasis on younger consumers than had been common in past advertising. The rejuvenated campaign was used for a brand restage in 1983–84, and in this advertising three varieties of Nescafé were featured.

2. In 1984, the main campaign was changed again, and the new advertising was directed wholeheartedly at young people. A series of realistic twenty-second face-to-camera interviews were filmed with the intention to communicate not only that Nescafé is a part of young people's way of life but also that it is easy to control the strength of the coffee by adjusting the spoonful dose in the cup (an argument having additional connotations of economy). For the first time in more than a decade, music played no part in the advertising.

3. An extremely innovative campaign was introduced in 1985 for iced Nescafé (Nescafé Glacé). This campaign has striking production values and intrusive music. Most importantly, it has struck a chord with the consumer, who looks upon this product as a highly appetizing drink in a hot country like Spain.

4. An umbrella image-building campaign was launched in 1985 for two varieties of Nescafé, plus Bonka (Nestlé's first brand of bean coffee), emphasizing their common Nestlé heritage.

5. The two new Nestlé varieties, Puro Colombia and Alta Rica, generated their own advertising campaign in 1985: another campaign enriched with magnificent production values, the setting for the films being a steam train crossing a Latin American landscape.

These aggressive responses to a changing marketplace made some progress, although their success was some way short of complete.

In the instant coffee market, the overall Nestlé market share eroded quite seriously—from 85 percent in 1981 to 74 percent of a smaller market in 1986—despite the introduction of the new Nescafé varieties already mentioned. Significantly, the loss of market share went primarily to store brands, which occupied 14 percent of the market in 1986 (compared with only 2 percent in 1981). The growth in store brands in this and other product categories is the result of two factors—their relative cheapness in comparison with manufacturers' brands and the expansion in the numbers and importance of retail chains, a virtually universal trend during the past thirty years.

To offset this (possibly inevitable) loss of business in the instant coffee market, Nestlé has made significant strides in the bean market, achieving 23 percent by weight, shared among its four brands in 1986. But in contrast to its still-dominant position in instant coffee, Nestlé is only one of three evenly balanced oligopolistic competitors in bean coffee; General Foods and the large Dutch firm Douwe Egberts each has a share of 20 percent, closely behind Nestlé.

Nescafé Advertising: Quantitative Considerations

The increased competition in the coffee market during the 1980s was accompanied, as might have been expected, by a huge increase in advertising expenditures, as shown in table 7–2. Since the bean coffee segment represented the setting for most competitive activity, the share of voice of brands in this market segment increased, and the share represented by all brands of instant coffee fell more or less progressively, from 81 percent to 45 percent in 1986.

Table 7–2
Advertising for All Brands of Coffee

	Millions of Pesetas	Index
1980	467	100
1981	712	152
1982	788	169
1983	1,122	240
1984	876	187
1985	1,524	326
1986	1,835	392

Source: J. Walter Thompson, Madrid, June 4, 1987.

This quadrupling of total advertising expenditure would have put an unacceptable pressure on Nestlé's margins had the company maintained its traditionally dominant share of voice. Nestlé could not therefore keep this up, and although the company's total advertising expenditure increased in absolute terms during this period, its share of voice (table 7–3) fell dramatically each year until 1984, after which it recovered to a limited degree.

Besides showing the dramatic reduction in Nestlé share of voice, table 7–3 also shows how the Nestlé advertising effort became dispersed and, in

Table 7–3
Nestlé Share of Voice in the Coffee Market

	Nestlé Total Share	Nescafé	Other Nestlé Instant	Nestlé Bean
1980	93	52	22	19
1981	91	40	36	15
1982	90	34	40	16
1983	68	29	27	12
1984	48	31	6	11
1985	55	22	21	12
1986	59	25	17	17

particular, how the proportion accounted for by the main Nescafé campaign was progressively pushed down (despite some recovery in 1986).

It is tempting to draw oversimplified conclusions from these data—that underinvestment in advertising has played a large and direct role in Nescafé's present problems. But before considering this point in more detail, we should emphasize our belief that dominant brands like Nescafé benefit from advertising-related scale economies, which means that such a large brand can commonly be supported successfully with an advertising share of voice below the "normal" level of advertising investment that is suggested by its share of market. But we must be careful in how we act on this supposition. Empirical observation of many such brands suggests that there are real, although not always easily perceived, limits to the extent to which the share of voice can be reduced below the brand's market share. Indeed, in chapter 20 we describe some aggregated data that show that too much reduction will cause sales to decline.[17] It is also reasonably clear that the prime determinant of the effect of advertising pressure is share of voice, not absolute expenditures. In other words, advertising pressure is essentially a *share* game.[18] As we have seen, Nescafé was a heavy loser in share of voice. We think that this loss affected the brand's sales.

Nestlé's Present Position

The main problem that has assailed Nestlé during the 1980s has been the emergence of serious competition from brands of ready-ground bean coffee. The company responded effectively by joining this growing market sector, an extremely wise step, if for no other reason than that some consumers may prefer the taste of ground coffee to instant coffee, so that Nestlé had to be in the ground coffee market in order to protect its overall company franchise. With its four brands of ground coffee, Nestlé has an aggregate market share similar to—in fact, slightly ahead of—that of its main rivals,

General Foods and Douwe Egberts. The establishment of the Nestlé brands (like the establishment of its competitors' brands) has meant significant investment costs, not least in advertising. These costs were, of course, inevitable, although there could have been an important carry-over benefit from consumers' familiarity with the Nestlé name.

The downside of this advertising investment in Nestlé's ground coffee is that the growth in this market segment has meant a significant erosion of sales of instant coffee. In this declining market, Nestlé, with its dominant (and therefore vulnerable) position has lost 14 share points over the course of the five years 1981 through 1986, mainly to food-store brands, with their lower prices. Nescafé, with 66 percent of the instant coffee market, is still huge, but it dominates the market somewhat less securely than it did in 1981 (with its 80 percent share in that year).

Although Nescafé remains a powerful and profitable brand, its situation is not entirely comfortable. This circumstance is mainly because of the competitive pressures discussed above, but we believe that the advertising, too, has contributed to the situation to some degree.

1. As already suggested, a reduction in Nescafé's share of voice in its main campaign from 52 percent in 1980 to 25 percent in 1986 may very well have contributed to a loss of business. In the market as a whole, we have seen that advertising quadrupled. That Nescafé's expenditure in 1986 in absolute terms was less than twice what it had been in 1980 is what caused the brand's share of voice to be cut in half. This is a matter of great importance and should not be left to judgment alone. It is something that could fruitfully be evaluated with the use of econometric analysis, a planning tool that indeed holds generally interesting possibilities for the study of Nescafé's position in the Spanish market.

2. These expenditures on the main Nestlé campaign do not take into account any carry-over effect of other Nescafé advertising (such as the current umbrella image-building campaign, which makes much of the Nescafé name). But experience in other markets suggests that consumers tend to look upon brand extensions as entities on their own. Such markets can effectively expand a franchise by attracting consumers who do not often buy the main brand. But there is not much mutual support between the *advertising* for the main brand and that for its extensions.[19] We suspect that this has been the case with Nescafé and that the advertising for the subsidiary brands has meant more dispersion than synergy in the total advertising effort. Again, econometric analysis could help us evaluate this point.

3. The creative experimentation that has taken place since 1984 has not achieved completely satisfactory results. Some of the creative developments (for example, Nescafé Glacé) have worked extremely well. The feeling remains, however, that the "Nescafé moment" campaign, which had done so much to build the brand during the decade on the 1970s, may not have been

strong enough to maintain sales of the brand after such a heavy reduction in Nescafé's share of voice (although we are not sure that any other campaign could have done much better.)

Five Lessons from the History of Nescafé in Spain

1. Consistent and Well-Directed Advertising Helped to Build the Brand. There is little doubt that during its first twenty and more years in the market, Nescafé benefited from advertising that, by its consistency, well-judged concentration on motivating arguments, and—not least—emotional content that encouraged the involvement of the viewer, helped to build both the instant coffee market and the brand. Nescafé was (and is) a brand with a strong and coherent personality. Few brands in any markets maintain shares of upwards of 60 percent, and Nescafé's ability to do so is a tribute both to its product quality and to the effectiveness of the advertising.

2. Massive Market Shares Mean Vulnerability. It is virtually inevitable that a brand with a dominant market share in any market will suffer, if determined and functionally effective newcomers enter into competition with it. If at the same time the dominant brand's market segment erodes, then the brand will most probably lose some of its franchise—in particular, occasional users. Both these things happened to Nescafé; Nestlé was forced to respond to the situation, and Nescafé's strategy inevitably had to be directed at ways to minimize the inevitable damage. The consequent expansion of the marketing effort has wide implications, not least for the brand's advertising budget. The vulnerability of a large brand makes it important for its psychological added values to be refreshed and reinforced continuously, and this calls for competitive advertising appropriations and a continued degree of concentration of expenditure.

3. Even Successful Advertising Requires Contingency Planning. The ability of a brand to hold a dominant market share over even a long period does not mean that it is able to do so forever. It is always wise for a strong brand, no matter how successful it may be, to develop and test advertising to meet an unexpected competitive situation. By doing this before the competition emerges, the brand will manage to maintain the initiative in the market. Contingency planning is an expensive process, but response to the emergence of competition is even more expensive and generally less effective after the event. The story of Nescafé in Spain during the 1980s is about the emergence of competition from two sources: store brands and (even more importantly) the branding of ground coffee. Nestlé met the challenge of the latter by a successful introduction of its own ground coffees, but the feeling remains that the cost for this measure was to some extent paid by Nescafé.

4. The Erosion in Nescafé's Share of Voice Affected Its Market Shares. Although a brand with a large market share does not require the support of an equally large share of voice, there is nevertheless a crude causal relationship between the two variables, and there are dangers in substantial reductions in the latter. We think it is very possible that the reduction that took place in the share of voice of Nescafé's main campaign between 1980 and 1986 adversely affected the sales of the brand. And the advertising for other Nescafé lines was not heavy enough, nor did it work synergistically enough, to compensate for the reduction in Nescafé's share of voice. Econometric evaluation (possibly involving test-area experiments) would be a useful technique in assessing specifically the loss of business that may have resulted from the reduced share of voice. We believe that such a tool of analysis might be generally very helpful to the brand.

5. Product Diversification in the Instant Coffee Market Led to a Dispersal of Effort. Production diversification was carried out to protect—and to some extent to extend—Nescafé's consumer franchise. Although the new varieties introduced have been reasonably successful, they have in turn tended to divert advertising resources (as well as management attention) away from the main Nescafé campaign. Nescafé has always been, and remains, Nestlé's largest and most profitable brand in the market, and the scale economies from which it almost certainly benefits make it a prudent policy to fight to preserve every point of the brand's large market share. Although some erosion may be inevitable, such erosion must obviously not be encouraged.

In conclusion, we must reiterate the point that Nescafé remains a highly profitable and successful brand (although slightly less so than formerly). As with other cases in this book (for example, Listerine), stability at a reduced yet still-strong market share is a practical objective for a large brand suffering from intensive competitive pressure. It is entirely possible to arrive at a market share that provides security as well as profitability. This we see as the future for Nescafé and as a situation for the brand that is compatible with the strength of the company that manufactures it.[20]

8

Oxo

Oxo gives a meal man-appeal.
—Advertising slogan.

A Durable Brand

The slogan that prefaces this chapter was first used nearly thirty years ago and has played an extensive part in the Oxo advertising during the intervening period. In a small way, the longevity of this advertising idea typifies the durability of Oxo, the oldest of all the brands of packaged goods considered in this book.

In its most familiar form, Oxo is a beef extract cube a little less than an inch square, manufactured in a moist but crumbly consistency. Although chicken and onion varieties were added to the range during the 1960s, beef has always been the biggest seller. And the strong masculine association of beef (echoed in the red of the packaging and the in-store display material) is well expressed in the slogan and the advertising associated with it.

Although the story of Oxo is set in Britain and intimately concerned with both British cuisine and British society, the product was in fact invented by a German, Baron von Liebig, as long ago as 1847. Its original purpose was as a diet supplement for individuals who needed concentrated nutrition—undernourished people, sick people, and explorers. It was endorsed by Florence Nightingale and the Duke of Wellington; it was taken to Africa by Henry Morton Stanley in his search for David Livingstone; and Scott and Shackleton took supplies on their expeditions to Antarctica.[1]

Oxo was not always a cube. In fact, between 1847 and 1910, it was produced in the form of a thick black liquid. Supplies came from the beef-producing countries of Latin America, and the letters O-X-O were codes on the packing crates, marks with no specific meaning. Thus, a brand name that was to become immensely familiar and important emerged serendipitously. The bottles of liquid Oxo were too expensive to find a mass market, but the technical process enabling the product to be made into cubes that could be sold for a penny each opened the door to an enormous expansion in sales of the brand, an expansion that took place steadily, though with some interruptions, between 1910 and 1975. (During the most recent twelve years, sales have more or less stabilized at a high level, although in some of these years they have shown improvement.)

Oxo is a strong-tasting product. It is used in Britain to add flavor to gravy, stews, casseroles, and soup; when dissolved in boiling water, it makes a bouillon that is powerfully fortifying on a winter day.

Oxo is particularly appropriate for the normally rather bland English cuisine. It provides a punch and a zest that are lacking in many of the ingredients and in most of the traditional recipes made in British homes.

The poorer cuts of meat are greatly improved with Oxo. And it is no coincidence that when meat was in shortest supply, during the two world wars, Oxo sales grew faster than at any other time. This growth was not only because Oxo was used by the armies in the field[2] but, even more importantly, because it could eke out the rations of the civilians on the home front. Indeed, only four years after the original launch of the cubes, World War I broke out, and sales of Oxo rose rapidly. The period between the wars was difficult economically; incomes rose only slowly and unemployment was high. These conditions led to a modest but steady and continuous increase in Oxo sales.[3] Sales shot up again during World War II, stabilized during the latter part of the 1940s, but showed signs of erosion during the 1950s. That erosion took place because working-class people were experiencing higher incomes and lower unemployment than ever before. Moreover, they were beginning for the first time to enjoy Continental vacations, which led them to experience a more adventurous and varied cuisine than they or preceding generations had ever known or even thought possible.

It was at this time that the manufacturers of Oxo made the brave decision to dig in their heels and fight for their market. Conventional product life-cycle theory pointed to the brand having passed its apogee and indicated that forces in the market were now leading inexorably to the decline phase, during which (the theory propounds) the brand could be milked for profit until its extinction. This theory is self-fulfilling, because belief in inevitable decline will actually encourage brand managements to milk brands (and thus bring about their decline). Many cases, however—and Oxo is not the least important of them—demonstrate that the downward phase of the life cycle is by no means inevitable.

Indeed, with Oxo the possibility of cyclical decline was faced but quite simply not accepted. The company "invested in Oxo in 1958–59. There was a new marketing management and a strengthened sales force; the cubes were completely repacked; a new unit size was introduced; rather more was spent on advertising and a new agency was appointed, with a new campaign and media plan."[4] This campaign forms an important part of this study and deserves to be evaluated in some detail.

The Birth of Katie

In 1958, the two main problems for Oxo were that it was a very old brand and that it was thought of in terms of cheap, dull food. It was something from the "bad old days." J. Walter Thompson resolved to meet these problems head-on by endeavoring both to rejuvenate the brand and to associate it with a much more versatile and adventurous cuisine than that with which Oxo had traditionally been associated. The way the agency tackled these difficult tasks was to make a long series of television commercials starring a young housewife called Katie who demonstrated how she used Oxo in all her meat dishes. By the extent and variety of these dishes, Katie gradually persuaded the British public that Oxo was suitable for the dining tables of a public that, in the words of the Prime Minister at that time, Harold Macmillan, "had never had it so good."

The personality of Katie was carefully planned. Her husband, Philip, was a young executive who had a job with prospects. The house they lived in, as well as their style of living, was to a nicely judged degree above the market. (Oxo was a stubbornly working-class brand.) The average Oxo user could recognize Katie and Philip's position in life, and the strategy of the advertising was that Oxo users should aspire toward that position. The couple were a symbol of a gradually upwardly mobile society. But in addition, there was one important basic point in all the Katie advertising—namely, that there was also a reward for the housewife in the gratitude of her family for giving them delicious food. This argument was never weakened, and it provided a bedrock appeal that all housewives could appreciate.

But despite the meticulous planning of the campaign and despite the craft that went into the filmmaking, the Katie advertising was not an immediate success. At this time the client and agency began the tradition of continuous measurement of the brand's image attributes, and there were encouraging improvements in Oxo's association with "modern people" and "good cooks." Despite these favorable signals, however, sales measured both by ex–factory shipments and via the Nielsen retail audit stubbornly refused to move upward. In fact, seven Nielsen periods passed (a span of fourteen months) before the needle started to swing. During this long time, both client and agency demonstrated a remarkable strength of nerve.

The early stage of the Katie campaign is therefore a case—one of the few documented examples—of advertising that appears to have had a slow-burning effect. The reasons for this phenomenon are not clear even now. Most likely, the advertising had little effect on consumer penetration, which was, and has remained, exceptionally high, with 60 percent of British housewives using the brand every week. Within this vast body of users, the frequency of use varies and household inventories of the brand are quite high. It is possible, if not probable, that the Katie campaign in the early stages increased the frequency of use, which in turn led to a running down of inventories in the home. And it was this cushion of Oxo supplies in households that caused the delay before consumer purchases in the grocery store started going up in response to the advertising.[5]

Whether or not this is the right reason for the delay in response, a shot of adrenaline was eventually pumped into the sales, and five years after the beginning of the Katie campaign these sales had gone up by as much as 35 percent. As further evidence of the strengthening of the brand, the company successfully implemented two price increases during those five years. (In 1957, a year before the first Katie film was exposed, an Oxo cube had cost the consumer the same penny it had cost in 1910.)

Over the course of the seventeen years during which the Katie campaign ran, the advertising evolved through a number of phases. These need not concern us in detail, but the important point is that the agency contrived to keep Oxo users continuously interested in Katie and the progress of her family (she produced a son, David, in 1965), by subtle changes in the advertising, in the emphasis devoted to Oxo in Katie's kitchen and to Katie's family and life-style. As mentioned, the Oxo imagery was carefully and continuously monitored by regularly replicated consumer surveys.

At times, this consumer research provided diagnostic clues that led to improvements in the campaign. In 1967, for instance, the campaign was shown to be developing in ways that were growing too far above the market, so that Katie was losing her all-important aspirational appeal. As a result of this finding, Katie and Philip changed houses and the family went to live in the country.

Shortly afterward, research showed that people were eating more snack meals and that the average household cuisine was changing quite rapidly in a much more adventurous direction. Katie was not thought to be keeping up with the times. This finding led to Philip's employer transferring him to the United States, and the agency produced a series of exciting commercials featuring Katie in her new surroundings. In no time at all, Katie was using Oxo to improve her "cookouts", to the enlightenment and pleasure of the family's American friends. One of her new dishes, baked beans with Oxo, became the best remembered of all the many recipes introduced during the seventeen-year life of the campaign.

But in the early 1970s, with economic depression in the United Kingdom, Katie and her family had to return to the rigors of their homeland in order to maintain the empathy of their audience. And Katie was soon showing how to prepare dishes as mundane as liver and leeks with Oxo and demonstrating her customary panache despite the unpromising ingredients she was using.

The importance of the regular monitoring of image attributes cannot be overemphasized. This practice not only enabled the Katie campaign to be fine-tuned—adapted to a changing environment—but, even more importantly, provided advance warning of potential problems with the campaign, those which might have led to eventual sales declines. As noted, the brand's high consumer penetration and heavy household inventories provided a cushion that worked to delay the effects (both positive and negative) of advertising on sales.

By the mid-1970s, two fundamental problems were emerging from the image tracking data, although these problems had not yet begun to affect sales seriously, despite some evidence of a weakening in the average frequency of purchase. First, Katie, who seventeen years before had been a young, widely admired figure, was now being seen (particularly by young people) as rather staid and unadventurous. In fact, by 1975, Oxo was considered far less strongly associated with "modern people" and with "good cooks" than it had been in 1969. Second, the advertising was losing the interest and involvement of consumers: it was becoming part of the background, resembling (as it was described at the time) the wallpaper in a suburban living room.

The decision was therefore made to abandon the Katie campaign, although both client and agency had come to grips with the possibility of doing so a number of years before. This aspect of the case is a matter of considerable interest.

Regular Contingency Planning

When a brand has the benefit of a campaign that worked as well as the Katie one did over such a long period, the vast majority of clients and agencies will opt for a quiet life and continue running the campaign unthinkingly, rationalizing their decision with platitudes like "if it ain't broke, don't fix it." In the case of Oxo, the company and agency took a much more thoughtful and enlightened position. Without losing real confidence in the campaign, from the earliest years of its exposure they constantly considered the possibility of what would happen to the brand if the advertising ran out of steam of if Katie were killed in a car crash. There was also the likelihood that, although most people liked Katie, substantial numbers never would, so that it was at least possible that an alternative campaign might be developed to have an even greater effect in the marketplace.[6]

These arguments led to an operating procedure by which alternative campaigns were written and evaluated; not only were these campaigns developed into finished films, but they were also exposed in test areas. Here, their effectiveness was monitored by measuring sales and image associations of the brand in comparison with the national advertising, which of course featured Katie. In some cases attitudinal data were used to fine-tune the test-market advertising in order to improve its effects. Work on these alternatives was not a token endeavor. Full agency resources were put into it in a genuine attempt to find something that might outperform Katie. In at least one case, four films were made for a test campaign that was exposed and monitored for three years.

The experience of this work was, however, uniformly discouraging. In some cases, the alternatives gave promising early signals, but these all eventually weakened. Katie—at least until the mid-1970s—seemed unassailable.

When in 1975 it was decided, for good reason, to discontinue the Katie campaign, it was perfectly clear that new advertising would be required to rejuvenate the brand's image and to reinforce Oxo's position in the housewife's mind as a big and important brand. Oxo needed to be reappraised rather dramatically by the consumer. The agency was, however, some way short of finding a creative solution, and the tension surrounding its efforts to produce one is remembered to this day. Some early alternatives were even finalized and put into consumer test, where they failed.

The agency did, however, in time develop a promising campaign, which it entitled "Crumble Cameos." The central visual idea was the cook's gesture of crumbling the Oxo cube in the fingers to drop the product into a sauce or casserole. This signal had strong brand associations, because Oxo was then (though not long to remain) the only important stock cube on the market. The campaign employed characters cast with extraordinary flair and imagination, each film containing five vignettes of people crumbling the Oxo, planning to crumble it in delighted anticipation of the food to come, or commenting on the deliciousness of the food they were eating by making the crumbling gesture to show what went into it. The films were all good-humored and soon became popular with the public. They demonstrated a markedly confident and self-assured tone of voice. The public, of course, is widely familiar with Oxo, and the films said nothing whatsoever about the brand explicitly. But by their style and in particular their use of the crumble gesture, they said a great deal implicitly. They were a classic example of advertising that succeeded in building nonrational added values.

The campaign was exposed in most parts of the United Kingdom in 1976. Not only did sales respond, but diagnostic data from image monitoring soon showed a superiority of performance over the Katie campaign, which continued to be exposed and monitored as a control in one television region. The improvement associated with the Crumble Cameos campaign was not only in how Oxo users were perceived (Oxo was seen to be used more by "modern people," "young women," and "good cooks") but also in how the brand itself was seen (more as a versatile brand and an important part of home cooking). All this was consonant with the campaign's objectives.

The brand and the advertising seemed set for a long run. But trouble arrived from an unexpected direction.

Enter the Competition

During the decades of Oxo's growth, Oxo was the only beef stock cube on the market. But there was an old, established rival brand, Bovril, that for years had sold reasonably well in the more expensive liquid form. Oxo was no longer sold in liquid at this time. Indeed, Bovril was virtually the only brand in the liquid-stock market and it was well regarded by housewives for its strength of flavor, although it could not compete effectively with Oxo cubes on price.

During the 1970s, Bovril was acquired by the large and well-established Cavenham Foods organization, owned by the aggressive entrepreneur Sir James Goldsmith. The sales value and profitability of Oxo were obviously an attractive lure and target, and a cube formulation was quickly developed for Bovril. The Bovril cubes were launched into a test market in 1976. Cavenham had done its homework. Not only were Bovril cubes preferred to Oxo in blind tests by a ratio of 60 to 40,[7] but the brand also received massive promotional support (including sampling in 70 percent of homes in the test region) and an advertising budget larger than Oxo's. The advertising, appropriately enough, was based on discriminating arguments demonstrating Bovril's superiority over other cubes (which everyone knew meant Oxo).

The impact of Bovril's launch on the makers of Oxo and its agency, as well as on the public, can well be imagined. In the brilliantly clear illumination of hindsight, the thought emerges that had the company and agency been as punctilious in product development as they had in contingency planning for the Oxo advertising, they would not have been caught on the wrong foot by the launch of Bovril. They did, however, make good the deficiency by the fruitful energy expended in tackling the problem. During the year and a half in which Bovril cubes were in test market, the beef flavor of Oxo was improved to eliminate any advantage Bovril would claim when it was rolled out nationally (which occurred in early 1978).

The emergence of Bovril also had an effect on the Oxo advertising. It was judged that the Crumble Cameo gesture was no longer appropriate as the central feature of the campaign, because it was not unique to Oxo now that Bovril was on the market. The Crumble Cameos idea was popular, but on its own it was not considered distinctive enough.

Although in the Bovril test market Oxo lost about 30 percent of its sales, the client and the agency had the courage and good judgment to continue to treat Oxo from all points of view as the brand leader it was. The new campaign developed in response to the Bovril threat concentrated on men and Oxo's heritage of beef, and in so doing it continued to emphasize its dominance and natural superiority in the market—its "big brand" quality. The Crumble Cameos gesture was retained, but, as noted, it was no longer used as the central part of the story. The campaign emphasized more strongly than ever before the brand's masculine user associations. Most of the men in the commercials, press advertisements, and outdoor billboards were themselves beefy, a point reinforced by the red Oxo T-shirts they were shown wearing.

Although the new campaign was exposed before the reformulated Oxo was available in grocery stores, it was deemed important to reassert many months in advance Oxo's "man-appeal" as the best means of containing possible inroads by Bovril. This thinking proved sound, and the campaign itself was easily adjusted to include the slogan "Beefier Taste" (which also appeared on the Oxo packaging) when the reformulated cubes were in full distribution. This step took place, it will be remembered, just before the national expansion of Bovril.

To jump ahead in time, Bovril eventually became a national brand, and it was joined by Bisto (a brand that had been available for decades as a powder used exclusively for gravy making), which launched Rich Gravy Granules in 1984. Bovril also introduced granular versions of beef and chicken cubes in 1986. The market has thus become much more competitive and fragmented than during the long years of Oxo's growth. Nevertheless, Oxo has held its own.

With the new competition during the past decade, the total market has grown. In fact, with the national launch of Bovril it went up by 25 percent and then stabilized within two years. Most importantly, Oxo did not lose sales. The real menace of Bovril (and Bisto) was contained, and sales of Oxo have held satisfactorily. In an expanding market, however, the brand lost share: from absolute domination to the still-extraordinary level of more than 70 percent.[8] It is in these circumstances, which are rather different from those operating during the brand's decades of growth, that the Oxo advertising during the 1980s must be evaluated. The larger market was an accepted fact. Oxo clearly had to maximize its share, although that share was clearly not going to be quite so dominant as formerly.

Oxo Advertising in a Competitive Market

The advertising for the reformulated Oxo communicated straightforwardly and powerfully that Oxo was now better than ever before, and the restage was considered a success. The company and agency believed, however, that a long-term campaign could not depend so substantially on a simple functional argument and considered it essential to steer the advertising toward a return to the brand's emotional heritage—its prominence in the kitchen (the brand is used in a third of all British hot meals)—and to its small but not unimportant contribution to family life.

A good deal of quantitative and qualitative research was carried out that reinforced the wisdom of focusing on the family, and this research led to the development of two 60-second commercials. Enriched with a high standard of craftsmanship, the commercials featured a series of vignettes of rather humorous but also warm and friendly scenes from family life (a father rescuing a kitten from a tree, a father kicking a football over the fence into the neighbor's garden, children responding to their father making faces from outside a car window on a winter day). The campaign aimed at—and to a degree succeeded in—continuing to preempt the stock cube market for Oxo, a point distilled into the slogan "Only Oxo Does It," which was reiterated by the strongly paced music.

These films and others derived from the same creative idea ran between 1978 and 1982, during which period sales of Oxo maintained their supremacy in the market. As noted, the total market now also accommodated Bovril, which, although outsold by Oxo by a ratio of more than 4 to 1, maintained its by-now established position. While the Oxo campaign was running and having some success in the marketplace, the client and agency gradually moved to the view that the advertising, although popular with Oxo users and effective in doing a protective job for the brand, was too rigid and, in the last analysis, perhaps not distinctive enough for Oxo in a newly competitive environment.

As had happened during the life of the Katie campaign, alternatives were developed and tested, with generally disappointing results. But an alternative idea—or, rather, an imaginative development of the existing campaign—eventually evolved. This alternative was partly the result of studying the gradually shifting psychographics of British family life during the 1980s. The direction the campaign took was to depart from the normal, idealized, anodyne "advertising family" and to move toward a family possessing a very special and arrestingly realistic character. The family in the new campaign was carefully planned to echo, although not imitate, some of the families in the best of the modern television situation comedies. The result was unlike any other advertising in this or any other product field, and there began an advertising campaign whose tone of voice was unique to Oxo.

The campaign and the family it featured achieved considerable réclame and are perhaps best described by an editorial in a leading British popular newspaper: "Family life was about kids being noisy and refusing to eat—a kind of 'domestic war and peace,' as one woman said."[9] The heroine of the series, actress Lynda Bellingham, is a slyly humorous and at the same time unobtrusively but highly competent mother. The father, actor Michael Redfern, also has depth of character; he has an underlying humor and tolerance

1. *Dad:* Not here yet, then? *Mum:* No. Only half an hour late. *Dad:* I don't know why we're going to all this trouble.

2. *Mum:* He's your brother. *Dad:* Yes. And you invited them . . . *Mum:* Alright. Alright! Just give me a hand will you.

3. *Alison:* Who's all this for?

4. *Mum:* Uncle Bob and Auntie Jean, of course.

5. *Alison:* But they rang this morning to say they couldn't . . . . . come. Ah.

6. *Mum:* Alison. *Dad:* No.

Thirty-second television commercial first screened in Britain in 1987.
Note the very low-key treatment of the Oxo brand name.

but is rather more self-effacing than his wife. There are three teenage children, two boys and a girl, who have some of the charm of their parents but also the gaucherie and bloody-mindedness of most young people their age. The campaign is notable for the sparseness of its dialogue. The Oxo brand name hardly appears. And much of the tension and the humor are powerfully unstated.

The campaign, first exposed in 1983, led to a sales improvement.[10] But there was a six-month lag before any sales movement took place—a shorter period than at the outset of the Katie campaign, although the reason for the delay was probably the same as in 1958: the high level of household inventories of the brand.

In the competitive situation of the late 1980s, Oxo has maintained its high market share, but the market has reached stationary conditions. In fact, there is at the moment a modest annual reduction in total market sales, reflecting a severe reduction in sales of beef, a phenomenon at least partly connected with an increasing health consciousness on the part of the British population. The beef stock cube market in general and Oxo in particular have done well to maintain relatively stable sales in light of this trend in beef consumption. Oxo remains a very large and profitable brand.

The effects on the Oxo campaign in the marketplace have been tracked with continuous studies of how consumers recall it. Although this evaluative technique is imperfect, the use of continuous measures eliminates some of the contaminations associated with the "single shot" measurement of recall.[11] Oxo's ability to add flavor, as well as its versatility, seems to be communicated strongly to consumers by all the many commercials in the campaign; in addition, recall of the situations in the commercials is high. Brand image data are also collected, and Oxo shows a clear lead over its competitors in all image attributes. This, of course, is to be expected because of the strength of the brand.

Research also confirms the popularity of the campaign with the public. Not surprisingly, based on this popularity the campaign has been chosen for four years running as one of the "Top Ten" campaigns by the popular magazine program guide *TV Times*. The campaign is yet another example of a popular campaign that is successful in selling the brand—a further case demonstrating that relentless hard-selling is not the only successful advertising technique. Advertising that entertains provides an obvious reward to the consumer for the trouble he or she takes to switch on attention. If the brand is also popular, enjoyable advertising provides a note of harmony with— even a metaphor for—the brand.

The campaign is also pregnant and has not lost its appeal to the public after the exposure of as many as fourteen different films over a five year period.

Oxo is a profitable brand. The 1986 advertising budget ($13 million) is reasonably substantial by British standards. It is carefully arrived at: heavy enough to help generate sales, while not so high as to jeopardize the brand's advertising-related economies of scale. Oxo's share of voice is 60 percent, which is dominant yet below the brand's market share of more than 70 percent. Like virtually all major brands in all categories, Oxo can be effectively supported by a share of voice somewhat lower than the "normal" level suggested by its market share, but the extent of this deliberate underinvestment is—as it needs to be—nicely calculated.[12]

Six Lessons from the History of Oxo

1. Brand Life-Cycle Theory. The company's continuous and successful determination to maintain and, where possible, boost the sales of Oxo is evidence that conventional life-cycle theory does not have universal validity. The investment in the Katie campaign in 1958 and the response to Bovril in 1976–1978 are good examples of the dogged aggressiveness of the company's attitude; on both occasions, this aggressiveness was more than justified by results in the marketplace. The manufacturers of Oxo are not the only major marketers that refuse to accept life-cycle theory because of its essentially self-fulfilling nature. Nevertheless, this attitude is rare enough to deserve comment. Only a small number of other companies also think the same way, but some of them are the most successful. As Thomas J. Peters and Robert J. Waterman, Jr., say in their best selling book *In Search of Excellence*, "One Former [Procter and Gamble] brand manager notes: 'The first thing they tell you is, "Forget product life cycles and cash cows! One of the soaps has been reformulated over eighty times and is thriving." ' "[13]

2. A Clear Statement and Sensitive Evolution of Advertising Strategy. The underlying strategy of each phase of the Oxo advertising has always been clear:

- *Katie,* to rejuvenate the brand and to emphasize its versatility and contribution to good cooking
- *Crumble Cameos,* again to rejuvenate the brand and to persuade people to reappraise its value in home cooking
- *Beefier Oxo,* to meet a real competitive assault, by emphasizing both Oxo's better taste and its "big brand" qualities: its general importance in the kitchen
- *Oxo Family,* to emphasize without exaggeration Oxo's role in family life, by showing a typical family with an unusual veracity

Each strategy has been expressed by advertising that in every case has made a creative leap and whose success was largely because of the extent of this leap. But the direction of the leap was determined to an exceptional degree by the soundness of the initial strategic evaluation. This was not static. Indeed, the brand's strategy has continuously evolved in response to subtle signals from the market that emerged from research.

3. Effective Use of Research. Our knowledge of Oxo is exceptionally rich because of the productive use that has been made of research during all phases of the advertising over a long time. Two types of research, in particular, deserve notice. First is the continuous tracking of image attributes, which has provided a valuable illumination of the ways in which the various campaigns were working and an even more valuable flagging of danger signals as the campaigns were almost imperceptibly weakening. Such tracking also provided a multidimensional evaluation of campaign alternatives. Second, and especially valuable, is the continuous study of the psychographics of both Oxo users and the population as a whole. An understanding of these elements led directly to a number of successful evolutions of the Katie campaign. More recently, an understanding of trends emerging from such research led to the Oxo Family campaign, which is paradoxically both true to life and extremely unorthodox in the context of British advertising (which itself is considered unorthodox by international standards).

4. Advertising Contingency-Planning. The search for campaign alternatives during the long and successful life of the Katie advertising—for national exposure only if Katie showed signs of weakening—is a strategy notable for its rarity in the marketing field. When the Katie campaign did eventually lose its impetus, many months of fruitless labor were saved because the client and the agency were psychologically prepared for the search for alternatives, and in any event many alternatives had already been developed and tested. Client and agency were in effect halfway to finding a solution as soon as the decision was made to abandon Katie. And appropriately enough, the expensive but immensely effective mechanism of continuously keeping an alternative in a testmarket also paid off after the Katie advertising had been discontinued in national use. Katie was in turn exposed in a single area, where a continued weakening of Oxo in terms of both sales and image confirmed the wisdom of stopping the national exposure of the campaign.

5. Product Improvement. With a brand that has no direct competitors—Oxo's position until the arrival of Bovril—there are less pressure and less incentive to carry out regular functional improvements in the product than is the case in the sort of evenly balanced oligopolistic markets that are normal for most fast-moving consumer goods.[14] This is a dangerous situation.

It might have had disastrous consequences for Oxo when Bovril cubes were launched with a formula preferred by consumers in blind product tests. With Bovril on the scene, the Oxo scientists moved quickly to improve the brand's formula in order to protect its preeminent position in the market, and the day was saved, although by a perilously short margin of time. But it is impossible not to conclude that small but continuous improvements over the course of the preceding years might have led to an Oxo that was less potentially vulnerable. It should be remembered that during this whole period, advertising contingency-planning was being carried out continuously and that this is in essence a procedure that might also have been adopted in product development.

6. The Reasons for the Slow-Burning Effect of Oxo Advertising Are Unclear. Advertising effects in the marketplace tend to be immediate.[15] The exceptionally slow-burning initial effect of Katie and the (less pronounced) slow-burning effect of the Oxo Family campaign are both exceptions to the general rule. In this study it has been hypothesized that the reason is related to the frequency of use of Oxo and to the size of household inventories of the brand. Oxo advertising works to reinforce attitudes (operating at the "indirect" extreme of the King Continuum). As discussed in Chapter 1, this slow-acting reinforcement operates as a lagged effect, but with Oxo, it may be operating in conjunction with a second delayed effect caused by the extra purchasing being put back by the cushion of existing kitchen inventories. Research should be carried out to explore this hypothesis. It is important to know with greater certainty how the Oxo advertising works, because such knowledge should make a difference to our predictive powers and therefore to our skills in forward planning.

9
Quaker Kibbles 'n Bits

If this business were to be split up, I would be glad to take the brands, trademarks, and good will, and you could have all the bricks and mortar—and I would fare better than you.
—John Stuart, president of Quaker Oats, 1922–1942[1]

An Old Business Finds a New Market

The roots of the Quaker Company lie in the breadbasket of America—the fertile, arable lands of the Midwest. These roots were planted in the middle of the nineteenth century. The company was an amalgamation of a group of oats millers (not Quakers in the religious sense) who had built a secure organization well before their joint enterprise began using the Quaker name and trademark in 1877.[2] The decades following the Civil War were significant for the growth of a vast national marketplace, and this movement was spearheaded by the rapid development of branding and consumer advertising.[3] In the van of this movement was Quaker Oats, one of the earliest of that select group of substantial advertisers which have powerful, widely familiar, and very old brands that are still strong in the marketplace. The contributions of Claude Hopkins, such as his slogan that Quaker Puffed Wheat is "shot from guns," are remembered today. Indeed, the use of imaginative and intensive advertising has been an important part of the operating policy of Quaker Oats from the 1880s to the present.[4]

Quaker was for many years a rather narrowly focused organization and remains today one of the six major manufacturers of products eaten for breakfast, with a business primarily concerned with a group of large and indirectly competing categories of breakfast foods (hot cereals, cold cereals, pancakes, and pancake syrups). Quaker Oats, however, like certain of its competitors in these same categories, made a successful diversification into the burgeoning field of pet foods when this field was still undeveloped.

Pet foods may appear far removed from the human breakfast table, but the new business fulfilled a need for the company to diversify: an important matter in the judgment of the Quaker management at the time. The move turned out to be remarkably prescient. It was brought about by what seemed at the time—1941—to be a risky decision to acquire the equity of a company that traded under the name Ken-L-Ration. But with the support that Quaker Oats eventually gave to this operation, Quaker's pet-food business developed after the end of the Second World War in a most spectacular fashion.

This chapter is concerned with dog food and with a period after the market had become fully mature—the 1980s. Quaker Kibbles 'n Bits was launched in July 1981.

The factor that sets a natural top limit to the dog-food market is, of course, the population of dogs or, rather, the relatively stable population of households that possess dogs. As shown in table 9–1, which covers adults who own dogs, the numbers are large, but it should not be forgotten that more than 60 percent of all adults lie outside the target group.

Table 9–1
Adults Possessing Dogs

	Number of Adults	*Percentage of All Adults*
Adults with any dogs	64,200,000	37.6
Adults with one dog	40,500,000	23.7
Adults with two dogs	13,100,000	7.7
Adults with three or more dogs	10,600,000	6.2

Source: Annual report on the dog-food market prepared by the Simmons Market Research Bureau, 1986.

There is, however, a countervailing force to this limitation in the breadth of the market. Like many other markets, that for dog food is characterized by a high frequency of use. In fact, the net value of total sales was estimated at $2.9 billion in 1981, or $45 per dog-owning adult, making the market one of an obvious attractive size in absolute terms (although the per capita figure is kept down by the common habit of feeding dogs table scraps).[5] Prima facie, there was still some growth during the early 1980s, but this was substantially an inflation-related phenomenon. In terms of volume, the market exhibited the stationary conditions commonly associated with mature categories of packaged goods.

In 1981 there were five major manufacturers in the field, with value shares as follows. (The large group of "all others" represented substantially regional brands):

Total market	100%
Ralston Purina	29%
Carnation	11%
General Foods	9%
Quaker Oats	8%

Liggett Group	5%
All others	38%

The market, besides being large and highly competitive, is also complex and fragmented. In 1980, a total of sixty-five national brands were grouped into four functionally different market segments. Here are the segment shares by value, based on 1981 data:

Total market	100%
Dog biscuits and snacks	7%
Canned dog-food	27%
Dry (complete) dog-food	56%
Semimoist dog-food	10%

The first of the above categories comprises both biscuits (the first products made especially for dogs) and the more recently introduced snacks, neither of which offers a complete balanced diet on its own. (When different types of dog food are served, they are commonly, though not universally, mixed.) The original growth of the market in the decades of the 1920s through the 1950s was the result of the successful development of canned dog food. The remaining two categories—dry (complete) and semimoist—expanded during the postwar period, notably the decades (also of rapid total market growth) of the 1960s and 1970s. As we shall discover, Kibbles 'n Bits is categorized in the dry (complete) segment, although in effect it straddles this and the semimoist segment.

As in most mature markets, the manufacturers of dog food are all multibrand companies, and each has varying strengths in different segments. And, as might be expected from a market containing so many different brands, individual shares tend to be low. In 1981, the largest brands were (a) a dry (complete) dog-food, Dog Chow (from Ralston Purina), with 10.2 percent by value, and (b) a canned dog-food, Alpo (from Liggett), with 6.1 percent by value. There was a long tail of viable (and in many cases advertised) brands with shares of 2 percent or less. Quaker was (and is) represented in all market segments. The shares referred to so far relate to the total market and are measured in value, not volume or weight. The aggregate total market for dog food is not commonly analyzed in volume, because there are large differences in value per ounce in the different market segments, making it potentially misleading to compare market shares based on volume across the market as a whole. In the rest of this study, therefore, when we look at volume shares they will be based on individual market segments, where the brands are comparable.

The competitive nature of the market means that advertising and promotions play an important role in it. Total market advertising is estimated at an ongoing level of $150 million above-the-line, or an advertising-to-sales ratio in the market as a whole of rather less than 5 percent. (This figure covers both advertised and nonadvertised brands; the ratio for advertised brands alone would, of course, be higher on average.) To these amounts spent above-the-line should be added very considerable promotional expenditures. Although estimates are difficult to arrive at, projections based on what is spent in the dry dog-food segment put promotional expenditures about 50 percent above the advertising levels, suggesting that the advertising plus promotional ratio for all brands taken together is in the 12 percent range. Again, the figure for the advertised/promoted brands would on average be higher, and for new brands higher still.

Based on expenditure for the dry (complete) dog-food market (the segment that accounts for two-thirds of total advertising), advertising and promotional expenditures rose rather rapidly between 1980 and 1984, when they peaked, and then subsequently fell back somewhat. Very importantly—and typical of many other packaged goods markets of all types—the balance of expenditure moved away from advertising and toward promotions during much of the period. The pendulum is now swinging the other way, although not yet far enough to return to the advertising-promotional balance of the period before 1981. These trends can be seen in table 9–2.

Table 9–2
Dry Dog-Food Advertising: Promotional Ratios

	Advertising	Promotions
1980	44%	56%
1981	36%	64%
1982	34%	66%
1983	29%	71%
1984	36%	64%
1985	37%	63%
1986	39%	61%

The market exhibits in total many of the quintessential characteristics of mature packaged goods. It is large and characterized by high frequency of purchase. It is functionally segmented and divided among a large number of brands. It is oligopolistic, and the major manufacturers are represented in all or most of the segments. It exhibits high activity, with relatively substantial advertising and promotional ratios, indicating that advertising and promotions are—or are perceived to be—important sales-generating activities. Over the long term (and despite recent short-term reversals), the advertising:promotional balance has tipped away from advertising and toward promotions.

Despite the high degree of activity in the market—new brand launches as well as high noise from advertising and promotions of existing brands—the market is characterized by generally stationary conditions, as evidenced by the overall lack of volume growth, the generally small degree of movement between segments in the short term, and the accompanying stability of manufacturers' total shares and also of individual brand shares. Much of the activity is, in other words, self-canceling. Against this background—and we should emphasize that the overall pattern is typical rather than untypical—we will now trace the fortunes of a new brand, one that was an exception to normal experience and became successful.

Kibbles 'n Bits: An Uncertain Beginning

The lack of volatility in the shares of the individual market segments on a year-by-year basis conceals certain long-term movements that are measurable only over a three- to five-year span. The most pronounced of these movements was a very gradual increase in the size of the dry (complete) segment, from 47 percent of total market value in 1978 to 52 percent in 1982. This increase was to some extent a reflection of brand activity; it will be remembered that this segment represented two-thirds of the market's advertising expenditure. The small subsegment of combined moist/dry dogfood, which was an offshoot of the dry segment, was also showing buoyancy.

It was in this subsegment that Quaker Oats positioned Kibbles 'n Bits, and indeed the brand was a pioneer in this subsegment.

Formulated in an unusual way, the product was made up of separate types of nuggets, or chunks: one hard/dry (named Kibbles) to provide crunchiness and the other semimoist (named Bits) for extra taste. It was thus positioned to appeal to buyers in both the large and slowly expanding dry (complete) segment and the much smaller semimoist segment. (The existing brands in the combined moist/dry subsegment were individually too small to be an attractive source of business.)

The new brand was supported by advertising that was demonstrably liked and remembered by consumers (it was subjected to standardized recall and persuasion testing) and was exposed to an "investment" rate. High levels of trial were achieved, and within months the brand exceeded its share objective and peaked at a volume of 4.2 percent share of the dry market (which, it will be remembered, represented about half the total market when this is measured by value). Although it is normal for new brands to achieve an initial peak, followed by a decline to an ongoing stable level of brand share, the reduction in Kibbles 'n Bits was larger than what would normally have been expected. Indeed, there was evidence that the brand was achieving inadequate levels of repeat purchase.[6]

This was not the first time that a brand had suffered from such a problem; almost invariably, the matter is related to some perceived deficiency in the product's performance. Such indeed was the case with Kibbles 'n Bits. Upon investigation, it was discovered that the difficulty lay with the taste of the product and was caused by the way in which the two separate types of chunks separated in the bag during storage, the heavier Kibbles working their way to the bottom of the package. When the bag was first opened, the dogs enjoyed a product with much more taste and little crunchiness, but as the pack was used up, they got progressively more crunchiness and less taste. This was a genuine formulation problem, which only manifested itself after the bags has spent some time on supermarket shelves; it could not therefore have been discovered in normal prelaunch product-testing. It was, however, a problem that could very well have been mortal. The market share became gradually depressed and eventually got down to 2 percent by volume of the dry market.

In test market, the product was a new idea, and some buyers thought it lived up to expectations, although some did not. But the initial success of the launch spurred competitive retaliation, and within two years four new brands of dry dog-food were launched and three established brands restaged, so that Kibbles 'n Bits soon lost its functional uniqueness.

It is against this rather forbidding background that Quaker Oats decided to pick up the pieces of the Kibbles 'n Bits launch and correct their formula, before making a redoubled effort in the marketplace.

The resultant new product was composed of four instead of two nuggets: There were now two different crunchy pellets and two chewy ones. The problem of the chunks settling in the bags was solved, and consumer tests confirmed that the new formulation was a real improvement (although some potential buyers remained skeptical). The name was changed to Kibbles 'n Bits 'n Bits 'n Bits (which, for simplicity, will be shortened in this study to Kibbles 'n Bits 3), and advertising was developed to communicate that there was now a new and much better product. This was done without laboring the point that the old one was unacceptable. The launch of the restaged brand began in August 1983.

A High-Profile Advertising Campaign

In this section we will describe and evaluate in some detail the advertising campaign for Kibbles 'n Bits 3. It was (and is) a campaign remembered and liked by consumers, and there is no doubt that it has been successful in the marketplace. But before examining how the campaign sticks in people's minds and generates warm feelings toward the brand—and how it stimulates the consumer to buy—we must consider briefly a few generalized points about the relationship between memorability and the sales effects of advertising.

The relationship between recall and sales has been an important yet controversial topic in advertising research for the past quarter-century. The received wisdom that advertising that is remembered also succeeds in selling was generally accepted during the 1960s and 1970s, the evidence for such acceptance being the virtually universal use of day-after-recall testing by large advertisers in the United States. Yet underlying evidence to support the connection between advertising recall and sales has always been very scarce. And the decline in the use of day-after-recall research during the 1980s has been, if nothing else, a confirmation that some advertisers have begun to doubt the empirical basis of the underlying assumptions and indeed have begun to realize that the research was supported more by myth than fact, except in certain narrowly defined circumstances. Such circumstances include brand launches and relaunches, when there is value in establishing public awareness of brand attributes, irrespective of whether such knowledge can be related to how well the commercial tested sells the brand.[7] Because Kibbles 'n Bits 3 was a new brand, not all the customary criticisms of recall testing apply.

A recent film in the campaign *(Spike and Speck)* demonstrates the underlying features of the advertising most clearly. The film is a tour de force, irresistible to the average viewer. Its heroes are a purposeful bulldog and a skinny, febrile terrier who accompanies the bulldog in a leaping, dancing gait: trotting behind, alongside, and on occasion jumping over his friend. Male voices represent the two dogs in human terms—the bulldog gruff and the leader; the terrier anxious, dependent, and the follower. They are making for their Kibbles 'n Bits 3. What we are shown of the product identifies it clearly as the restaged (four-pellet) formulation, one that is very obviously enjoyed by the dogs. And we *do* notice what the product looks like: The two dogs capture our attention and lead us unerringly toward it. The film is an ingenious and effective synthesis of nonrational and rational communication.

In recall testing, the campaign scored significantly above the norm. Its "persuasion" scores were considered good in comparison with expected levels. These data demonstrate that the commercials passed a basic "quality control," but the figures were not necessarily predictive of what sort of success would be achieved in the marketplace, the details of which will be described shortly.

After the campaign had been exposed for a short while, an important independent organization provided interesting and encouraging evidence that the Kibbles 'n Bits 3 advertising was being perceived extremely favorably by the public. This information came from a large-scale national poll conducted by Video Storyboard Tests and published in the *Wall Street Journal*.[8] The Kibbles 'n Bits 3 campaign was shown to be ranked by the public as among the most memorable advertising campaigns in the United States, taking twenty-fifth place among all advertisers in 1983, thirteenth place in 1984, and tenth place in 1985. Interestingly, all the brands that scored higher had the benefit of larger advertising budgets—anything from four to thirty times as large. Only two other pet-food commercials were in the top twenty-five in 1984, only one in 1985, and all these scored lower than Kibbles 'n Bits 3.

Although this research into the popularity of the campaign is not reliable enough for sales prediction, the brands of the "top twenty-five" list do include several that were widely recognized successes in the marketplace: Pepsi-Cola, McDonald's, Ford, Bartles and Jaymes, Snuggles, and Wendy's (in 1984). The Kibbles 'n Bits 3 campaign was, to say the least, in very good company.

The best evidence of success, however, is the market share figures. From its low point of 2.0% (by volume) of the dry dog-food category in 1983, Kibbles 'n Bits 3 progressively rose to 2.6 percent in 1984, 3.3 percent in 1985, and 3.5 percent in 1986 before settling at a stable 3.3 percent in 1987.[9] This brand share has been held despite competition from dual-textured brands subsequently introduced by competitive manufacturers—Praise, Lucky Dog, Kibbles 'n Chunks, and Tender Chops.

As with all soundly based brands of fast-moving consumer goods, the marketing effort must be adjusted over time away from building penetration and toward increasing usage from an established penetration base. This aspect of the brand repays some study. A good deal is known about Kibbles 'n Bits 3, on the basis of consumer panel data, and the following points are the most salient ones, as they relate to the brand during its first two years following the 1983 restage.[10]

1. Overall product penetration (of all brands) is at relatively stable levels among dog-owning households, and the overlap between these penetration figures indicates the amount of multiproduct buying. This is illustrated in table 9–3. Note that the ratio between market share and penetration is an index of the regularity of use of a product. Contrast dry complete dog-food, for instance, with its 58 percent share and 83 percent penetration, indicating

Table 9–3
Types of Dog-Food—Market Share and Penetration

	Value Market Share 1982	Penetration 1982	Penetration 1985
Dog biscuits and snacks	8%	48%	49%
Canned dog-food	26%	43%	45%
Dry (complete) dog-food (including combined moist/dry)	58%	83%	84%
Semimoist dog-food	8%	25%	22%

high purchases per buyer, with dog biscuits and snacks, whose 8 percent share and 48 percent penetration are evidence of very low purchases per buyer.

2. Penetration of Kibbles 'n Bits 3 was 13.6 percent in 1985, down from a peak level of 16.5 percent in 1984, the brand having lost a fringe of infrequent buyers. As we have seen, the brand's market share was higher in 1985 (3.3 percent) than in 1984 (2.6 percent). With the fall in brand penetration, this increase in market share can be explained only by an increase in the quantity purchased by the average buyer. This is in fact what happened, with a progressive increase—from an average of 16.5 pounds in 1982 (before the restage) to 18.0 pounds in 1984 and 23.0 pounds in 1985. This increase in the average quantity bought is decisive evidence of consumer satisfaction with the brand.

3. As evidence that added values are being built in the mind of the consumer (the prime function of the consumer advertising), the quantity of Kibbles 'n Bits 3 that sold with deals (mainly price-cuts) actually fell from 68 percent in 1984 to 53 percent and resulted in a rise in the average price actually paid. The added values in the brand can be seen, then, as justifying a price of 52 cents per pound in 1985 (up from 48 cents in 1984 and 37 cents in 1982). The reduction in the amount of Kibbles 'n Bits 3 sold on deal is rather unusual in the market, where price dealing has not decreased since 1982; indeed, promotions as a whole have gone up. It is normal for successful advertising to create added values, making it possible for the brand in question to support a premium price. The interest of the Kibbles 'n Bits 3 case lies in the way this process is tracked over three years—a period of steady growth.

4. The growth in average consumer purchases of Kibbles 'n Bits 3 is faster than that for competitive brands (but, of course, from a lower base). In its purchase frequency, the brand is now approaching that of the leading brands in the market, and it achieved this position in little more than two years after its restage.

5. There is some growth in sales of the larger packs of Kibbles 'n Bits 3. And although such growth has been less than expected, it has signaled consumer satisfaction with the brand.

These data are all encouraging, particularly those which indicate consumer satisfaction: the key to repeat purchase. The cost of achieving trial and early repeat usage has, however, been quite significant relative to the advertising voice level in the market. With an ongoing market share of rather more than 3 percent, investment levels are still being maintained—a share of voice twice as great as the share of market.[11] This can be seen in table 9–4. The brand's advertising-to-sales ratio in 1986 was an estimated 5.5 percent, marginally above the market average.[12]

In addition to these investments above-the-line, rather greater sums are

Table 9–4
Quaker Kibbles 'n Bits Advertising Investments

	Estimated Advertising ($ millions)	Share of Voice in Dry Dog-Food
1982	10.0	12%
1983	4.9	6%
1984	7.5	7%
1985	4.1	4%
1986	6.1	6%

spent on promotions, although Quaker Oats can now afford to cut these back to some extent. As noted, the brand can now achieve worthwhile repeat purchase without an excessive level of deal support.

Extending the Mileage from the Kibbles 'n Bits Name

Given the competitive nature and fragmentation of the market, it was soon realized that, once a solid franchise had been established for Kibbles 'n Bits 3, it might be economically attractive to extend that franchise by introducing complementary products that employed the same brand name, if this could be done without cannibalizing the parent product too much.

The segment of the dry dog-food market devoted to puppy food was relatively undeveloped, with only one major brand (Ralston Purina's Puppy Chow, with 6.5 percent by volume of the dry market), plus three smaller entrants. Product development for a new Quaker brand concentrated on the need for extra nutrition for growing dogs, in addition to good taste. Like Kibbles 'n Bits 3, Puppy Kibbles 'n Bits was developed with a four-part formula: two different crisp chunks and two soft ones. The final product pleased veterinarians[13] and—more importantly—puppies.

Although directly derived from Kibbles 'n Bits 3, the advertising features puppies in settings usually associated with human babies—a notion developed partly as a result of qualitative research.[14] The female voice-over talks about the puppy in terms a human mother would use to talk about her baby, and the props—the pink and blue nurseries, the pacifier in the puppy's mouth, the sound of the musical box in the background—dramatically enhance this impression. Partial evidence of the popularity of these commercials comes from a record amount of correspondence that members of the public have sent to Quaker Oats.

The brand has been reasonably strongly supported above-the-line. Following the launch in July 1984, the client committed $7.5 million in 1985 (an 8 percent share of voice in the dry dog-food market) and $4 million in 1986 (a 4 percent share of voice). No attempt was made to launch the brand with low advertising support in the expectation that some of the added values of the Kibbles 'n Bits name would carry over and presell Puppy Kibbles 'n Bits. According to extensive Nielsen evidence, such a strategy invariably fails. Quite simply, people look upon brands as products first and brands second. This means that people do not automatically associate a brand in one field with the same qualities of a brand in another field, although the names may be the same.[15]

The brand's market share was initially very satisfactory. And although this share was not maintained when support was cut back, the brand remains a not-unimportant supplement to Kibbles 'n Bits 3. Dogs do not long remain puppies, and it is a reasonable supposition that the contented Kibbles 'n Bits puppy will have good reason to become a Kibbles 'n Bits dog.

Six Lessons from the History of Kibbles 'n Bits

1. Correct Positioning. Kibbles 'n Bits succeeded as an entry into a buoyant market segment: complete dry dog-food. It offered a unique formulation—a significantly more interesting type of dry dog-food—one intended to take business at the fringe of this market: primarily from consumers who buy dry dog-food but also from some who buy semimoist dog-food. The functional superiority of the brand was demonstrated in product testing, certainly for the reformulation that was urgently brought onto the market as a result of the problems encountered with the first version of the brand. The reformulation meant no repositioning. The basic correctness of the brand's positioning remained a fundamental reason for the success of Kibbles 'n Bits (as is indeed true of the vast majority of successful brand introductions in all fields).[16]

2. An Initial Problem with Functionality Need not be Fatal to a New Brand. This point is not meant to imply that manufacturers and agencies should underrate the importance of functional superiority in at least some respects for new brands, nor does it mean that manufacturers should carry out product testing before the launch in anything less than a thorough and comprehensive way.

The experience of Kibbles 'n Bits did demonstrate, however, that if an unexpected functional deficiency is revealed after the launch, this setback need not turn into a disaster. Yet the situation must be handled with energy and imagination. Kibbles 'n Bits had to have a complete reformulation and reintroduction to the retail trade, requiring in turn a high level of promotional support and the development of fresh advertising emphasizing the improved formulation. It was fortunate that this message was expressed in an advertising campaign for Kibbles 'n Bits 3 that has both high impact and pregnancy. It was also necessary to continue to commit funds above-the-line at an investment level to establish and cement the brand's consumer franchise. It is sometimes necessary to make this sort of investment for a period of up to five years in a competitive market.

3. A Popular Campaign Need Not Be Ineffective. One of the myths of the advertising business (a myth still believed by a surprising number of practitioners) is that advertisements must force consumers into submission—that those advertisements which seduce do not work as well as those which drive their points home by relentless hard-selling.[17] The fact is that there is no robust aggregated evidence to prove or disprove this myth, although there is directional evidence that the use of humor in advertisements has a real, though somewhat ambiguous, value.[18]

The Kibbles 'n Bits 3 campaign provides a reliable piece of evidence at the "micro" level that popular and memorable advertising can also be effective in the marketplace. It is part of the received wisdom of the advertising business that children and pets are devices that automatically provide memorability.[19] But among the campaigns favorably ranked by the *Wall Street Journal* are very few for other brands of pet food, and none ranks as high as Kibbles 'n Bits.

One of the secrets of the Kibbles 'n Bits campaign is that it is an artfully contrived synthesis of the nonrational and the rational; the advertisements tell a story that has a rational substance, but they do so in an unexpected, humorous, and highly involving fashion. By the use of lighthearted hyperbole, the dogs in the commercials are given human characteristics. This strikes a chord with viewers. The commercials also sell effectively.

The product concept, the name, and the advertising work synergistically. The degree to which the advertising is liked makes a major contribution to building the brand's added values.

4. As a New Brand Grows, the Marketing Emphasis Must Change from Penetration Growth to Usage Growth. With a new brand, achieving trial is not the greatest of its problems. Indeed, in the dry dog-food market, an advertising-intensive field in which more than 60 percent of advertising/promotional budgets are deployed below-the-line, much of the initial advertising and virtually all the promotions are directed to building penetration. With Kibbles 'n Bits 3, a reasonable level was achieved: a peak of more than 16 percent within a year of the relaunch.

With virtually all new brands of fast-moving consumer goods, ongoing penetration levels are a few percentage points below the introductory peak, reflecting the fact that a small proportion of the new trialists are going to be disappointed with the functional performance of the brand. On the assumption that this amount of falloff is acceptable, the challenge for a new brand is to boost purchase frequency quickly. The manufacturer's success in doing this depends on two factors: the consumer's satisfaction with the brand's functional effectiveness and the added values that are being built by the advertising. Evidence of success in these endeavors can be provided in the more successful cases—such as Kibbles 'n Bits 3—by the brand's ability to grow in spite of reductions in below-the-line promotional support or—another way of looking at the same phenomenon—with a very gradual increase in the effective price paid by the consumer. This is objective evidence for the existence of added values created in the main by the advertising. In the last analysis, this is the real advertising payoff.

5. Range Extensions Require Realistic Support Levels. The policy of range extension has attracted large numbers of manufacturers in many product fields, on the grounds of the commonsense—but essentially fallacious—argument that added values built for one brand can be easily and cheaply transferred to another. Quaker Oats did not follow this line of reasoning by launching Puppy Kibbles 'n Bits with inadequate support, in the belief that there might be a carryover of added values. The Kibbles 'n Bits 3 advertising campaign demonstrated its pregnancy by the way it could be adapted to range extensions. But a franchise for Puppy Kibbles 'n Bits required an advertising investment. The initial investment yielded a good market share.

Nevertheless, despite some erosion in sales when the introductory support level was cut back, Puppy Kibbles 'n Bits represents the most natural type of long-term reinforcement to Kibbles 'n Bits 3. Puppies grow. They will, it is hoped, eventually graduate from the puppy to the adult product. This range extension thus represents sound long-range marketing thinking. The subtlety of this reasoning is that Puppy Kibbles 'n Bits is not so much a conventional range extension as a *consumer* extension. It is not a case of selling additional products for the same dogs but, rather, of using common brand values to sell an additional brand for dogs that are not yet in the primary market.

6. Client Input. One of the problems advertisers face as they expand in size is that discussion about advertising proposals tends to become repeated and diffused among numerous layers of marketing management. This leads to delays, and it is often thought that the system leads also to erosion and distortion of advertising ideas that may have started off strong and coherent.

One of the characteristics of the Quaker Company is that discussion with its agencies about advertising proposals is carried out in the company at a decision-making level. This leads to a clean and rapid acceptance or rejection of advertising proposals, besides much wisdom in advertising evaluation. There is a strong feeling within JWT Chicago that Quaker gets good advertising at least partly because the company is a good client. In marketing and advertising circles, it is often believed that operating procedures geared to ensuring the best, most experienced, and most continuous contribution from the client to the judgment of advertising campaigns are the hallmark of a sophisticated client. This point is compatible with that made at the beginning of this chapter—that advertising has always been a high-priority activity for the Quaker Company.

10
Slice

> I share my outrageous goal for the brand: Slice as the third-biggest
> trademark in the industry. An annual sales volume of 500 million
> cases—over $2 *billion* a year at retail.
>
> —Roger Enrico[1]

Against the Odds

Slice is the story of an extraordinarily successful new brand introduction.
New brand launches are common; they represent mostly the best efforts of
talented people. Yet those launches which achieve anything like the success
of Slice are rare indeed.[2] In this chapter we shall attempt to answer the
question, Why has Slice worked so spectacularly when so many other new
brands have failed?

The market for carbonated flavored soft drinks in the United States has
three important features. Two of them are typical of most repeat-purchase
packaged goods, and the third (which we shall address first) is rather
untypical.

1. The market shows reasonable growth. Per capita consumption has
been expanding by an average compound rate of 4 percent per year over the
entire period 1972–1985.[3] Average consumption is currently more than 44
gallons per person per year, or approximately 470 twelve-ounce bottles/cans,
equal to a good deal more than a bottle or can per day of the year for every
consumer.

The carbonated soft drinks category is by a large margin the biggest
among all types of drinks. Coffee consumption is more than 40 percent
smaller; beer, 45 percent smaller; milk, 55 percent smaller; and other beverages, vastly less. Coffee, beer, and milk consumption is on a plateau or
even a decline. To a varying degree, the same is true of most of the less
important drinks: juices, tea, powdered drinks, wine, and distilled spirits.
Only bottled water in its different variations—spring water, mountain water,
seltzer and club soda—shows strong growth, but such growth is from a
relatively low level, approximately 5 gallons per capita per year.

The growth of soft drinks has to some extent been at the expense of
other beverages. But this is not a matter of straightforward substitution.

What tends to happen is that children early acquire the soft-drink habit. When they leave their teens, they do not develop the habit of drinking coffee, beer, and so forth, quite so strongly as previous generations did. This means that the markets for these more traditional beverages are not "replenished from below" quite fast enough to maintain growth in them. Any endemic growth gets siphoned off into soft drinks, as young people continue drinking these beverages in large quantities as they grow older. (There is even evidence of an increasing consumption of soft drinks in the morning and even for breakfast.)[4] Among the beverages that have suffered from these changes, the coffee industry in particular has been fully aware of what has been happening and has devoted substantial advertising funds to attracting young people, although with little notable success.

2. As in so many other markets for fast-moving consumer goods, the soft-drink market has become fragmented. In the 1960s, there were two major colas, Coca-Cola and Pepsi-Cola, and a tail of smaller, although profitable, brands of variously flavored drinks, the most important being Seven-Up, Sprite, Dr Pepper (becoming nationally distributed), and Royal Crown Cola. During the 1970s and 1980s, a number of functional innovations caused the market to fragment at a high rate. The market saw the introduction and success of diet soft drinks, caffeine-free soft drinks, new varieties of old flavors (such as New Coke), and new flavors, the most notable being cherry. By far the most important of these innovations was diet soft drinks, using artificial sweeteners. The consumer's response to the concept of taste without calories has been overwhelming.

As a result of these movements in the market, Coca-Cola currently markets sixteen different brands and brand variations, most of which come in at least three different pack sizes (12 ounces, 16 ounces, and one or more of the 1-, 2-, and 3-liter bottles). Pepsi-Cola markets eighteen different brands or variations, again with a range of pack sizes. The large amount of innovation has meant that the corporate market shares of the major companies are now spread over larger numbers of individual varieties than ever before. The existence of such large numbers of brands, varieties, and sizes, together with the bulky packaging (some of it breakable), makes for problems with in-store distribution, although the large size of the market puts pressure on the retail trade to maintain stocks of all major lines. The importance—and the difficulties—of maintaining full retail distribution lead to strong weight being given to promotional activities, which are generally very heated. For some brands, 80 percent of sales in supermarkets are made on deal.[5]

3. The soft-drink market is, as indicated, very large indeed. Recent estimates report that people in the United States drink a larger quantity of soft drinks than of tap water, and a brand with a 1 percent market share has annual sales of $250 million.[6] Like the markets for virtually all repeat-purchase consumer goods, the soft-drink market is oligopolistic. Coca-Cola and

Pepsi-Cola are reasonably balanced in size, each accounting for approximately a third of all grocery soft-drink sales.[7] Seven-Up has 7 percent, Dr Pepper (which now owns Seven-Up) has 4 percent, and Royal Crown Cola also has 4 percent. Private-label brands account for 8 percent. Finally, there are an extensive number of independent and very small trademarks, many of them regional.[8]

Coca-Cola and Pepsi-Cola each market a repertoire of varieties, including the diet and caffeine-free alternatives already cited. Seven-Up, Dr Pepper, and Royal Crown Cola have a much more restricted range, each having only three varieties using the main trademark.

The market is dynamic. Within the growing volume of consumption, competition during the past decade has been characterized by the introduction of many functional innovations, which in most cases were quickly followed by similar introductions by the competition.[9] The pace of new product introduction does not provide the total explanation for the market growth; other markets exhibit a similarly high volume of new product activity without any aggregate upward movement in the market. But it probably does act as a spur to the latent growth that is caused essentially, as noted, by the strength of teenagers' taste preference for carbonated soft drinks over other beverages. An important characteristic of the market that also makes for growth is the seemingly endless flexibility provided by new packaging innovations and new distribution channels.

Not surprisingly, advertising plays a large part in the competitive process. Roger Enrico, president of Pepsi-Cola U.S.A. during the launch of Slice, was the driving force behind the brand. One of the striking features of his published account of his career at Pepsi-Cola is the considerable role that advertising activities have played in his professional life. Later in this chapter, we will review the development of the Slice campaign and Enrico's role in it.

The Growth of Lemon-Lime

The lemon-lime market segment has traditionally been second in importance to cola, although trailing a long way behind. In the early 1980s, lemon-lime drinks accounted for 12 percent of the market, compared with more than 60 percent for cola. The two most significant lemon-lime brands were Seven-Up (manufactured by an independent company acquired by Philip Morris in 1970, which subsequently sold it to the organization that owns Dr Pepper) and Sprite (from Coca-Cola). Seven-Up, the earlier brand, outsold Sprite by a ratio of 2 to 1.[10] Between them, these two brands accounted for three-quarters of all the lemon-lime drinks sold. Very importantly, this market segment was growing in volume at a rate of 15 percent per year.

Pepsi-Cola was, of course, conscious of this growth and believed strongly that it was losing an opportunity by not having a competitive lemon-lime brand, despite the much smaller size of the lemon-lime segment in comparison with the cola one. A number of arguments were put forward to explain and emphasize the potential and growing importance of fruit drinks, in particular lemon-lime. Studies of consumers showed them to be monitoring their eating and drinking habits more than ever before, in the interest of better health. Within the Pepsi-Cola stable, Pepsi Free, a caffeine-free cola and a brand with connotations of good health, has been a notable success. Consumers' interest in better health was leading them in minor but significant ways to switch from darker to lighter beverages (for example, from whiskey to vodka and white wine); from snacks having limited food value (like candy) to snacks having greater and better balanced food value (like Granola and yogurt);[11] and from lower priced to premium priced brands in many product fields. One of the functional superiorities of many premium brands was thought to be extra ingredients, a point that was to be echoed with Slice, with its fruit juice content.

Lemon-lime drinks were judged consonant with these trends.[12] Indeed, the demographics and psychographics of lemon-lime users showed them to care more than the average person about health and fitness. Users also tended to be gregarious and sociable, upwardly mobile, and rather self-centered.[13] These habits and personal characteristics all seemed to be of growing importance. There was a genuine evolution of habits and attitudes, so that underlying trends in the market were moving in an encouraging direction for growth in the sales of fruit drinks, lemon-lime in particular. Indeed, Pepsi's own brand Mountain Dew, which falls between a lemon-lime and an orange drink, had for some time been showing strong growth.

In view of these factors, Pepsi-Cola was engaged in applying serious resources of research and development to producing a lemon-lime product directly competitive with Seven-Up and Sprite. It was at this time, the fall of 1982, that Roger Enrico became executive vice-president, reporting to John Sculley, president of Pepsi-Cola U.S.A. Enrico realized immediately that if Pepsi-Cola were to launch a lemon-lime product without some pronounced physical difference from Seven-Up and Sprite, the brand could never hope to overtake them in the market. Extensive Nielsen evidence from many product fields confirms the general correctness of this reasoning.

Earlier in his career with Pepsi-Cola, Enrico had had successful experience in both Japan and Latin America. In both regions, he had seen firsthand the success of carbonated soft drinks that contained a percentage of fruit juice. In Japan, the Coca-Cola brand HiC (which was based on a fruit juice formula) had been dramatically successful, and the vending machines in the streets of Tokyo were selling orange soda mixed with five different strengths of orange juice. In Latin America, Pepsi-Cola itself had introduced fruit juice into its lemon-lime Teem and its orange drink Mirinda. This was done to take advantage of local tax laws; drinks containing juice were exempt from tax because of the Brazilian and Argentinian governments' anxiety to protect their fruit juice industries.[14] But the question was whether the experience of Japan and Latin America could be applied to the United States. Those executives who have actually worked in overseas markets—like Roger Enrico—tend to be generally optimistic in answering questions of this sort, but other people tend to be much more skeptical.

The first difficulty to be overcome was developing a suitable formulation. Technically, there were a variety of problems: the high raw-material cost because of the price of the fruit juice, the difficulty of controlling quality uniformly through long manufacturing runs, and the stability-related problems of producing an all-natural formula. One suspects that some of the initial difficulties were unconsciously exaggerated by the scientists working on the project, because of the unorthodox nature of the proposed new drink. Enrico succeeded, however, in driving the venture forward, at one time by threatening that he would get the job done by outside consultants. Good laboratory batches of an experimental formula were soon produced; the diet variety was especially promising. But hazards soon emerged with quality control, as the scientists had originally predicted—the second batch was very disappointing in comparison with the first. It was at this stage that Roger Enrico became president of Pepsi-Cola U.S.A.; the time was the spring of 1983.[15]

Laboratory work and product testing proceeded for a further six months before the basic problems were solved. The product testing was carried out against Seven-Up, the market leader in lemon-lime drinks. In earlier tests, consumers consistently preferred Seven-Up, because it is a clear, sparkling drink such as they were used to. They only began to prefer the Slice formula when it was explained to them that the new drink contained real fruit juice.[16] Blind product testing is as important with carbonated soft drinks as in any other product field, but the comparative tests against Seven-Up illustrate special problems. What is especially difficult is to test the important variable of product imagery. In order to do this, extra information must in some way be given to consumers in addition to their tasting the product, to enable them to evaluate the brand's functional and nonfunctional values.[17]

Despite all the initial difficulties with the formulation and the product testing, the project eventually began to look promising. In particular, a small but significant edge over the competition had been developed in blind taste tests. The name Slice had not yet been agreed on (although the company owned the trademark, it was inactive and registered by the Frito-Lay division). Rather grandiloquently, the project was code-named Overlord.

The Most Productive Working Relationship.[18]

During his early weeks as head of Pepsi-Cola U.S.A., Roger Enrico had been preoccupied with his bottlers. Pepsi-Cola makes its money by selling soft-drink concentrate to these bottlers, who in turn add sweetener and carbonated water, before selling the bottles and bulk supplies of Pepsi-Cola and other beverages to retailers and fountain suppliers. The major costs incurred by the bottlers are in packaging and delivery; packaging includes keeping up-to-date with the plentiful packaging innovations that characterize the soft-drink market. Quality control in the manufacture is carefully monitored by Pepsi-Cola, which also effectively controls the marketing of the brand. Pepsi-Cola plans, supervises, and pays for national advertising and merchandising, and the large amount of local advertising and merchandising, which are controlled by the bottlers, is coordinated with the national plans.

Not unlike automobile distributors and fast-food franchisees, soft-drink bottlers are powerful independent businesspeople. It is essential for soft-drink manufacturers to work in active cooperation with their bottlers, who are, of course, the sole point of contact between the brand and the retail and fountain customers, who are in turn the link with the public.

During the time when the Slice formula was being developed, Enrico was persuading his bottlers to accept two important changes in the Pepsi-Cola business—an increase in the price of the concentrate and a change in the formulation of the finished product, through the use of high-fructose corn syrup in place of half the sugar used as the sweetener. The corn syrup was less expensive than sugar, but there were doubts (which were in fact proved to be unfounded) about the effect of the change on the flavor of Pepsi-Cola. The substitution of corn syrup would, of course, reduce the manufacturing costs borne by the bottlers.

These two changes were deemed critical by the company, because they would provide both Pepsi-Cola and the bottlers with additional funds to finance marketing activities, not to mention the capital costs needed for product innovation in an increasingly aggressive marketplace.[19] This was vital for the Pepsi-Cola brand. The changes were also important because of the need to finance the heavy marketing investment that would have to be put behind Slice.

J. Walter Thompson was appointed to handle the advertising for the new drink. The senior people at JWT were known to Pepsi-Cola; indeed, the agency had for some years handled brands from the company in a variety of world markets. In New York, the chemistry between client and agency made a powerful brew, although the relationship (as is the case with the best of such cooperations) was not always an easy one. Enrico played an active—at times decisive—role; his description of the client-agency relationship, which prefaces this section of the chapter, is both gratifying to the agency and true.

The first matter to be resolved was the name. The proposed name Slice was pushed emphatically by the brand management at Pepsi-Cola and supported by JWT. It was eventually accepted—despite initial reluctance—by Enrico. Fruit comes in slices, and those slices can be picked up with great effectiveness in the advertising and on the packaging, to suggest both fruit and juiciness. In fact, the name is one of the key reasons that the entire brand personality is so strongly coherent—the name is embedded in the intrinsic qualities of the product.

The central idea in the launch advertising was for slices of fruit to shoot through crystal-clear liquid. A schematic form of this idea appeared on the storyboards, but it was extensively developed in the subsequent filming. It was not only an appealing visual symbol but one that was shown in research to communicate deliciousness, refreshment, and lightness (the opposite of heaviness), points echoed by the music and the reiterated theme line "we got the juice," a slogan that makes a strong preemptive claim for the brand.

The preliminary versions of the films put great emphasis on Slice drinkers; this is the normal language of soft-drinks advertising, which relies heavily on user associations as a means of brand differentiation. There was a dispute with the client over this emphasis, and in an atmosphere of some crisis, this element in the commercials was edited out. The resulting campaign was oriented to the product more powerfully than any competitive soft drink. And in retrospect, this orientation can be seen as correct, because the essence of the brand is the product differentiation—something best demonstrated directly. However, in the heated atmosphere of the launch, when the bottlers' convention was looming within a few days, it was not easy to be objective.[20] But the right decision was made, and in essentials the campaign followed this format in the three generally successful years that followed.

A subtle feature of the campaign, one that can only be detected by research, is that although the advertising when described in words appears more oriented to the product in comparison with advertising for other soft drinks, in reality the consumer responds to the Slice advertising by taking sensory, rational, and—very importantly—emotional signals from it. The models, the pace of the commercials, and their overall tone of voice all communicate the psychographics of the Slice drinker. Like most effective advertising, the Slice campaign works as a totality, a gestalt. The life-styles and values of the users actually seem to come out of the presentation of the product.

The chronology for the launch of Lemon-Lime Slice was that test marketing was begun in May/June 1984 in four markets, representing regions in which lemon-lime sales were strong, average, and weak.[21] This effort was followed by limited expansion to the West Coast in October 1984 and by a full national rollout in the summer of 1985. It can—correctly—be inferred from this progress that the brand was an immediate success.

1. *MVO:* Get the soft drink that's got 10% real juice

2. *MVO:* Get Slice!

3. *Jingle (male voices):* We got the juice, An icy blast, A burst of taste in every glass.

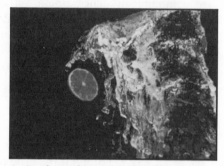

4. *Jingle (male voices):* We got the juice, We got the twist, We got what Sprite and Seven-Up have missed! *MVO:* Real juice!

5. *Jingle (male voices):* We got the juice, We got the splash Slice! Slice! We got the taste that no one has. On ice. We got the juice!

6. *MVO:* Diet too, with 100% Nutrasweet *Jingle (male voices):* Slice! Slice!

Introductory thirty-second television commercial screened in the United States in 1985.

The brand and its advertising were strongly sold to the bottlers, whose support turned a well-founded and imaginative idea into a marketing reality.

The result of the launch, in summary, was that the lemon-lime segment, which, it will be remembered, had been increasing at a rate of 15 percent per year, surged upward by 70 percent with the arrival of Slice. This happened partly as a result of existing lemon-lime drinkers consuming more and, even more importantly, by new consumers coming into the market segment on an occasional basis. Much of the extra sales were accounted for by Slice, which for a time measured 3 percent of the total soft-drink market: a very high rate of sale for a new brand in this category.

Range Extension

One of the initial—and continued—problems with Slice is the relatively high cost of raw materials. After careful consideration of the alternatives, Pepsi-Cola decided that the extra costs had to be absorbed by the company and the bottlers, to avoid making the consumer pay a premium price. This decision meant that to the bottlers, Slice is marginally less profitable than Pepsi-Cola (besides, of course, being very much smaller in terms of volume). In view of Slice's rapid and seemingly secure establishment in the market and its ability to grow without posing any threat to the sales of Pepsi, the bottlers proved themselves willing to bite the bullet, although some of them experimented with charging a premium price for Slice, without notable success. The decision to avoid a premium price was arrived at because of the obvious risks of damaging a fragile consumer franchise. General experience from other markets suggests strongly, however, that consumers are happy to accept a higher price for a product that is demonstrably different from and superior to competitors in functional terms—which is the case with Slice.[22] At some future date, there could well be merit in studying the price elasticity of the brand, based on actual data from the marketplace. Such research would provide the necessary information for manipulating the price to maximize the earnings of the brand in the long term, possibly by a price increase.

During the period of rather more than a year when Lemon-Lime Slice was being expanded geographically to the whole United States, the brand management group was moving fast to develop other fruit flavors. One of the unusual merits of the name and brand concept was that Slice was adaptable to range extensions—so long as two conditions were met. First, the new flavors had to offer the consumer a degree of functional reward similar to that offered by the Lemon-Lime variety. Second, the new flavors had to be introduced quickly, while Slice was still perceived by the public (not to mention retailers, caterers, and bottlers) as exciting and innovative and before the Lemon-Lime flavor had become so deeply entrenched that people could think of Slice only in terms of Lemon-Lime.

One of the factors that hastened the rollout of the first of the Slice range extensions was the fact that Coca-Cola's brand, Minute Maid Orange Soda, was already in test market with 10 percent fruit juice.[23] This is an excellent example of the speed and responsiveness of the oligopolistic competition in this market, a matter that has already been referred to in this study.

The new flavors for Slice were carefully explored and evaluated. Orange was a natural choice for a second flavor, although the image of carbonated orange drinks was not favorable, tending to be both cheap and child-oriented. The decision to develop an orange flavor was made long in advance of the news of Minute Maid Orange Soda with 10 percent fruit juice. True to the Slice tradition of product differentiation, the new Slice flavor became something different—Mandarin Orange, which was rolled out over the country during the twelve months beginning in November 1985 (following immediately on the heels of the national extension of Lemon-Lime). The fact that Mandarin Orange was different from the flavor of competitive orange drinks meant that the advertising for this variety, like that for Lemon-Lime, could be based on discriminators intrinsic to the product.

Most importantly, research soon demonstrated that because the strategic concentration was strongly on the 10 percent fruit juice—something that applied to all flavors—a crossover effect developed between the different commercials in the campaign. Consumers took the idea of Mandarin Orange flavor out of the Lemon-Lime advertisements. Generalized Nielsen data suggest that a favorable crossover effect between advertising for different brands using a common umbrella name is an unusual phenomenon.[24] In the case of Slice, the mutual interaction of the different advertisements seems to suggest that it was the branding that came through most strongly, possibly more than the product differentiation, because the campaign had such a powerful and uniform tone of voice.

Mandarin Orange posed a problem with some bottlers, since a few of them had to sacrifice more profitable business from other orange drinks (not from Pepsi-Cola) in order to be able to handle Mandarin Orange Slice. But again, the strong track record of Lemon-Lime Slice convinced them, and their faith was to be justified. Following the launch, brand awareness and usage of Mandarin Orange Slice shot up. And the new brand expanded the small orange market segment by 20 percent, and soon occupied 24 percent of this larger segment, to become the number-one orange soft drink in America (6 percentage points ahead of its target). This performance in the marketplace led to a gold Effie award for Mandarin Orange Slice in 1987;[25] the Effie is an advertising industry prize based on the marketplace effectiveness of brands and advertising campaigns.

Following the success of Mandarin Orange, Apple and Cherry Cola flavors were developed, and these were rolled out from April 1987. The Cherry Cola was introduced partly to counter Cherry Coke, but there was some feeling at the time that Cherry Cola, with its dark appearance and rather heavy flavor, was not an entirely appropriate range extension for Slice.

None of the four flavors of Slice covers the United States comprehensively, but the brand (in one flavor or another) is national; it covers 97 percent of the total population. In the summer of 1987, Slice accounted for 3 percent of total soft-drinks sales in food stores. It will be remembered that this was the initial peak share level of the Lemon-Lime flavor in 1985. The normal sales pattern for brand launches in all fields is that sales invariably drop below the initial peak to something approaching an ongoing stable level, in those cases in which a brand looks as though it will succeed.[26] With Slice, the decline has been quickly picked up or, rather, made good, by the new flavors.

An important characteristic of Slice is that the original two flavors did not cannibalize each other. (Seventy percent of users of one flavor were exclusive to that flavor; only 30 percent also drank the other flavor. The diet versions had a particularly stable user base.) This meant that the brand originally achieved an interesting combination of attributes. There was a commonality of appeal that stemmed mainly from the claim of 10 percent juice that links all the varieties. But there was also, and somewhat paradoxically, a differentiation, in that the rewards from the two different original flavors were sufficiently separate from one another that they attracted substantially different people. And Slice's overall four-weekly household penetration of only 17 percent suggests that the brand still has growth potential,[27] although increases in consumer penetration will probably cause the mutual cannibalization between flavors to increase. Indeed, this is what began to happen with the introduction of the Cherry Cola and Apple flavors.[28]

Fourteen films were made in the original campaign. The advertising remained continuously fresh (in the estimation of consumers), a result achieved partly by injecting new elements into the advertising—for example, the introduction in 1987 of minor celebrities not well enough known to become what are called Video Vampires. This type of evolution took place without eroding the campaign's strategic essentials—in particular, its emphasis on delicious taste (from the juice) and its lightness and refreshment. The commercials were researched sensitively, with no reliance on standardized recall procedures. The commercials, which were screened before consumers alongside commercials for a variety of brands in different fields, were evaluated by measuring the salience of brand image attributes in the minds of these consumers. The questioning was both closed- and open-ended, and each sample of consumers who viewed the show-reel that included Slice was matched by a sample who viewed a reel that did not include Slice.

As might have been expected, the introductory advertising represented a substantial investment: In 1985, the total advertising budget on Slice above-the-line exceeded $40 million. This heavy expenditure was comparable with that for Seven-Up (a brand with twice the market share). As a share of voice in the carbonated soft-drink category, Slice's advertising, excluding the heavy expenditures spent below-the-line on promotions, represented a proportion in excess of 11 percent—more than three times the brand's peak market share. This is, of course, a required investment for a major brand with ambitions, in a dynamic product category.[29] Pepsi-Cola quite correctly sees the task of establishing a major new trademark as something that will require decades of investment to accomplish. However, the initial investment policy obviously had major implications for Slice's earnings, and the subsequent need to make some reductions in expenditure had a negative effect on the brand's sales.

Pressures in the Marketplace

This case study is concerned essentially with the launch of Slice, an introduction that was uniformly successful and owe that reflected great credit on both client and agency. The story did not have a happy ending, however, for JWT.

During 1987, the market for soft drinks continued to be hyperactive, and a combination of forces began to cause a faltering in the sales of Slice. One factor was the emergence of new competition, in particular, directly competitive brands with a percentage of fruit juice, which in effect removed Slice's uniqueness in the market. The new competitors included Coca-Cola's Minute Maid, which was originally in orange flavor but soon also in lemon-lime.[30] Another difficulty was caused by the growing cannibalization of existing flavors by the new Cherry Cola and Apple varieties (a point we have already mentioned), and this problem was compounded by distributional difficulties caused by the now rather overextended range of Slice flavors and packs.[31] In fact, the distributional system was becoming overloaded by the range of flavors, varieties, and bottle sizes. There were also some manufacturing problems in the bottling connected with the difficulty of keeping the fruit juices fresh, although these difficulties were eventually overcome. (Minute Maid also had some manufacturing problems, connected with its product stability.)

A reduction in the advertising investment behind Slice to the more economic ongoing level of $20 million also had a predictably dampening effect on sales.[32] This was caused at least partially by a refocusing of attention on Pepsi-Cola, in response to competitive pressures by Coca-Cola earlier in 1987.

The success of Slice also caused competitors to reevaluate their businesses. New campaigns were launched for both Seven-Up and Sprite, increasing to a measurable degree the amount of competitive pressure on Slice. Seven-Up had a new advertising agency, and shortly afterward Philip Morris sold the Seven-Up operation.

In addition, there was the growing feeling on the part of Pepsi-Cola that the Slice advertising—despite its track record in lifting the brand off the ground so spectacularly—was developing problems. In particular, it was thought to be losing its effectiveness in building brand discriminators in a situation in which Slice was no longer functionally unique: now that competitive soft drinks with fruit juice were emerging in the marketplace.[33]

Interestingly, qualitative research was also demonstrating that (a) some consumers were beginning to think that 10 percent juice made the taste of the drink rather heavy and syrupy and (b) Slice was losing some of its original connotations of lightness and crispness. These findings led to experimentation with different formulas containing lower amounts of fruit juice—and naturally also to a change in the direction of the advertising.[34]

The point of maximum sensitivity had been reached. But there was no extended agonizing. There was a speedy break, a parting of the ways. Not surprisingly, in view of JWT's contribution to the brand, the divorce between client and agency was characterized by truthful expressions of mutual respect and gratitude.

It should be remembered that Slice is still a successful brand, with a current sales value not far short of $1 billion.[35] The remarkable success of the launch justifies our concentrating on the reasons for this in the lessons we draw from this case.

Why Has Slice Succeeded? Ten Lessons

At the beginning of this chapter, we raised the question, Why has Slice succeeded when so many carefully planned and apparently promising new brands have failed? We also said that we would make some attempt to provide an answer. Combing through the facts of this case, ten lessons seem to emerge, but it is difficult to give them a firm order of importance, indeed even to disentangle those which were critical to the success of the brand from those which were of lesser importance. Most likely, what mattered was the very coming together at one time of a number of these ten elements—perhaps all of them. This meeting of disparate forces, which was a matter of luck as well as judgment, caused a spark to ignite. The odds against such a thing happening are long, but so are the brands as successful as Slice. The ten factors we have isolated are briefly described below. The reader will note that they are not isolated factors; indeed, a number of close interconnections exist among certain of them.

1. A Growing Market. Before the arrival of Slice, the market for carbonated soft drinks was expanding quite positively and at the same time showing evidence of internal changes: It was fragmenting and also moving toward increasing sales of lighter, fruit-based beverages. All this provided fertile soil for the new brand. By the standards of other packaged goods, the overall market growth was an exceptional circumstance, although movements within stationary total markets are by no means uncommon.

2. Ripeness. The concept of ripeness was conceived by Arthur Koestler, in his exploration of the circumstances conducive to discovery and invention: ". . . the statistical probability for a relevant discovery to be made is the greater the more firmly established and well exercised each of the still separate skills, or thought-matrices, are."[36] The analogy with Slice lies in the development, or ripening, of the attendant circumstances in the marketplace that provided a current that the new brand could ride. These circumstances were the overall buoyancy and growth of the soft-drink business; the lifestyle changes that were encouraging the consumption of lighter, especially fruit-based beverages; the reemergence of well-established lessons from overseas markets concerning the sales potential of carbonated soft drinks with fruit juice; the inability of those who marketed Seven-Up and Sprite to be innovative enough to tap into the latent growth; and finally the flair of Pepsi-Cola in synthesizing its conclusions from these different trends. The last point is important, for as Koestler reminds us, ripeness on its own is "merely a necessary, not a sufficient, condition of discovery."[37]

3. Differentiation. Experienced marketers are aware that a second brand entering a market with a strong resemblance to an innovative brand is likely to achieve a much smaller market share (on average, less than half the share of the innovator).[38] This is more or less the situation today with Seven-Up and Sprite. It is also widely known that a third brand will achieve a still-smaller share. It follows that despite the extensive work carried out by Pepsi-Cola on the product development of a clear lemon-lime formula, it was absolutely correct that this formula should have been rejected in favor of one offering an obvious functional difference from the competition: the inclusion of fruit juice.

4. The Value of Overseas Experience. In many product categories, the experience of brands in some markets will be repeated elsewhere, a matter deriving from the likelihood that consumers in different countries will have similar tastes and habits and will respond similarly to the same marketing stimuli. This similarity between consumers is known to many multinational marketing companies, some of which use smaller markets as test markets, or precursors, for larger ones. Such a use of precursor markets is, however, less practiced in the food and drink fields than in, for example, detergents and toiletries—a matter concerned with idiosyncratic differences in eating and drinking habits in many foreign countries.[39] These differences are sometimes exaggerated and occasionally used to rationalize a reluctance to accept ideas from overseas because they were "not invented here." Enlightened companies, though, will tend to give ideas from overseas the benefit of the doubt and put them into consumer test. This is a policy that emphatically paid off with Slice.

5. Resources. The cost of entry into the soft-drink market is high. The success of Slice could not have been achieved without the expenditure of the most significant resources in research and development, management effort and attention, and marketing and advertising. Such a program was more than a one-year project. Slice, with its range of flavors, is potentially a very profitable brand. But to realize that potential, Pepsi-Cola has had to mobilize major resources and be willing to deploy them to secure a long-term (at the expense of a short-term) return. This point is related to the next one.

6. A Lower Rate of Return. As explained earlier, Pepsi-Cola decided against setting the consumer price of Slice above the average in the market. Because of the brand's above-average cost of raw materials, this meant trimming the company's (and the bottlers') margins in order to make funds available for the necessary production, distributional, and marketing investments. This policy was correct in its priorities, although it imposed a squeeze on earnings from the increased business that was added. An increase in the consumer price would make for more comfortable margins—a step that may repay study in the future.

7. The Integration of the Brand. Essentially as a result of good judgment, Slice has been developed into a brand that attracts consumers in two seemingly opposite ways. The different flavors have a similarity, even a commonality of appeal: They all communicate a sensory attraction—refreshment and juiciness, together with an emotional appeal—those values associated with modern life-styles which are becoming associated increasingly strongly with the name Slice. Despite the links of the common heritage, the original flavors are substantially drunk by different people. However, the third and fourth flavors began to overload the bottlers' production and distributional capacity, as well as causing some (perhaps predictable) mutual cannibalization between the different varieties.

8. The Advertising Gestalt. The name Slice is of great value, not least because the advertising grew out of it. Like all effective advertising, the introductory Slice campaign worked synergistically at the sensory, rational, and (above all) emotional levels. Sensory and emotional appeals are important for all soft-drink advertising. But, in addition, a rational appeal was essential for Slice, in view of the brand's all-important functional discriminator: its juice content. The most dramatic illustration of this synergism that emerged from consumer research was the way in which the psychographics of the user came out of the essentially product-related advertising. This leads us to the next point.

9. Intrinsic Arguments. In view of the functional difference between Slice and competitive brands, it appears in retrospect entirely natural that the advertising campaign should have been oriented so strongly to demonstrating that difference. This approach was different from the traditional language and imagery of soft-drink advertising, which are concerned almost exclusively with the enjoyment and life-styles of the brand's users, the intention being that brand differentiation can be achieved gradually by associating the brand with the type of user shown in the advertising. This strategy has been highly successful for pioneer brands like Coca-Cola and Pepsi-Cola. It is, however, a device that is increasingly difficult for smaller brands to employ. It is typical of the differentiation that has always been the hallmark of Slice that the advertising should also have been differentiated. There was no downside to this concentration on the product, because, as we saw in point 8, this concentration on the product did not prevent the advertising from also communicating the psychographics of the user subtly and indirectly but quite distinctively.

10. Cross-Over Effects of the Campaign. This factor greatly eased the launch of the different flavors and has more than a short-term value. Advertising can work cumulatively, from subject to subject in the campaign, only when brand associations, especially the rational and nonrational values connected with the juice content, are being built by the advertising. It would be reasonable to conclude that the future of the brand will depend more than anything else on a continuation of this process—a process that, in the judgment of Pepsi-Cola, is a task needing decades rather than years to accomplish.

11
Smarties

> . . . [P]ictorial thinking is an earlier form of mentation than concep-
> tual thinking—in the evolution of the individual as in that of the
> species. The language of children is "picturesque"—in the literal sense
> of the word.
>
> —Arthur Koestler[1]

More Than a Children's Candy

Smarties is a major brand marketed by Rowntree, one of the three oligo-
polists dominating the British confectionery industry. The term *confectionery*
is the most accurate description for what are popularly called sweets in the
United Kingdom and candy in the United States; all three words will be used
on occasion in this chapter. Rowntree is a British company in origin, recently
taken over by Nestlé. It operates both in the British market, under the Rown-
tree-Mackintosh name, and overseas, including in the United States where it
markets certain of its brands via licensing arrangements with Hershey. Of
the other two major manufacturers, Cadbury-Schweppes is also British,
whereas Mars Confectionery is American, a massive subsidiary of its American parent organization. Mars Confectionery markets M & Ms, a direct
competitor to Smarties and a brand that will be discussed later in this chapter.

The British people eat an enormous amount of candy. Consumption per
capita is among the highest in the world—approximately 12 kilograms per
year for every man, woman, and (particularly) child in the country; the
comparable figure for the United States is less than 9 kilograms.

The British have always had a sweet tooth, and the confectionery market
is both huge and relatively immobile, although with an annual volume change
that has varied during the post-decade from a low of −1.7 percent to a high
of +4.7 percent, it is not absolutely stationary. The market is segmented,
and the segment in which Smarties is positioned is defined as being directed
at children, the products in it coming in a number of different sizes and
shapes and being sold in boxes, envelopes and tubes. This segment accounts
for less than 10 percent of the aggregate confectionery market by volume, a
proportion that is related to the child population, which in recent years has
declined. The size of this segment, however, is such that it can accommodate
a number of substantial and profitable brands. In this as in other product

categories, all the major manufacturers tend to have at least one brand in each of the separate segments, although not every manufacturer has filled every gap. This tendency for a manufacturer to match the competition in each segment is a characteristic of oligopoly.

Brands directed at children are bought by 39 percent of all British households. The figures are 75 percent for households with children ages one to four years and 68 percent for households with children ages five to nine.[2]

Within this children's market segment, Smarties is by a wide margin the largest brand, with a 55 percent volume share; its net sales value in 1986 totaled nearly $50 million. The brand was launched in 1937, was first advertised in 1938, and first appeared on television in 1955 (the year commercial television was introduced in Great Britain).

Smarties can be described as hard chocolate buttons or beans in eight separate bright colors. They contain a milk chocolate center (except for the popular orange color, which has orange-flavored chocolate in the middle). The color comes from a polished sugar coating, which gives the sweets a very attractive appearance. Smarties has developed over the years extrinsic as well as intrinsic values. The brand has grown to be more than a candy to be nibbled. As J. Walter Thompson described the brand: " . . . children count with them, use the tube as a cannon or telescope, sort them into colors, and so mothers who can remember Smarties as part of their childhood are happy to continue the tradition."[3]

The brand represents a typical amalgam of functional and nonfunctional values for its consumers. These values have been succinctly described by JWT in the following eight words: "fun, liveliness, children, play, quality, chocolate, color, *LOTS*." The advertising has always exploited these features, which research indicates are meaningful and accurate descriptions of what Smarties stand for to the separate target groups of consumers (children) and buyers (mothers). The existence of these two target groups is an important characteristic of the brand, and the reader should keep in mind the fact that the advertising has always addressed both groups. Indeed, it has always been an explicit objective that mothers should like the advertisements and should feel that their children would benefit in some way from seeing them. It has always been the general intention that mothers should respond in a way indicating that "these advertisements (and this brand) are not cheap and nasty."

The Smarties advertising has always been most successful in striking a harmonious chord between the two target groups. Much research has shown that the extrinsic arguments—the educational "play" aspects of Smarties—have appeal to mothers. Many mothers are looking for things with which to amuse their offspring harmlessly and are conscious of the potential problems with candy and teeth, although they also appreciate that Smarties contain high-quality milk chocolate, which is nutritious as well as delicious.

Sales of Smarties grew strongly during the 1950s and 1960s, and experience during these decades demonstrated that television was a potent selling medium. In the 1970s the tactical reintroduction of outdoor billboards alongside television represented a highly effective extension of the media mix. Print advertising has occasionally also been used. The brand's media have provided a remarkably ubiquitous presence for Smarties. Campaigns in particular media have always been imaginative in exploiting the special features of those media. JWT has produced and exposed an ever-fresh flow of advertisements characterized by a warmth and approachability that have communicated the fun, liveliness, and, more recently, intrinsic (chocolate) values of Smarties. The advertising strategy was itself substantially unchanging, but there was a large variety of creative executions during the course of the 113 different commercials made between 1955 and 1987.[4]

Some of the commercials used live action featuring children enjoying the play value and taste of Smarties; others were animated; and still others employed a combination of the two techniques. One notable film that is remembered today, at least in professional circles, was influenced by the innovative filmmaking of the *Sesame Street* television series that has had such a long and successful run on the Public Broadcasting Service in the United States. Interestingly, a key characteristic of many of the animated Smarties commercials has been the density of the imagery. Many of the films contained as many as thirty separate vignettes—an average of one per second. The vignettes were expressions of visual fantasy—for example, a leopard licking off its own spots, which are Smarties, and a statue of Admiral Nelson looking through his telescope, which turns out to be a tube of Smarties. Not only were such vignettes a fascinating source of interest to children, but research demonstrated that children comprehended more easily than adults the range of often subtle and evanescent images packed into the commercials. (This point confirms Koestler's perceptive observation prefacing this chapter, on the pictorial nature of children's thinking and self-expression.) Often there has been an oscillation between this type of advertising, for which parental endorsement is more difficult to obtain (given the much slower degree of comprehension by adults), and live action, in which children enjoy a Smarties fantasy world, normally to the accompaniment of an appropriate contemporary music track. The latter type of advertising often has more potency with parents, who can identify with the children featured, but is not so effective as a stimulus to children.

Emerging Difficulties in the Marketplace

A central factor determining the health of the brand is, naturally, the size of the target group—the population of children of the appropriate ages. In this, the rate of increase decelerated during the 1970s and the number of children actually began to fall after 1973. Although Smarties continued to be an important and profitable brand, sales began to stagnate, a development connected not only with the falling size of the target group but also with another factor.

The live action advertising remained attractive to very young children and was as popular as ever with mothers. But the feeling was emerging that such advertising was appealing progressively less to eight- and nine-year-olds; there was thought to be a danger of these older children growing out of Smarties and graduating to other brands in the large, fragmented, and competitive confectionery market. At the end of 1983, a major piece of qualitative research was commissioned to help understand the child's world and Smarties' place within it and also to evaluate what the mothers were thinking.[5]

The potential danger for the brand was that it was digging a hole for itself. The more it continued to appeal to the declining number of younger children, the more difficult it was becoming to sell Smarties to older children. Success with the younger target group was reducing the campaign's impact on the older group. The research was planned to find a way of getting the brand out of this perceived hole.

The problem that the brand was facing in the 1980s, therefore, was the need to broaden its appeal. It had to reinforce its attraction to older children without weakening its strong franchises among both young children and mothers. It also seemed sensible to retain, if possible, the strengths of the long-established heritage of the Smarties advertising, so long as the campaign could be made to change slightly (rather than merely to confirm) what people already knew about the brand. Using the discipline of the King Continuum, the role of the advertising had to be changed to nudge it from the "indirect" extreme of the model to a slightly more direct role.

The advertising now had to be planned to work more aggressively to modify some people's existing attitudes toward Smarties, a task often considered more difficult than merely reinforcing existing perceptions, the previous aim of the advertising.[6] It needed to reaffirm core brand beliefs but to do so in an idiom intended to appeal to a slightly wider age range of Smarties consumers, at the same time reemphasizing the brand's intrinsic (chocolate) qualities.

A Creative Restaging

The agency approached its task not only with an instinctive feeling for the strengths of the brand with consumers but also with a willingness to use qualitative research first to help reevaluate the brand's strategy before planning the advertising and then to guide judgment of the creative directions proposed.

With this latter use of research, however, there was a problem. Partly as a result of the large qualitative investigation carried out in 1983, the agency, pressed strongly by the client, was thinking seriously about the use of computer animation, a relatively unusual film technique that might be creatively appropriate for Smarties, besides providing an unquestionably fresh look to the campaign. This meant revisiting the world of animation, because of its appeal to children, after a period of live action advertising. But there was a hazard in giving up live action, because showing real children was a long-established and important tradition of the Smarties campaign. Abandoning them was a calculated risk, but it was felt that the risk had to be taken.

The next stage of research—finding out how consumers respond to preliminary creative ideas—is normally carried out when those ideas have been expressed in a schematic, sometimes even crude, form, and there is a large gap between a creative idea expressed in a storyboard or an "animatic" (a videotaped storyboard), and that same idea expressed with the production values of a finished commercial. One of the valuable lessons of this case is that it demonstrates that such worries may be groundless and that good research pretesting is indeed able to work with relatively primitive storyboards and animatics.

Although the proposed new commercials maintained the traditional aura and atmosphere of previous Smarties advertising, they had a very fresh look. The new strategy directed the Smarties advertising to be associated with slightly more adult symbols than formerly. In campaign development, television game shows and contests were chosen as interesting to older children as well as to young ones. The Smarties themselves were shown to be the heroes of these games and contests, and the proposed films were also packed with symbols of the brand (making it a game in itself for the viewer to recognize them).

The advertising pretesting was carried out by assembling six small groups of children of varying ages and six small groups of parents. They were (in their separate groups) first shown a series of films made with the computer animation technique planned for Smarties and then shown an animatic and a storyboard representing the creative idea planned for the first new Smarties commercial. The groups then discussed the films, the animatic and storyboard, and, most importantly, the brand. The conclusions of this research were extremely clear and are briefly summarized below, although we unfortunately do less than full justice to many interesting but less important findings.[7]

1. The commercial was very favorably received by children. It made a

strong impact on children of all ages as an enjoyable visual experience: for its "abundance of visual treats."[8]

2. Older children understood the visual images more comprehensively than younger children did. The commercial could be enjoyed as much by the older as by the younger children, but it had a stronger cognitive effect on the older ones. The research report stated, "As might be expected, the degree of sophistication associated with this level of enjoyment differed between younger and older children."[9]

3. Parents enjoyed the commercial as much as the children did, but they found it less easy to assimilate; some said it was "too fast" or "too noisy." (This conclusion is consistent with other Smarties research we have mentioned, which suggests that children can comprehend fast-moving visual imagery more easily than adults can.)

4. The commercial was seen by both children and parents as being targeted at older children; however, all children could (in the words of the research report) "take out what they need/want from the ad."[10]

5. Both children and parents appeared to understand that the animatic they viewed fell some way short of how the finished commercial would look. The deficiencies of the former were largely compensated for by the viewer's imagination.

In summary, and bearing in mind the small size of the investigation, the results generally confirmed that the proposed new creative approach would work in accordance with its strategy. "It is a radical step forward for the brand, tapping an unspoken need for 'refreshment' of the advertising."[11]

A first commercial, *Get Smarties,* was produced, serving as the springboard from which a number of ten-second versions were subsequently developed. The commercial had striking production values, at least partly a result of the freedom the client allowed to the animation studio. The client was wise enough not to require detailed storyboards before the work began, although he participated in regular supervisory meetings as the animation progressed.

Get Smarties is characterized by a high level of obtrusiveness balanced by an essential friendliness; high noise and dynamic music; brisk pace; bright colors; and a remarkable three-dimensional effect derived from the computer animation. It also has a real relevance to the brand, for two reasons: (a) although the commercial is quite different from past Smarties advertising, it has a similar aura, in that it makes an unmistakably similar use of visual fantasy, and (b) the commercial is packed with images of the brand (every viewing seems to disclose new ones). The puzzle thought of "only Smarties has the answer" echoes the intriguing play value of the brand.

Three commercials were produced initially: *Get Smarties;* a film entitled *10% Extra,* emphasizing an increased quantity of Smarties in the tube; and *Chocodiles,* described below. (A fourth commercial was subsequently introduced, with the promotional objective of launching a new Smarties color, blue.)

Chocodiles, the third commercial in the series, is modeled on an obstacle race in a stadium. It has an echo of the television program *Jeux sans Frontières* ("Games without Frontiers"), which has been popular in a number of European countries. Unlike *Get Smarties,* the *Chocodiles* commercial has a narrative element through its use of a number of different but interrelated storytelling vignettes. The competitors are different-colored Smarties; the animation even succeeds in conveying the idea of their limbering up before the contest. The competing Smarties race through a game of "Snakes and Ladders" (the snakes having spots like a tube of Smarties, and prominent eyes that resemble Smarties). The competitors slide through a plastic maze and negotiate a pool with crocodiles (the liquid is melted chocolate, and the crocodiles are Smarties tubes—inspiring, incidentally, the name *Chocodiles*). The winning post is an elevated plinth surmounted by an Olympic torch— a Smarties tube, naturally.

This campaign made an impact almost immediately after its first exposure in 1985. Total sales of Smarties in that year were 9 percent above those in 1984. In 1986, the brand's position was strengthened by the additional quantity of Smarties in the tube advertised in the *10% Extra* film. *Get Smarties* and the other films in the new campaign emphatically and seemingly effortlessly took the brand past the point of maximum sensitivity. The sales improvement has been continuous since the middle of 1985, as we can see from table 11–1's moving-average index, which has been calculated from bimonthly retail audit volume sales figures.

As noted, the 1986 sales increase was helped by the 10 percent extra quantity in the pack, although the advertising was obviously also working. The reader will note from table 11–1 how much greater was the sales increase in 1986 than in the second half of 1985 and that the pace of the upward movement was continuing in 1987 with little abatement. This acceleration and continuation in the sales increase is presumptive evidence of repeat business—a rising volume of consumption by children of a wide range of ages.

Data on consumption by children of different ages show (a) a slightly increased share of total Smarties sales accounted for by children under age five and (b) a stabilized share accounted for by five- to eight-year-olds.[12] Against the background of an increasing total volume of Smarties sales, the consumption by both these age-groups therefore increased in absolute terms. The particularly good performance of the brand with young children was not foreseen by the initial research, possibly because the campaign had a lagged effect, in that it took repetition to establish effective communication in addition to its initial impact, which was related to its pure entertainment.

Qualitative research carried out four months after the first exposure of

Table 11–1
Smarties Moving-Average Sales Index

Year Ending	Sales Index
July/August 1985	100
September/October 1985	101
November/December 1985	103
January/February 1986	104
March/April 1986	108
May/June 1986	110
July/August 1986	114
September/October 1986	117
November/December 1986	123
January/February 1987	127
March/April 1987	129
May/June 1987	131
July/August 1987	134
September/October 1987	137

Source: A. C. Nielsen Audits of the Food and the Confection-ery-Tobacconist-Newsagent (CTN) trade.

the campaign demonstrated its appeal both to mothers and older children: "It's more for older children, there's more going on . . . unlike the other ones with little children at parties."[13] Eighteen months after the beginning of the campaign, qualitative research confirmed its impact in even stronger terms: "In general, there was an unusually high degree of spontaneous recall of the current advertising across the age spectrum, and it has apparently 'universal' appeal."[14]

The campaign was not only effective in the marketplace. It also created a considerable stir in professional circles and won four major creative awards, even before any unambiguous evidence of its sales success. As in a number of other cases in this book, the Smarties campaign demonstrates that prize-winning advertising can often also sell brands.

A series of outdoor billboard advertisements used alongside the television campaign in 1985 attempted to stimulate a direct involvement from passers-by by getting them to solve puzzles on the posters. On one poster, there was a triangle of ten Smarties, the puzzle being to turn the triangle upside down by moving three Smarties. A second poster showed six Smarties tubes, the puzzle being to add five more tubes in such a way as to make nine. It is rare for outdoor advertising to generate a direct behavioral response; however, the client received many hundreds of replies to the puzzles, thus providing additional evidence that the campaign was achieving an intellectual and emotional engagement with the public.

The situation for Smarties has looked extremely buoyant during the past three years. Yet as long ago as 1985 a cloud that was a good deal larger than a man's hand had appeared on the horizon, and it is there still.

A Transatlantic Competitor

From a description of the physical properties of Smarties, it will strike some American readers that Smarties bear a strong resemblance to M & Ms, a large brand manufactured by Mars that is securely established in the confectionery market in the United States. M & Ms are, in fact, worldwide, a 150,000-ton brand, and with 14 percent of the American market alone, they are the single largest brand of confectionery sold anywhere. There are certain physical differences between Smarties and M & Ms: The latter are more simply packaged in a coated paper envelope (simple packaging being a general characteristic of brands from Mars), are available in only six colors, and come with two alternative types of centers—(a) plain chocolate and (b) peanut and milk chocolate.

Mars Confectionery was faced with substantial problems in launching M & Ms in Britain. The company already marketed two brands based on the M & Ms concept, Minstrels and Treets, which accounted jointly for a sales volume 25 to 30 percent higher than Smarties'. These two brands had to be withdrawn to facilitate the launch of M & Ms, with its stated volume target of three times the Smarties sales level (that is, more than twice the existing sales of Minstrels and Treets combined). A decision as major as the one to launch M & Ms takes a long time in the making, and rumor has it that certain people in the Mars operation in the United Kingdom resisted it. It is fairly clear the the launch of M & Ms has called for a long-term investment, with the possibility (though by no means the certainty) of a long-term payout.

The launch area chosen was Tyne-Tees in the northeastern part of Great Britain, a relatively self-contained region containing upwards of 5 percent of the British population and possessing an effective local television station that does not overlap with neighboring stations.

The most striking characteristic of the M & Ms launch was the investment level, particularly in consumer advertising. This is best appreciated in comparison with Smarties. The overall national advertising expenditure for all confectionery brands in Great Britain was approximately $150 million in 1987. The Smarties share was 2 percent—below the brand's market share in the aggregate confectionery market of 3.7 percent.[15] A lower share of voice than of share of market is normal for a large, well-established brand and is (as noted in many cases in this book) one of the manifestations of the scale economies associated with such brands.

The Smarties appropriation had been gradually moving upward, reflecting the brand's increasing sales. Even more importantly, the Smarties expenditure in the Tyne-Tees area was lifted above the national rate, in anticipation of the struggle with M & Ms, to about twice the national level, or about a 4 percent share of voice in the region. In comparison with this statistic, M

& Ms invested at twice Smarties' effective level (measured in Gross Rating Points) during the year beginning July 1985; thereafter the expenditure came down in the second year but was still comfortably ahead of Smarties. In addition, there were heavy promotional investments.

In crude terms, M & Ms were deploying an initial investment of 8 percent of total market advertising expenditure in the test area. Such advertising contributed to a market share of 3 percent, which was a reasonably good performance but below that of Smarties, as we shall see. This degree of investment spending is not unusual, although it is perhaps a little on the high side, according to extensive evidence from A. C. Nielsen.[16]

What is slightly unusual, however, is the resultant level of sales of M & Ms. In normal circumstances, a second brand introduced into the market in the wake of a successful pioneer can only expect an ongoing sales level of less than half of the latter.[17] M & Ms did better than this—but not without vicissitudes.

M & Ms sales almost immediately hit a high point, coinciding with the high initial burst of consumer advertising, and stabilized after about two years at a level approximately 35 percent of the initial peak. This drop from peak to ongoing stable level is larger than average, even in comparison with other British brands, which in turn show a greater average drop than brands in the United States.[18] The M & Ms launch has therefore been a high-cost operation in terms of advertising investment (among other factors), because the brand has taken an above-average drop from its initial peak.

Nevertheless, its ongoing sales level is about two-thirds that of Smarties, and this level appears to be stable. The up-front cost has yielded above-average ongoing sales despite the substantial initial drop. We guess, however, that it will be some years before the brand will yield any profits. But Mars Confectionery has the resources and resolution to continue this level of investment, since plans have been announced to roll the brand out into new regions, to make it fully national at about the time this book is published. The likely advertising investment will be in the $12 million bracket, a historical level of expenditure for any confectionery brand in the British market. And to this, Mars will add very significant sums in promotions.

One of the fascinating features of the launch of M & Ms in the Tyne-Tees region is that the brand has increased the size of the market. This outcome may have been partly the result of the targeting of M & Ms advertising at teenagers. Smarties has been essentially unaffected, an outcome unquestionably related to the influence of the *Get Smarties* advertising campaign, which was, of course, planned quite independently of the launch of M & Ms but was available for exposure in the Tyne-Tees region during the period when M & Ms were being introduced. Judgment suggests that the *Get Smarties* campaign prevented M & Ms from picking off the important group of eight- to nine-year-old children.

The overall strength of Mars Confectionery makes it likely that M & Ms' performance in Tyne-Tees will be replicated in other regions, although the loss of sales of Minstrels and Treets (brands that have been withdrawn) must be set against the sales of M & Ms. Although general marketing experience suggests that national brands settle at share levels slightly below those in test markets,[19] it should be remembered that there was extra advertising expenditure behind Smarties in the Tyne-Tees region. The national rollout of M & Ms should therefore be evaluated in light of the national advertising policy for Smarties, which may or may not be the same as in Tyne-Tees.

Judgment suggests that M & Ms could, within a couple of years, become a national 3 percent brand, although for some time after that still an unprofitable one. The Tyne-Tees experience suggests that Smarties will not suffer directly, although further growth of the brand may be inhibited. This outcome, which is relatively favorable for Smarties, would not have been possible had Smarties not built up over a period of decades the strength of its functional and nonfunctional attributes. Nor would it have been possible without the significant reinforcement and refreshment of these attributes that resulted from the new advertising discussed earlier in this chapter.

Incidentally, a simple technique is available to forecast the likely ongoing M & Ms sales level in each area in which the brand is distributed. The same relative drop from initial peak that was experienced in Tyne-Tees can be applied to each new area in which the brand is introduced, despite the likelihood that the initial peaks will vary area by area.[20]

Six Lessons from the History of Smarties

1. Demographic Targeting and Its Influence on Creative Thinking. The *Get Smarties* campaign, with its imaginative impact and its success in enhancing consumers' perceptions of Smarties without disturbing the strength of existing perceptions, was a natural campaign evolution guided by a strategic change concerned with the definition of the target group. The new campaign that resulted was planned to give a fresh look to the brand in the eyes of all age-groups of children, not just the eight- to nine-year-olds. This change was partly intuitive and represented campaign development, but it was also supported by a redefinition of the demographics of the target group, a change that confirmed the desirability of thinking in more radical creative terms than had been done for some years.

2. A Twin Target Group. For many brands of confectionery, including Smarties, there is a double target group of consumers (children) and buyers (mothers). It has been a sine qua non of all Smarties advertising that its appeal to each target group must be in harmony with that to the other target group. The success of the client and agency in maintaining this harmony has been a key reason for the brand's great success and ultimately was the result of the establishment of the extrinsic associations of Smarties. The strength of the brand has been seen most recently in its ability successfully to resist the threat posed by M & Ms.

3. The Value of Qualitative Research. This case offers yet another example pointing to the value of qualitative research, both in the preliminary strategy-setting stage and in the evaluation of rough creative ideas. The research was valuable in the light it threw on both target groups of consumers and buyers, although it did not actually fully predict the effect of the advertising on younger children. It did, however, demonstrate the way in which the new advertising had a more all-embracing effect than the previous advertising on older children.

4. The Media Mix. The combination of television (used strategically to build added values) and billboards (used tactically to provide a ubiquitous presence) is a potent media mix that has demonstrated its effectiveness for brands in the confectionery market (not just Smarties) for more than three decades. It is rather surprising that this book contains so few examples of two or more media operating with particular suitability in specific product fields. Although television is shown to be of almost universal value in the cases in this book, it is always a medium with a high absolute cost, and there are too few examples of how other media can be employed to extend television's effect with power and economy of force.

5. The Contribution of Production Values. The *Get Smarties* film and the subsequent advertisements in the series are characterized by spectacular production values. These values represented an important extra ingredient to reinforce success. The results of the qualitative research, which was based on an animatic and a storyboard, predicted fairly well (although with one possible inadequacy—see point 3 above) the strategic correctness of the advertising and its likely effectiveness. The production values added something on top of this. We hypothesize, however, that had the creative idea been conceptually weaker than it was, the production values alone would not have compensated.

6. Investment and Other Ratios. This case presents a number of ratios that echo general experience in the marketing field, including that in other cases in this collection.

a. The Smarties share of voice in the total British confectionery market (2 percent) is smaller than the brand's market share (3.7 percent). Such a difference is normal for large established brands.

b. M & Ms' initial share of voice in the Tyne-Tees area (8 percent) was well above its achieved market share (3 percent). This difference is not unusual, although it is a little above the average for important launches and is likely to have influenced the brand's remarkably high initial sales peak.

c. M & Ms' ongoing stable market share in the Tyne-Tees area is approximately 35 percent of the initial peak. This drop is larger than average (compare point b above) but is likely to be consistent in the new areas into which M & Ms are launched, although the *absolute* size of the initial peak may vary.

d. The national share of M & Ms is not likely to exceed (and could turn out to settle below) the test-market experience. It is possible that the brand will lose money for a number of years, although it has a good chance (in view of its American as well as its Tyne-Tees experience) of eventually becoming a stable and profitable entry.

e. The launch of M & Ms has not taken many sales from Smarties, which is a considerable tribute to the strength of the latter. M & Ms have, however, increased the size of the market segment in which both they and Smarties are positioned. This circumstance is unusual, since brand advertising only rarely has such a "macro" effect. We hypothesize, however, that the situation will be replicated in new areas as the distribution of M & Ms is extended.

f. The conclusions above do not take into account the possible future complications that could be caused by new brand activity by Mars Confectionery—notably, the introduction of a new brand called Skittles and the reintroduction of Minstrels under the Galaxy name. Such developments could cause modifications in the expected drop in M & Ms sales from peak to stability in new areas (point c above) and in the anticipated increase in the size of the Smarties/M & Ms segment (point e).

12
Timotei Shampoo

> The Scandinavian love of nature has made [Scandinavian women]
> natural. . . . [T]o see girls with unfussed hair and uncaked skin, the
> blood near the surface of unlipsticked mouths, is to rediscover a lost
> beauty.
>
> —Marya Mannes[1]

A Nordic Shampoo for a Nordic Market

Timotei Shampoo can be understood only if one also understands its origins.
It was a brand constructed for a specific type of consumer in a specific
market, Sweden. Timotei has been an international success, but this achieve-
ment was brought about by its manufacturer and the agency taking a clearly
defined brand concept that had been successful in its original market and
expanding its geographical reach into other markets. Timotei was emphatically *not* an "international" brand constructed for a (mythical) "international" consumer.

People who are acquainted with Sweden will attest to the considerable
impact the country can make on the visitor. This impact stems from the
formal beauty of its cities and the austere beauty of its landscapes, the generally dignified and usually diffident (although on occasion extroverted) de-
meanor of its inhabitants, the splendor of the culture and of the cuisine, and
the elegant design and construction of the furniture and other artifacts for
living. Most of all, one is struck by the summers, which arrive without
warning during the second week in May and disappear suddenly, early in
October. The summers are full of sunshine because the days are long and
the climate generally dry. During the great festival of Midsummer Eve—a
Christian celebration with pagan origins—there is virtually no night in the
northern latitudes, and much aquavit is drunk. The importance of this joyous
occasion is exceeded only by the beginning of the crayfish season in early
August.

It is not surprising that the Swedes consider summers very special. Factories and offices contrive to provide extralong vacations, so that workers
can, as it were, store up sunshine for the winter nights ahead. Outdoor living
in the summer has always been taken seriously, and there are more "summer
houses" relative to the size of the population in Sweden than anywhere else

in the world. Many of these dwellings are in the vast hinterland; many others are on the literally uncounted islands of the Stockholm archipelago, which stretches to Helsinki across the south of the Gulf of Bothnia.

The summer houses are mostly simple; they are generally secluded and often rather beautiful wooden cabins, with crude arrangements for supplying power and water. But this simplicity is not devoid of sophistication. Elements of the primitive are accompanied by elements of the well ordered. Swedes will entertain their friends endlessly and rather formally at meals that make use of Persson stainless steel flatware, Arabia china, and Orrefors crystal. Swedish summer living is simple but far from barbaric.

It is not a coincidence that movements to protect the environment and to return to nature have always received strong support in Sweden. These, together with populist antiwar sentiment, the generous provision of social welfare for rich and poor alike, and endorsement of economic and political self-sufficiency, have for many years characterized Swedish social democracy. The paradoxical coexistence of this political creed with an economic organization based on advanced capitalism for the production of goods and services is unique to Scandinavia, if not to Sweden.

We now come to Timotei.

During the early 1970s, as part of routine investigations into how, and how often, people wash their hair, Gibbs AB (the Unilever company in Sweden that markets "personal products") discovered that people were beginning to wash their hair much more often than previously. This increased frequency was attributable to the fact that more people were preferring shorter, casual hairstyles and were washing their hair in the shower and blow-drying it. All this was good news to a company that manufactured hair products and could now foresee an optimistic expansion in its markets. But a slightly less obvious reason soon also emerged: the possibility of marketing a brand specifically directed at frequent hair-washers. This meant that such a brand had to be both effective and mild—efficient enough to wash the hair demonstrably effectively, yet not drying or destructive, so that users would be able to shampoo with it as often as once a day.

In 1973, the client and the agency began a series of concept tests. These tests embraced alternative ways of positioning a brand for frequent use. The most promising of them was accompanied by a product formula incorporating an ingredient that was distinctive, evocative, and very Swedish. This was *timotei,* or timothy grass, a wild grass known also in other parts of Europe and in the United States. In Great Britain it is called cat's tail; in the United States, timothy, after Timothy Hanson, the man who introduced it into colonial America in 1720 for use as cattle fodder. There is a special folklore connected with this grass in Sweden, where it is associated with Midsummer Eve, a time when young women wear garlands of wildflowers and grasses in their hair. There is a charming tradition that, if a girl picks seven (some say nine) different varieties of wild plants, each from a different field or ditch, and if she sleeps with this bouquet under her pillow, she will dream of the man she will marry.

Timotei is therefore rich with appealing and very feminine associations for Swedish users—associations of great value were it to prove possible to appropriate them and communicate them effectively. Although the idea of using *timotei* had first been suggested for a brand of deodorant in Finland, the concept had failed in test. Fortunately, however, the concept was not forgotten. Gibbs passed the idea on to JWT, Stockholm, and the rest, as they say, is history.

The brand as it was marketed did its hair-washing job well, that is, by providing its promised effectiveness allied to mildness.[2] Its ingredients included a number of natural herb extracts, such as chamomile, sage, and osier leaf. It was sold in a single variety and in one size (a 220-milliliter green bottle with a white and green label). The package was designed to be distinctive and practical and was indeed found to appeal to all types of women. The shampoo, and in particular its green color and high-quality herbal perfume, was also found to be extremely attractive to consumers. This well-planned and demonstrably appealing product mix was accompanied by advertising that subtly captured the spirit of a young Swedish woman in the setting of a Swedish summer house, advertising that will shortly be described in more detail.[3]

Both client and agency had given the brand their best efforts. Such is, of course, the case with the vast majority of new brands that are prepared for the marketplace. Yet only a tiny proportion—perhaps as few as 5 percent—of such brands are demonstrably successful.[4] What is so special about Timotei that enabled it to defeat the odds? Before attempting to answer this question, we should examine in some detail how Timotei was launched in Sweden and how it progressed there.

The Success of Timotei in Sweden

The shampoo market in Sweden resembles that in most developed Western countries: It is relatively large, functionally segmented, extremely crowded, and rather volatile. Because, as noted, people were tending to wash their hair more often, the total market was showing some growth when Timotei was launched. One other characteristic of the market is significant to note. Sweden, together with Norway and Denmark, had no commercial television until the mid-1980s (when limited satellite broadcasts began; local commercial services began in the late 1980s). The markets into which the brand was subsequently introduced possess this medium almost without exception, which means that an important change had to be introduced into the Timotei media mix once the brand began to be widely expanded into fresh markets. Cinema advertising, which was used in Sweden, is a relatively small advertising medium, although a particularly effective way of reaching a young target audience.

Gibbs AB already marketed Sunsilk, the then-leading brand of shampoo, together with important brands in other product categories. The company therefore had a good deal of credibility with the retail trade (which in Sweden is extremely concentrated, with a small number of buying points). As a result, it was relatively easy to achieve effective distribution and display for Timotei. There was, however, an immediate complication. It so happened that a competitor, Helene Curtis, having arrived at the same conclusion as Gibbs AB about the growth in the frequency with which people washed their hair, launched its own brand Varje Dag ("Every Day") coincidentally with Timotei. In normal circumstances, a second brand on the market with conceptual similarities to a first innovative brand can expect to achieve an ongoing market share below half the level of the pioneer.[5] That Timotei soon climbed ahead of Varje Dag says something special about Timotei.

Timotei was launched in September 1975, with a value market share objective that was exceeded by February 1976, when it achieved 8 percent. (Varje Dag was by then at 9 percent.) Timotei grew to 12 percent in 1976 and to 15 percent from 1977 through 1980 before settling at its relative stable long-term share, which is below this peak.[6] The brand was holding 10 percent of total market value in 1984–1986 and was the leading brand in the Swedish shampoo market. It had handsomely overtaken Varje Dag, which was down to a 3 percent share.

With hindsight, what seems important about Timotei was that in addition to a strategic rightness and recognizably effective formula (characteristics shared by Varje Dag as well), Timotei offered the *timotei* ingredient. Although this was prima facie a largely rational product advantage, judgment suggests that the ingredient was such that it became possible to build upon it an advertising story rich with nonrational—indeed highly emotional—brand discriminators.

The advertising was directed at the substantial number of Swedish women who prefer natural and mild products and who wish to look well groomed in a natural way. All ages from fifteen to fifty were targeted, but primary attention was focused (as with so many toiletry products) on the age group fifteen to twenty-five. The copy for the consumer advertisements was, as is common in Sweden, extremely simple and direct, emphasizing the propositions that Timotei is so mild that you can wash your hair as often as you like and that the shampoo contains specific named herbs. The copy being short and factual, the all-important emotional added values came from elements in the execution of the magazine and film advertisements.

Advertisements in both media are characterized by the extraordinary richness of their production values, and these values are most evident in the films (a considerable advantage when the campaign was extended to new markets in which television became the main medium employed). In the films, the viewer is struck by the models—both male and female, and the hint of romance between them; by the settings—the simple and picturesque wooden cabins and the antique appointments, such as the wooden pail in which the girl washes her hair; by the delicious countryside and the flowers—the emphasis on nature in summertime; by the special quality of the Swedish summer sunlight, which is intensely bright, yet has no suspicion of sultriness but, rather, the tiniest hint of winter ahead; and finally by the subtle sound effects and the background music of the rustic violin that brings to mind the ritual dancing on Midsummer Eve. These signals are all highly distinctive to Sweden, and although certain of them are subtle, their combined impact is unmistakable.

The campaign was launched with substantial use of magazine and cinema advertising, together with a major below-the-line program involving coupons distributed by direct mail for consumer sampling. The main weight of the campaign was in magazines, but cinema was an extremely important auxiliary because of its ability to reach effectively the younger end of the target audience.

The coverage of the schedule was considerable for a nontelevision market. It was estimated, on the basis of awareness studies, that 60 percent of the target group had been reached by February 1976 (about six months after the launch), and the target group had been virtually completely covered by February 1977 (eighteen months after the launch).[7]

It is worth reiterating that the success of Timotei in Sweden and elsewhere was not an advertising success alone. It was the success of a marketing mix that created a total and coherent brand personality. The elements of the mix included product, fragrance (very distinctive, herbal), packaging, and product line (one product, one size, no variants, initially one pack size).[8]

In view of the immediate success of the brand, client and agency soon embarked on a modest program of product extension, although it was found that apart from hair conditioner, additional products with the Timotei name did not have the staying power to maintain a franchise in most markets on a long-term basis. (The exception to this appears to be Japan, which will be discussed later.)

JWT, Stockholm, which with some justification is proud of the success of Timotei, has produced since 1975 a wide range of advertising material, including nine different commercials. These have all managed to maintain their freshness and unique identity. Many Swedish films have also been used outside Sweden, and the JWT International Unilever Unit, located in London, has developed systems by which Swedish advertising material (and also a limited amount of material from other countries based closely on the Swedish campaign) can be supplied to other markets, prepared with the correct technical specifications and legal clearances. Everything possible is done to maintain the original integrity of the campaign: the element that is considered the central reason for its success. The campaign was evaluated by qualitative (in some cases by quantitative) research in the majority of new countries before it was exposed.

We have already referred to the generally disheartening failure rate for new brand introductions. We have also described the strategic soundness of the original planning of Timotei and the executional finesse of both the product and its advertising. The fitness of the strategy is what gave the brand its potential salience to consumers. What translated this potential salience into something the consumer was persuaded to buy, and buy repeatedly, was the wholeness, coherence, and integrity of both the brand and its advertising. Judgment suggests that those elements are the central reason for the success of Timotei.

The Spread of Timotei Outside Sweden

It was not long before Unilever companies outside Sweden began to express a practical interest in Timotei and to explore its suitability in their own markets. After Sweden, the first market to launch Timotei was Finland, where it unfortunately proved a failure. But shortly afterward the brand was launched in Norway and Switzerland, where it became, and has remained, a considerable marketplace success.

The timing of these original launches was as follows:

1975—Sweden
1976—Finland
1977—Norway
1978—Switzerland

Some analysts would judge this to have been a prolonged rollout. But there are two important factors to bear in mind in understanding this timing. First, in a volatile market such as that for shampoo, there was at the beginning the arguable possibility that Timotei might have gone down as rapidly as it went up. Operating companies were therefore, for reasons of self-interest, eager to get some idea of the level at which the brand was going to settle in Sweden. Second is a point concerned with the organization of Unilever. Internationally, Unilever is rather a decentralized company—far more so than certain of its competitors. This means that much, if not most, of the initiative in new product launches comes from local operating companies. It is certainly true that the various central organizations, such as the product group Coordinations, exchange market intelligence rapidly, and encourage vigorously the spread of successful ideas. Nevertheless, in most circumstances, and subject to discussion and persuasion, brand policy in individual markets tends to be determined by the local operating companies.

What results from this procedure is a brand extension policy that is generally soundly based and that is able to accommodate local inputs when they give evidence of being able to improve on international concepts by adding a local flavor. But time has on occasion been lost. The trade-off has been between sureness of progress and rapidity.

Sweden has for a long time been regarded by Unilever in a special way. Because of the advanced living standards in that country and the sophistication of most of its consumer goods markets, Sweden is sometimes regarded as a precursor market.

Timotei was demonstrating long-term staying power in Sweden, Norway, and Switzerland when, in 1981, it was launched into four new markets: two large and two small. These markets were France, Germany, Portugal, and Austria. The brand has proved successful in all of them.

France was a particularly interesting case. Timotei was launched with strong advertising and promotional (sampling) support and reached a 6 percent market share in 1982. The leading manufacturer of hair products, L'Oréal (which has a 50 percent market share with its seven brands combined), counterattacked with its own new brand entry directed against Timotei. This brand, called Ultra Doux, was introduced with massive advertising and promotional support. It quickly achieved a market share of 9 percent, pushing Timotei down to under 5 percent. But as soon as the support expenditures for Ultra Doux were reduced to a more normal ongoing level in 1984, Timotei's share recovered to 6 percent. Timotei is now the fifth largest brand in the market. Although it is outsold by Ultra Doux, Ultra Doux has succeeded only by cannibalizing other L'Oréal brands.

Timotei has kept a 4 percent market share in Germany. Its share in Austria is 10 percent. Note that in the shampoo market, as in most others, a large brand in a large market tends to hold a smaller market share than a large brand in a small market does. This point relates to a growing heterogeneity within product categories in more economically developed countries.[9]

In the 1980s, the pace of expansion began to pick up. In 1983, Timotei was launched in South Africa, the Netherlands, the United Kingdom, and Venezuela. It was a reasonable success in all of these countries except Venezuela.

In 1984, Timotei went into Denmark,[10] Greece, Spain, and Japan. Although the experience in Denmark was disappointing, the situation in Japan has been extremely promising, and indeed Timotei achieved market leadership in the fall of 1987, with a volume market share of 14 percent. Herbs have a special meaning in Japan because of their association with oriental medicines (something that contributed, for instance, to the success of a Timotei on-pack premium of a miniature herb garden). The Timotei range has

Music background from "Picnic at Hanging Rock" Male voice over:

1. Timotei Shampoo.

2. So mild

3. you can wash your hair as often as you wish.

4. Containing natural herb extracts. Timotei always leaves your hair soft and shining,

5. with the fresh smell of summer meadows.

6. Timotei.

Twenty-second television commercial used internationally and first screened in May 1984.

been extended in Japan and includes the shampoo, a conditioner, a special treatment product, a facial cream, and a body shampoo.[11] In 1985 and 1986, Timotei was launched or market-tested in Thailand, the United States, Canada, Chile, Malaysia, Taiwan, Singapore, Hong Kong, and a number of small export markets.

It was not, incidentally, until 1984 that Timotei had its first restage in Sweden, to offer a modest functional improvement concerned with care of the hair.

In summary then, Timotei has, over a twelve-year period, reached out into a total of twenty-six markets. It has been a success in eleven (which include the lucrative markets of Germany, France, the United Kingdom, and Japan), a failure in three (the relatively small markets of Finland, Venezuela, and Denmark), and in the remaining twelve countries no clear picture of long-term success or failure has yet emerged, although initial progress is very satisfactory. In the eleven countries in which Timotei has been launched successfully and reached a reasonably stable share, it is the leading brand in four (Sweden, Norway, Switzerland, and Japan) and the second brand in four others (Germany, Austria, South Africa, and the United Kingdom).

Timotei has therefore succeeded in building a valuable brand property in a wide and varied range of countries. There still, however, remain a number of markets for it to penetrate. By its progress to date—a ratio of eleven successes to three failures—we can hazard the guess that the brand will succeed in the majority (although not the overwhelming majority) of markets into which it will be introduced in the future.

The reason for our optimism and our caution is as follows. The reader will have noticed that the brand has made its greatest headway in three of its four original markets, and the progress was made here during the first few years of its introduction. In countries in which Timotei was subsequently launched, its progress has been slightly inhibited by a number of exogenous factors, such as competition from monolothic existing brands (for example, Johnson and Johnson Baby Shampoo) in certain markets, the preemptive activities of competitors in other markets, and the possibility that in developed countries consumers may now be looking for functional properties in a shampoo that will not be provided by Timotei. Nevertheless, in view of the manifest difficulty of sustaining any brand that shows strong growth, the best clue to the future almost certainly lies in the maintenance of Timotei's total brand personality.

If Timotei eventually reaches a substantial number (say, upwards of forty) markets and succeeds in about twenty of them, the brand will represent an extremely important property to Unilever in its ability to generate immediate and future earnings.[12]

All the advertising in all Timotei's markets has been derived from the Swedish model, and the actual Swedish material has been used in the majority of countries with a minimal amount of adaptation. Much of the success of the brand has stemmed from the discipline of this approach, which has also meant financial savings in advertisement production.

Four Lessons from the History of Timotei

1. The Integrity of the Original Brand Concept. Timotei has provided a model example of clear targeting. It was developed as a brand with specific planned characteristics developed for a Swedish consumer, who was carefully described psychographically and demographically as well as in terms of her shampooing habits. All elements in the marketing mix including, notably, the consumer advertising, were planned as a coherent totality. The ingredient *timotei*, which, as suggested in this study, was probably the key product and advertising discriminator in the brand's early days, has very special and valuable nonrational values to Swedish consumers. Many of the signals made by the brand and its advertising are subtle, but the total impression made by them together is extremely distinctive. And this distinctiveness has staying power. Indeed, the original advertising ran unchanged in Sweden during the entire period 1975 through 1984, and the brand's restage during the latter year did not even then change the strategic essentials in any significant way.

It is interesting to speculate what would have happened to Timotei had it been planned as an "international" brand. We think it highly unlikely that the brand would have advanced as far as it has today, essentially because it is difficult to define and target an "international" consumer.

2. The Maintenance of This Brand Integrity. As discussed in the last section, the distinctive characteristics of the Timotei brand were maintained intact in Sweden during the whole of its first decade. Equally importantly, the integrity of the brand has been maintained when Timotei has been extended geographically. A real and consistent effort has been made to avoid what might be called balkanizing the brand concept, by subjecting it to piecemeal adaptations, all carried out for supposedly good reasons, but which could, in the end, lead to an irreversible and fatal erosion of what the brand originally stood for.

Resistance to imported ideas on the (unstated) grounds that they were "not invented here" has meant the ruin of many important brands in the past. Perhaps conscious of such past experiences, the custodians of Timotei—both client and agency—managed to preserve the strategic essentials intact. This was an act of notable persistence and sound judgment.

3. The Rollout of the Brand has Taken a Long Time. Although it is easy to understand why it has taken rather a long time to extend the geographical reach of Timotei, it is still true that the brand was launched in Sweden in 1975, had become an established success by 1978 at the latest, but only in 1981 was expanded beyond four markets. Timotei can be found today in a total of twenty-six markets, a wide spread indeed, but the rollout was rather prolonged. Delay means that the competitive situation in new markets can change, with a real danger that Timotei might be preempted in markets it has not penetrated, by new competitors who are sharp and aggressive enough to steal the concept.

4. The Original Media Mix was Not a Prerequisite for a Successful Introduction of Timotei into New Markets. This point is simple but important. Sweden had no commercial television for many years of Timotei's life. Nevertheless, television has been the main medium for the Timotei advertising in the majority of new markets the brand has reached. Most of these new markets have adapted the Swedish cinema commercials in the simplest way possible, and these films have been demonstrably as effective when shown on the small screen as on the large. This does not mean that we can generalize and say that all commercials made for the cinema will work equally well on television or vice versa. But the creative concept of the Timotei cinema advertising—perhaps because it made effective use of close-ups—adapted well to television.

13

Diamond Gemstones (De Beers)

> Under the simple test of effectiveness for advertising, we should expect to find leisure and the conspicuous consumption of goods dividing the field . . . while the conspicuous consumption of goods should gradually gain in importance, both absolutely and relatively.
> —Thorstein Veblen[1]

"Memory Treasured in the Depths of Her Engagement Diamond"[2]

Campaigns to advertise diamonds, which have been exposed for some decades with an unchanged basic strategy, have a number of unusual features, among them that diamonds are a commodity, virtually never branded.[3] Such campaigns are a combination of generic advertising and cooperative programs with the trade, inasmuch as De Beers speaks for the industry as a whole, for reasons we shall shortly review.

Diamonds are measured by weight. Eighty percent of all diamonds produced are used for industrial purposes, since the diamond is the hardest natural substance on earth (according to the best-known scientific measurement, known as the Mohs Scale) and, accordingly, has no rivals as a cutting edge in machine tools.[4] But industrial diamonds, being the smaller and less perfect stones, are absolutely and relatively much less valuable than the larger gemstones. This means that the aggregate value of industrial diamonds is very much smaller than 80 percent of the total (as it is by weight), and they will not be discussed in this chapter. Instead, we shall devote our attention to the jewelry market, in which the marketing and advertising activities of the industry are concentrated and in which sales are more responsive to marketing inputs than sales of industrial stones are.

The weight of diamonds is measured by metric carats. A carat weighs one-fifth of a gram, or 0.007 ounces. Each carat is in turn divided into 100 points. The greater absolute and relative value of larger stones applies to different sizes of gemstones as well as to gemstones in comparison with industrial diamonds.

Although diamonds are unique, in the making of jewelry they have indirect competitors. As an investment for major personal assets, they have even more competitors, which accounts to a large degree for their price sensitivity. Diamonds are among the highest value products known to humankind. They are also among the advertised products with the highest ticket price. Consequently, the target group for the advertising has always had an upper-income bias, although this element has become less pronounced as the penetration of diamond jewelry has, as a result of growing affluence, reached out fairly widely into the population as a whole, to levels bracketing 50 percent in the main markets.[5] (This is a fulfilment of Thorstein Veblen's prophecy, which he made as long ago as 1899.)

Diamonds offer three rewards or benefits to the consumer. First, they are things of beauty, and form the centerpiece of often incomparable jewelry. The appearance of a diamond gemstone is evaluated by four criteria (known as the Four C's: color, cut, clarity, and carat weight). Second, as a result of both their beauty and their rarity (and their high value), they are gifts of love worthy of marking the high points in people's lives, particularly betrothal and the most important anniversaries. They symbolize the love of the giver toward the receiver, and the giving of the gift is profoundly gratifying to both parties. De Beers, by the consistency and continuity of its advertising and promotional efforts, has made a major contribution to building the value of this reward to the consumer. Third, diamonds represent a store of value, if not an investment. (As such, however, their track record in comparison with that of other assets has not been impressive during the past decade, a point that should be borne in mind when we come to review how the sales of diamonds have progressed during this period.)[6]

As will be obvious to the reader, the aesthetic appeal of diamond jewelry is substantially sensory, with emotional overtones (because a diamond is a symbol of love, not to mention the strong element of conspicuous consumption it embraces). The reward from giving and receiving diamond gifts is essentially emotional. Buying diamonds as an investment is an essentially rational activity. However, people tend to buy gemstones for a mixture of all three reasons, so that the advertising—which is, of course, aimed at stimulating demand, both directly and indirectly—must be, as a diamond itself, multifaceted; it must, even more than most advertising, embrace sensory, emotional, and rational appeals, although the last of these is normally covered implicitly rather than explicitly. The evocative piece of advertising copy in the heading for this section, and which dates from 1948, illustrates rather well this multifaceted nature of the De Beers advertising.

There is, incidentally, a trade in diamonds for men that is relatively small in comparison with that for women (with an annual purchase rate in the United States of less than 20 percent of that for women's diamond jewelry).[7] But although men's diamond jewelry represents a market with growth potential, our study will concentrate on women's diamond jewelry, because of its greater past and present importance.

"The Twin Problems of Organizing the Market and of Controlling Output"[8]

Diamonds were found and soon became treasured possessions in the fourth century B.C., when they were discovered and first mined in India. India remained the main source of supply for more than two millenia, a period during which diamonds spread to the Western world. They were greatly prized, although esteemed somewhat below certain other precious stones—rubies and emeralds, in particular. Diamonds played a spectacular part in much of the ecclesiastical and secular art of the Middle Ages.

During the first centuries of production, the number of gems emerging from the diggings every year was very small, although what were to become some of the most celebrated individual stones in the world were mined at this time. Diamond mining, however, is no exception to the general rule that supplies of mineral mines eventually become exhausted, an outcome that gradually occurred with Indian diamonds.

But during the time when the Indian mines were running down—the first part of the eighteenth century—diamonds were discovered in Brazil, which, for much of the nineteenth century, served as the source of most of the world's supplies. It was during this period that diamond finishers and diamond merchants set up their flourishing businesses in Amsterdam and Antwerp; late in the nineteenth century, New York became the third main diamond center of the world. The diamond finishers, who cut and polish the stones, bring a fine aesthetic sense and a wondrous manual dexterity to their trade. Their operations, as well as those of the merchants, are quite separate from and independent of the diamond producers'.

Brazilian supplies, too, gradually became exhausted, but while that was taking place, from the late 1860s onward, unparalleled quantities of diamonds were discovered in South Africa. It was these supplies which led to an enormous expansion in the use of diamonds both in women's jewelry and (later) for industrial purposes and also to a gradual improvement (in which advertising played some part) in the already-high regard in which diamonds were held by the public in many countries.

The name De Beers came from two Boer farmers: brothers named De Beer, who owned an estate on which diamonds were discovered in 1871 at Vooruitzigt, near Kimberley in the Cape Colony. This site became an important mine and grew rapidly in size.

The discovery of diamonds in South Africa naturally attracted swarms of prospectors to the diggings, which for a short period remained small individual enterprises. But because of the difficulty of keeping the individual mines separate from one another as the open-cast diggings went deeper into the ground, and also because of the rapidly growing need for expensive capital equipment, the mines quickly amalgamated into larger units. A num-

ダイヤモンドは永遠の輝き De Beers

光彩の、君。

Advertisement first exposed in color magazines in Japan in 1983.

You sparkle with brilliance.

Carat Diamond
Exceptional quality diamonds for your wonderful life.
"I've reached this level of happiness only because you've always

been at my side. For you, the ultimate woman for me, I've chosen the ultimate gift. The Carat Diamond. A top quality diamond, is the perfect way for me to show how much I value you. I've chosen it according to the standards known as the 4C's: Cut, Color, Clarity and Carat. The Carat Diamond's crystalline beauty and inimitable rarity symbolize my love and our wonderful life together. I give you the brilliance of a carat or more with all my love and gratitude.''

A diamond is forever. De Beers

4C's your guide to diamond value.

ber of pioneers became famous and immensely wealthy in this drive toward concentration, the most prominent being Cecil Rhodes and the Barnato brothers.[9] But there was a whole generation of vigorous pioneers, of which Rhodes was the most energetic of all. By 1889, he was head of the De Beers Mining Company and controlled 90 percent of the world's output of diamonds.[10]

It was Rhodes who realized (partly, it was said, as a result of a basic education in economics he had received at Oxford University) that the worldwide demand for diamonds was unstable and susceptible to economic vicissitudes, income elastic in the language of microeconomics. (This describes the direct association between the demand for diamonds and the level of personal incomes: High personal incomes mean a high demand for diamonds, and growing personal incomes mean a growing demand. The opposite also holds.) This income elasticity meant that the price of diamonds was likely to go up and down erratically unless there were some system of adjusting the output reaching the market in response to the demand. Controlling and adjusting output was a feasible strategy while output was in the hands of a virtual monopoly, as it was during Rhodes's time. But if De Beers lost its dominant market share, as in fact happened after Rhodes's death, the strategy could only be implemented by means of all the producers getting together and agreeing individually to sell their output to a central organization.

People buy diamonds with the conviction that they are a store of value, a long-term protection of their assets. People have, moreover, an exceptionally pronounced price-value perception of diamonds: The stones are valued for the very reason that they are scarce and high priced. These are the basic principles which unerringly and continuously motivated Cecil Rhodes. He saw that the owners of diamonds would be as displeased as the producers if oversupply were at any time to bring about a collapse in price. It was therefore in the buyers' as well as the producers' interest that supplies of diamonds should be regulated continuously, with the objective of maintaining stable prices in the market.[11] This matter is important, and it would be helpful, before continuing the historical narrative, to emphasize briefly the economic value of the organization established by Rhodes.

The central body in the diamond industry was developed by Sir Ernest Oppenheimer, later a chairman of De Beers, and came to be called the Central Selling Organization (CSO). It is widely thought to operate to everyone's benefit, for the reason mentioned. As a result, it shows no sign of weakening with the passage of time. The actions of the CSO have generally meant that diamonds have not been subjected to the degree of erratic price fluctuation that has characterized silver, gold, and platinum since the early 1970s.

Although nearly nine decades have passed since Rhodes's death, the mechanism he set up for regulating output with the object of maintaining industry stability has remained intact. The general economic advantages it provides have led the mechanism to continue to work in essentially the way that was established a century ago. In 1933, what we today know as the CSO was set up and named the Diamond Producers' Association. This body guarantees the purchase of the stones that are mined by the producers of some 80 percent of the world's annual rough diamond output. The CSO is associated with De Beers and its affiliated companies, and it is De Beers that funds and directs the worldwide advertising campaign for diamond gemstones, although in many local markets there are supplementary campaigns funded by the retail trade (but often based on the main De Beers campaign).

Sir Ernest Oppenheimer, the dominant personality in the diamond industry for four decades, beginning in the early 1920s, made many contributions, including bringing important new sources of supply into the regulatory system. Oppenheimer also guided the industry through the desperate difficulties caused by the world depression, when despite a reduction in production, enormous inventories of diamonds were built up, and only run down—a very gradual process—after the end of the Second World War. Oppenheimer was also much involved with a major expansion in the use of industrial diamonds during the 1930s, 1940s, and 1950s. And it was he who helped reestablish a solid and expanding world market for gemstones during the 1950s, when he was reaching the end of his long tenure as chairman of De Beers Consolidated Mines and the Anglo-American Corporation of South Africa.

Sir Ernest Oppenheimer was always much concerned with the American market. In the growth of the market for diamond gems that took place during the second half of the twentieth century, the United States has always had a special position, as the largest and in some ways the most dynamic of all the many world markets supplied by diamonds that, in their uncut state, had been controlled by De Beers.[12]

"The Demand for Gem Diamonds Has Far Exceeded the Production of the Mines"[13]

The quotation in the heading above comes from a speech made by Sir Ernest Oppenheimer in 1957. It summarizes the powerful postwar consumer boom as it affected the diamond industry, although at the time, of course, no one knew the situation would continue for at least two further decades. More recently, new sources of rough diamonds, including major discoveries in Botswana and Australia, have increased supply of newly mined diamonds substantially.

This study is primarily concerned with the worldwide demand for diamonds during the 1980s and the role of advertising in stimulating that demand. This was a period when sales were generally healthy but also when some problems had manifested themselves, mostly as a result of the fact that the demand for diamonds is both income elastic and price elastic. (Price elasticity describes the sensitivity of the demand for diamonds to price. In price elasticity, unlike in income elasticity, the relationship between the two variables is inverse. A high price means a low demand for diamonds; an increasing price means a falling demand. The opposite also holds.) It is the pronounced price elasticity that makes the CSO's maintenance of market stability such an important activity.

The general economic problems during the 1970s and the 1980s caused some distortions in the market. We shall attempt to isolate these effects, as well as undertake the more difficult task of assessing the influence of the advertising. The consumer advertising campaign for gem diamonds was first exposed in the United States in 1939[14] and extended to all major world markets from 1962 onward.[15]

Reliable data are available from twenty-eight world markets—the most important ones for the sales of diamond jewelry. De Beers commissioned surveys in all the countries in which it operates marketing programs.[16] In 1985, the last year for which we have comprehensive information, the aggregate value of diamond jewelry sales in these markets (including men's as well as women's pieces) totaled more than $18.1 billion at retail value. Although the retail margin in the jewelry trade is traditionally high (which would call for a substantial reduction before arriving at any estimate of net sales value), the dollar figure for total sales of diamond jewelry is still massive: Diamonds are probably one of the fifty largest businesses in the entire world.[17] We are looking at a very considerable industry, although because of its worldwide ramifications and its susceptibility to exogenous influences on demand, it would be fair to say that the mining, finishing, and marketing of diamond gemstones is a more volatile business than most other enterprises of comparable size. The worldwide advertising budget ($70 million in 1983)[18] is not high by the standards of such large businesses.

We shall look in some detail at the sales of diamonds in the twenty-eight markets covered in the De Beers research, in order to isolate some of the more important of these exogenous influences. But before doing so, we must briefly review the aggregate sales in all the markets added together. In 1985, these totaled, as we have seen, $18.1 billion, a 6 percent advance on the 1980 total of $17.1 billion. It is, unfortunately, rather misleading to rely on these dollar estimates, in view of the general strengthening of the U.S. dollar that took place between those two dates. In simple terms, this means that in a market like the United Kingdom, where sales advanced quite significantly over a span of five years when measured in sterling, they actually showed a reduction when the sterling is converted into dollars at the appropriate year's parity; this reduction measured in dollars also reflects the effect on price of increased world supply of newly mined rough diamonds.

Looking at the value of sales in each market individually, twenty-four markets show a healthy growth in value; however, if we take into account inflation, the rate of which differs country by country, the number of markets that show an increase in real terms is reduced to fifteen. Reviewing all twenty-eight markets together, the growth rate in value measured in local currency, after correction for inflation, was probably slightly above the 6 percent improvement measured in dollars (up to 1985, the year for which data are included in the tables). In terms of value, the growth of only 1 to 2 percent per year masked the dramatic rise and fall of the speculative years 1979–1981.

The complication of computing the different currencies, with their varying inflation and dollar parity, makes it more sensible to look at the market on the basis of the "real" measures—the weight of the diamonds and the number of pieces sold. In weight, the 6.3 million carats sold in all twenty-eight markets in 1980 grew to 7.7 million in 1985, an overall increase of 21 percent, or an average compound annual growth of about 4 percent. In terms of pieces sold, there have been increases in sixteen markets (which include eight of the largest ten). Such a rate of growth is unusual in developed product fields; it is an optimistic feature of the diamond industry and to a degree a tribute to the advertising. There has, nevertheless, been an unusual variability in the average price paid for diamond jewelry in different markets. This variability is partly an artifact of the differences in exchange rates, but it is also influenced by a reduction in the average caratage of each diamond sold. This reduction in the average weight of the stones sold was fairly general in the 1970s and continued in the 1980s in certain fairly large markets—Italy, Mexico, West Germany, Spain, and France (although the situation in other, even more important markets is quite different—a point to which we shall return).

Before we move closer to specific markets, we are listing below three hypotheses that seem to be raised by the empirical data, and we shall use the information from the individual markets to amplify them.

1. The demand for diamonds is strongly influenced by personal income. This means not only the absolute level of income but also changes in the level of income. Also important is the distribution of income (a pronounced skew, with a minority of very high incomes, encourages the demand for diamonds); also the progression of direct taxation (high progression discourages demand because it cuts off an increasing share of income as the latter rises).

2. The demand for diamonds is strongly influenced by a number of price and fiscal factors, especially the price of diamonds themselves (in particular, price changes). It is also influenced by the level of inflation. Steady inflation encourages investment in diamonds because of their ability to preserve their value in real terms, although hyperinflation—as in Brazil—can have an op-

posite influence on demand because of its disruptive effect on personal incomes. The level of indirect (sales) tax on diamonds also has a direct bearing on their consumer price.

3. The demand for diamonds is influenced by diamond advertising—its absolute amount—and also by the share of voice it represents; also the trend in advertising expenditure over time. The content of the campaign exerts an influence, although the changes in the De Beers campaign, real though certain of them may have been, have remained confined within strategic parameters.

The data are not robust enough for us to allocate weights to these three influences on demand. We suggest, however, that the third factor is a good deal *less* important than the first two. We shall endeavor to refine this point in the subsequent discussion; in this, we shall be referring to five statistical tables (tables 13–1 through 13–5), which appear in the text of this chapter.

The most obvious feature of table 13–1 is that the value of the diamond market is very widely spread among the different countries (as reported up to 1985), with pronounced extremes. The top quartile (representing the seven most important markets) accounts for 79 percent of the total value of sales; the second quartile accounts for 14 percent; the third for 5 percent; and the fourth for only 2 percent. This means that it is important for us to pay more attention to the larger markets than to the smaller ones. And we suggest that an appropriate grouping of the markets for analytical purposes be as follows:

First Group: Markets with Stability or Reasonable-to-Strong Growth in Diamond Sales

Nine Large	*Ten Small*
United States	Switzerland
Japan	Australia
Italy	Hong Kong
Mexico	Belgium
West Germany	Austria
Canada	Sweden
Spain	Netherlands
France	Norway
United Kingdom	Denmark
	Finland

Second Group: Markets with No Growth

Five Large	*Four Small*
Brazil	Indonesia
Korea	South Africa
Philippines	Singapore

Table 13–1
Sales of Diamond Gemstones, 1985

	Total Retail Value ($ millions)	Acquisition of Women's Diamond Jewelry (%)	Average Price of Diamond Jewelry ($)	Pieces of Diamond Jewelry Sold (index 1980 = 100)	
United States	8,133	11.6	477	136	
Japan	3,174	5.6	854	134	
Italy	869	7.1	410	163	
Brazil	702	5.7	399	95	
Mexico	489	6.2	320	191	
West Germany	478	4.3	356	102	
Canada	475	7.6	395	151	
Spain	395	5.8	378	152	
Korea	390	1.7	710	57	(1983 = 100)
France	357	2.3	567	103	
United Kingdom	356	3.7	283	127	
Philippines	350	9.1	185	88	(1982 = 100)
Thailand	321	3.3	494	72	(1982 = 100)
Taiwan	275	3.8	933	77	(1982 = 100)
Switzerland	184	10.6	555	186	
Indonesia	170	0.8	380	19	(1982 = 100)
Australia	164	6.5	274	132	
Hong Kong	147	13.8	437	102	(1982 = 100)
South Africa*	126	8.5	502	91	
Singapore	101	12.9	720	65	(1982 = 100)
Belgium	90	5.0	362	100	(1983 = 100)
Austria	83	6.5	363	108	
Malaysia	76	4.5	304	91	(1982 = 100)
Sweden	70	6.7	247	98	
Netherlands	48	3.1	287	115	
Norway	27	5.5	281	178	
Denmark	21	3.8	223	211	
Finland	16	4.1	201	100	(1982 = 100)

*In South Africa there is a significant difference between the economic development of the white population and that of the nonwhite population. The data in this and the other tables refer only to the white population.

Thailand	Malaysia
Taiwan	

Note: The descriptors *large* and *small* refer to sales of diamonds, not (necessarily) to the size of the population.

The First Group of Markets

1. In tables 13–1 and 13–2, we see that the nine large markets in this group are the strongest diamond markets, taking into account both their absolute

Table 13–2
Diamond Sales and Selected Economic Indicators

Group One Markets	Pieces of Diamond Jewelry Sold in 1985 Compared with 1980 (index 1980 = 100)	Private Consumption per Capita, 1985 ($)	Change in Private Consumption per Capita, 1980–1985 Calculated at Constant Prices in Local Currency (%)
United States	136	10,879	+9
Japan	134	6,235	+11
Italy	163	3,988	+6
Mexico	191	1,150	+4
West Germany	102	5,726	+2
Canada	151	7,673	+4
Spain	152	2,872	−2
France	103	5,981	+5
United Kingdom	127	4,830	+7
Switzerland	186	8,855	+5
Australia	132	5,931	+11
Hong Kong	102 (1982 = 100)	4,320	+26
Belgium	100 (1983 = 100)	5,281	−1
Austria	108	4,956	+11
Sweden	98	6,097	+5
Netherlands	115	5,057	−6
Norway	178	6,308	+6
Denmark	211	6,043	+7
Finland	100 (1982 = 100)	5,615 (1984)	+9 (1984)

size and their growth. Two other large markets—Brazil and Korea—are excluded because they show sales declines. The United States is almost in a category of its own in its development, which clearly reflects the momentum generated by nearly fifty years of marketing investment, compared with a fraction of that time elsewhere. As one might imagine from the history of strong marketing support and the overall value systems that exist in the United States, diamond jewelry is a good deal higher on the American public's list of aspirations than it is for people in any other country. And growth in the United States has continued strongly since 1985.[19]

2. Table 13–2 shows that sixteen of the nineteen markets are economically rich, in that they have a high level of consumption per capita. (We have used private consumption per capita as the best available surrogate for personal income.) The three exceptions are Italy, Mexico, and Spain, but these markets have an unequal income distribution, with a sizable minority cluster of high-income families. Italy and Spain also have a large "black economy" (people with undeclared income on which they pay no direct taxes). Private consumption advanced in sixteen of the markets over the period 1980–1985; only in three markets did it retreat.

Table 13–3
Diamond Sales and Selected Economic Indicators (continued)

Group Two Markets	Pieces of Diamond Jewelry Sold in 1985 Compared with 1980 (index 1980 = 100)[a]	Private Consumption per Capita, 1985 ($)	Change in Private Consumption per Capita, 1980–1985 Calculated at Constant Prices in Local Currency (%)
Brazil	95	605	−28
Korea	57	1,228	+15
Philippines	88	383	−7
Thailand	72	488	+10
Taiwan	77	1,615	+24
Indonesia	19	323	+21
South Africa[b]	91	5,792	−2
Singapore	65	3,322	+15
Malaysia	91	1,023	+5

[a]Because of gaps in the data, the base years for these estimates are 1980 for Brazil and South Africa; 1982 for the Philippines, Thailand, Taiwan, Indonesia, Singapore, and Malaysia; and 1983 for Korea.
[b]See footnote to table 13–1.

3. Table 13–4 shows that in fifteen of the nineteen markets, the average price of diamonds fell when measured in real terms, after adjustment for inflation. Some reductions were quite substantial; indeed, in Japan, Hong Kong, and Austria, the average price went down in absolute terms even uncorrected for inflation. Some of the reductions were partly a reflection of the fall in the average caratage of the diamonds already mentioned in connection with five markets. Others reflect the effect of comparatively sluggish growth in private consumption per capita. Overall, with greater numbers of people coming into the market, the democratization of diamond jewelry ownership inevitably resulted in a reduction of average price. But even bearing these points in mind, the downward trend in the real "ticket price" is quite unmistakable, and the influence of this trend on demand is equally unmistakable. (Contrast the second group of markets in table 13–5.)

4. The influence of general inflation on the specific demand for diamonds is a little more pronounced than the data in table 13–4 suggest. In each country, the five-year averages smooth the general decline in inflation that took place over the period. This means that the incentive to buy diamonds as a hedge against inflation was more pronounced during the earlier years, although the inflation rate in Spain, Italy, and particularly Mexico remained much above the general rate over the whole period.

5. The amount of diamond advertising was relatively low when measured as a ratio of sales value. The figures, however, are much ahead of those in the second group of markets. Four of the markets in the first group

Table 13–4
Diamond Sales and Selected Economic Indicators (continued)

Group One Markets	Pieces of Diamond Jewelry Sold in 1985 Compared with 1980 (index 1980 = 100)	Average Annual Inflation Rate 1981–1985 (%)	Change in Average Retail Price of Diamond Jewelry, 1980–1985 Calculated at Constant Prices in Local Currency (%)	De Beers Advertising as a Ratio of Retail Sales Value, 1985 (%)
United States	136	5.5	− 14	0.4
Japan	134	2.8	− 39	0.5
Italy	163	13.7	− 40	0.3
Mexico	191	62.1	+ 1	0.1
West Germany	102	3.9	− 13	1.0
Canada	151	7.5	− 14	0.5
Spain	152	12.2	− 26	0.5
France	103	9.6	− 28	0.8
United Kingdom	127	7.2	− 4	0.6
Switzerland	186	4.3	− 18	0.3
Australia	132	8.3	− 25	0.6
Hong Kong	102 (1982 = 100)	7.2 (1983–1985)	− 29 (1982 = 100)	1.3
Belgium	100 (1983 = 100)	5.6 (1984–1985)	− 10 (1983 = 100)	0.6
Austria	108	4.9	− 26	0.4
Sweden	98	8.9	+ 11	0.4 (1984)
Netherlands	115	4.2	− 3	1.0
Norway	178	9.1	+ 25	0.5 (1984)
Denmark ·	211	7.9	+ 6	0.7 (1983)
Finland	100 (1982 = 100)	7.1 (1983–1985)	− 18 (1982 = 100)	0.4

spent between 0.8 and 1.3 percent. Virtually all the remaining markets had expenditures clustering around the overall median (0.4 percent for all twenty-eight markets in 1985), most of them above it. The sole major exception is Mexico, where the expenditure level was only 0.1 percent. A smaller exception is represented by the Scandinavian markets, which have had gaps of a year or two in their advertising programs.

6. It is important in this as in other fields to avoid drawing oversimplified conclusions from the relationship between advertising expenditures and sales levels. One particular problem concerns the direction of causality—in any one year, is a specific level of advertising the cause of the sales, or does the anticipated volume of sales determine the advertising appropriation? Nevertheless, in the majority of markets, the De Beers campaign is a long-running one, and its effects in the marketplace have been evaluated, at least judgmentally, for many years. Over the period 1980–1985, the De Beers advertising-to-sales ratio has *increased* in every one of the nineteen countries, with the exception of Mexico, Switzerland, and Norway. Such an increase suggests strongly that the advertising has contributed to sales or at the very

least that it is judged to have made such a contribution. Additionally, the impact of the campaign on the consumer is demonstrable, a point that will be examined. In strategic terms (both creatively and in media), the campaign has been substantially unchanged, despite alterations in emphasis.

The Second Group of Markets

Examining these markets after reviewing the first group is like turning over a coin and looking at the reverse side.

1. Of these nine markets, seven are in the Orient and one is in Latin America. Many of them have endemic economic problems.

2. Table 13–3 shows that the nine countries include seven that have a low level of personal consumption per capita (six of these are the poorest in our total list of twenty-eight countries). The exceptions are South Africa and Singapore. Much of the problem in South Africa can be attributed to the exceptionally depressed state of the economy (the gross national product has fallen in real terms in three of the five years under review). In Singapore, there is no obvious economic explanation for the decline in the market for diamonds; many of the economic indicators are moving in a positive direction. But it may be that the demand for diamonds in Singapore is an exceptionally speculative phenomenon and that the combination of a low inflation rate and the greatly increased price of diamonds has discouraged demand.

3. Table 13–5 shows that the average price of diamond jewelry has *increased* at a higher rate than inflation in eight of these nine countries. The only country in which there was an effective reduction was Brazil, but here the hyperinflation, with its deleterious influence on personal incomes, makes comparisons of consumer prices over a five-year span virtually meaningless. Korea has a punitive (200 percent) sales tax on diamond jewelry.

4. Table 13–5 also demonstrates that five of the nine countries have an exceptionally low inflation rate. This situation has not encouraged an investment in diamonds as a protection of the value of personal assets.

5. The nine countries are virtually all low advertisers, both in absolute terms and in comparison with the first group of markets. The only market in the second group to have an advertising-to-sales ratio (just) above the overall median is Singapore, with a level of 0.5 percent in 1985. In most cases, the ratios (which mostly bracket 0.1 percent of net sales value) are moving slowly upward. But the strong impression remains that in these markets (they are not advertising-intensive economies), the De Beers advertising has been exposed at a level below the threshold of effectiveness. The campaign has also not run for long in many of them and has not succeeded in breaking a possible consumer "inertia barrier." The critical level seems to be an advertising-to-sales ratio in the range of 0.4 to 0.6 percent, but there are probably local exceptions. These could be efficiently investigated by a

Table 13–5
Diamond Sales and Selected Economic Indicators (continued)

Group Two Markets	Pieces of Diamond Jewelry Sold in 1985 Compared with 1980[a] (index 1980 = 100)	Average Annual Inflation Rate 1981–1985[b] (%)	Change in Average Retail Price of Diamond Jewelry, 1980–1985 Calculated at Constant Prices in Local Currency (%)	De Beers Advertising as a Ratio of Retail Sales Value, 1985 (%)
Brazil	95	153.7	−29	0.2
Korea	57	2.3	+34	0.1
Philippines	88	27.8	+17	0.1
Thailand	72	2.3	+265	0.1
Taiwan	77	0.4	+17	0.1
Indonesia	19	9.0	+86	0.2
South Africa[c]	91	14.5	+35	0.1
Singapore	65	1.6	+55	0.5
Malaysia	91	2.6	+25	0.3

[a]Because of gaps in the data, the base years for these estimates are 1980 for Brazil and South Africa; 1982 for the Philippines, Thailand, Taiwan, Indonesia, Singapore, and Malaysia; and 1983 for Korea.
[b]The average inflation rate has been calculated for 1981–1985 for Brazil and South Africa; 1983–1985 for the Philippines, Thailand, Taiwan, Indonesia, Singapore, and Malaysia; and 1984–1985 for Korea.
[c]See footnote to table 13–1.

program of pressure testing, monitoring consumer awareness and attitudes as well as measuring sales.

"A Diamond is Forever"

The picture that emerges from these twenty-eight disparate markets is surprisingly clear. The absolute level of diamond sales and the growth in the market are related directly to two key phenomena: one exogenous (the amount, growth, and distribution of wealth) and the other substantially endogenous (the price of diamonds and certain related fiscal variables). Of a lower order of importance is the consumer advertising, and it is now appropriate both to review what the campaign has attempted to accomplish and to describe what we know about its success.

The characteristics of diamonds as a product are as follows:

- They are mainly gifts from men to women.
- They are major occasional purchases (with little repeat).
- They offer a synthesis of sensory, emotional, and rational rewards.

Although there are semantic problems in attempting to apply to diamonds the terms *functionality* and *added values* that normally pertain to packaged goods, it can be argued that the rewards of owning diamonds are virtually exclusively a matter of added values. In building these values, advertising has a role. Indeed, as diamonds have been presented in the advertising, the major emphasis has been on the emotional reward, which is of virtually equal importance to the giver and to the receiver of the gift. A further significant added value is the extension in the ways in which diamonds are worn and the occasions on which they are used, both of which have been influenced by the advertising. That De Beers has also been imaginative and energetic in fostering the art of jewelry design in many parts of the world has served to underpin and provide specific direction for the advertising.

The sensory reward—the beauty of the stone itself—comes from how the diamond is shown in the advertising and is a matter of some importance. The rational reward—the investment because a diamond is a store of value—is essentially implicit, although there is no shortage of evidence that people are fully conscious of this aspect of a diamond's appeal.[20] The thrust of the advertising argument has always been motivating, not discriminating. Since the campaign speaks for all diamonds and since diamonds have no direct competitors, the argument has inevitably been based on general benefits.

The advertising wheels were set in motion by N. W. Ayer, the American agency that has always handled the De Beers account in the United States. The first advertisement featuring the slogan "a diamond is forever" appeared in 1939. Anecdotal evidence suggests that the potentially immensely powerful emotional appeal of diamonds had eroded for some years during the 1930s but that the N. W. Ayer campaign managed to rebuild this appeal, bringing a fairly speedy improvement in sales in the marketplace.[21]

The basic advertising idea distilled into this astonishingly durable slogan has remained unchanged over the years since it was first used—years during which the De Beers advertising has been extended to the majority of economically active world markets, mainly under the direction of J. Walter Thompson. The main media used have been television (plus some cinema) and color magazines. These media are the most appropriate ones for the highly charged emotional story that has always been built into the advertising.

The campaign has two obvious tasks: (a) the long-term or strategic one of building added values—to reinforce and add to people's already high perceptions of diamond gemstones—and (b) the tactical task of selling certain types of jewelry, for example, engagement rings (traditionally the main concentration); necklaces, earrings, bracelets, and eternity rings; and men's jewelry. A major effort has been made since 1982 to sell larger stones.

The advertisements say very little explicitly (the word count of the films is exceptionally low). But they communicate their message with high artistry, in visual terms and also with the use of atmospheric music. The tone of the advertising is mostly serious: emotionally involving in a way that evokes sentiment and not sentimentality. Such a tone is a long-standing tradition of the campaign, yet there is no constraint against using humor when doing so is meaningful and relevant. One recent commercial for eternity rings shows the recipients' names written by a skywriting airplane, illuminated in the sky with fireworks, and lit in huge neon letters on a suspension bridge. The spectacular way in which the names are featured is stylish hyperbole; we smile when we see the commercial, and it registers with us.

This *Skywriting* film was made in Great Britain. De Beers advertisements outside the United States originate in Britain, France, Germany, Italy, Japan, and Spain. But it is a matter of policy that all the films must be able to travel; they must be usable in many other countries. (In this, the spareness of the use of words is an advantage.) Although there are natural economies in the international syndication of advertising material, they are seen (as in the case of Lux Toilet Soap) as a means of maximizing the value of an already-high investment in advertising production. The syndication procedures are quite complicated, and the system is made possible by a small international coordination group situated in J. Walter Thompson's London office.

All the films and magazine advertisements are enriched by exceptional production values. In particular, the film and still photography is of a uniformly impressive quality and features the most up-to-the-minute fashion trends. High production values are, of course, complementary to and not a substitute for strong advertising ideas.

As stated, the task of the advertising is both strategic and tactical. In its strategic role, the enduring slogan "a diamond is forever" is a valuable tool that has been used for almost a half-century. It has entered the public consciousness (with spontaneous awareness levels of 66 percent in France, 62 percent in Italy, and 50 percent in Germany and with much higher scores for defined target groups of the population).[22] The slogan has been used continuously, and, even more importantly, the imagery and tone of voice of the campaign have also been exceptionally consistent.

The total promotional activity for diamonds is led by the theme advertising campaign. But the advertising is by no means the sole activity. There are two other major programs: (a) product publicity and (b) cooperative programs with trade associations and with jewelry manufacturers and designers. There is also an enormous output of brochures and selling literature for use by the trade. All these activities are integrated and add further mileage to the theme advertising effort.

The best evidence of the strategic effectiveness of the advertising and promotional activities is the striking number of engaged couples every year who mark the event with the gift of a woman's diamond ring. This practice is true even in countries in which the custom is relatively new. In Japan, for instance, the level of engagement ring-giving has reached 68 percent. Over a twenty-year period, the diamond engagement ring tradition was virtually created in Japan by the combined advertising, public relations, and publicity programs run by De Beers.[23] There is also respectable generalized evidence of the tactical effectiveness of the campaign: its ability to steer demand in specific directions. Most recently, such evidence has taken the form of an increase in the average caratage of the diamond jewelry purchased in the important markets of the United States, Japan, and Canada, as well as in a string of smaller countries. Since the thrust of much of the advertising during the 1980s has been toward selling larger stones,[24] this marketplace response is presumptive evidence of effectiveness.

But these have not been the only signals of the campaign's success. Others have included the reestablishment of the diamond engagement ring tradition during the late 1970s, after a decline during the Vietnam War, the flower-child period, when formal betrothal and marriage suffered a partial eclipse. Another example was the way in which the campaign enabled the diamond market to withstand competition from mixed-stone engagement rings.

Five Lessons from the History of De Beers

1. Advertising is the Third Influence on Sales. The evidence examined in this study demonstrates that three of the main influences on the demand for diamond gemstones are the wealth of the purchaser, the price of the stones, and the advertising. The income elasticity of demand and the price elasticity of demand are both high. Advertising—both quantitatively and qualitatively—is of a lower order of importance. It does, however, have an influence on sales, both in the long and the short term, and the advertising can take some of the credit for the clear growth in the market that has taken place since the end of World War II.

2. A Synthesis of Three Appeals. The rewards from receiving and giving diamonds are an amalgam of the emotional, the sensory, and the rational. The advertising has traditionally been based on the first two of these. There is good evidence of widespread public awareness of the rational reward: an awareness of diamonds as a store of value, particularly in inflationary times. Diamonds carry a particularly high price-value perception. Partly as an investment but also partly as a manifestation of conspicuous consumption by both the giver and the receiver of a diamond gift, they are valued partly if not mainly because of their rarity and high price. Since this is all well understood by the public, the advertising does not have to labor the point.

3. **Unvarying Continuity of the Advertising Strategy.** The main lines of the advertising strategy were laid down almost five decades ago and have been uniformly applied in the twenty-eight world markets in which diamonds have been advertised. The slogan "a diamond is forever" has always played a pivotal role, and it is a tribute to its depth and pregnancy that the campaign based on it continues to be involving, fresh, and effective. Since diamonds are not only mere jewelry but also a signal and celebration of the high points of people's lives, the advertising is able to mirror these high points in an affecting way, one in which advertisements for many other high-ticket items are unable to do. The central emotional content of the campaign is a source of both its power and its durability. A diamond is forever; a diamond is love; therefore, the love expressed in the gift has the durability of the diamond.

4. **The International Syndication of the Advertising.** De Beers provides one of the best examples available anywhere of the ability of effective advertising to travel. The central feature of the campaign is that it has been able to tap into those consumer desires and aspirations which seem to be similar in country after country. This ability has made it a classic case of success in single markets followed by rollout into others, and the commonality of consumers' attitudes has enabled a single advertising strategy to be universally employed. But the advertising syndication goes further. Specific advertising material, both for film and print media, is created in seven markets and syndicated to all the others in which the De Beers campaign is exposed. This means that the widest use is made of the best creative talent available. In many cases, an individual market has access to advertising of a much higher class than it could afford were it to produce its own campaign. There are cost savings in this procedure, but the reason for syndicating advertising material is more than economic, it is to maximize quality.

5. **A Threshold Budget Level.** One of the conclusions from this study is that the advertising has been effective in those markets in which the campaign has become established and has overcome initial inertia and in which it is being supported by a meaningful budget, at least in the bracket of 0.4 to 0.6 percent of the retail value of sales. In these more successful markets, budgets of that level are minimal and they have also gradually increased, a point not unrelated to their effectiveness. The data seem to point strongly to the likelihood that in the less successful markets, where the budgets bracket the level of 0.1 percent of retail sales value, the campaigns are ineffective because they are subthreshold. This hypothesis could be explored by a limited program of pressure testing. The evaluation procedure would need to include a monitoring of consumer awareness and attitudes as well as sales.

14
The Discover Card

> The new company operated according to Sears's traditional methods,
> particularly those resulting from economies of scale.
>
> —Gordon L. Weil[1]

A Part of the American Way of Life

The opening quotation for this chapter says something important about Sears, Roebuck and Company. But the quotation is not a reference to the Discover Card. It pertains to an event that took place fifty-four years before the arrival of the card and describes an even more important broadening of the company's business: its very first move into financial services, with the launch of Allstate Insurance in 1931. General Robert E. Wood, the fourth head of Sears, was the driving force behind this move. Seizing upon an idea given to him by a friend outside the company, Wood drove it forward to success despite the inauspicious time during which this step took place. The general was one of the early pioneers who did so much to make Sears, Roebuck and Company an American legend.[2]

In 1921, the thirty-five-year-old Sears was still exclusively in the catalog mail-order business, closely tied to agriculture. This specialty was admittedly successful and profitable, but it needed Wood's imagination and energy to transform the enterprise into something altogether larger and more powerful. He did this first by moving the thrust of the business from mail-order to retail selling, through opening a chain of well-located department stores during the 1920s, and second by exploiting a completely new business opportunity in insurance, one that was to lead eventually to a full range of financial services. This move into financial services is the central concern of this chapter.

The company was digesting these changes when the Great Depression of the 1930s struck the American economy. Sears weathered the storm by tightening its centralized controls, reducing costs, and sweating out the reductions in sales volume, and it lost money in only one year, 1932. Purchasing had always been highly centralized, an arrangement deemed necessary to garner the maximum profit from the company's vast scale of operation. General Wood's instinct was, however, toward decentralization, and the rapid growth of the business after the Second World War was spurred by his drive to decentralize the retail operation and to encourage local initiatives—moves accompanied by a progressive opening of new stores, many in new shopping malls, their size geared to the dimensions of the local community. In this, and also in the way the business was broadened to attract large numbers of male as well as female shoppers, the general demonstrated his admirable grasp of demographics. Like all good marketing people, he benefited throughout his life from the treasures of actionable information that can be found in the pages of the *Statistical Abstract of the United States.*[3]

It would need a study many times the scale of this one to analyze fully the reasons for the success of Sears, Roebuck and Company. But it is important for us to comprehend at least something of the culture of the organization if we are to understand how the Discover Card was planned and nurtured, because the card's positioning and launch were carefully worked out in light of both the intensely competitive nature of the market and Sears, Roebuck and Company's strengths. Those strengths were of great value, despite the fact that the launch would be taking the company some way out of its area of primary expertise.

Four aspects of Sears were especially key to the launch of the Discover Card. First, the company has, since its birth in 1886, been in the business of direct contact with the public. Unlike virtually all packaged goods manufacturers, which sell their goods via the retail trade, the Sears business *has been* the retail trade. This activity is, from one point of view, highly demanding: There is no cushion between the retailer and the end user of the goods and services sold. And it is fast moving, because marketing tactics achieve an immediate response (which can, of course, be negative as well as positive). It follows that the more successful retail operations have their antennae well tuned to the demands of the consumer. And it is no coincidence that the Sears merchandisers have developed a profound understanding of their customers when they "prepare the specifications and styles for the goods they think Sears should sell."[4] Indeed, the group entitled the Chicago merchandising brain trust is regarded as the most critically important management body in the company.

Second, the hundred-year growth of Sears has been driven by a massive and virtually continuous growth in population and income in the American market. Economies of scale—mainly in buying but also to some degree in merchandising, advertising, and the location of stores—have expanded the volume and profits of the business, this despite the traditional and even increasing intensity of retail competition. Since Sears has for a number of years been the largest retailer in the United States, with a credit card that in turn is the largest store credit card operation in the country (44.2 million cards were issued by mid-1987), the company is in that select group which achieves the greatest scale economies in the retail business, economies that the company puts to work to achieve even greater growth.[5] Scale of operations is a matter of vast import in the market for credit cards. A related point is that the gigantic Sears customer base provided an obvious ongoing target group for the Discover Card. The more than 44 million households in the United States represent an obviously valuable data base for direct mail.

Third, the company decided in the early 1980s to extend radically its business in financial services. At the time, Allstate was large, soundly based, and accounted for a large proportion of the Sears pretax income but was confined to providing insurance services alone. Although the range of these services had been progressively broadened, there remained defined limits to what it was felt could be provided under the Allstate name. In 1961, Sears began operating a savings and loan bank in California, doing so by the acquisition of the Commonwealth Savings and Loan Association, whose name was changed first to the Allstate Savings and Loan Association in 1964 and then to the Sears Savings Bank in 1984. This is today a big operation—the twenty-fifth largest in the United States—but for a variety of reasons savings and loans operations are relatively unattractive to investors and therefore have low growth potential. The company also owns the Sears Mortgage Corporation and Sears Consumer Financial Corporation (which provides larger loans to individuals than those needed for the purchase of Sears merchandise).

In 1981, Sears acquired the real estate and mortgage brokering firm of Coldwell Banker and the investment brokering firm of Dean Witter Reynolds Inc. Both were prominent national organizations and were acquisitions of great significance. The pieces were being put in place for Sears, Roebuck and Company to build a broad-based financial services organization, the equivalent of a national bank. Indeed, the stated intention of the company was to make Sears during its second hundred years a major force in the financial markets, with all needs served by one company.

The Discover Card was planned to be a vital part of this program, to provide the "access vehicle" for the different financial services, such as all transfers of funds, including mortgage payments, and purchases of certificates of deposit. First, though, it had to establish its position as a profitable credit card. The Discover Card was seen in the planning stages as equally important as a credit card and as an access vehicle for other financial services. That the advantage of the latter was not entirely obvious to the consumer was, however, a potential source of problems. The consumer does not seem to accept fully the concept of one-stop financial shopping.

Sears had long experience in financing and handling consumer credit on a vast scale. Indeed, more than 60 percent of Sears merchandise is sold on credit. The Sears store card was introduced in 1953, and today, as noted, there are Sears cardholders in more than 44 million households in the United

SONG: THIS IS THE DAWN

THE DAWN OF

DISCOVER.

THE DISCOVER CARD.

NOW YOU HAVE A BRIGHTER DAY IN STORE.

ANNCR: In this world there are very few things that cost you nothing to get

and pay you back every day. Just the important things.

And now the Discover Card is one. (MUSIC BEAT)

It costs you nothing to get

and pays you back with Real Dollar Dividends on every purchase,

and a unique savings plan that not

only pays you high money market rates,

the higher your savings level, the higher the rate climbs.

SONG: A WAY TO SAVE

A WAY TO FIND THAT BRIGHT TOMORROW.
ANNCR: Very few things work that way.

SONG: THE DISCOVER CARD CAN

PUT YOUR DREAMS IN SIGHT.
ANNCR: Just the important ones.

SONG: THIS IS THE DAWN

THIS IS THE DAWN

THE DAWN OF DISCOVER.

THE DISCOVER CARD.

THE DISCOVER CARD PUTS MONEY IN A WHOLE NEW LIGHT.

ANNCR: From a member of Sears Financial Network.

Sixty-second television commercial first exposed in the United States to launch the Discover Card in July, 1985.

States. The Sears card will, incidentally, remain in existence no matter how successful the Discover Card becomes.

The fourth characteristic of Sears is that consumer advertising has for a long time been an important activity, and the company is sophisticated in its use. Traditionally, advertising-to-sales ratios are lower in the retail field than in packaged goods—a direct result of the relatively low profitability of retailing in comparison with manufacturing. But when Sears's relatively modest advertising-to-sales ratio is applied to the enormous sales volume generated by the business, the company is shown to be a large advertiser indeed, with an estimated expenditure of slightly more than $1 billion in 1986.

Sears is the third largest advertiser in the United States. Retail advertising as a whole has been expanding at a faster rate than packaged goods advertising has during the past twenty years, and Sears has led this trend (although the Sears budget did not increase in 1985 or in 1987). In 1961, Sears was the only retailer among the hundred leading advertisers in the United States and ranked twelfth on the total list. In 1986, there were seven retailers among the hundred leaders, and Sears ranked third on the total list; it was still the largest retail advertiser but now relatively a much bigger one. Most importantly, the Sears advertising-to-sales ratio climbed progressively from 1.1 percent in 1961 to 3.1 percent in 1986, indicating how markedly the advertising intensiveness of the business had increased over those twenty-five years.[6]

The Credit Card Phenomenon

Among the significant changes in society occurring during the 1970s—political instability both in the United States and abroad, low economic growth, unemployment, inflation, and demographic flux—a seemingly more modest revolution took place that in retrospect may have had just as much long-term import as these other, higher profile phenomena. This was the explosion in the use of credit cards that took place during that decade: something that was engineered by the emergence of brands and made possible by the technology that enabled debits and credits to be transferred electronically.

The credit card was, and is, seen by customers as something that offers considerable convenience to them, not to mention the all-too-easy possibility of increasing their personal debt. To the bankers who operate them, card systems provide the opportunity to make large and expanding profits in the long term. We should emphasize *the long term*, however, because the cost of establishing a network of retailers who accept the card and of building a worthwhile franchise of regular card users requires gigantic investments during the early years of operation, sums that must sometimes be measured in hundreds of millions of dollars. Launching a successful card calls not only for a clear plan, preferably with differentiating brand benefits, but also for energy, a steady nerve, and large resources.

The Discover Card was, of course, launched as a credit card. And although it is projected that it will have a broader range of uses in the 1990s, transforming it fully into a financial services card, it must establish a firm user-base in the 1980s: as a credit card in competition with other credit cards.

By the mid-1980s, the penetration of cards had reached a plateau, a situation similar to that in the majority of consumer goods markets. It is probable that consumer penetration will only slowly climb beyond its present level of 75.3 million cardholders, or 44 percent of adults living in the United States. This figure is based on a broad definition of credit cards and includes store cards, gasoline cards, and telephone cards, as well as those credit cards against which the Discover Card is most directly competing. The penetration and market share of its largest competitors are shown in table 14–1.

There is, of course, an overlap in ownership and usage. Note also that the original American Express card (before the launch of the Optima card) was, and is, a payment (or "travel and entertainment") card: The customer's bills have to be paid in full when they are presented. MasterCard and Visa, in contrast, need be paid only in part, and both offer extended credit at a high rate of interest.[7] As a result, these latter two cards are the most direct competitors of the Discover Card.[8]

As might be expected, the demographic bias of MasterCard, Visa, and American Express is toward people who have higher incomes and managerial occupations and who live in cities. American Express is more extremely

Table 14–1
Penetration and Market Share of Credit and Payment Cards

	Adults Using Each Card[a]		Sales Based on Each Card[b] (three cards only)	
	Millions	*Percentage*	*$ Billions*	*Percentage*
Total (any card)	75.3	44	205.0	100
MasterCard	27.7	16	71.7	35
Visa	33.8	20	88.1	43
American Express (green)	7.2	4	45.2	22

[a]Simmons Market Research Bureau, *Annual Report on the Credit Card Market,* 1986. The estimates yielded by this research are approximations. This leads to some exaggeration in the figures when the basic data are extrapolated to estimate volume use per card; however, the *comparisons* between the volume uses of the different cards are reasonably accurate.

[b]"Credit-Card War Looms," *Advertising Age,* March 16, 1987, pp. 1, 84.

skewed in these ways than the other cards. And, as can be seen in table 14–1, American Express accounts for a larger annual volume of transactions (an average of $6,300) than either MasterCard or Visa ($2,600 each).

That the market has reached a plateau in consumer penetration is a reflection of the top limit to the number of people whose discretionary income is large enough to make them profitable customers. Thus, long-term penetration growth can come only as a result of (a) the gradual increase in personal income that will follow a rising gross national product or (b) a change in transaction practices—in how money is managed. And although long-term changes will probably eventually take place in both these areas, we shall have to wait rather a long time for any substantial movement, and the establishment of the Discover Card cannot depend on such a long-range outcome. Success must depend on its ability to take business from its most direct competitors, MasterCard and Visa, although it can be expected that the *use* of all credit cards will continue to rise progressively, despite the plateau in overall penetration. In fact, growth in usage is still strong, American Express transactions having grown by 90 percent in 1980–1987 and usage of MasterCard and Visa having climbed by 68 percent.[9]

The thrust of the promotional effort for Discover therefore had to be in three directions:

1. to build rapidly the number of merchants that would accept the card until a satisfactory level were achieved
2. to build rapidly a base of retail customers who would use the card
3. to build frequency of consumer usage

Of these tasks, the first two were urgent necessities in the short term. It was, however, the third task—a longer term endeavor—that would determine whether or not the Discover Card would become a permanent marketing entity with substantial profit potential.

Since Discover came relatively late into the market, in the wake of a number of well-established competitors, the card had to offer well-defined discriminating benefits, or competitive advantages, and not rely on the generic appeal offered by credit cards as a category (convenience, credit, and so on). Ultimately, the success of the Discover Card will depend on the strength of these discriminating appeals, particularly since the strong position of Visa, MasterCard, and American Express in the market will continue to make them tough competitors for several years.

It was considered important—quite correctly—to provide discriminators that were intrinsically rational, but this did not mean that the way in which these discriminators might be expressed in advertising had to be exclusively rational. To people unacquainted with the ways in which advertising works, this distinction may appear overly subtle and perhaps unnecessary. But it is a significant one. It is well known, for instance, that with many successful advertised brands, emotional discriminators are critically important to consumers' selection of the brand, yet the advertising for such brands may incorporate lengthy rational argument, mainly for the reduction of cognitive dissonance *following* purchase. This use for rational argumentation is particularly prevalent with products and services with a high ticket price.

There are other cases in which the emotional-rational balance is consequential; the Discover Card was such a case. Real rational discriminators were planned for the card, and as a first step, two rounds of qualitative research were carried out to evaluate consumers' response to them. These discriminators comprised a sizable collection of money-saving advantages, such as no annual fee, money savings (the "Cashback Bonus") on purchases made with the card, and savings account earnings on credit balances, with an upward sliding scale of interest rates.

None of these advantages is individually unique, but taken together they can be used in a preemptive way. Note, incidentally, how these rational discriminators are consonant with the bedrock benefits associated with Sears in customers' minds. The research confirmed that these benefits are all meaningful to potential consumers. It did, however, make it clear that the benefits needed to be clothed in human, personal terms if they were to form the foundation for a viable advertising strategy. Propositions based on relatively bald statements of rational product advantage were rejected.

The preliminary planning and research pointed the way to a campaign that emphasized human values but was underpinned by a rational discriminating argument (or series of arguments). The balance of rational and emotional benefits was a matter of great importance for the brand. It was appreciated at the very beginning that it was vital to create a distinct brand personality differentiated from that of competitive cards. This meant the use of emotional signals about the brand to help build that personality. As a result, some (perhaps inevitable) dissonance developed between the creation of the image and the need to encourage card usage by means of retail-oriented advertising.

The Launch Advertising

The launch campaign was planned for one 60-second and a number of different 30-second television spots, with tactical support provided by radio and print advertising.

The television commercials were visually striking. They were introduced with the sunrise motif that is echoed in all advertising and promotional material, not least in the design of the card (with the sunrise represented by the letter *o* in the word *Discover*). Besides being visually arresting, the symbol of dawn is a rich, evocative means of communicating that something new is happening. The idea of newness has a traditional power in advertising communication; it was conveyed in the Discover advertising subtly but unmistakably, and without allowing the notion to degenerate into a cliché.

The remainder of each Discover commercial was devoted to visual vignettes of people living life fully, engaged in activities that most people can aspire to, yet are slightly unusual and very appealing. Production values were high. Underlying the visual images, the copy communicated simply and directly the rational arguments for using the Discover Card.

The commercials made a strong impression on the viewer, an impression derived from an amalgam of visual imagery, music, and rational argument. The advertising for certain competitive brands (Visa and, to a lesser degree, American Express) relies equally on a combination of visual imagery and rationality. Yet the introductory Discover advertising had a unique flavor—an essential requirement for a brand introduced rather late into a developed and competitive market—and its distinctiveness was essentially a function of its *visual* impression (which is why it is inappropriate to use the more usual phrase *tone of voice* to describe it).

The commercials were tested as concepts and as finished films, with favorable results. The method used was to screen the advertisements in a theater on closed-circuit television and to research them among controlled samples of potential customers to gauge their persuasion, their impact, whether they were easily understood, and whether they generated interest in the card. A number of such tests were carried out, mostly employing a technique proprietary to Sears, Roebuck and Company that has been used to screen three thousand advertisements. The reader will be aware that tests of this sort are subject to a number of limitations; they are nevertheless not as open to criticism as the much more common day-after-recall technique.[10]

The results of the research into the advertisements for the Discover Card exhibited a number of interesting points. Although there were some differences in responses to the different commercials, in general the points of similarity outweighed them. The principal conclusions were the following:

1. The majority of the films scored well above normal levels, or "evaluative benchmarks" (advertisements for competitive brands). This was the most important finding.

2. There seemed to be a real degree of consumer interest in the use of the Discover Card, particularly by men.

3. The commercials were demonstrably entertaining, in both sight and sound. Although there was some diffusion in the communication of the rational verbal messages, television was not designed to communicate all the product details; doing so was the particular task of the direct mail. The use

of television was directed mainly at establishing and differentiating the brand personality of the Discover Card.

4. Greatest interest was expressed by Sears customers. (This is what would normally be expected, through the operation of selective perception).

5. The production values of the sixty-second commercial led to a significant increase in the impact of the finished version of the commercial over the animatic (videotape storyboard) that had been researched earlier. This is what knowledge of such testing would lead us to expect; however, persuasiveness was unaffected—again an expected outcome.

The conclusions from the research were richer and fuller than this short summary allows. It provided reasonable reassurance that there did not seem to be any problems with the communication of the advertising. It showed a green light to expose the campaign, although both client and agency appreciated, then and later, that more than effective advertising was needed to ensure the success of the Discover Card.

The Discover Card in the Market Place

JWT Chicago had been working on developing advertising since mid-1984. During 1985, two regional test markets (Atlanta and San Diego) were established, followed by three more (Albany, Denver, and Milwaukee) in early 1986. The purpose of this sequence was to evaluate the marketing program and to iron out any operational problems. Results were promising. Indeed, they encouraged the client to launch the Discover Card nationally on January 26, 1986 (the Sunday of the Superbowl), four years ahead of the time proposed at the earliest planning stages. The launch was loud. The program moved quickly into high gear, with the use of direct selling, direct mail, and advertising and promotions to build quickly the consumer base, concentrating on Sears, Roebuck and Company's own customers. Equally or even more importantly, a great effort was made to build speedily a reasonably extensive list of retail and other establishments that would accept the card.

As mentioned, the cost of entry into this market required investments of hundreds of millions of dollars. In advertising alone (excluding promotions), a budget of more than $40 million was needed in 1986 to match competitive noise levels.[11]

Based as it was on the strategy of mounting the effort against the vast captive audience of Sears customers, the Discover Card was an immediate success in building consumer penetration. Increases in penetration took place at a high and steady rate over the whole of 1986, the average monthly growth during the second half of the year being more than 17.9 percent. By the end of the 1986, there were more than 6 million accounts and more than

11 million cards issued. The Discover Card had established a good start on its consumer base.

The numbers of retail and other establishments accepting the card had also increased, and the impressive total of 525,000 outlets, which was achieved by the end of the year, gave the card a promising start (although it had a long way to go to approach the 2 million establishments accepting Visa or MasterCard). The figure had grown to 725,000 by the end of 1987.[12] This satisfactory growth was attributable partly to the size and strength of Sears, with its ability to provide large numbers of creditworthy customers, and partly to the relatively inexpensive fee the Discover Card imposes on the retailer. Certain retailers that are directly competitive with Sears, however, continue to refuse to accept the Discover Card.

But these statistics are not in themselves enough to prove the success of the Discover Card. We need to know some facts about the development of usage in order to predict how the card might fare in the long term.

1. Usage climbed faster than penetration (number of accounts). This fact is presumptive evidence of consumer satisfaction with the card. This is evident from table 14–2. Although the date on usage growth looked reasonably good, the absolute levels remained below those of the competition, a problem that soon assumed a degree of urgency.

2. More growth was coming from the use of the card *outside* Sears stores than within Sears stores. Non-Sears transactions in early 1987 accounted for 72.3 percent of sales volume—a figure that was climbing fast.

3. In almost three-quarters of cases, the Discover Card joined the customer's repertoire of cards. But in an important minority of cases, it was a replacement (for instance, 7 percent of Discover Cards replaced the MasterCard).

4. Awareness of the rational discriminators offered by the Discover Card was high. The communication of these discriminators has been the main initial task of the advertising and direct mail, which appeared to have done their first job. These rational discriminators—notably no annual fee and the Cashback Bonus—were perceived by consumers as valuable advantages.

Table 14–2
Discover Card–Growth Index

		Growth (index)	Transaction Volume (index)
1986	July	100	100
	September	138	171
	November	196	238
1987	January	240	257

Source: Data from Dean Witter Reynolds Inc.

5. One-fourth of customers were unhappy with the relatively limited retail acceptance. (As we have seen, competitive cards still have a much larger merchant base.)

6. Advertising awareness (averaging 60 percent) was comparable with that for competitive cards, although the levels in different regions varied considerably. It can be argued that advertising awareness is a much less important measure of success than awareness of and attitudes toward the card itself.[13] Among card users, attitudes were favorable. And in the early days, these attitudes were, as we have seen, being translated into increasing usage.

Nevertheless, despite these indications of the early success of the advertising campaign, the Discover Card was perceived, before the end of its first year, as suffering from two problems. First, although usage had gone up a great deal, it was still below usage of competitive cards. Second, although the dollars spent per transaction were comparable ($63 per purchase for Discover, compared with $60 for Visa and MasterCard), the average monthly balance was only $550 for Discover customers, compared with $1,000 for Visa and MasterCard customers.[14] There was a clear need for a medium-term improvement in these levels, despite the fact that by the end of 1987, 22 million Discover cards had been issued (representing a penetration of 14 percent of all U.S. households).[15]

The client and agency were highly satisfied with the initial and growing levels of consumer penetration. Cardholders recruited by direct mail from the Sears list were considered the best customers. Indeed, some advertising aimed at stimulating penetration was canceled because it was found to be bringing in customers who were not sufficiently creditworthy.

However, despite the very satisfactory recruitment of a user base, both client and agency were soon conscious of the need to stimulate card usage. Before the end of the first year after the launch, a new television campaign was introduced. This showed the Discover Card being taken out of a wallet in preference to other cards, something described as a "Smart Move," because of the Cashback Bonus. This campaign gave particular emphasis to the Discover Card's product features, with the object of boosting usage. It made headway in the market, but after a year of exposure the client encouraged a further increase in the emphasis on usage by the introduction of a campaign embodying the slogan "For People Who Expect Value." This advertising was significantly retail oriented, and it listed a number of mass-market retail outlets that accept the Discover Card. By the final quarter of 1987, usage levels had grown ahead of expectations.

With a user base in late 1987 of 22 million cardholders, many of whom had only just begun to use the card, the total volume usage reached more than $6 billion during the course of 1987, an average of $484 per account (or $895 per active account). This total represented a huge increase over the

1986 figure of $1.8 billion and was caused by increases in both the number of users and in the average volume of use—up from $287 per card in 1986 (or $626 per active account). The Discover Card nevertheless has a long way to go to catch up on its nearest rivals, because use of Visa averaged $909 in 1987 and use of MasterCard averaged $840.[16] It was because of this continued strength of the competition that the emphasis on the usage of the Discover Card became such a pressing matter, despite the success that was already being achieved in boosting both penetration and usage.

As can be seen in a number of other cases in this book, a change in marketing emphasis from penetration growth to usage growth is common. This change, however, took place more quickly for the Discover Card than in many other product fields. For the Discover Card campaign, this transition represented the point of maximum sensitivity.

JWT lost the Discover Card business at the end of 1987. Since this study is concerned essentially with the successful launch of the Discover Card, we shall not explore in detail the reasons for this loss, although two points that bear on it deserve brief consideration.

First, the marketing of the Discover Card, which had originally been in the hands of Discover Card Services (located in Lincolnshire, Illinois), was gradually taken over by its parent in the Sears organization, Dean Witter Financial Services (located in New York City). There was a feeling on the part of the latter that fresh advertising thinking was required, despite the unquestionable contribution the advertising had made to the launch and during the first two years of successful development of the brand.[17]

The second point concerns the role—in effect, the dual role—of the television advertising. On the one hand, it was, and is, expected to encourage use of the card, which means that it must have an appropriately retail orientation. On the other hand, it was, and is, required to boost the image of the Discover Card, which implies a degree of upgrading and the establishment of a clear differentiation from competitive cards in terms of image. As noted earlier, there is some dissonance between these objectives, as is underscored by the fact that the Discover Card is recognized as a product of Sears, which by its sheer size and ubiquity is the most mass market of all brands in the United States.

JWT was always fully sold on the need to use the television advertising for image building. The agency recognized that although the functional differences between the Discover Card and competitive cards were important, they needed to be underpinned and reinforced by nonrational image-oriented communication aimed at differentiating the Discover Card even more strongly from the competition. This consideration was a matter of maximum importance to JWT during the more than three years of its cooperation with Sears, Roebuck and Company on the Discover Card. It should also be remembered that by many objective measures, those years were generally very successful for the card.

Seven Lessons from the History of the Discover Card

1. Discover is an Organic Extension of the Sears Business. The Discover Card is clearly outside Sears, Roebuck and Company's traditional main business, yet it is a new field in which the company's strengths and expertise are useful assets, which can carry over. In reaching out in new directions, the company has always had its eyes fixed on the long term: the next century rather than the next decade. The seeds for expansion into financial services were planted more than fifty years ago. With a business of the weight and momentum of Sears, in which there are such great rewards for success—and such enormous penalties for failure—new ventures cannot be entered into precipitately. But once entered into, they require the most massive resources to make them work. It is this organic attitude to growth that distinguishes a company like Sears, Roebuck and Company from a conglomerate. Sears is interested in profit but in long-term, stable—and substantial—profit, which has to be punctiliously planned and built.

2. In a Stationary Market, a New Brand Requires a Powerful Discriminator. The existence of relative product advantages has been the underlying theme of the Discover Card from its earliest planning stages. Not content with a single functional advantage—which could be copied by competitors—Sears built a whole range of meaningful functional discriminators. It is the *range* of rational discriminators that makes for a preemptible proposition. The desired response of the customer to the Discover Card is that it is *superior* because of this whole range of specific advantages. This superiority becomes a tone of voice that is not easily copied by the competition. It is "a unique blend of appeals."[18] The downside of this undoubtedly correct strategy is that these real rational discriminators cost money; they therefore erode the card's profitability, thus lengthening the already-extended investment period for the launch.

3. An Underlying Advertising Argument Based on Rational Discriminators Does Not Require Exclusively Rational Advertising. One of the salient features of the introductory Discover campaign is that the advertising avoided a laborious and literal presentation of rational arguments. What was considered important was the input of the consumer—his or her interest and participation in the mutual process of advertising communication. Concept testing at a very early stage confirmed the need to present the story in human terms, and both client and agency had the imagination to accept this requirement. It was the visual impact of the commercials that impressed them on the attention of the viewer and communicated the Discover name. But the visual symbolism was more than an attention-getting device; it opened the viewer's mind to an argument, partly emotional and partly rational: a benefit-oriented reason for the viewer to obtain and use the Discover Card.

4. To Launch and Develop a Major Brand Requires Major Resources. The launch of any major new brand, especially one with a payout as extended as a credit card, needs the depth of resources, the staying power, and the long-term commitment that only a gigantic organization can provide. The estimated investment costs that have been published are $200 million after tax over a two-year period.[19]

5. The Rollout Needed Careful Phasing. With a triple task of building consumer penetration concurrently with a base of retail establishments, followed shortly afterward by a high-pressure drive to increase consumer usage, all types of selling activity had to be planned and mobilized in a scheme constructed with military precision. Personal selling, direct mail, promotions, and advertising all had to work together coherently and synergistically, all the individual communications making much of the appearance of the card, with the dark background and the bright o. (The card itself represents Discover's most pervasive communications vehicle). While it cannot realistically be claimed that the launch was dominated by the advertising, it is evident that some of the visual imagery generated in the advertising, notably the symbol of the rising sun, had an overall influence on all aspects of the communications effort and consequently a value beyond the commercials alone.

6. A Dual Constituency. With a new brand whose success depends on its appeal to two separate groups—retailers and customers, who must both accept the card if it is to be successful—the advertising must naturally appeal to both. (In this, the Discover case study bears a resemblance to certain others in this book—for example, Ford and Slice). The Discover campaign succeeded in appealing to both groups in its early stages, and it is entitled to a share of the credit for the rapid initial growth in the merchant base and in the consumer penetration.

7. Campaign Evolution. In common with many, if not most, brands in all product fields (for example, Campari, Mumm, *Kodak*, Listerine, Quaker Kibbles 'n Bits, and TSB), the advertising for the Discover Card was required to change in strategic emphasis from building penetration to encouraging usage. The need for this change represented the point of maximum sensitivity for the Discover Card campaign, and an important feature of this case is that this point arrived earlier than it did in most other cases.

The advertising, which had been very successful in building penetration and was also doing a good job in stimulating usage, was in addition required to contribute to the critical task of building—perhaps upgrading—the image of the Discover Card: necessary in order to provide a strong and clear differentiation from competitive cards. There was a dissonance between these tasks, and it was emphasized by the Discover Card's known association with Sears, Roebuck and Company, with its vast ubiquity and mass-market connotations.

15
The Ford Escort

> Detroit is mainly product-oriented, not consumer-oriented. To the extent that the consumer is recognized as having needs that the manufacturer should try to satisfy, Detroit usually acts as if the job can be done entirely by product changes.
>
> —Theodore Levitt[1]

"His Real Genius Was Marketing"[2]

The quotation that prefaces this chapter was published more than a quarter-century ago. So was the quotation that forms the heading for this first section; those words describe the acumen of Henry Ford I, founder of the Ford Motor Company. Both quotations come from Theodore Levitt's widely read article "Marketing Myopia," a succinct, well-illustrated, and persuasive synthesis of the marketing concept. As the reader will appreciate, this concept was not extensively employed in the American automobile industry in the 1950s.

The thrust of that part of Levitt's argument which describes the car industry is that the success of the industry's pioneers was based essentially on their ability to anticipate what the consumer wanted—reliable personal transportation at a very low price indeed—and the vast extent of the consumer demand made production-line manufacture economically viable. (Note the order of events.) As the industry grew, however, profits became increasingly dependent on the growing production economies that stemmed from the very large scale of operations. This gave the whole industry a powerful vested interest in its existing products, leading in turn to a practically irreversible—and in the event almost catastrophic—change of emphasis in management policy away from the needs of the consumer. This change did not go unnoticed by economists and journalists, but many of those observers—even figures as eminent as John Kenneth Galbraith—were seduced by the car industry's confidence in its apparent ability to manipulate its market.[3]

But such confidence was not to last forever. Although there were signals from the marketplace as early as the 1950s that sections of the American public were turning toward small cars, in the late 1960s the average gasoline mileage for the American motor industry was "a dreadful thirteen miles a gallon."[4] It was about this time that the American car industry began to lose serious, though not disastrous, amounts of market share to imports, especially to small models from Japan. But it was the shock of sharply increased gasoline prices in the early 1970s that was to provide a decisive extra pressure and urgency to this earlier situation of grumbling danger.

What made the problems of the major American car manufacturers especially difficult was the extended lead time—normally about four years—needed for planning and "tooling up" new models.[5] Neither was the situation helped by the kinds of power struggles that are often endemic to giant industrial enterprises. One such struggle within the Ford Motor Company during the 1970s—that between Henry Ford II and Lee Iacocca—was an underlying force beneath the prolonged dispute about whether the company should enter the American small-car market with the subcompact Ford Fiesta, a successful European design featuring front-wheel drive, or with downsized versions of Ford's larger American models.[6] It was this same power struggle that also defeated the unorthodox proposal—perhaps better viewed as one that was in advance of its time—for a joint venture in 1975 between Ford and Honda.[7]

One of the central causes of the dispute between Henry Ford II and Lee Iacocca centered on the technical feature of front-wheel drive, in particular, its specific cost benefit. Front-wheel drive was used in a number of imports on the American market during the 1970s and also, as noted, in the Ford Fiesta, which was enjoying high sales in Europe. Front-wheel drive is lighter, less cumbersome, and (once the manufacturing plant is installed) less costly than rear-wheel drive, the system that until the 1970s was the norm for cars produced in Detroit.[8] Front-wheel drive is also more energy efficient and—a particularly important feature—gives better traction in snow and slush, thus providing an obvious consumer advantage in the large regions of the United States that suffer severe winters. Tooling up for front-wheel drive, however, is an extremely expensive proposition, and the decision in the 1970s not to install this modern technology was made with the object of saving the Ford Motor Company an investment on the order of $2 billion.[9]

There is little doubt that this decision, taken before the second shock of increased gasoline prices that followed the dramatic events in Iran in 1979, was a major setback to Ford, especially since its major American competitors were moving fast to produce their own small cars, in some, though not all, cases with front-wheel drive.

Nevertheless, the size of the American automobile industry is so massive, its inertia so profound, and its financial reserves so substantial that the industry is able to ride successfully for quite prolonged periods the most adverse market pressures. (This is perhaps psychologically why the industry as a whole is so sluggish in its response to market changes.) Eventually, wiser counsels prevailed in the Ford Motor Company, although not before a painful delay. Four decisions made during the late 1970s and early 1980s combined to produce the long-term effect of dramatically transforming the fortunes of the company, making it by 1986 a significantly more profitable operation than General Motors, despite the fact that the latter's worldwide sales volume ($103 billion) was more than 60 percent greater than Ford's ($63 billion).[10] Those four decisions have an intimate bearing on this study.

The first was a move toward front-wheel drive. The pioneer model to use this technology was the Escort, which reached the American market in the fall of 1980 (for the 1981-model year). This early introduction was made possible through a dramatic reduction in production lead time, because the car had been designed and first manufactured in Europe, where Ford had successfully developed, with the Fiesta, the front-wheel drive technology. The Escort was followed by the midsize Tempo in 1983 (named Topaz when sold by Lincoln-Mercury) and by the larger Taurus in 1986 (the same basic design as the Lincoln-Mercury Sable).

The second decision, also influenced by Ford's European experience, was to move to radically more "liquid" streamlined designs. The Escort was not to benefit immediately from this move, but much of the success of the Tempo and Taurus has been attributed to their distinctive difference from the more boxy, hard-edged products of General Motors.[11]

The third decision was to embark on a major cost-cutting program. This was to have a significant long-term payout during the 1980s, when, as noted, Ford became more profitable than General Motors.

The fourth decision was arguably the most important of all. In response to incontrovertible and long-standing evidence that many car drivers were less than happy with Ford's product quality, the company began the onerous, expensive, and extended task of improving the finish and workmanship of all its cars and of policing this with rigorous inspection. The widely used advertising slogan "Quality Is Job One" was not puffery; on the contrary, it represented something real and important that was taking place on the Ford production lines. The effort yielded no results for two full years. Then in 1982, signals from the marketplace indicated that things were improving. As David Halberstam tells us in his best-selling book *The Reckoning,* "The warranty reports got better. Letters from owners became more positive."[12]

Although repeat purchase (and its intimate relationship with good product performance) is not as regular a source of business with automobiles as it is with packaged goods, neither is it a factor that car manufacturers can ignore without fear of the consequences. Indeed, Ford now puts a good deal of emphasis on repeat purchase. Obviously, the more satisfied customers are with their present Ford model, the more likely they are to buy a Ford again. It is indeed interesting that when the importance of efficient product performance—an article of faith in the marketing of packaged goods[13]—eventually began to make an impact on the consciousness of the automobile industry, it contributed to a reversal of fortunes for the Ford Motor Company that was little short of dramatic.

This study is concerned with the launch and continued success of the Ford Escort, a model that from the beginning has led the way in the renaissance in Ford's fortunes. Although the story is of an advertising success, in evaluating it we should keep a broad focus and be continuously aware of Bill Bernbach's words that "it's the product itself that's all important."[14]

"A Brand-New World Car"[15]

When the Ford Escort was launched, it was not received well by the motoring press, on the grounds of its supposed sloppy handling and lack of power.[16] Although the car has subsequently been improved to deal with these problems, it is fair to say that they did not at any time trouble the public, who liked the Escort from the beginning; indeed, their liking was so strong that the Escort became the largest selling automobile in the United States in 1982.[17] It also earned the professional respect of Ford's competitors—witness the following extract from a contemporary appraisal by one of them: "It is the only domestic front-wheel-drive econobox coupe actually competing against the real import strength: Toyota Corolla, Datsun B210, Honda Civic, and Volkswagen Rabbit. The car is honestly represented in its advertising and is priced competitively."[18] From the beginning, the Escort design was also sold by Lincoln-Mercury, using the Lynx name. The Lynx is sold at a price averaging $600 more than the Escort, and although it is successful in the marketplace, its rate of sale is less than 20 percent of the Escort's. This study concentrates on the latter, as the more typical mass-market expression of the basic product concept.

The Escort was recognized by the public as offering modern engineering, good workmanship, interior space, fuel economy, and inexpensive servicing backed by the vast Ford dealer network, as well as a low sticker price and reasonably good resale value.[19] If the exterior design of the car lacks the smooth lines of the Tempo and Taurus, which were to follow the Escort onto the market, it at least gives a strong impression of gutsy practicality and strength. And from the first there was glamour stemming from the Escort's international origins, because it was indeed the pioneer car to be manufactured simultaneously in a number of international centers, thereby making it the first "World Car"—a concept recognized and conceptualized by J. Walter Thompson and effectively exploited in the consumer advertising.[20]

(The common international design does not, however, extend to standard-ization of parts and components. But this is a technical matter and probably does not affect consumers' perceptions of the Escort as a "World Car.")

Let us now consider the market at which the Escort was directed, and evaluate in specific terms its considerable success.

The basic shape of the automobile market is simple to describe. According to U.S. government statistics (1980 data):

> 17.7% of households own 3+ vehicles
> 33.9% of households own 2+ vehicles
> 35.7% of households own 1 vehicle
> 12.8% of households own no vehicle

In 1980, there were 161.6 million motor vehicles on the road (159.1 million privately owned), and of this total, 121.7 million were passenger cars, the remaining 39.9 million being trucks, motorcycles, and buses.[21] The market shows little annual growth, the most typical estimate of annual market de-velopment being +1 to +2 percent in 1987.[22] (These relatively low figures should not make us forget, however, that even a 1 percent growth means an increase of $100 million in sales value; such is the vast size of the car mar-ket.) Annual sales of passenger cars are currently running at a level of 11.2 million vehicles.[23]

The market is large, mature, and stationary. This last—and most im-portant—point refers to a stable level of overall sales, plus a relative degree of uniformity in the aggregate brand shares of the leading manufacturers. One element contributing to this stability is, of course, the upper limit (de-termined by government agreement) of Japanese imports—currently 2.3 mil-lion vehicles per year.[24]

Simple market segmentation—the division of markets into subgroups based either on the functional characteristics of the brands in the market or on the demographic or psychographic characteristics of brand users—is a common planning tool in packaged goods marketing. In these markets, func-tional segmentation is the most reliable technique. There is a good reason for this. If, as normally happens, consumers buy brands in different market segments on a regular basis, it is difficult to allocate these consumers into discrete categories in their brand buying. This means that demographic/psy-chographic segmentation, although frequently carried out, is often based either on impure data or on arbitrary assumptions about consumers' brand preferences.[25]

The automobile market is, however, different from that for packaged goods. As we have seen, a substantial number of car owners (41 percent of the total) possess only one vehicle. This is the equivalent of "sole buyers" in packaged goods (the numbers of whom are mostly minuscule).[26] In addition, 39 percent of car owners own two vehicles. We do not have full knowledge of the multibrand buying that goes into the composition of "family fleets." But there are many instances (although probably in total a minority) in which the second car is in a market segment similar to that of the first.

These facts about the car industry that demonstrate a relatively high level of single-brand ownership open the door to using demographic and psychographic positioning as a reliable tool to describe buyers of particular types of cars and of specific car models. These techniques have been explored extensively, and JWT Detroit has constructed a market model that comprises as many as twenty-three demographic/psychographic groups of owners. This model represents one of the major points of interest of this study, and we will outline its construction. The description is simplified for ease of exposition and also to veil certain confidential aspects of the analysis.[27]

The essence of the model is its ability to relate market segments covering specific categories of vehicle (and within these, specific models) to consumer groups. These groups are defined demographically: age, income, and education being the most important criteria. The demographic classifications are also extrapolated, with the help of additional research, into psychographic territory—to take account of life-style and attitudinal groupings.

The stages in constructing the model can be summarized as follows:

1. The population is grouped into eight categories according to people's career paths and the stage they have reached in these paths. The first determinant of career progress is education, but age and income later become important additional measures. Although the eight categories are determined essentially by demographic criteria, psychographic elements are now gradually introduced into the description of these groups.

2. These eight groups are then related to specific market segments. We are able to pin down, as far as possible, how far each group concentrates on particular types of cars. Some interesting patterns emerge from this analysis, and they in turn are used for the next stages.

3. The market segments are now refined, and eight specific car categories, based on size and price, are isolated. These categories are Large, Luxury, Upper Middle, Middle Specialty, Low Middle, Mini Van, Small Specialty, and Basic Small.

4. The categories of consumers are also refined, to include a stronger psychographic emphasis (although this still remains basically an extension of the demographic data, which are full and reliable). Four categories emerge, and these pertain not so much to people's education, age, and income as to the conservatism of their tastes and preferences. It is also possible to quantify the proportion of the automobile market accounted for by each of these groups:

People with:

Mature Values	28.0% of the market	(stable)
Traditional Values	27.0% of the market	(declining)
Bridge Values	15.5% of the market	
embracing some features of Traditional and New		(growing)
New Values	29.5% of the market	(growing)

5. Eight car groups and four consumer groups should theoretically yield thirty-two subcategories (or cells.) Not all the groups of consumers, however, buy all types of cars, a factor that reduces the final number of categories to twenty-three.

6. The final analysis enables us to categorize the buyers of the leading 134 models sold in the United States. (These represent far and away the greatest percentage of automobiles sold, although the total market actually includes more than 300 different cars.) Each named category (the names also being given psychographic meanings) covers a market segment. These segments embrace 6 models on average, although the number of cars in the segments vary from 3 to 12.

7. This categorization of buyers makes it possible for us to see which car models actually compete with which. Very importantly, this comparison is seen from the angle of the consumer. We can also get some idea of the selling arguments that must be reinforced if a car is ever to be projected outside its basic category, a prospect that can represent an important long-term marketing opportunity for models that—like the Escort—have reached high levels of consumer ownership and already dominate their basic category.

8. The analysis is from first to last based on sound and extensive empirical data, and it is as statistically robust as it is thought-provoking.

How does the Escort fit into all this?

The Escort is in the Basic Small category. Its buyers are mainly people with Traditional Values. The combination of these two categories yields a fairly large consumer group, called the Practical Plus, which accounts for 11.2 percent of total car sales. (The measurement of the market is in car units; the figure would be smaller if it were by value.) The simple demographics of people in the Practical Plus category are as follows:

Age. Median of 36. This is in the youngest quartile of car buyers.

Income. Median $30,000. This is in the lowest income category. (People who earn less tend to buy used cars).

Education. Thirty-five percent have received advanced education. This is almost halfway up the car buyers' education table.

Other demographics. Forty-seven percent of Escort buyers are women. Escort buyers have a professional and white-collar orientation.

In short, Practical Plus buyers in general and Ford Escort buyers in particular have a low income compared with that of other buyers of new cars. But they are young; substantial numbers have received advanced education; and many are in professional jobs. What all this points to is that the Escort is a car for young families with their feet on a vertical ladder—a target group of rather obvious present and long-term potential.

The Practical Plus category comprises, besides the Escort and the Lynx, nine directly competitive vehicles:

General Motors. Chevette, Pontiac 1000, Spectrum, Sprint

Chrysler. Horizon, Omni

AMC/Renault. Alliance

Nissan. Sentra

Yugo. Yugo

Total sales in the market segment amounted to 1.2 million cars in the 1986 model year—a number substantially unchanged from the 1985 level. The Escort's strength was maintained, and with sales of 416,000 units in 1986, it was responsible for 35 percent of total category sales. Its nearest rival, the Nissan Sentra, accounted for only 14 percent.[28] The reasons for the Escort's comparative strength are discussed later in this chapter.

"Honestly Represented in its Advertising"[29]

The advertising for automobiles, like that for most durable goods with a high ticket price, has traditionally been characterized by what advertising professionals describe as product orientation. (Contrast the advertising for most packaged goods, which concentrates mainly on end benefits for the consumer—for example, deliciousness and nutrition for breakfast cereals, white teeth for toothpaste, and clean clothes for laundry detergents). Although automobiles are a means to an end (this, of course being speedy, safe transportation), the advertising has always concentrated essentially on these *means*. This generalization applies even to what has always been considered the most innovative advertising in the field, such as the Getchell advertising for Plymouth in the 1930s; the Doyle, Dane, Bernbach Volkswagen campaigns; and the Ogilvy advertising for Rolls-Royce. In these cases, the new ground broken by the campaigns was essentially a matter of concentration on selected product features; it was in no way a departure from the use of product features as the basic creative strategy.

There are a number of reasons for this product orientation, including the sensory and emotional rewards for the consumer from a car's appearance and styling, as well as certain rather subtle rewards connected with its mechanical features. Among these rewards are the provision of discriminating benefits for the rather small number of technically oriented car buyers and arguments needed by many buyers for postrationalization of a major purchase decision with the object of reducing any latent cognitive dissonance.[30] (This is an important reason that press advertising for cars has long technical copy, which often impresses nontechnical readers as much by its length as by its content.)

Like all other car advertising, that for the Ford Escort has always concentrated on product features. Indeed, the initial campaigns, exposed in 1981–1983 and launching the Escort as the "World Car," were based on a straightforward amalgam of its product features and (an increasing) emphasis on the Escort's popularity with the public. In 1983, the advertising went the last step and made the powerful claim that the Escort was number one in America and number one in the world and that (no less importantly) "nine out of ten Escort owners would buy it again."

It is, however, a later campaign—one that was first run in 1983 and derivations of which have been used for most of the time since then—that had the greatest effect in the marketplace. This is the advertising that will be evaluated most fully in this study. This campaign (which uses the Johann Strauss waltz "The Blue Danube" as the rather unlikely background music on the sound track) has one important difference from the previous Escort advertising and an even more substantial point of departure from the general run of advertising in the automobile field.

The first point of difference—that relating to the earlier Escort advertising—is that the Escort's closest competitors are actually shown in the television commercials. (In some of the earlier advertisements, competitors had been mentioned in the voice-over, but comparisons had gone no further than that.) Since the strategy of the "Blue Danube" campaign had originated in the isolation of the Escort's specific competitors through the segmentation analysis described earlier in this chapter, it is a natural extension of this strategy for comparison with competitors to form an important feature of the campaign. The comparisons are, however, understated. The competitors are usually not even named, although they are clearly shown. The commentary refers to them in a lighthearted, even friendly fashion; one competitor featured to demonstrate the superior gas mileage of the Escort is even a Japanese motorcycle.

A consistent attempt is made to avoid a hectoring, aggressive approach—a style of advertising that is regrettably still rather common in car advertising all over the world. This brings us to the second, and even more important, feature of the Escort campaign.

The advertising has a highly distinctive aura and atmosphere. The commentator is friendly and accessible and manages to prod the television viewer in a cajoling fashion into making comparisons between the Escort and the competitive cars shown in the films. The commentary treats the viewer as an intelligent person, someone who brings something to the communication and will not respond to being browbeaten. The distinctive atmosphere of the commercials also applies to their relaxed pace. Various Escort models are shown being driven left-to-right and right-to-left across the screen—at first slowly, and then in some cases progressively quickly—and passing the competition parked at the curbside, competition whose inferiority to the Escort is being described in the commentary. The tempo of the "Blue Danube" fits the pace of the commercials surprisingly appropriately, and it adds not only a quality of ease and familiarity but also an edge of distinctiveness.

In all the commercials, the Escort's technical features (front-wheel drive, four-wheel independent suspension, rack-and-pinion steering) are mentioned in the voice-over, together with the more familiar and easily understood consumer benefits of gasoline economy and interior space. All these features are introduced in a low-key way. From quantified consumer research into the commercials, the general performance and quality come through strongly, and—not surprisingly, in view of the unique tone of the campaign—brand awareness consistently exceeds the norms for the product field.[31]

Some commercials concentrate virtually exclusively on specific features. One film, made in 1985 and entitled *Bumper Cars,* shows a number of close-up shots of the Escort's bumpers doing their job gracefully, to the "Blue Danube" music, in order to make the point of the car's safety and durability—and its ability to attract favorable rates from Sears, Roebuck's Allstate Insurance Company. But throughout the campaign, despite detailed variations in the types of claims, there is absolute uniformity of the all-important tone of voice.

The Escort advertising has always been exposed at a competitive rate.[32] By 1983, this was running at $33 million, representing 2.8 percent of the total volume of consumer advertising expenditure in the automobile industry. In 1984, the Escort budget had come down to a more economic level of $20 million. Thereafter, reflecting rising sales, the expenditure increased to $26 million in 1985 and (an estimated) $41 millions in 1986. The latter figure accounts for a share of voice in the total automobile category of 2.8 percent, precisely the same ratio as in 1983.

The 1986 budget was spent in the following media:

Television network	58%
Television spot	13%

Television cable		1%
Radio spot		1%
Outdoor		1%
Magazines		23%
Newspapers		3%
	Total	100%

The concentration on network television is normal in the automobile field, as it is in most mass markets. The deployment of a substantial proportion of the budget in more selective media (especially the 24 percent spent on magazines and cable television), however, is in harmony with the demographic targeting that has always been an important characteristic of the Escort campaign. Indeed, it is a manifestation of what Ford President Donald E. Petersen described as Ford's overall media strategy in 1981: "[T]he time is past when one could create a single great mass message and reach millions of consumers effectively."[33]

The advertising-to-sales ratio in the automobile industry normally brackets 1 percent, although the data on which this estimate is based are not analyzed by the value of the sales of different car models.[34] In terms of numbers of vehicles, the Escort represented 3.7 percent of total car sales (both domestically produced cars and imports) during the 1986-model year.[35] Bearing in mind that the Escort has a relatively low sticker price (which means that its market share by value would almost certainly be below 3.7 percent), its advertising-to-sales ratio is probably marginally above the overall industry average. This suggests that the Escort's current advertising budget represents a conscious investment in the Escort as a brand, especially since its profitability probably still remains low.[36]

The World's Best-Selling Car

Worldwide sales of the Escort were a massive 940,000 units in 1986.[37] Sales in the United States totaled 416,000 (plus 72,000 Lynx). The car had been an immediate success when it was launched, achieving sales of more than a quarter-million vehicles in 1981.[38] Annual sales grew more or less progressively to the current level, which in turn shows no sign of flagging.

It is difficult to deny that the launch and the growth of the Escort have been very impressive achievements. It is also difficult to argue against the proposition that its success has been due in the main to its being the correct product for the market. The Escort's engineering, its economy, its design— notably the glamour that stemmed from its being the first "World Car"— made it the right car for its time. Its continued success over its seven-year history is the strongest possible evidence of consumer satisfaction, which is expressed both in repeat purchase and in favorable word-of-mouth communication from owner to potential buyer.

It is also fairly certain that advertising has made a contribution to the Escort's progress. The low advertising-to-sales ratios in the automotive field sometimes create the impression that consumer advertising is a low-priority activity in that field. But it should be remembered that these ratios are applied to huge dollar sales volumes, which means that advertising budgets for car models can be very large indeed. The 1986 Escort budget of $41 million would be considered massive for a brand of packaged goods. Not surprisingly, it is among the four largest advertising budgets for all individual car models on the United States market.

Perhaps even more important than the quantitative aspect of the Escort campaign is the advertising's creative content. The campaign, certainly during the past five years of the Escort's greatest success, had an absolute distinctiveness that set it apart from all other advertising in the field. The campaign has been persuasive, yet in its understated way it has reflected its target group of ambitious and well-educated young people with progressive careers.

The last word regarding the Escort should, however, recapitulate the crucial point that the Escort, like the rest of the Ford range in the 1980s, has high product quality. This is something whose importance is far wider than a single product field. It is, in fact, a "red thread" that runs through the majority of successful advertising case histories.

An anonymous Ford executive made the most telling statement about the Escort in this regard:

> The first real effort we made to improve our quality came when we started the Escort line. . . . There were 7,500 [interior door] panels in the shipment. We rejected nearly 5,000 of them. The vendor was in a state of shock. He'd been using the same quality standards for years, but suddenly they didn't apply anymore. Frankly we'd been making do with second-rate work for years.[39]

Five Lessons from the History of the Ford Escort

1. The Right Car for Its Time. During the latter part of the 1970s, the American automobile industry made enormous efforts to produce well-designed small models that could compete effectively with Japanese imports. By the intensity of its effort, it made up to some degree for its late start. The Ford Motor Company won the race with the Escort, this despite the belatedness of the decision by the company to proceed with front-wheel-drive engineering. But Ford managed to make up for lost time by exploiting technical and design innovations that it had made successfully in Europe. The Escort, the first "World Car," had the engineering, the economy, the reliability, the design, and the low sticker price that the American public wanted. And the public responded immediately. The technical specification for the Escort has also not remained static; indeed, over its seven years on the American market, there have been a substantial number of engineering improvements.

2. **"Quality Is Job One"**. The general strengthening in the position of the Ford Motor Company during the 1980s was attributable to at least four factors, the most important of which was the rigorous effort made to improve product quality: one that (after two years' lead time) resulted in a major upgrading in public attitudes toward Ford products. In this improvement, the Escort led the way, and the importance of superior product quality to its success cannot be overestimated. One of the major favorable outcomes of the emphasis on product quality is that now that enough time has elapsed, there is repeat purchase. And word-of-mouth has been favorable since the time of the car's introduction.

3. **Demographic/Psychographic Targeting.** Because multibrand buying is not a majority activity in the automobile field, it is possible to analyze car buyers reliably in terms of their demographic and psychographic characteristics, and as a result, demographic and psychographic clusters can be used to isolate target groups for car types and specific models. JWT Detroit has advanced this technique and demonstrated its operational value. As an example, the definitions both of the target group for the Escort and of the group of cars with which the Escort directly competes in the eyes of the consumer provided a secure platform for the Escort advertising. This type of initial marketing analysis has been carried further with the Escort than with any other case in this book.

4. **A Distinctive Tone of Voice for the Escort Campaign.** The Escort campaign was written on the basis of a sound understanding of the consumer and of the competition. But the distinctiveness of the campaign, especially the advertisements exposed since 1983, has been based on an unusual combination of strong product claims and an understated tone of voice. This tone of voice is, however, very much in harmony with the target group: educated young people with relatively low incomes but on an upward career path. The Escort is perhaps not the only car directed at such a target group. What is remarkable about the campaign is that it makes it *seem* that the Escort is the only car targeted at these consumers.

5. A Realistic Budget Level. The increases since 1984 in the Escort's advertising budget, reflecting growing sales, have acted as a reinforcement of success. The 1986 budget of $41 million was a major investment, bearing in mind that it was the Escort's seventh year—a time when many manufacturers might have been inclined to cut advertising to boost profit. The sum of $41 million probably represented an above-average advertising-to-sales ratio in comparison with the rest of the automobile industry, and the seriousness of this investment was thrown into higher relief by the Escort's continued low profitability. This budget was, however, a strong confirmation that client and agency then visualized—and continue to anticipate—continued success and also a long-term future for the first "World Car."

16
Goodyear Corporate

I don't know who you are.
I don't know your company.
I don't know your company's product.
I don't know what your company stands for.
I don't know your company's customers.
I don't know your company's record.
I don't know your company's reputation.
Now—what was it you wanted to sell me?
—Advertisement for McGraw-Hill Magazines[1]

"The Positive Values in Familiarity"[2]

The copy for the McGraw-Hill advertisement that prefaces this chapter, accompanied as it was by a stark cutout photograph of a sour and skeptical-looking businessman in an office chair, created a notable impact in advertising circles when it first appeared more than twenty years ago. It forms an apposite introduction to a case that—unlike any other in this book—illustrates the value to a manufacturer of its corporate reputation: how well the corporation is known and what it stands for in the public estimation.

The subject of this study, the Goodyear Tire and Rubber Company, is the brand leader in the automobile tire market and one of the hundred leading advertisers in the United States. Goodyear had an overall advertising budget of $162 million in 1986, derived from a domestic sales value of $5.8 billion ($9.1 billion worldwide). From these figures it can be seen that the company's advertising-to-sales ratio was 2.8 percent, an above-average figure in the automotive field.[3]

The reader may be puzzled about how such a well-established and substantial organization, which holds more than 30 percent of the U.S. tire market and whose main product is a household name, could have experienced any problems in communicating its corporate identity. And the skeptical reader may also ask whether such problems are anyway a matter of much importance. We shall be discussing the first of these points later in this study, but we shall start by attempting to answer the second one and shall evaluate it with the help of some substantial factual data.

This information comes from a piece of research carried out by Yankelovich Clancy Shulman in 1986, on behalf of Brouillard Communications, the J. Walter Thompson subsidiary that specializes in corporate communications and that handles the Goodyear corporate account.[4] The research, aimed at assessing the value of a company's communications with its public (or "publics"), was based on 1,038 personal interviews:

- 655 with affluent consumers (people with incomes of more than $50,000; 20 percent having incomes of $100,000; and 75 percent being investors)
- 217 with corporate executives (people in companies with $100 million revenues or more; 86 percent being decision makers in those companies)
- 62 with directors of the top fifty brokerage firms
- 104 with portfolio managers from the top one-hundred investment institutions

This spread of respondents reminds us that there are many audiences ("publics") for a company's corporate communications. They include not only actual and potential stockholders and their advisers but also the company's customers, suppliers, and employees; politicians; journalists; and the public as a whole.

Before the interviews took place, pilot qualitative work examined a number of specific companies and drew up a short list of those with excellent corporate reputations. These were provisionally identified as winners (the best description that emerged for the kinds of companies the research was intended to examine). Most importantly, the attributes contributing to the winner's status were tentatively isolated. The 1,038 respondents also had views on the importance of those attributes, as we shall shortly discover.

Although we shall give here only a truncated summary of the main conclusions of the research, this general information will help us to put into perspective the specifics of the Goodyear corporate case. The research interviews covered three main areas of investigation, the first two of them being mere preliminaries to the third. But we will summarize all three parts, starting with the two less important areas.

The Rewards of Being a Winning Company

The respondents were asked to consider and evaluate specific companies, some winners and some not. (The word *winner* and indeed the notion that some companies were different from others were not, of course, introduced into the questioning, because of the bias that doing so would have introduced at this early stage). Each of the companies was judged according to the following four criteria:

1. whether the respondents would be "very likely" to buy a new product from a company

2. how much they would be prepared to invest in the stock of the company
3. whether they would recommend that manufacturing plant for the company be located in their home area
4. whether they would recommend a family member to work for the company

The thrust of the respondents' judgments was clear and unambiguous. The companies identified as winners had a consistent edge over the nonwinners in the minds of all four groups of people. And the margin of preference was in every case quite large—in a number of instances, two to one or even more.

There is nothing very surprising about these findings. They are in a sense tautological, a mere confirmation that the winning companies had been reasonably well identified beforehand. But identification of the *qualities* that actually make a winner in any decisive sense is a more complex matter; the second and third parts of the investigation were devoted to exploring it.

What People Say Makes a Winning Reputation

The respondents were next shown a list of attributes bearing on the winning reputation of a company and asked to rate each attribute on a six-point scale, ranging from "not at all important" to "absolutely critical." There was no mention of specific companies, merely a total of fifteen different attributes in the abstract. What emerged was unanimity between the four groups of respondents about the particular importance of the following:

- quality service
- honesty and ethics
- quality products
- high-caliber management
- flexibility

There was also support for the following attributes, but with less than unanimity:

- clearly defined goals
- good value
- concern for employees
- staying power
- financial performance

It is an interesting characteristic of this type of research—so much of which is carried out both in the United States and overseas—that respondents will generally produce the answers that are expected of them. These tend to be rational rather than "gut." But since we know that gut reaction often influences behavior, rational (or rationalized) answers are often rather misleading. Indeed, most of the responses to this part of the research could almost have been predicted in advance. These "blinding flashes of the obvious" confirm some of the things we may intuitively believe about winning companies, and knowledge of such things may have a limited value. But they are much less useful in helping us *discriminate* between the winning companies and the others. Fortunately, the research did not end here.

Yankelovich Clancy Shulman has a high reputation and much experience in the field of tracking public attitudes, and in the third part of the investigation they found a way of getting below the surface to ferret out some more unusual truths.

What Differentiates Winning Companies?

The approach that distinguished this third part of the inquiry from the second was that the respondents were now asked first to think about specific companies and then to rate them as to how well they were judged to be winners. The questioning then turned to the attributes of these specific companies, and by means of a multivariate regression, the attributes influencing people's choice of winners were coaxed out of the statistical analysis. This procedure ensured not only that there was a direct empirical basis for the evaluation of attributes but also that those which discriminated were scientifically isolated.

What emerged from this procedure was rather unexpected. Among a number of attributes considered important, one unusual discriminator came out that distinguished the winning companies from the others. This was the quality of a company's communications.

In the second part of the investigation, people had been asked to respond from the "top of the mind," which led them to give the sort of rational and sensible answers they thought were expected of them; in these circumstances, effective communications were dismissed as a relatively insubstantial and unimportant matter. Yet when people were asked, in the third part of the research, to think about specific companies, all the factors entering into their choices had an equal chance of consideration. Good communications floated to the top of the list of attributes. This does not mean that good communications are all that matter. But good communications added on top of other favorable features make a major difference.

Their importance, defined in this way, was no surprise to Brouillard Communications. Indeed, according to Brouillard, it "ties in with a traditional corporate communications axiom: familiarity breeds favorability. . . . Among all audiences, if a respondent felt he knew a company well, he was much more likely to rate that company a winner."[5] This finding applied to all the groups of respondents, and in the case of the affluent consumers, a known company was rated a winner by two and a half times as many respondents as an unknown company. Also—rather significantly—Brouillard stated that "every single company in the study which was rated overall as a winner was credited with having good communications."[6]

This research, with its rather unexpected conclusion, provides an appropriate starting point for our evaluation of the situation facing the Goodyear Tire and Rubber Company in 1982.

"The Amiable Goliath"[7]

The problem with Goodyear's corporate communications was not so much that the company was unknown as that people had a one-sided and somewhat distorted perception of it. This meant that the task was to modify rather than build perceptions about the company, a task often regarded as even more difficult than building "from the ground up."

The Goodyear corporate advertising that had been run during the 1970s and until 1982 was communication with an undeniably high profile. It was aimed at the task of keeping the Goodyear name in people's minds during the long period of time between their buying one set of tires and their buying the next. The commercials featured the Goodyear Blimp as the symbol of protection, of "Goodyear watching over us." The commercials themselves were warm, human, and witty—showing, for instance, a newly married couple in a car, or a pair of nuns driving along with the Goodyear Blimp hovering in guardian attendance. The commercials won a number of advertising awards and produced very high consumer recall. As discussed in connection with a number of the cases in this collection, this is a matter about whose value we have considerable skepticism, except in limited circumstances. [8]

Despite the popularity of the campaign with the public and in advertising circles and despite the general support it received within the Goodyear organization, the newly appointed Goodyear chief executive officer, Robert E. Mercer, requested in 1982 that the objectives of the campaign be carefully reevaluated. In particular, he questioned whether the campaign was doing all the jobs that a corporate campaign for Goodyear should have been doing. This is the sort of intermittent questioning of basics that is healthy in good client-agency relationships. And it prompted Brouillard to reappraise the basic communications tasks for Goodyear in a most rigorous fashion.

To help this reappraisal, a research technique was used that, although relatively common in the field of consumer goods, was much less often practiced in research about manufacturing companies. The technique is based on interviews with members of the public, who are asked to describe brands (or, in this case, companies) in human terms: "If Campbell's soup were a person, what sort of person would he or she be? What age and sex and income? What does he or she look like? What sort of character and temperament does he or she have?" Respondents are encouraged to talk freely, at their own pace and in their own words.

Brouillard has had long experience with this technique, and the general feeling about it is that, if carefully handled, it can be applied with as good an effect to companies like Goodyear as to brands like Campbell's. Consumers can be persuaded, even in front of a videotape camera, to shake loose some interesting and original ideas and to provide, without much prompting, numerous insights into the image of a brand or company that are both interesting to the researcher and illuminating to the client and agency. One characteristic of this type of research that makes it ring true is that brands and companies are normally seen as having a mixture of good and bad features in people's minds. There is almost always a downside to people's favorable impressions, which normally comes through with surprising consistency from the responses of numbers of different men and women. The name used to describe this research technique is "Who Is a Company?" It has, over the years, provided extensive and generally constructive information that has been of direct help to Brouillard Communications and a number of its clients.

In the case of Goodyear, there was no doubt that people knew a good deal about the company. Goodyear was considered "big," "reliable," "nice," and "responsible." But it was seen as rather dull, particularly in comparison with Michelin, a French tire firm that had a smaller tire share in the United States but was perceived by the public as "dashing and European," "exciting and interesting." Goodyear was seen as important in the tire field but not in any way an innovative organization.

Another important finding of this research was that although Goodyear was widely known for its tires, people were simply not aware that the company was becoming an increasingly technologically driven operation, as well as a dynamically diversified one. The change of pace within the organization was in fact influencing the mainstream tire business, with a growing use, for instance, of electron microscopes, lasers, and computers to measure the ways tires wear out. And it was also influencing the organic growth of the company into related but new fields—moving, for instance, from synthetic rubber into plastics, with products ranging from synthetic arteries and mechanical hearts to bulletproof materials and large bottles for soft drinks (sometimes impolitely referred to as hernia packs because of their size).

The products of the company were widely spread in 1982—even more than they are today—and included important interests in aerospace and energy. (These interests, unfortunately, had to be closed down to help finance a stock buy-back in response to a hostile—but unsuccessful—takeover bid in 1985.[9] Nevertheless, the business of the Goodyear Tire and Rubber Company during the 1980s remains far wider than tires and rubber alone.) But the public in 1982 was shown to be completely unaware of this considerable breadth. This lack of awareness set an urgent new task for the company's corporate communications.

"Here's Goodyear as a Little Guy"[10]

Not surprisingly, the findings of the research caused client and agency to return to the advertising drawing board. It was judged that a more radical approach was needed than fine-tuning the existing campaign. Brouillard, working in close cooperation with the Goodyear Public Relations Department, developed a range of fresh campaign ideas, of which seven were formally presented for the client's evaluation. After fairly extensive consideration and discussion, the client eventually agreed to proceed with a highly unorthodox creative concept, one that was far distant in tone from earlier Goodyear corporate advertising. This had portrayed Goodyear as a Goliath; the new advertising aimed to portray the company more as a David.

The most unusual feature of the new campaign was its use of animation—in particular, a very spare, stripped-down, abstract style of animation. In each film, three amorphously shaped characters representing conventional wisdom use the phrase *"They say* that . . ."* to tell us about the things that can or cannot be done (most commonly, the latter). There is also a fourth cartoon character—a busy technician who stands for Goodyear—who says and demonstrates the opposite of what the other characters say.

The idea is simple but highly unusual for the field of corporate communications, which is normally extremely serious in tone. It is also extraordinarily pregnant, in that it can be used to promote an endless series of products which Goodyear makes but about which most people know (or knew) little. In this fecundity, it is the opposite of the Goodyear Blimp, which was—by the values built into it during a long-running advertising campaign—a symbol specifically tied to Goodyear tires. (In all the cartoon commercials, a Goodyear Blimp appears drawn in the same style of animation, and this representation has been gradually adapted as a more versatile symbol to stand for the broad range of Goodyear products. But we do not know how well it has succeeded in broadening the communication in this way.)

There is also a not-unimportant use of humor as an attention-getting device. Humor was a part of the earlier "Blimp" campaign, but it was not central to it, being added essentially by the dialogue in the individual commercials, which had a rather understated wit. With the cartoon campaign,

They say a new roof is messy and expensive. But Goodyear said, "Top this," and invented a synthetic rubber roofing that simply rolls on and seals with a hot air blower. Waterproof. Weatherproof. It comes in black. And in white to reflect the sun and save energy. It's fast, easy and economical for schools, factories and buildings anywhere.

They say you have to give up comfort to wear dress shoes. But Goodyear said, "Try this on for size," and created Wingfoot SP™ replacement heels. They absorb 87 percent of heel-strike shock. So your feet can feel as good as they look.

They say you can still train pilots in a flight trainer that teaches only instrument flying. But Goodyear said, "Obsolete," and helped create a new flight simulator that gives pilots the sights as well as the feel and sound of flying. And with computerized projectors that react to a pilot's every move, the sky is the limit.

See all the dynamite things you can do when you don't listen to what "they" say.

GOOD*Y*YEAR

Newspaper advertisement first run in *The Wall Street Journal* in September, 1986.

by contrast, the idea is intrinsically humorous, while still allowing the copy to make serious points about Goodyear.

In one commercial, in the voice of the animated characters, the audio goes: *"They say* there's just no way to make today's lighter cars ride like yesterday's heavy cars." This provides the opportunity to tell the story of Goodyear's airsprings for lighter cars. In another, the statement *"They say* it takes a big computer company to build a big computer" introduces the story of the Goodyear computer that was built for NASA. In a third commercial, the statement "To photograph the earth's resources from the air, *they say* you need a camera that can see through clouds" is followed by a description of how Goodyear went ahead and solved the problem with their radar. In another, the words *"They say* there's no easy way to move California oil to Texas refineries" is rebutted by "until Goodyear built a pipeline." And in yet another, the statement *"They say* a new roof is a big deal" leads to the story of Goodyear roofing, with its special synthetic rubber strips that can be rapidly rolled out and heat-sealed to make a secure, weatherproof roof for schools, factories, or a domestic garage or shed.

For each of these very different products, Goodyear's answer is similar: "So much for what *they say.*" "We say, 'Is that so?' " "Want to bet?" "Let's try a new way." "Let's break new ground." "Try and top this." The tone of the copy is light, its quality of understatement similar to that of the earlier campaign featuring the Blimp. Experts who say no are familiar figures to most people; there is an instinctive sympathy with someone who shows such experts to be wrong.

The format of the advertising is unifying, in that the range of products and the all-important Goodyear identity are communicated to the television viewer when he or she sees a number of commercials in the series. The media weight of approximately $7 million per year is large enough to ensure a reasonably high average level of "opportunities to see," especially since the media are targeted to men—and in particular, to the fairly homogeneous demographic group of businessmen. To achieve effective targeting, the media are concentrated in sports television programs and a limited print schedule composed of the *Wall Street Journal, Business Week, Forbes,* and *Fortune.* Much of the television buying is made on short notice, because such opportunism can increase the media cost-efficiency sometimes dramatically.

The campaign has an undeniable impact that comes from its very unorthodoxy in the otherwise rather straight-faced field of corporate communications. By its humorous and unexaggerated tone of voice, it seems to have succeeded—in line with the original strategy—in putting across the points that Goodyear is more nimble, exciting, and technologically oriented than people had previously imagined and that Goodyear is a company that makes many more things than automobile tires.

When the campaign was first exposed, it acted (perhaps surprisingly) as a direct stimulus to the Goodyear business. There is evidence that Goodyear was now being asked to bid for many more government contracts than formerly, because the advertising had increased awareness of the width of the product range. This was true of the Goodyear aerospace business and of Goodyear rubber roofing. When the rubber-roof commercial appeared on television in various Christmas holiday football programs in 1985, it generated a huge number of inquiries (three hundred on the first day of exposure), including an invitation to bid for roofing for all the schools in Texas: "Our roofing sales people have collected millions of dollars in orders they can trace directly to this commercial."[11]

The data about such sales successes are anecdotal. They are nevertheless extensive enough over a five-year period to have convinced Goodyear of the value of the campaign. The company feels strongly enough about the advertising idea to employ the cartoon characters in many of its own communications with the financial community. The 1984 annual report featured them.

The campaign is still working to modify and broaden the public's perceptions of Goodyear, and there are positive signals (for instance, from repeats of the "Who Is a Company?" research) that it is moving people's awareness and attitudes in the right direction, although the job has naturally not yet been completed. An interesting and important side effect of the campaign is that there have been a number of reports that it has stimulated public interest in buying Goodyear stock. Goodyear itself reported, "One letter from a broker cited the campaign as the catalyst behind the sale of over 300,000 shares to his local customers alone."[12]

The word *catalyst* is interesting in this context. By using it, the broker was acknowledging that although stock buyers may evaluate a company by a number of criteria, it takes a dramatic piece of communication to increase the salience of that company in their minds and to turn latent interest into action. The value of such communications is naturally just as great to all the company's "publics," including the public as a whole, as it is to its actual and potential stockholders. It is however only possible with stockholders to evaluate the result of such communications in behavioral terms. But if a company's communications have had a demonstrable effect on actual and potential stockholders, research suggests that it is highly likely that they are having a positive influence on other groups as well.[13] Such an effect acts as general confirmation that the Goodyear campaign has been working in accordance with its original strategy.

Five Lessons from the Goodyear Corporate Case

1. Good Communications Can Discriminate Between Winning Companies and Others. This finding is well supported by research, but it is nevertheless rather unexpected. The value of being a winner in the eyes of an organization's many "publics"—both the specific groups (customers, suppliers, employees, stockholders) and the public as a whole—is very important to the organization. But it is vital to remember that corporate communications are not an isolated factor unconnected with other aspects of a company's operations. A winning company must also have other winning characteristics, among them quality service, honesty and ethics, quality products, high-caliber management, and flexibility. But even with these characteristics, it may not be *perceived* as a winner unless it has good communications. This case provides good evidence that it is good communications that act as the catalyst to make the marginal but critical contribution to turn an otherwise deserving company into a winner.

2. Advertising Problems Can Be Unexpected. Goodyear's "Blimp" campaign had many things going for it, not least its popularity within the company, in the agency, and among the public. Yet it is fairly clear, in retrospect, that the campaign was doing an inadequate job in communicating Goodyear's innovativeness and the extent of its product range. It took fresh eyes—those of a new chief executive—and some unusual research to uncover the deficiencies of this campaign. After those deficiencies had been fully comprehended and appreciated, the client and the agency had to abandon an advertising idea to which they had both become emotionally attached and instead had to apply imagination, energy, and enthusiasm unreservedly to the search for something new. This represented the point of maximum sensitivity. In passing it, both client and agency gave evidence of notable mental flexibility in planning and executing a revised communications strategy.

3. A Strong Advertising Idea Can Be Limiting. This is the main point about the Goodyear "Blimp" campaign. It made a considerable impact and was extraordinarily relevant to what Goodyear originally needed to communicate to its tire buyers. Yet the more it put across its message to tire buyers, the more it limited the image of Goodyear in the eyes of the general public—not least to potential buyers of the company's many new products. The Blimp appears as a subsidiary element in the commercials featuring the cartoon characters; it will be interesting to discover (nothing is known as yet) whether this symbol can indeed be given a broader application, to embrace the full range of the company's products.

4. Humor Is No Handicap to Serious Advertising. The corporate communications of Goodyear, like those of other major companies, are a serious matter that impinge on virtually all aspects of its operation. Yet it is a mistake to conclude that a serious objective will always require a serious means to accomplish it. People respond to all communications—not least, advertising—in unexpected ways. They are more easily seduced and persuaded than browbeaten, and humor has a value (although admittedly not a ubiquitous value) in this process of persuasion.[14] There is an interesting parallel between Goodyear's use of humor for a serious purpose and, as described elsewhere in this book, the British Trustee Savings Banks' use of lighthearted commercials to persuade young people to open a bank account.

5. **"Who Is a Company?"** The research technique of asking people to describe brands of consumer goods in human terms, as if those brands were to come to life, has long proved its value in analyzing the psychographics of packaged goods markets. This case demonstrates that the same technique is equally valuable in a different context. People's images of companies are as subtle and multifaceted as their images of brands are. "Who Is a Company?" is a means (as it were) of drawing a map of what a company stands for in the public's estimation. This case demonstrates not only the intrinsic value of this research technique as a means of discovery, but it also shows its operational value in guiding both the development of advertising strategy and the evaluation of campaign effects.

17
Orkin

Termites are found only in warm climates, where they are sometimes very destructive. They are vegetarian. . . . The basis of their alimentary regimen is woody matter.

—Anon.

[Cockroaches] are voracious and omnivorous, devouring, or at least damaging, whatever comes in their way, for all the species emit a disagreeable odor, which they communicate to whatever article of food or clothing they may touch.

—David Sharp, *Encyclopedia Britannica,* 1910[1]

"An Organized and Determined Destroyer"[2]

Many people are surprised to learn that the main cause of damage to American homes is not the forces of nature that receive such wide publicity. It is not hurricanes, or floods, or fires. It is in fact termites, with their gradual, insidious, and almost invisible assaults on the whole fabric of clapboard and shingle houses and on the floors and joists and doors of brick ones. Termites are estimated to cause $800 million worth of damage in the United States every year, almost as much as the *combined* damage caused by all tornadoes, hurricanes, hail, flooding, and windstorms. And they attack 625,000 homes (compared with the 550,000 homes that are damaged by fire).[3]

A great swath covering more than two-thirds of the land mass of the continental United States is susceptible to termite attack. Although termites are found in every state except Alaska, the problem is especially serious in the warmer parts of the country—the states south of the Mason-Dixon line, and California. In these warmer regions there are often as many as four termite colonies on every quarter-acre house plot, each colony holding some 260,000 termites.

Termites are insects that are unpleasant in both their appearance and their habits. They live in colonies with an astonishingly high level of social structure, an organization that includes a division of labor among those subspecies of termites which reproduce, those which provide the food, and those which protect the nests. Because termites need warmth, moisture, and cellulose (their main food) for survival, the colonies grow beneath the earth. It is the cellulose in wood that attracts them, and the workers, or food providers, wander as far as 150 yards away from their habitat to find wood to feed the colony. In this they contribute to the cycle of nature by cleaning up the remains of trees and bushes that have fallen or have died from natural causes. But termites are indiscriminate in their taste for food and will attack the wood of a house with as much enthusiasm and destructiveness as they would consume a dead tree in a forest. In most cases, the owner of the house is unaware of what is going on, because the termites work below the surface.

Roaches and similar pests pose a different problem, although, like termites, they flourish and breed with remarkable fertility in a warm climate, which means that the areas of the country infested by termites tend also to be infested by roaches. Seventeen species of roaches and other common pests cause a wide range of troubles—diseases, painful bites, destruction of clothes and books, and the contamination of human food.

People in the warmer parts of the United States are conscious of the need to protect their homes from termites and roaches, although some of the facts about how much damage these insects cause are, as we shall see, often a surprise. To many people, protection is something they are prepared to provide for themselves by (generally inadequate) do-it-yourself efforts. Other people go to one or other of 14,000 local specialists, whose work is variable in quality but who are generally inexpensive. Of the 16.3 million people who used professional exterminators in 1986, approximately 28 percent used one or the other of two services, Orkin and Terminix, 2.6 million going to Orkin (16 percent of the total) and 1.9 million to Terminix (12 percent).[4]

Those 16.3 million people who used a professional exterminator were concentrated, as might be expected, in the warmer states (48 percent in the Southeast and Southwest alone). They also had an upper-income orientation, with 47 percent of them in having a household income of $40,000 or more, which means that most of them were probably living in high-class housing (76 percent own their houses). Beyond a further demographic leaning toward people with a college education and professional and managerial jobs (matters connected with the bias toward high incomes), users of professional exterminators have no other important demographic skews, nor are their patterns of media exposure in any way exceptional.

The figure of 16.3 million customers for professional exterminators is, on the face of things, relatively high, although it represents individuals and not homes. Those individuals account for 9 percent of the total adult population in the United States; in the Southeast, the figure is 15 percent, and in the Southwest, 16 percent. About four times as much roach treatment as termite treatment takes place. Controlling roaches is a simpler process but is one that must be repeated at intervals. Termite control is a bigger job, but the work is more permanent; indeed, Orkin currently guarantees its termite protection to last for seven years (if monitored by annual inspections and if annual renewals are paid for).

In August 1987, the most widely used chemical for termite control, chlordane, was withdrawn by its manufacturers because the U.S. government's Environmental Protection Agency wanted to carry out additional tests to determine potential risks. The alternative chemicals now used for termite protection have a much shorter effectiveness period (two to seven years) than chlordane (thirty years or more). This means that although the total market for termite control will be flat or even slightly declining (for reasons we shall discuss shortly) for the next five to seven years, thereafter it is likely to pick up again, as houses begin to need retreatment. It will be a long time indeed before the entire American housing stock of more than 80 million dwellings has been substantially protected.

The actual process of termite treatment is carried out by injecting the soil around the house with chemicals and also by treating all parts of the structure through which termites might enter. (A termite can crawl through a space as small as one sixty-fourth of an inch). Protecting a house takes about a day. Prices vary with the size of the house, but $800 is an average figure. (It was $300 in the mid-1970s).

Roach protection is, as mentioned, a simpler process, involving first locating where the roaches and other pests live and breed and then putting down pesticides at regular (normally, monthly) intervals.

The Orkin Exterminating Company is by a reasonable margin the most prominent in the market and is part of a larger enterprise, Rollins Inc., a public corporation with significant interests also in security systems and lawn care. Orkin, established in 1901, is the world's largest company in its field; it has always been a leader in scientific developments in termite and pest control and was a pioneer in setting up a research department to develop the best equipment and chemicals for various types of protection. The company has 5,000 employees, including a large staff of trained technicians, located in forty-seven states, the District of Columbia, and Mexico.

"People Who Can't Afford to Settle for Less than the Finest"[5]

The Orkin story has much in common with a number of other cases studied in this book. The company is the market leader and offers the best product available in functional terms. But there is a price premium. The Orkin service is approximately 20 to 30 percent more expensive than the competition. Orkin's business is approximately half termite control and half roach control. This division, as we have seen, is out of line with the total market's, which is directed 20 percent at termites and 80 percent at roaches. The split of the Orkin business dictates a similar split of the advertising budget: 50 percent to termite protection and 50 percent to roach protection.

Orkin is the most familiar name in the field, its level of consumer awareness at 94 percent in July 1987; *unaided* awareness was at the extraordinary level of 73 percent. (Comparable figures for Terminix were 69 and 22 percent, respectively).[6]

The Orkin advertising has a point in common with a number of other cases studied here—that it aims at building added values, using a careful balance of rational and nonrational arguments that emphasize the quality and reliability of its service. These added values stem from the company's long experience, large size, and know-how. The advertising features these characteristics, with the aim of justifying Orkin's above-average price. Orkin is different and better because of its experience, size, and expertise, and the advertising is used to demonstrate this superiority and the reasons for it.

To use advertising for this purpose is common in many advertising campaigns for other types of goods and services, but it is interesting that it has an application in fields like termite protection that are prima facie so far distant from the repeat-purchase packaged goods field with which we mostly associate it.

The "bundle of consumer benefits" that Orkin offers is concentrated on protection for the home; it is underpinned by substantially unconditional guarantees that are an argument in themselves, because customers appreciate that Orkin would not offer them if the service were not completely reliable. These are all essentially rational points. But protection of one's home also brings peace of mind, a powerful nonrational motivator. The very word *protection* is emotive, and it opens the door to the use of strong arguments involving the protection of one's family from the diseases carried by roaches and the protection of one's home—most people's largest single capital asset—from being undermined and eventually destroyed by colonies of repulsive insects. It follows that Orkin's advertising, although essentially rational in tone, is not devoid of nonrational overtones.

The advertising campaign, which is concentrated in spot television, acts as a direct stimulus to generate business. The numbers of inquiries telephoned to Orkin regional centers are a measure of the campaign's effectiveness. Since the ticket price of the Orkin service is high, the advertising, although it works directly, stimulates people to find out more and in some locales to get a free inspection; such inquiries are handled by the customers' contacting one of the 350 local branches of the company. The advertising is addressed primarily to new customers, although there is naturally some cross-selling of termite prevention to roach-extermination customers and vice versa. The role of the advertising is direct, but not at the extreme of directness; it is in the "seek information" category of the King Continuum described in chapter 1. Each commercial sells the Orkin service strongly, operates to build the image of Orkin, and is not looked on as a means of generating leads alone. (There is no telephone number included in the spots, since experiments have demonstrated that this does not produce any extra inquiries).

JWT Atlanta has handled the Orkin business since 1976. (Previously, the advertising was planned and written in-house). During JWT's tenure, the advertisements produced have been different executions of a basic strategy, which has itself changed only once in the past decade.

The argument in the commercials follows a logical sequence of problem and solution. In a 1987 spot devoted to termite protection, a householder greets the new day at the door of his handsome brick house. (This kind of house was chosen deliberately, to demonstrate that not only wooden frame-houses are vulnerable). The man notices slight decay in the door frame. He scratches it with his fingernail and only too easily uncovers the trail of destruction left by a colony of termites. The Orkin technicians come on the scene, and one of them says, "For about the price these people are having to pay to fix this one door frame, we could protect your whole house."

Both the sequence of the commercial and its general tone are rational. Yet the very ease with which the homeowner scratches the wood surface of his door frame to show how far it has rotted, the brief but repellent close-ups of the blind worker termites gnawing the wood, and the description of their depredations (" . . . termites hiding just below the surface, destroying your home from the inside out") are all contrived to stimulate an emotional response. And so also, in contrast, is the calm proficiency of the uniformed Orkin technicians as they make sure the same thing does not happen again (30 percent of the spots offer free inspection, an attractive benefit, though a not-uncommon one in the industry).

A 1987 commercial devoted to roach protection opens with a small boy who has awakened in the night, and this scene leads quite naturally into the argument (spoken by the uncommon choice of a female voice-over) that although one may do everything possible to keep one's family healthy, roaches in the house are capable of bringing in six different types of disease. The answer is the Orkin pest-control treatment. The story is strong, simple, and believable. And the commercial—like that for termite protection—does not shy away from showing the most disagreeable types of insects, whose very appearance has a shock effect.

The argument in this, as in the termite protection film, is based essentially on motivators rather than discriminators—arguments describing the general benefits of controlling termites and roaches. Although Orkin is strongly identified and the high quality of its service demonstrated, the commercials do not devote their main emphasis to the competitive strengths of Orkin. On the contrary, more is said about the general benefits of termite and pest control, a line of argument entirely appropriate for a leading brand

(MUSIC: ACCENTS ACTION.)
ANNCR: Even with all you spend to keep your home beautiful, you may be overlooking something...

Termites. Hiding just beneath the surface. Destroying your home from the inside-out.

Call Orkin.

ORKIN MAN: You know, for about the price these people are having to pay to fix this one door frame, we can protect your whole house.

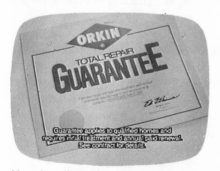

After that, if termites ever damage your home, we'll repair it—whatever the cost.

Call number one. For termites, we just might be all the protection you'll ever need.

Thirty-second television commercial first exposed in the United States in 1987.

like Orkin in a market that has not yet reached saturation. Motivating arguments stimulate total market growth.

The strategy and execution of the campaign are clear and logical. They are also successful, which means that any change in the medium term will be no more than a strategic evolution, mainly by reinforcing Orkin's brand values. The competition is getting stronger, and competitors are also branding their services. Orkin is responding to these developments by placing additional emphasis on the careful selection of its employees, the careful training of them, and the friendly service they provide.

Research is carried out to help evaluate people's interest in specific copy claims. A recent investigation confirmed not only that termites and pests are emotional issues with customers but that specific "statements that deal with numbers have a strong ability to surprise"—for instance: "Roaches are proven to carry at least six known diseases."[7] Rather importantly, the research also confirmed the strength of the argument that the "cost of prevention versus the cost of damage is the most motivating factor in the termite statements."[8] The reader will remember how these points were fitted appropriately into the two commercials described in this study.

Orkin's advertising budget makes it by a substantial margin the largest advertiser in the field, although it is, of course, one of only two organizations that attempt to build brand values for their services on anything approaching a national scale. Audited estimates of advertising expenditure are misleading in the termite- and pest-control field, because they cover inadequately the advertising expenditures of small local operators. But even accounting for this factor, Orkin's expenditures still represents a *higher* share of voice in the market then the company's 16 percent of the total number of users of professional extermination services.

The Orkin budget is deployed on spot television in 130 markets, supported by a low level of network television, spot radio, and outdoor advertising. JWT's spot buying is generally very efficient in comparison with the average cost-per-thousand of the schedules of the majority of advertisers using spot television. JWT's efficiency stems from the opportunism and local expertise of the buyers in the agency's regional offices.

The campaign is supported by a variety of color brochures that do a full educational job of explaining the dangers of termite and roach pestilence. They also describe how the different Orkin treatments are actually carried out, how the technicians do their job, and how fully Orkin's work is guaranteed.

Vicissitudes in the Marketplace

There is, as we have seen, a generally low level of market penetration of termite- and pest-control systems. As a result, the potential for long-term market development is substantial. Remember also that there is a small increase every year in the aggregate housing stock, which contributes to a growth in the size of the potential market (despite the fact that a number of newly built homes are treated during their construction).

But in spite of the attractive potential of the market, the growth in usage of pest and termite control has flattened in recent years.[9] There are a number of reasons for this change. One is the point already made that many new houses do not need termite protection, because it is carried out while they are being built. Another is the (very gradual) decline in the aggregate size of the market as an increasing proportion of the total housing stock is protected, although, as we have pointed out, the recent introduction of termicides that provide protection for only five to seven years means that, by the mid-1990's, there will be an increasing market represented by houses that need renewed treatment. The third difficulty stems from the cost of termite protection, which has more than doubled during the past decade, uncorrected for inflation. Even taking inflation into account, the cost has increased significantly. The price increases are related to restrictions placed by the government on the chemicals that can be used in and near homes. The cost of liability insurance has also gone up dramatically, increasing by 132 percent between 1983 and 1986.

At the same time, the increase in the rate of house buying, which in turn is influenced by the reduction in mortgage interest rates that has generally taken place during the 1980s, has been favorable for the extermination business. In many states, it is often necessary for the house seller to provide a certificate that the property has been inspected and is free from active termite infestations.

Yet in the market as a whole, the downward pressures have predominated, and it is against these background trends that we must judge the performance of Orkin, the company that offers by far the most expensive service in the market, albeit one of the best. Orkin's success against the odds forms a fitting conclusion to this case study.

The termite market is seasonal, with maximum sales in April and May; thereafter, sales decline slightly but remain above average through September. The consumer advertising is usually first exposed in February, March, and April, to lead up to the expected seasonal uplift, and it is then continued through the summer.

Partly as a result of Orkin's relatively high level of investment, the consumer advertising has always been a rich source of inquiries. The number of Orkin inquiries, already substantial when JWT was appointed, has been exceeded every year JWT has handled the business, reaching a total of more than 124,000 for termite protection alone in 1987. It is estimated that Orkin accounts for 17 percent of all consumer inquiries in the pest-control industry (compared with Terminix's 8 percent).[10] This large number of leads is, of course, a direct measure of the effectiveness of the advertising, and such a level, with frequent annual increases within a stagnant total market, is clear evidence of the productivity of the Orkin campaign. Judgment suggests that the improvements in this area are more than can be accounted for by increases in the advertising budget alone.

The present campaign for Orkin's termite-control service, which has been described in this chapter and represents merely a new expression of an unchanged basic strategy, was tested in the spring of 1986 in thirteen markets, mainly in the Sunbelt, split between areas of high and moderate market development. It generated a 22 percent increase in inquiries above the preceding year's level. It was then extended nationally during the summer of 1986, and the increase in leads (24 percent) was even higher than in the test markets. The goal for 1986 had been a 7 percent increase.

The impetus of the campaign was maintained in 1987, with an increase of 14 percent over 1986, although its productivity did not increase quite as fast as in 1986. This buoyancy provided an encouraging situation for both client and agency, although it posed for the latter a real enough problem in how to build on success. Nearly all advertising, and in particular advertising that works directly to achieve a behavioral response, produces almost-immediate diminishing returns to incremental pressure. This means that campaigns that prompt action, even if short of finally closing a sale, require experimentation with alternatives in their creative execution and media strategy and tactics, to maintain their pulling power.[11] Despite the fact that the present campaign is so successful—which is extremely flattering to the agency—it is always rather perplexing for an agency in such a situation to know what to do for an "encore" in order to maintain and increase the drive generated by the client's advertising investment.

Five Lessons from the History of Orkin

1. Branding Works in Unlikely Product and Service Categories. The Orkin case provides further evidence that branding is a virtually ubiquitous phenomenon in the marketing field. The essentials for the process are for a known organization to provide a product or service and for advertising to build nonrational added values in the mind of the consumer. In the case of Orkin, these values embrace confidence in the effectiveness and reliability of its service. Building added values is a long-term task, but it can accompany shorter term tasks, such as generating inquiries. As far as we can tell from the Orkin campaign, the advertising's short-term role has not worked at the expense of the long-term one or vice-versa. The advantage to Orkin of establishing its brand—as it is to many other advertisers—is to justify its premium price. This reduces the price elasticity of demand, maintaining sales if the price has to go up (as it has in the past, partly because of exogenous forces). The need to continue building added values will not diminish in the medium term, because the company is operating in a field with a relatively low level of product penetration, which makes the building of added values a very gradual process.

2. Rational Advertising is not Devoid of Nonrational Overtones. Rationality is as much the characteristic of people's responses to the Orkin advertising as it is to the basic work carried out by the company. The advertising emphasizes a functional task and a price. Yet the advertising argument is enriched and reinforced with strong nonrational elements, because the health of one's family and the condition of one's house are matters close to people's hearts, and the campaign exploits the emotional quality of such arguments with balance and skill. In addition, the termites and roaches themselves are given enough emphasis to generate a prickle of distaste without switching off the viewer's attention to the commercials.

3. Advertising in Its "Seek Information" Role. The Orkin campaign operates at the direct end of the King Continuum. Viewers are encouraged to seek information to put Orkin on their shopping list. The ticket price of the Orkin service is too high for the advertising to operate on its own to close the sale. In common with campaigns for many other goods and services, the Orkin advertising is able to combine the roles of generating inquiries and building added values. (In this respect, the Orkin campaign has an unlikely parallel with the JWT advertising for the U.S. Marine Corps, discussed elsewhere in this book).

4. Problem-Oriented Advertising Can Be Effective. One of the half-truths of the advertising business is that advertising should present a brand or service in an essentially positive way and that negative elements (problems to be solved and the penalties of failure) carry the ever-present danger of cutting off the audience's attention. Of course, the validity of this contention depends on how dramatically the negative elements are presented, but the Orkin campaign shows that the advertising can go quite far in presenting unpleasant problems. In the Orkin advertisements, the distasteful presence of termites and roaches is quite dramatic, with close-up photography of the insects themselves. And while the campaign also has strong positive elements in the way it describes the Orkin service, the demonstration of *why* the service is needed is shown with full force, and the advertising argument is thereby strengthened without any apparent cost in reducing the audience's attention.

5. The Pressure to Increase Advertising Productivity. The advertising has operated with a demonstrably increased productivity during the past decade. This trend is unlikely to change in the future. As the market matures (with a probable increase in competition), there will be a continuous double pressure on the advertising campaign to operate with even further increases in productivity. But although this pressure to yield more leads per dollar in a tougher marketplace may seem prima facie to be a severe challenge, such an occurrence is common in the advertising business. Indeed, it is virtually universal in the field of repeat-purchase packaged goods, where it is caused essentially by the strength of the retail trade, which presses down manufacturers' margins (the source of the residuals from which consumer advertising appropriations are derived).

18

The Trustee Savings Banks

. . . [T]hese institutions, conceived by philanthropic individuals, started on their career of public usefulness towards the close of the eighteenth century, with the express purpose of procuring safe and remunerative investments for the industrial classes.

—Sir James Jaffrey[1]

"The Successful Progress of This Institution"[2]

In Great Britain before the Industrial Revolution during the latter part of the eighteenth century, there was no reason for the existence of an organization to care for and employ productively the savings of the working classes. This was so for the simple reason that workers' earnings were barely enough to pay for their living expenses in a society based essentially on subsistence agriculture, and there was no surplus for luxuries like savings. It is an interesting commentary on the Industrial Revolution that, for all the overcrowding, squalor, and relentless labor that were the lot of the workers in the "Satanic Mills," their standards of living gradually improved. There were, of course, vicissitudes in both money wages and real earnings corrected for inflation. Nevertheless, by the end of the eighteenth century, average real wages of workers in industry were strikingly higher than those of agricultural and industrial workers during the first decades of that century.[3]

It was this increase in working-class incomes that brought into being a national chain of savings banks in Britain that eventually numbered more than six hundred organizations (some called penny banks). Their function differed from that of commercial banks, which operated checking accounts and made loans, in that the savings banks were exclusively a conduit for savings and were carefully regulated by statutes (dating from 1817 in England, Wales, and Ireland; 1833 in the Channel Islands; and 1835 in Scotland) to maintain absolute probity and extreme caution in their operations. Indeed, they had been originally established by upright philanthropists and were continuously supervised by local worthies in all parts of the country, a tradition that has continued to this day. These savings banks were all quite separate organizations, although their function was similar. They did, however, gradually begin to merge, until—after more than 170 years—they became four linked banks.

The way in which they originally operated was simple. The savings of working-class people were taken in and recorded in the saver's passbook, and a modest rate of interest was paid at regular intervals. The funds were accumulated by each bank, and the law required that they be invested in British government securities, earning a slightly higher rate of interest than what was paid to the saver. The savings banks were, as noted, regulated by statute, but they were not, of course, government owned.

The cost of running each bank was financed by the difference between the higher interest rate the bank received from the government and the lower rate it paid its customers. The keynote of the operation was stability. Although depositors could take out their savings easily and the bank could equally easily sell its government securities, the banks in effect borrowed long and lent long.[4] With little inflation, the nest eggs of the working classes were protected; indeed, they were guaranteed by the continuity and permanence of the British government, whose long-term debt was to a small but important degree financed by TSB deposits. Government securities in Britain are still referred to as trustee or gilt-edged investments, a reflection of their solidity and the protection provided to the investor, although in inflationary times their safety as a store of value in real terms is highly questionable.

A notable characteristic of the Trustee Savings Banks was that they were nonprofit organizations. That they did not have outside capital or stockholders meant that their earnings were substantially added to reserves (which in turn increased the equity), and what was left over was used to augment the interest on depositors' savings, which were also free from British income tax.

During their more than 170 years of growth, TSBs built enormous reserves and became important, respected, and tranquil landmarks in their local communities—a position typified by the imposing premises they occupied in large numbers of industrial cities and county towns in England, Scotland, Wales, Ulster, and the Channel Islands. TSBs were as durable as the British government.

But in the 1960s and 1970s, two key changes took place. First, with serious inflation, there were increasing doubts about whether people would continue to invest their savings for the interest alone, with no possibility of capital appreciation. TSBs had for many years had very serious competitors for working-class savings—the building societies, the traditional British organizations for channeling mass savings into private real estate mortgages (at variable interest rates, not fixed rates, as charged by "thrifts" in the United States). With building-society loans, it was normally necessary for a borrower also to be a lender. With the emergence of the private property boom in the United Kingdom that got into its stride in the late 1960s and has continued relentlessly for two decades, savings in building societies began to be much more attractive than savings in TSBs. This was so because private real estate investments, which became possible for building-society savers, satisfied a deep-seated human need to own the roof above one's family's head, as well as offering a means both of sheltering income from income tax and—even more importantly—of enabling the building-society customer to benefit from a sometimes dramatic capital appreciation as house prices continued to rise.

This situation was potentially most damaging for TSBs; however, during the 1970s a second important change took place. For many years, British governments of all political persuasions had wanted to introduce more competition into British banking. The British commercial banking industry had been a classic oligopoly, with four major national organizations—the National Westminster, Barclays, the Midland, and Lloyds—plus a tail of much smaller, mostly regional competitors. Commercial banking means accepting deposits, handling checks, and making loans (mainly short-term) for personal and for industrial and commercial customers; the definition excludes merchant banking, which is concerned with raising capital for public and private joint-stock enterprises. The commercial banking industry has always been carefully regulated by the Bank of England (interest rates, for instance, are set more or less uniformly for all the banks)—a situation that is not conducive to aggressive competition. Indeed, economists and politicians had for decades felt that British commercial banks operated in an environment of only token competition while at the same time achieving economies of scale because of their huge size. As a result, they had accumulated enormous reserves, made large profits, and at the same time led rather a quiet life.

During the 1960s and 1970s, the opinion grew in political circles that TSBs should be encouraged to change their structure and purpose in order to provide a major new competitive force in the banking industry, and a government committee (the Page Committee), which reported in 1973, made the point formally and explicitly. This meant that the amalgamation of local TSBs—something which had been going on for years—would have to be accelerated in order to concentrate them into one more or less uniform national organization. This concentration was necessary to enable them to build scale economies comparable to those of the commercial banks. In addition to amalgamation, one important way of building the business would be to extend the range of the TSBs' services: They had to become more than old-fashioned savings banks. They would have to make loans and offer their customers checkbooks. They would also have to attract industrial and commercial as well as personal customers.

Such a change meant that the working procedures and attitudes of TSB management and employees would have to alter radically, a task that might not be easy, because many people in both groups had had long years of service and this factor would inevitably constrict their thinking. Just as importantly, the existing customers and the public as a whole (as potential customers of the transformed TSB) would need to modify their attitudes toward the organization. It is difficult in a competitive world for advertising and publicity alone to reverse or reconstruct public attitudes to a brand or organization; the most that can be hoped for is some gradual (albeit substantial) modification of such attitudes. What was needed for TSB was for the public to be persuaded to see it as a more multifaceted bank directly comparable with the "Big Four," without any change taking place in people's emotional attachment: that is, in how TSB was seen as friendly, local, and accessible to all sorts of people (points we shall shortly consider in more detail).

Accordingly, the objective of the communication was the rather uncommon one of effecting a major modification of public attitudes. Whereas the role of advertising (for instance, with large and successful brands in other product fields) is commonly if not quite universally a reinforcement of attitudes, so as to protect market share, the job for TSB was different, and the modification of public attitudes was to take a number of years. But when measurable progress had been made, it was inevitable that the role of advertising and publicity would gradually revert to the normal type of protection of the franchise that is so common with packaged goods.

A New Force in Commercial Banking

The British government supervises and regulates the banking industry, although most parts of the industry are privately owned. After the report of the Page Committee, what the government visualized for TSBs was that they would become the "third force" in British banking. The first force was the traditional commercial banks. The second was the post office, which in Britain as in other countries is a nationalized enterprise and which to some extent was being transformed by the introduction of the National Giro, an inexpensive system of transferring credit for the payment of small debts. This change in functions, however, was small in comparison with what was to happen with TSBs.

The move toward concentration proceeded rapidly and surprisingly smoothly. By the end of 1983, there were only four banks: TSBs of England and Wales; Scotland; Northern Ireland; and the Channel Islands. (Because these companies operate in an integrated fashion, we will begin using the singular to refer to the national TSB organization). After the amalgamations had been finalized, the legal status of TSB was changed to that of a public limited company and shares of stock were sold to the public (including many TSB customers). The offer price was very favorable to stock buyers, the flotation raising approximately $2 billion from 2.3 million new shareholders.[5]

While individual TSBs were being amalgamated, the range of banking services was being expanded through the whole network. Personal checkbook accounts had been introduced as early as 1965. By 1980, the organization had introduced personal lending and overdrafts, systems for direct crediting and debiting of accounts, cash dispensers, a credit card (part of the Visa network), mortgages, various types of insurance, travelers' checks, unit trusts (the equivalent of American mutual funds), and other services to attract corporate as well as personal customers. TSB had become a major financial group capable of competing on level terms with any of the commercial banks.

Advertising's role in broadening people's perceptions of TSB is the particular concern of this study. But before examining the advertising, we should first look at some rather important differences between TSB and its major competitors, the Big Four commercial banks.

In overall size (in capital, customer base, and number of branches, although not in assets) TSB is comparable with any of the Big Four. In particular the number of TSB customers is very large indeed. A recent estimate puts the number of TSB checking-account customers at 4.4 million, plus 3.5 million people with savings accounts. There is an overlap between these totals, but taking it into account, the net number of adults who have any type of TSB account still amounts to the very considerable total of 6.3 million. (Although other estimates have suggested an even larger number of TSB account holders, they include the substantial number of children who have savings accounts in their own names).

Adults with accounts at any British bank total 33.5 million—about two-thirds of the British adult population, a proportion that does not grow much over time. Of these 33.5 million adults, the percentages who have accounts with each of the four commercial banks, TSB, and the post office's National Giro are as follows:[6]

All bank account holders	100.0%
Those who have current and/or deposit accounts with:	
Barclays Bank	20.2%
National Westminster Bank	19.1%
TSB	18.8%
Midland Bank	16.0%
Lloyds Bank	13.8%
National Giro	5.0%

Just as notable as the absolute size of the TSB customer base—which is an order of magnitude similar to that of any of the commercial banks—is the difference between TSB's 18.8 percent and the National Giro's 5.0 percent. The former organization has clearly transformed itself into a major banking force with much more obvious effect than the latter.

The way in which TSB has built up the number of its checking accounts has naturally been by converting its existing savings accounts, and such conversion has been a successful strategy.

As noted, only two-thirds of the British adult population have bank accounts; furthermore, ownership of bank accounts is to some extent skewed demographically. As common sense would suggest, such ownership is biased toward the higher income groups and the higher socioeconomic (occupational) categories. Socioeconomic analysis is normal in British social studies, a reflection, perhaps, of the significant role that social class and education still play in British life.

For historical reasons connected with TSB's origins, its customers have a much more pronounced blue-collar orientation than customers of the commercial banks do (a third of TSB customers are Class C2 in the British classification, which broadly covers the skilled working class, and a further third are Class DE, the unskilled working class). There are also further skews. To a pronounced degree, TSB customers are concentrated in the older industrial regions of Scotland, the North of England, and the Midlands. They also have an older profile than the customers of the Big Four commercial banks do, although TSB is also of above-average importance among very young adults, the sixteen- to twenty-year-olds, as the result of a successful marketing strategy whose significance we will address later.

Another important difference between TSB and the commercial banks has already been mentioned briefly and is also a result of its history, in particular, its relatively humble and localized origins: TSB has always been regarded as more friendly and more interested in personal customers than other banks are. The other banks are all very large, national rather than local, and essentially impersonal, even intimidating—and perceived as such by the working classes. This perception has been a disadvantage for the Big Four commercial banks when they have sought working-class business. TSB, because of its accessible and friendly image, is seen as rather different from other banks and is also thought to be moving with the times and striving hard to attract new customers, especially the young.

From some points of view TSB has a lower profile than other banks; for instance, when people are asked for the names of banks they can remember, they invariably mention the Big Four significantly more often than they cite TSB. Nevertheless, people's consciousness of TSB as a major force in banking, as well as their perceptions of the organization generally, has climbed at a faster rate than perceptions of other banks during the past decade. And people's knowledge of the individual services offered by TSB—cash dispensers, home mortgages, insurance services, and so forth—is now at uniformly high levels and in many respects comparable with what people know about the four major commercial banks.[7]

Dancing to the *TS Beat*

The transformation of TSB has been the result of aggressive management policy. Coinciding with the amalgamation of the large number of individual banks into the four large national units as they exist today, change percolated down to the level of the smallest individual TSB branch.

The extensive switching of traditional savings accounts into checking accounts was the result of much effort at the local branch level, reinforced by national advertising and a large amount of widely disseminated literature. In the launch of the new banking services during the 1970s, the advertising also had an important role, in cooperation with widespread use of promotional material and other activities in the branches (although promotions are not as widely used in Britain as in the United States). During the 1970s, TSB became a major national advertiser. Advertising expenditures by all the commercial banks and the building societies increased continuously at this time—a symptom, and perhaps not the least important one, of the increased competition among all parts of the financial industry, a competition that was welcomed by many economists and politicians.

To jump forward in time, banks currently spend some $160 million per year on advertising above-the-line.[8] As a proportion of their total volume of business (or even of their net earnings), $160 million represents a minuscule fraction. This point emphasizes the fact that the importance of advertising as a business-generating activity is much smaller than the work of the individual branches. But advertising is still important, and the marginal productivity of banks' advertising expenditures is often monitored with sophisticated techniques, an example of which this chapter will describe. The estimated expenditure by TSB is currently $15 million, making TSB quite a substantial national advertiser, although the 9 percent share of voice that the expenditure represents is modest in comparison with the bank's 18.8 percent of all bank account customers. TSB's expenditures during each year of the past decade have nevertheless all been high in absolute terms, and the history of the various campaigns has some interesting features.

TSB became a major national advertiser during the mid-1970s with a campaign that featured as its presenter a popular actor from television and films, Gordon Jackson, whose performance as Mr. Hudson the butler in the long-running, extremely popular television series *Upstairs, Downstairs* made him a nationally recognized figure. His homely Scottish personality, together with Mr. Hudson's associations from *Upstairs, Downstairs* of well-merited success in life within the confines of a strictly working-class environment, made Jackson an extraordinarily suitable spokesman for TSB. In a long series of simply constructed commercials, he told the public in an unadorned but credible way how TSB was becoming a very different sort of bank from the way it had been commonly viewed in the past. The campaign was very popular, and this popularity rubbed off onto TSB, working synergistically with the bank's already-favorable image in the mind of the public.

But in 1977, the decision was made to devote a substantial proportion of TSB advertising to a campaign with an essentially different strategy. This study is much concerned with describing and evaluating that change in strategy and the effects on the marketplace of some of the advertising resulting from it.

The genesis of the change in strategy was a single demographic fact: People open bank accounts when they are young. In Britain, customers do not change their banks as often as in the United States, because British banks are national organizations and a change in a person's location does not necessitate finding a new bank, merely a new branch of the old one. It follows that if a bank successfully attracts a young customer and manages to provide a continuously competitive and acceptable service, then the bank has a good chance of keeping that customer for life. This simple fact led TSB to direct a large proportion of its advertising and promotional efforts toward young people who did not have a bank account and who might be persuaded to open one with TSB.

This strategy led to the development of commercials that were highly unorthodox by the standards of bank advertising and that were considered by some observers at the time as frankly bizarre—although they were strongly supported by TSB staff at all levels (which demonstrates that it is misleading to consider everyone associated with banking as staid and conservative). The findings of qualitative research were also encouraging. The commercials featured musical routines, with young people dancing to an adaptation of the song "Button Up Your Overcoat" (which had already been widely used in TSB advertising in conjunction with the slogan "It's the bank for me"). The music was specially arranged with a modern pace and rhythm, and although the commercials were designed to entertain, they also all contained solid information about TSB's banking services. Television was used extensively, as was cinema, an important advertising medium in Great Britain for reaching teenagers and young adults.

The campaign was immediately successful. Not only did it modify perceptions of TSB and in particular heighten perceptions of the bank among the young, but even more importantly it led large numbers of young people to open TSB accounts. At an early stage of the campaign, a leading British market research organization published the following tribute to the advertising: "With a new series of commercials currently being screened on television, the modest Trustee Savings Bank is substantially market leader in attracting new accounts, particularly among the C1 [that is, clerical], C2 and DE socioeconomic groups."[9]

The campaign directed at young people was not TSB's sole advertising effort; indeed, it accounted each year for only about a quarter to a third of the overall budget. It was, however, that part of the advertising which was most strongly directed at increasing the bank's customer base, and for this reason it was—and is—of above-average significance. It will be given prominence in this study not only because of this fact but also in view of the important advertising lessons it exemplifies.

Before describing a recent development of this campaign, we should give some attention to the rest of TSB advertising—in particular, to the continuing success of that advertising which was directed substantially toward existing TSB customers and which was aimed at selling the Bank's increasingly wide range of services. This is the campaign that continued to account for the lion's share of TSB's advertising budget.

This service-oriented campaign went through a number of evolutions over the years. Throughout the period, television was the main medium, although newspapers, magazines, and radio were used in a minor way until the mid-1980s, and afterward more significantly although at a lower level than that of competitive banks' campaigns. The strategic basis of the TSB campaign did not change, although at different times emphasis was given to different services, which meant that the role of the advertising was sometimes concerned more with modification of people's attitudes and sometimes more with reinforcement. Both the client and the agency agreed that the advertising continued to make an important marginal contribution to establishing the new banking services as permanent features of TSB, as well as helping them to grow.

A good example of how TSB successfully established a new service was the launch of TSB's credit card, the Trustcard, part of the Visa network. This was launched with enormous success in 1978, mainly by aggressive promotion in the individual bank branches, but also supported by an advertising campaign that relied heavily on TSB's associations of friendliness and trust.[10] The card attracted a substantial number of users within months of its launch and currently has 2.8 million cardholders.[11]

In 1980, a unifying device, the slogan "We like to say yes," was brought into TSB advertising. (It was the successor to the equally famous slogan "It's the bank for me.") It has been used in its original or its modified form ("The bank that likes to say yes") in all advertising, display material, and promotional literature ever since. The slogan has become extremely familiar to the public,[12] and its success stems both from its simplicity and distinctiveness and from the way it encapsulates the friendliness and personal service with which TSB has always been associated. The slogan "We like to say yes" has also been used consistently in the advertising directed at young people, and

Music: Modern, punchy, percussive, with clean, bright vocals.
Vocals: The answer's yes at TSB!
MVO: Wouldn't it be good if your bank could. . . . . get you what you want all over. . . . the country?
Vocals: The answer's yes at TSB!

MVO: Wouldn't it be handy to have a bank. . . that wasn't shut just because it happened to be closed?

Vocals: The answer's yes at TSB!

MVO: A bank that didn't charge you. . . if you stayed in credit? Where there really were friendly helpful people?
Vocals: The answer's yes at TSB!

MVO: A bank that offers. . . . discounts on music. . . . . . clothes and lots more? Well, it's for real at TSB!

Vocals: The bank that likes to say . . *Yes!*

Forty-second television commercial first exposed in Britain in July, 1986.

there has been an unquestionably real, although unquantifiable, synergistic relationship between the main campaign and the youth campaign. This point should be borne in mind when the success of the latter is judged.

During the late 1970s TSB was not alone in addressing the young, and indeed by 1983 the competition among the different banks for younger customers had become heated. In particular, the competition was taking the form of banks offering extremely attractive and increasingly expensive promotional packages (involving free banking, personal loans, and various cash and other bonuses) to attract young people who were learning to control their own finances for the first time. The Big Four commercial banks concentrated on students in higher education, whose incomes would (it was hoped) grow rapidly when they entered the real world. This strategy meant an investment in bank branches on campuses, an investment TSB was reluctant to make. Most importantly, all four of the large commercial banks were devoting substantial funds to advertising to young people, the largest slice of which was directed toward students.

TSB's reluctance to address its advertising to students was based partly on the relatively small size of the national student body (in Britain, fewer than a quarter of all graduates from secondary schools go on to any further education, broadly defined). It was also argued, with reason, that the more than three-quarters of young people who leave secondary school to enter the work force were more appropriate customers for TSB because of the traditional working-class nature of the bank.

It was therefore decided to devote the TSB youth campaign single-mindedly toward teenagers who had left secondary school and were starting their first jobs. Vis-à-vis the competition, the Big Four commercial banks, this was an indirect, or flanking, strategy. But it led to some remarkable results.

As this study has emphasized on more than one occasion, TSB advertising has never been planned to work in isolation; the efforts of the banks have always been much more important in generating new business. Now, with the decision to concentrate on persuading working school-leavers to open TSB accounts, it was recognized that the advertising could only work if it was used in cooperation with some sharp-edged promotions[13] (the kinds of promotions that, incidentally, had for years been used successfully by banks in the United States, although not in the more conservative British environment).

The first offers were made in 1982/1983. In 1984, the promotions took the form of three years' free banking (for an account in credit), plus discounts on tapes and records, hi-fi equipment, and musical keyboards. In 1985 the program was expanded to offer additional discounts on records and musical equipment. In addition, in 1986 a special magazine was launched, entitled *TS Beat* (a name anticipated by the most popular of the television and cinema commercials produced for the youth market as early as 1978). Although this magazine is primarily concerned with pop music, it also gives advice on financial topics, written unobtrusively but in a way that is intellectually accessible to young people. Copies are distributed free (on request) to youth clubs, leisure centers, colleges, and secondary schools (the most important outlets). They are given away at rock concerts and distributed in large quantities in TSB branches. *TS Beat* comes out three times a year, and on average, three-quarters of a million copies are printed of each issue.

As the promotions evolved, they moved toward pop music: a topic of inexhaustible interest to young people. By 1986, the promotions had become single-mindedly oriented to pop music. TSB has been perceptive enough to latch onto this, the most ubiquitously popular of all youth activities, and to preempt it as a part of TSB's brand personality. Relying on this, the advertising campaign could now be sharply directed to achieve a behavioral effect (which we shall shortly examine). Television was used until 1987 as the main advertising medium. As in the United States, it is not a very selective medium, carefully planned program-buying being the only means of targeting an audience. Television was supported by other, smaller media—cinema, magazines, and radio—that are able to attract a young audience without excessive waste.

The results of the campaign are easy to describe.

1. Some 33,000 youth accounts had been opened in 1983—considered at the time, and subsequently, as a base, or normal, level. With the advertising and promotional programs in 1984 and 1985, the numbers rose to 66,000 and 126,000, respectively, in those two years. (The target for 1985 had been 79,000). In 1985, out of 783,000 young people leaving secondary school, TSB's 126,000 accounts represented 16 percent of the potential total market. Considering the number of young people who do not open bank accounts at all, not to mention those who respond to the incentives of the Big Four commercial banks, 16 percent is a remarkable figure.

2. In 1985, of all young people in their first year of employment and opening a bank account, 32 percent had opened a TSB account—a figure almost twice as high as that for any other bank. This result is entirely consonant with TSB strategy; account opening peaks as the school-leaver enters the job market.

3. Data on the images of different banks in the minds of young people consistently favor TSB over the competition. And awareness of TSB's special promotions is higher than that for other banks and steadily increasing.

4. The month when new accounts are opened varies to some extent year by year, but it tends to coincide with when the advertising is concentrated. This is presumptive evidence that the advertising achieves at least a marginal behavioral effect, perhaps best seen as a trigger to action.

5. Using an econometric modeling technique, an attempt has been made to quantify the relative importance of the different influences on the opening of new accounts. Although the overall fit of the predictions to actual experience has been extremely good, the model has not been entirely successful in disentangling precisely the individual contributions of the different variables.

In 1985, assuming 33,000 youth accounts to be the base level (per point 1 above), the marginal additions generated by the advertising and promotional program totaled 93,000 extra accounts. The model computed that the advertising generated 27,000 (29 percent) of these accounts; *TS Beat,* 10,000 (11 percent). The remaining 56,000 accounts (60 percent) came jointly from the promotions, the lagged effect of previous years' advertising, and a contamination caused by imperfections in the measurement. A judgmental interpretation of these findings suggests the approximation that the advertising and promotions may have accounted for fifty-fifty shares of the total number of new accounts. Additional econometric work on the delayed effect of previous years' advertising might make possible a sharper estimate, and carrying out such work would certainly be a good idea.

Despite the difficulties of the analysis, this matter is important and has budgetary implications. In 1985, the total expenditure on sales-generating activities directed at young people was made 76 percent above-the-line on advertising and 24 percent below-the-line on promotions. This division of expenditure between advertising and promotions is some way different from the estimate above of their relative effectiveness, so that it is at least possible that a readjustment of the two ratios could lead to an improved overall result in the marketplace. Regrettably, there are no reliable historical data on the split of appropriations above- and below-the-line in the banking industry and the effectiveness thereof. The results of each program must therefore be evaluated independently.

The key to understanding TSB advertising (as with most successful campaigns in all product fields) is to look at its long-term or strategic effects. As far as the youth-oriented campaign is concerned, it started in the 1970s as something highly innovative and made an immediate impact. Over the years, the client and agency learned how to sharpen and improve it. As young people become mature and (it is to be hoped) prosperous adults, TSB in both its banking policy and its advertising must move to protect its franchise and encourage its customers to use the full repertoire of services. The role of the advertising will become increasingly indirect and protective—the equivalent of nurturing patterns of repeat purchase in the packaged goods field. In this respect, bank advertising, despite appearances to the contrary, bears strong resemblances to the advertising in most mainstream product categories.

Seven Lessons from the History of TSB

1. A Planned Evolution of the Advertising Strategy. During the 1970s and into the 1980s, the advertising was intended gradually to modify and broaden people's perceptions of TSB, so that they would visualize it as a national organization that is technologically up-to-date and quite capable of competing with the major commercial banks on level terms. Such modification and broadening have been substantially achieved, and the advertising is entitled to a share of the credit. The various campaigns used have moved gradually toward selling a range of bank services, an objective that has also been successful. The strategic evolution of the campaigns has been carefully planned. Although TSB is now seen as a realistic competitor to the Big Four commercial banks, the main perceived difference between it and them stems from TSB's essential friendliness and orientation toward personal customers. These values are the direct result of TSB's history, and they have been embodied in all the various detailed evolutions of the advertising strategy.

2. The Advertising Has Built on Existing Perceptions. Public perceptions of TSB have been, and remain, favorable; the bank has always been considered friendly and welcoming to small, personal customers. These are major strengths in the present competitive environment. The aim of the advertising and publicity since the early 1970s has been to modify and broaden people's perceptions of TSB, not to attempt to reverse or rebuild them. In terms of consumer response, the objective has always been to make people think, "This is the same friendly TSB I have always known, but it now does more for me than ever before." Much of the emphasis has been placed on doing more for the customer, by cross-selling the wide range of TSB services.

3. An Increasingly Protective Role for the Advertising. As people's perceptions of TSB are increasingly adjusted in line with the original strategy and as more TSB customers are persuaded to have checking rather than savings accounts, the role of the advertising will change to some extent. In the future, the objective will increasingly be to retain the loyalty of customers as a means of retaining and increasing the profitability of their accounts, as TSB manages to sell them the full range of services. Gradually, the advertising is likely to become more an engine for repeat purchase. TSB advertising still needs to sell the range of TSB services, but as the years pass, the role of bringing about progressive changes in public attitudes will slowly give way to that of protecting the franchise in a highly competitive environment.

4. The Youth Campaign Stemmed from an Analysis of Simple Demographics. Before the 1970s, the language and tone of voice of all bank advertising were essentially extremely serious: the result of the strong belief that money is a serious subject and of the equally powerful but mistaken belief that one needs always to be unsmiling in talking about it. In the late 1970s, an analysis of simple demographics demonstrated that one of the most important target groups for TSB ought to be the young, for the reason that the people who open bank accounts for the first time are young people either in their first jobs or in higher education. When it was decided to speak to these people in TSB advertising, the agency made a creative leap that led to an arrestingly unorthodox style of bank advertising, as well as to a campaign that had much success in the marketplace. But the genesis of its initial and continued success was the statistical analysis that isolated the target audience clearly.

5. The Success of a Flanking Strategy Against Competitors. When, during the 1980s, the major commercial banks were devoting substantial resources (in opening bank branches as well as in using promotions and advertising) to attacking the student market, TSB wisely—and successfully—moved its focus of attention. The client and the agency realized not only that there were three times as many working school-leavers as college students but also that the former were more suitable for TSB because of its working-class associations. The target group was precisely identified, and the new strategy was a striking success and exceeded expectations. It was also a reminder that in marketing (as in the science of war), indirect, flanking attacks are almost invariably more successful than direct, headlong assaults.

6. Innovative Media Planning. Young people are not an easy group to target effectively in media planning. TSB advertising has always gone as far in such targeting as marketing circumstances allow, with the selective use of television, cinema, radio, and magazines. But in addition to all this, the launch of *TS Beat* represented a media innovation of extraordinary originality and effectiveness.

7. A Growing Role for Econometrics. The econometric evaluation that has been carried out of the youth campaign has produced interesting but inconclusive results. Further work should be carried out to isolate with greater precision the contribution to sales of the different marketing variables. The specific value of this analysis would be to guide the budget split between advertising above-the-line and promotions below-the-line. The total budget is at the moment heavily weighted toward the former activity, but this split may not be optimally effective in view of the indications from econometrics of the very large contribution made by promotions to the success of the total effort.

19

The United States Marine Corps

And what about Cates? He'd get his shoulder straps shot off, his leggings, every part of his uniform would pick up fragments from shells, but never Cates. I think he even had his canteen shot off at one time. And it was the same at Guadalcanal in the Second War. I don't think anyone ever had the close shaves he had. I guess he was being saved to become commandant, because that's just what happened.

—Samuel W. Meek[1]

One of the Oldest Military Bodies in the World

During its more than two centuries of existence, the United States Marine Corps (USMC) has established a quite remarkable record of service to the Republic, one that is appropriately encapsulated in the Marines' motto, *Semper Fidelis* ("Always Faithful"). Bravery, resilience, and staying power are expected of individual Marines, but such intrepidity is combined with a hard-bitten self-reliance and independence.[2] There is a complementarity of qualities, and this is as true today as it was seventy years ago, the period described by Sam Meek in his account of his personal experiences with the Sixth Marines in World War I. Meek's graphic remarks about the early career of General Cates also say something about how promotion in the Corps is normally earned.

The USMC has been in continuous existence since 1798 (it was originally founded in 1775). It has fought in every armed conflict the United States has had with foreign nations and also fought in the Civil War. Originally a small band of men, numbering only 10,000 even in 1916, it grew rapidly during World War I, and its numbers were not significantly reduced during the interwar period—a tribute to its fighting record in 1917–1918.

The size of the Corps grew tenfold during World War II, in which it was mostly involved in the immensely wide-ranging amphibious operations in the Pacific. Although it was scaled down after 1945, it fought from first to last in both Korea and Vietnam. Its present active strength is approximately 200,000—more than 190,000 men, plus a few thousand women.[3] By the standards of peacetime armies, this is a reasonably large force. But despite its size, it retains its tight cohesion and special "family" feeling—qualities readily apparent to the reader of the *Marine Corps Gazette,* the "professional magazine for United States Marines" that has been published every month since 1916.

The USMC has always come under the Department of the Navy (and some of the regular officers are products of the U.S. Naval Academy). Nevertheless, the USMC is an independent service; the Marine Commandant has coequal status with the other members of the Joint Chiefs of Staff. The Marines are more than just seasoldiers; they have a large air component. Because of this component and the other supporting arms it commands, the USMC forms a more or less self-contained military formation, which again adds to the family feeling.

Because of the long history and prestigious status of the Corps, it is only natural that it should have a healthy regard for its own prowess. It is also not surprising that it is selective in its recruitment policies and that acceptance into the Corps has to be earned with some natural aptitude and no small amount of effort. The phrase *esprit de corps* excellently describes the special qualities of military efficiency, loyalty, self-reliance—and exclusivity—that the Marines stand for in their own eyes and also to a considerable degree in the eyes of the U.S. population, the source of its recruits.

Recruitment into the Marine Corps is a difficult task insofar as the standards are high, and some applicants do not measure up to the qualities needed. Yet paradoxically, the esprit is also a powerful attraction to men and women of the right type—those who have physical and mental resources and who respond to challenge. It follows that the advertising used to stimulate recruitment must reflect the marines' esprit de corps if it is to be truthful—and also if it is to be effective.

J. Walter Thompson has been associated with the USMC since World War II, although only in 1947 did the agency become formally responsible for the Corps' publicity and advertising. The association was the result of Sam Meek's position in JWT. We have read Meek's words at the beginning of this chapter. He had fought, as a temporary junior officer in the USMC, at the horrendous battle of Belleau Wood. After World War I, he created the powerful international arm of JWT and became a legend in the company.

Meek was one of the four powerful personalities (the others being Stanley Resor, Helen Lansdowne Resor, and James Webb Young) who dominated JWT for the four decades between 1920 and 1960. These four individuals not only created the largest and most prestigious advertising agency in the world but also, and even more importantly, created a new concept in agency work, a more or less equal partnership between the drive, vision, and resources of the client and the orchestrated analytical skills and imagination of the agency.

During his long tenure at JWT, Meek was involved at least occasionally with all international clients and also some domestic ones, including the

USMC. But there was in fact very little advertising for the Marine Corps until the early 1970s (almost a decade after Meek had retired), for the obvious reason that with conscription in the United States, voluntary recruitment was a matter of relatively small importance. The situation radically changed when the armed forces were established on an all-volunteer basis in 1974.

JWT originally handled the USMC advertising from its New York office. The account was then moved to the Washington office, which was amalgamated with the agency's Atlanta operation in 1986. Since 1986, the advertising has been serviced out of Atlanta, although JWT has a field representative in each of the six USMC recruiting districts in the United States. The appointment of JWT is reviewed every year, a matter of standard government policy. The agency has, however, continued to handle the business without interruption: presumptive evidence that the agency's work meets the goals of the Marine Corps and is effective in the marketplace.

The underlying strategy of the advertising campaign has been unchanged since national advertising began, although the execution of that strategy—the campaign itself—has gone through a number of evolutions. This study is mainly concerned with the advertising to recruit men into the enlisted ranks of the regular Marine Corps. This is the largest individual recruiting task, although there are smaller advertising campaigns to bring in male and female officers; USMC reserves; and women into the enlisted regular ranks. (The last of these is a relatively simple recruitment job; for most of the time the numbers of women applying to join are greater than the Corps requires).

"A Few Good Men"[4]

In common with all the other cases in this book, this chapter is not intended to prove anything, but to isolate salient facts so that readers can learn something about how advertising works in different circumstances.

The role of advertising for the USMC is in some respects different from that for any of the other organizations depicted in this book, inasmuch as the USMC is selling a comparatively higher ticket item. The price of joining the Marines is some years—perhaps a lifetime—of service, a factor that obviously needs to be carefully weighed and considered by potential recruits. Evidence indicates that as many as two-thirds of young men considering the USMC give serious consideration to other branches of the armed services as well. And 43 percent of those who do join the Marines request literature—half of them more than once.[5]

In chapter 1 we described the King Continuum, the device that JWT often employs to plan advertising's role according to how directly it is in-

Black-and-white advertisement in magazines first run in 1988.

tended to work. This device is helpful in describing JWT's advertising for the USMC.

One important part of this campaign—employing direct mail as the main medium—is a classic example of advertising intended to stimulate people to seek information. It is obviously unrealistic to expect the potential recruit to sign on immediately upon reading an advertisement. The advertising is therefore directed at encouraging him or her to make contact with the USMC by visiting a recruiting office and/or studying recruiting literature in order to find out more about life and career prospects in the Corps.

Another part of the campaign—and one just as important—employs the main advertising media, especially television, and does so with a total budget more than twice as large as that for the program geared to stimulate inquiries. The main media campaign operates at the opposite end of the continuum. It is aimed at reinforcing attitudes—confirming and augmenting the potential recruit's awareness of and respect for the USMC's esprit de corps. In advertising jargon, the advertising builds awareness of the image. It presells. By building favorable attitudes, it makes the work of direct personal recruitment more efficient and productive.

Despite the two separate tasks undertaken by the advertising and despite the fact that Marine Corps recruitment is sensitive to advertising pressure (with some time lag), it is important to remember that the advertising does not work in isolation. Indeed, the total recruitment effort is effective because its different parts work in close cooperation with one another. The advertising works rather as a catalyst.

When the interested applicant gets as far as to seek information, sometimes as a result of an advertising stimulus but sometimes not, that part of the advertising devoted to image building makes a contribution because it has (as it were) fertilized the ground. This is an indirect and almost imperceptible process, operating through a gradual underpinning of what the potential recruit has learned from many information sources about the Marine Corps' rather special style and esprit.

The image-building campaign, by its truthful concentration on all aspects of marine life—the hardships as well as the glamour—also does a rather important job of prescreening applicants. Most of those who talk to the recruiters have to a degree been self-selected and possess some of the characteristics the USMC is seeking.

Spearheading the recruiting effort are the recruiting offices in all parts of the United States, staffed by regular Marine officers and enlisted ranks, and there is evidence that potential recruits are impressed by these recruiters.[6] The contribution of the advertising is essentially to support their efforts. It makes the recruiters' work more productive by enabling the recruiters more easily to get face-to-face with suitable prospects.

Since that part of the advertising which stimulates inquiries is only one component of the repertoire of stimuli that persuade a potential recruit to join, it follows that the campaign must not attempt to oversell. And since the contribution of the image-building part of the campaign is probably very gradual, it must retain a strong continuity. The advertising exposed during the past twelve years has closely followed these two precepts. But before looking at the campaigns themselves, we must first examine the parameters that control where the "few good men" the USMC is seeking are actually going to come from.

We can isolate five forces that substantially determine Marine Corps recruitment. One of them—the size of the demographic group from which the recruits come—is a critical variable but one that cannot be influenced by any direct or indirect efforts. The other four factors all contribute to a second major determinant—what is referred to in recruitment planning as the propensity to join, an element that *can* to some extent be influenced. Such propensity is tracked by means of an extensive research study, the Youth Attitude Tracking Study (YATS), carried out by the Department of Defense on behalf of all branches of the military. Conducted every year, the study is based on long telephone interviews with more than 10,000 men and women ages sixteen to twenty-four: a fully representative national sample.[7]

Propensity to join is measured by the response "definitely" or "probably" to the question, "How likely is it that you will be serving on active duty in the Army/Navy/Marine Corps/Air Force?" This question is not especially subtle, but investigations by two researchers (Orvis and Gahart) have established "a strong relationship between enlistment propensity, as measured by YATS, and actual enlistment behavior."[8]

The five forces that go most of the way to determining Marine Corps recruitment are as follows:

1. The size of the demographic population pool from which the recruits are drawn,

together with four influences on the propensity to join:

2. General levels of civilian unemployment, as well as employment and educational prospects for the recruiting population pool specifically.

3. The objective attractions of the USMC—the pay, benefits, living conditions, travel, and training. There is also a downside—the potential physical dangers of a USMC career.

4. The subjective attractions of the USMC—the prestige, glamour, comradeship, and esprit de corps—and also how well the Corps is recommended by a potential recruit's parents, advisers and peers. (Ten percent of recruits had or have fathers in the Corps, and 19 percent of recruits

are persuaded by friends who joined.[9] These are remarkable tributes to the strong corporate identity of the Marine Corps).

5. The publicity and advertising. As noted, these elements are not decisively important in their own right. But they operate as a trigger and as a catalyst to maximize the effectiveness of factors 3 and 4.

We shall look briefly at each of these five points.

The Population Pool

Eighty-six percent of male recruits for enlisted service join at ages seventeen to nineteen.[10] The age-group we shall look at in most detail is ages sixteen to twenty-one, because this grouping covers (a) young men when they are high school juniors and are considering their future careers, (b) men during the three prime recruiting years, and (c) men ages twenty to twenty-one, when most of the remaining 14 percent of recruits sign on.

In any year, this pool is of a finite size; the size varies year by year, and it is on a declining trend. It was at its highest in 1984, with 8,065,000 men; fell in 1985; and fell again in 1986, to 6,775,000 men. These figures represent absolute top limits to the numbers on whom the Marine Corps can draw. In normal circumstances, the year-by-year changes are predictable long in advance.

Unemployment, and Employment Prospects

As common sense would suggest, recruitment into the armed services will be influenced by how many jobs and educational opportunities are available in the civilian world and by what prospects there are for jobs in the future. High national unemployment leads to high military recruitment, and the statistical correlation between the two variables over the eleven years 1976 through 1986 is reasonably pronounced ($r = 0.61$).[11] And at the level of the individual, the difficulty of finding a civilian job locally also has a clear influence on propensity to join.[12] This factor or combination of factors, however, influences *all* military recruitment and is not specific to the USMC, whose share of the recruitment market is determined more by the remaining points we discuss below, particularly the last two. Unemployment affects Marine Corps recruitment; however, it does not influence the advertising campaign.

Objective Attractions of the USMC

The pay, benefits, and other aspects of USMC life are attractive to recruits. Positive interest in joining increases, for instance, when potential recruits learn that the starting pay is more than $600 per month, with all living expenses and medical care provided.[13] There is also the GI Bill, which helps make it possible for service men and women to go to college when they have completed their active service. These objective attractions are motivators drawing young men toward enlistment in all branches of the military. The pay and other objective attractions of life in the Marine Corps have more similarities to than dissimilarities from the other military services. There is nothing special or very different about the USMC in this regard.

Subjective Attractions of the USMC

As already suggested, the intangible rewards of USMC life are the true discriminators between the Marine Corps and the other branches of the military. There is good evidence that more than half of Marine recruits, when asked why they joined the Marine Corps in preference to any other of the armed services, focus on the prestige of the corps.[14] This emphasizes the importance of the way in which the prestige and the other subjective attractions are projected by the last of our five factors. The role of advertising as a means of projecting the image of the Corps is a matter to which we shall return.

The Publicity and Advertising

Before evaluating the publicity and advertising for the USMC, we must emphasize the point that Marine recruitment is a competitive activity. The government-funded campaigns for the U.S. Army, Navy, Marine Corps, and Air Force are all aimed at the same sorts of people when these populations are measured demographically. (There are, however, psychographic differences, especially where the USMC is concerned).

The aggregate annual advertising budget for all military recruitment is approximately $200 million, out of which a joint campaign for all branches of the armed services together accounts for approximately $30 million. The remaining $170 million is devoted to individual campaigns for the army, navy, marines, and air force, with the army alone accounting for $100 million.

The total Marine Corps budget is under $20 million for all advertising and direct mail, booklets, and recruiting films. This figure represents 12 percent of the overall appropriation for the individual services' publicity and advertising campaigns and in absolute terms is a reasonably large sum of money. It contributes to USMC recruitment contracts with just under 45,000 men and women every year, out of a total annual military recruitment of 315,000 (in 1986). The USMC share of the total number of military recruits is therefore more than 14 percent—a figure *higher* than the USMC's 12 percent of the overall advertising budget.[15] The USMC's advertising therefore represents a smaller investment per recruit than that for the rest of the armed services taken as a whole (the latter being fairly heavily biased in favor of the army). To put this another way, the Marine Corps' advertising is expected to work, dollar for dollar, rather harder than that for the other branches of the armed services taken together.

"The Few, The Proud, The Marines"[16]

As noted, the direct-mail advertising is primarily aimed at stimulating inquiries. A huge volume of recruiting literature is produced; about 17 million pieces of direct mail are sent out every year. Judgment suggests that the quality of these pieces, especially in their design and presentation, is very high—perhaps higher than their competition, the recruiting literature produced by the other branches of the armed services.

It is worth noting that although the Marine Corps has a proud history, this history is given worthy but subsidiary treatment in the recruiting literature, the thrust of which is essentially forward-looking.

The style of the printed material is factual and rational. Questions are raised and answered, and potential recruits come back for more.[17] The copy and illustrations touch on the nonrational rewards of joining the Marines, but such rewards are seen as the main province of the campaign in consumer media, especially television. In this, there is no mention of toll-free (800) telephone number for inquiries, for fear of damage to the image orientation of the advertising. Moreover, inclusion of a toll-free number would be unlikely to generate a substantial number of leads. The two parts of the campaign—rational in direct mail and nonrational in consumer media—work in an essentially complementary and synergistic fashion. This is what makes it difficult to isolate their effects separately.

Television advertising is especially good at building the kinds of imagery and added values that are a part of what the Marine Corps stands for in people's minds. The esprit de corps is typified by the uniforms, the ceremonial drill, and the tempered steel of the marines' dress sword, and these are all portrayed in the commercials. But although the uniforms, drill, and dress sword are important symbols, they represent less than half the advertising story. The discipline, the high physical standards, the arduous training, and the inculcation of leadership receive much attention. (The array of battle armament was featured in the 1970s and early 1980s, but this is regarded today as a less important discriminating argument than the esprit of the USMC). The people responsible for the advertising at both the client and the agency have a good understanding that the tough image of the Marine Corps may put off the fainthearted, but it is a positive attraction to the kinds of men and women the USMC wants to attract.

The USMC is not interested solely in recruiting brawn. More than 98 percent of those who join in the enlisted ranks have graduated from high school, and two-thirds manage to score in the top 30 percent category in the armed forces aptitude tests. By both these criteria, the quality of recruits has improved significantly since the early 1970s.[18] The emphasis in the recruiting arguments on training for leadership is both truthful and realistic.

The advertising campaign for the all-volunteer force has, over the more than twelve years of its exposure, been consistent, with an absolute harmony in strategic essentials in what is communicated and in its tone of voice. At different times, however, varying aspects of Marine Corps life have been featured, and commercials have been produced under the main campaign umbrella to recruit women, officers, and reservists. The production values of all the advertisements have been uniformly high, with in many cases a stark and arresting simplicity that comes from dramatic close-up photography. The commercials have been expensive to produce. The style of the television advertisements, especially in their use of close-up illustrations, has been echoed in the press advertisements and on the covers of the recruiting literature.

The advertising generates approximately 330,000 leads per year. This body of inquiries eventually yields 12,000 recruits, a rate of conversion considered high by the normal standards of military recruiting. These figures mean that in recent years, the advertising has acted as the first stimulus to the recruitment of 12,000 men and women (27 percent of the total USMC intake), besides, of course, making an indirect and unquantifiable (but probably even more important) contribution to bringing in the remaining 73 percent. All this suggests that the campaign works hard in both its roles. It stimulates substantial numbers of inquiries. And in the next section, we shall evaluate the evidence of the campaign's success in its other role of dramatizing and underscoring the esprit de corps of the USMC in a way intended to augment its subjective attraction to potential recruits.

"The Services Show Distinct Patterns"[19]

If we track young men's propensity to join any of the armed services, this is how the percentages have differed year by year over the past eleven years:[20]

1976	30.5%
1977	34.1%
1978	32.4%
1979	30.0%
1980	33.7%
1981	34.3%

1982	35.8%
1983	35.4%
1984	29.9%
1985	29.8%
1986	32.0%

Many people would consider these figures remarkably high. They are certainly significantly above what they were during the latter phase of the Vietnam War. They provide a positive confirmation that the general status of the military has been substantially repaired and that service in the non-commissioned ranks of the armed forces is seen as offering an attractive career choice to a substantial minority of young men. The propensity to join is greatest (as common sense might suggest) to younger men, to blacks and Hispanics, and to the less well educated, although these populations do not represent the largest groups who actually enter the service.

The rise in the figures in 1980–1983 generally reflects the increased level of unemployment of young men during those years. The exceptionally high unemployment figures for 1982 (21.9 percent) and 1983 (21.1 percent) have not recurred in subsequent years.

These trends in propensity to join must in turn be applied to the trends in the total number of men from whom the recruits are drawn, in order to arrive at an estimate of the size of the effective recruitment pool. As noted, the trend in the size of the appropriate demographic group was downward in 1985 and 1986, which means that even with the increase in propensity to join in 1986, the size of the effective pool was smaller than in 1985. That it is becoming progressively more difficult to maintain the targeted number of recruits each year also means, among other things, that the advertising must work progressively harder. (Remember, too, that the USMC's share of recruitment advertising dollars is already below its share of total military recruits).

The overall upward and then downward trend in propensity to join any of the armed services during 1976–1986 was closely followed by the figures for each of the services individually, although these, of course, were at lower absolute levels. Prima facie there is nothing striking about the data for the individual services, but there is an interesting internal movement within the figures that can be isolated without too much trouble.

To do this, we should look at the figures for each of the individual services in a given year and express them as a percentage of the overall figure for all the services. Table 19–1 shows the data for 1976: The figures in these columns do not add up, because many young men who are interested in joining the armed services are unsure which service, and express interest in more than one branch.

If we track the figures for the individual services over time, movements

Table 19–1
Propensity to Join Individual Branches of the Military, 1976

		Percentage of All Young Men	
Propensity to join	Any of the services	30.5	100%
	Army	11.4	34%
	Navy	13.8	45%
	Marine Corps	9.3	30%
	Air Force	15.4	50%

Table 19–2
Propensity to Join Individual Branches of the Military, 1976 and 1986

		1976	*1986*
Propensity to join	Any of the Services	100%	100%
	Army	34%	49%
	Navy	45%	35%
	Marine Corps	30%	35%
	Air Force	50%	50%

appear. These can be demonstrated in a somewhat simplified way, as shown in table 19–2, by comparing the first and last years for which data are available.

These figures show clearly that the army and the marines have increased their attraction to young men. The army has done better than the Marines, with a gain of 15 percentage points in comparison with the Marines' 5. But the superior performance of the army must be related to its $100 million publicity and advertising budget—by far the biggest of any of the service appropriations, and five times the size of the marines'.

Response to the Marine Corps by potential recruits tends to be polarized. To some—those who are physically, psychologically, and intellectually the best material—the Corps has a powerful attraction. To many others, it stimulates them to active rejection.

The propensity-to-join figures are influenced by the advertising in its secondary, image-building role, although, as stated earlier, advertising's influence on the recruit's final decision to join is as a catalyst working in cooperation with the other stimuli. Nevertheless, if we acknowledge that advertising plays at least some part, the evidence suggests that the USMC's advertising is—as it is expected to be—more productive dollar for dollar than that of the army (whose success in boosting propensity to join is a function of its overwhelming advertising budget) and of the navy and air force, whose propensity-to-join figures have made no net advance over the past decade.

These data do not allow us to isolate the influence of the USMC advertising in any precise scientific way, but recall studies (despite their imperfections)[21] demonstrate that the advertising has made a considerable impact. Research among a sample of 1,000[22] Marine recruits shows that 87 percent of them recall the USMC campaign, 79 percent recall the television advertisements, and 65 percent judge the advertising "extremely believable" or "very believable." It is dangerous to infer from these figures that the high awareness of the advertising and belief in its claims work in a persuasive way to convert former unbelievers. It is just as likely that the already interested potential recruit, when he is studying the options, pays particularly close attention to the advertising. But, despite this qualification, there is a strong correlation between advertising awareness and propensity to join. In addition, the credibility score is extremely high. And equally remarkable are the extraordinary richness and density of those elements in the advertising which are actually recalled. The slogan "The Few, the Proud, the Marines" is alone recalled spontaneously by 51 percent of the respondents.

This research into the recall of the campaign does not provide us with evidence that the advertising has done anything to convert the unconverted. But it has, without any question, made a strong and favorable impression on young recruits who have actually joined the Corps. Judgment suggests that it works, in cooperation and synergistically with all the other influences on the individual recruit's decision, and this is surely as much as could be expected of an advertising campaign for as high ticket an item as recruitment into the ranks of the USMC.

Five Lessons from the USMC

1. A Trigger to Stimulate Inquiries. Advertising, particularly lead-generation advertising, makes a positive contribution to recruiting 12,000 Marines every year. Within its limits, this campaign is critically important in providing the potential recruit with an initial stimulus to action. But it does not "sell off the page" (or television screen); the ticket price of joining the Marine Corps is too high for that. And the actual decision to join depends on many things in addition to the advertising, which itself must not attempt to oversell. The tone of voice of all the advertising for the Marine Corps is, however, strong and confident, in keeping with the image and style of the Corps.

2. Building Awareness of the Image. The publicity and advertising, particularly in consumer media, consistently endeavor to project the esprit de corps of the USMC—its combination of discipline, leadership, toughness, military pride, and exclusivity. In projecting the image of the Corps in this way, the advertising has an inevitably slow-burning effect that is difficult to evaluate.

Studies of recall and credibility are exceptionally positive (although such studies admittedly suffer from technical imperfections). The campaign operates in a competitive environment, and there is presumptive evidence that the USMC advertising works harder than that for the other armed services. Judgment and research suggest that its success stems from the fact that the USMC's esprit has potent selling appeal and that the advertising has managed effectively to tap into it.

3. Strategic Continuity. A point closely related to the preceding one is that both sides of the campaign—that devoted to stimulating inquiries and that intended to build awareness of the imagery—have been unchanged in essentials over the more than twelve years the advertising has been run, although the campaign has proceeded through a number of different phases. As far as the direct mail is concerned, this continuity has obeyed the professional adage that a campaign that keeps pulling should not be changed. With that part of the campaign which is aimed at building awareness of the USMC image, continuity is important because the Marines themselves have not changed, and advertising has a *progressive,* albeit unquantifiable, effect on the potential recruit. The campaign works slowly and continuously, making strategic change undesirable. The advertising has indeed succeeded in maintaining a notable freshness and impact over a long period of exposure, despite an unvarying strategy and a continuity of executional style.

4. The Value of Tracking Studies. The USMC case, like a number of other cases in this book, demonstrates the value of continuous research. YATS, conducted annually, covers all aspects of the recruiting effort (including the impact of competitive activities: the effects of the recruiting efforts for the other branches of the armed services). The particular merit of this type of research is that it is diagnostic and thus enables weaknesses to be corrected and strengths reinforced. It is also multifaceted, in that it scrutinizes all aspects of recruiting activity and helps us judge how the publicity and advertising cooperate with the other stimuli.

5. A Pressure to Increase Productivity. Trends in the U.S. population and a reduction in youth unemployment will provide a diminishing pool from which the USMC can recruit; any increase in the propensity to join will therefore be operating in a weakening total market. This factor puts an extra pressure on the advertising. Although the Marine Corps campaign has worked in these circumstances with an increasing efficiency during recent years, the pressure is unlikely to weaken in the future. This situation makes an interesting parallel with the advertising trends for packaged goods in most repeat-purchase product fields. (For these products, the problems are caused by the prevalence of stationary market conditions, allied to the increasing strength of the retail trade, which presses down on retail margins and leads to reductions in advertising investments.)[23] This book contains a number of examples of these trends in operation.

20

A Bird's-Eye View of a Thousand Brands

> Our precision will be a mock precision if we try to use partly vague
> and non-quantitative concepts as the basis of a quantitative analysis.
> —John Maynard Keynes[1]

Some General Hypotheses about Markets

The eighteen chapters describing cases (chapters 2–19) have been devoted
to the advertising history of specific brands, and we have attempted to evaluate the contribution of advertising on a case-by-case basis. Before we try
to put some of the lessons of these cases together (the focus of chapter 21),
we think it important to return to three of the points raised in chapter 1—
points that the reader will by now have seen confirmed in a rather piecemeal
way by the case histories. We shall now examine these points more fully,
with the intention of having this chapter serve as a bridge between the individual cases and chapter 21's discussion of general patterns that cut across
the cases.

The three hypotheses to be examined are:

1. advertising scale economies (point 18 in chapter 1)

2. a growing heterogeneity (point 2 in chapter 1)

3. maturity equals flatness (point 1 in chapter 1)

The way we tackled the analysis needed to evaluate these hypotheses
was by mobilizing the resources of J. Walter Thompson. In the fall of 1987,
we sent to all JWT offices around the world a questionnaire calling for a
limited amount of clearly defined and solidly based factual data. (This questionnaire is reprinted in the appendix). We received back 242 completed
questionnaires, each referring to a single product category in a single country. Data were sent in from twenty-three markets: Argentina, Australia, Austria, Brazil, Canada, Chile, Colombia, France, Germany, Greece, Hong Kong,
India, Italy, Japan, Malaysia, Mexico, the Philippines, Portugal, South Africa, Sri Lanka, Thailand, the United Kingdom, and the United States.

The sample in postal surveys is always uncontrolled (that is, we cannot
predetermine who will reply). In mitigation of any such criticism, however,

we can state that the majority of people to whom we wrote completed their questionnaires. And the resultant coverage of total JWT business is large— about 25 percent of the markets in which the agency operates.

In fact, we collected basic information pertaining to 1,096 advertised brands. This number of readings represents an excellent gross sample size, so long as we avoid breaking it down into too many subsamples to examine special groups based, for instance, on product types, brand sizes, or blocs of countries. In this chapter, when we fragment the sample in any way, we shall warn of the statistical dangers, and when percentages are computed on a total of less than 100, they will be put in parentheses.

These 1,096 brands represent, as noted, a substantial proportion of those product fields in which JWT conducts its business. Of the 1,096 brands, 866 (79 percent) are repeat-purchase packaged goods and 230 (21 percent) are other types of goods and services. As a proportion of the aggregate expenditure on advertising by all advertisers in all markets, packaged goods represent a considerably smaller share of the total than in our sample—probably less than 40 percent, although the business handled by all the major advertising agencies is concentrated at least 60 percent in packaged goods.[2] The JWT proportion of packaged goods is therefore high, but it is probably not an excessively distorted representation of JWT's business, largely because of the traditional importance to the agency of its international clients in a range of packaged goods fields.

Packaged goods are both less volatile and more advertising intensive than other types of goods and services. The preponderance of packaged goods in our sample is an advantage from these points of view. At the same time, packaged goods do not represent advertising patterns *different* from those of other sorts of products, merely more consistent patterns with fewer eccentricities, and this is again an advantage.

The findings of the investigation are distilled into several statistical tables and one diagram, included with the discussions below. Although we carried out a number of additional tabulations of the data, they did not materially add to what is in the tables and thus have not been included here.

First Hypothesis: Advertising Scale Economies

We have looked at the first hypothesis by examining advertising intensity and how it differs for brands of different sizes. The best way to examine advertising intensity is to calculate a brand's advertising-to-sales ratio, which requires reliable estimates of both its advertising expenditure and its sales value. While it is not difficult to arrive at an estimate of advertising expenditure, it is virtually impossible to make a tight estimate of sales on the basis of retail audit or consumer panel data. We are therefore forced to find an alternative system of evaluating the importance of advertising in relation to sales.

Fortunately, such a system exists and is the method used in this investigation. It consists simply of comparing a brand's share of market (on a volume or value basis, volume being used here) with its share of voice (the brand's share of the total value of the main media advertising in the product field).

The rationale for this method of calculating advertising intensity is that the cost structure of one brand in a market tends to be similar to that of any other. That the manufacturers of competitive brands are also conscious of one another's advertising expenditures is a characteristic of oligopolistic competition, the most prevalent type of market organization in all but the most undeveloped categories and countries. The result is that brands of similar size will tend to spend similar amounts on advertising; moreover, a brand that is twice the size of another will tend to spend twice as much on advertising. This quantitative relationship between the advertising appropriations of different brands introduces the concept of a normal approximate equality between a brand's share of market and its share of voice. Obviously, there are some erratic exceptions to this similarity, and we can do nothing to allow for them. But there are also *consistent* exceptions, which pertain to brands of different sizes. The purpose of this analysis is to examine those consistent exceptions.

One mathematical quirk must be understood before we go any further: In every market there are some brands that are unadvertised. This means that the average share of voice (shared among fewer brands) is, for mathematical reasons, *above* the average share of market (shared among more brands). Thus, it is not quite true to say that the normal and stable relationship for any brand is a parity of share of market and share of voice. The normal relationship for an advertised brand is in fact between the brand's share of market and a *higher* share of voice. In some markets, the difference is only fractional. But in others—those in which there are many substantial but unadvertised store brands—the difference can be quite large. In all circumstances, however, if a brand spends the same share of voice as its share of market, then it is (at least slightly) underspending.

In this investigation, we started by organizing the data into two categories:

1. *profit-taking brands* (or underspenders): those whose share of voice is the same as or is below their share of market

2. *investment brands* (or overspenders): those whose share of voice is clearly above their share of market

In table 20–1 we have put all the brands into groups covering 3 percentage points of market share (1 to 3 percent, 4 to 6 percent, and so on).

Table 20–1
Profit-Taking and Investment Brands

	All Brands	Profit-Taking Brands (Share of Voice Equal to or Smaller than Share of Market)	Investment Brands (Share of Voice Larger than Share of Market)
Total	1,096 = 100%	= 44%	= 56%
Share of market:			
1 to 3%	224 = 100%	= 27%	= 73%
4 to 6%	218 = 100%	= 37%	= 63%
7 to 9%	153 = 100%	= 41%	= 59%
10 to 12%	112 = 100%	= 45%	= 55%
13 to 15%	(77 = 100%)	(= 56%)	(= 44%)
16% and over	312 = 100%	= 59%	= 41%

Note: We have covered only advertised brands.

This has been done because the sample cannot be reliably broken down to allow an analysis based on single percentage points of share. As we can see in this table, profit-taking brands are in a minority among those with small market shares, but the proportion consistently increases as the brands get larger. The movement is quite continuous: from 27 percent for brands with a 1 to 3 percent share of market to 59 percent for those with a share of 16 percent or higher.

The picture is remarkably clear, and we believe that at work are three forces that are responsible for it.

First is that new and burgeoning brands (which are, of course, nearly always small) normally receive advertising investments deliberately calculated to exceed their market share percentages. Indeed, A. C. Nielsen has long recommended this budgetary policy on the basis of extensive empirical knowledge of successful and unsuccessful new brands.[3] This factor accounts for many small-share brands having relatively high shares of voice.

Second is the all-too-common practice of "milking" older and often quite large brands. This strategy is tempting to manufacturers, because stopping advertising and promotional support can bring about a sometimes dramatic increase in a brand's earnings in the short term (although sales will almost certainly be adversely affected, which will lead to a sometimes rapid demise of the "geese that lay the golden eggs"). Manufacturers are sometimes persuaded to adopt this strategy by a belief in brand life-cycle theory. This is essentially self-fulfilling, because the very act of reducing support when a brand's sales are turning down, in the expectation that such a downturn is inevitable, will actually cause the downturn to be accelerated.[4] An examination of the 389 larger brands in our sample (table 20–2 shows that a third—but only a third—of the profit-taking brands are on a slightly

Table 20–2
Brands with 13 Percent Market Share or Greater

	All Brands	Profit-Taking Brands (Share of Voice Equal to or Smaller than Share of Market)	Investment Brands (Share of Voice Larger than Share of Market)
Sample size	389	226	163
	100%	*100%*	*100%*
Brands with:			
Slightly rising share	43%	39%	49%
Static share	26%	28%	24%
Slightly falling share	31%	33%	27%
Premium price	32%	28%	37%
Average price	51%	54%	46%
Below-average price	17%	18%	17%
Handled by JWT	33%	28%	41%

Note: We have covered only advertised brands.

falling sales trend, which suggests that many, if not most, of them are being milked. (Further evidence for saying this can be found in the table 20–4, which appears at the end of this discussion of our first hypothesis).

Third is the most interesting and possibly the most important of the forces at work. Many large brands (two-thirds of them, according to the data in table 20–2) flourish in the marketplace with shares of voice consistently below their shares of market. This means that for such brands, advertising works harder, dollar for dollar, than it does for most smaller brands, and their strength in the market illustrates a clear advertising-related economy of scale for such large brands. Such an economy can be expressed in a dollar value representing the difference between (a) these brands' appropriations with a normal relationship of share of market and share of voice and (b) the smaller dollar amounts actually spent on them. This scale economy is one of the real strengths of the branding phenomenon. Another of its strengths clearly visible in table 20–2 is that 28 percent of the profit-taking brands are able to command a premium price in the market.

The cause and operating mechanism of this scale economy are not known with certainty, but they are thought to relate to a characteristic of consumer purchasing behavior: a tendency for large brands to benefit from above-average frequency of purchase and repurchase. The phrase *penetration su-*

percharge has been coined to describe this phenomenon, and it is one that appears to have a wide application.[5]

The analysis so far has been based on unweighted data relating to the number of brands in the profit-taking and investment categories. We have not yet looked at the *amounts* by which they underinvest or overinvest in advertising.

In the next analysis (table 20–3), we have, in a search for the most consistent data, concentrated on balanced packaged goods markets. We chose these markets by examining each packaged goods category in turn and selecting the more normal markets that contain at least four advertised brands and are not dominated by any brands with exceptionally large shares. This process reduced the number of markets under analysis to 117 (48 percent of the total sample) and the number of brands to 666 (61 percent of the total sample). This means that some of the subsamples in this analysis are getting rather small, but there are nevertheless advantages in looking at this rather homogeneous group of brands.

We grouped the 666 brands into families covering 3 percentage points of market share, and for each brand we calculated the difference between share of voice and share of market and averaged those differences within each family of brands; such differences vary according to the size of the brand. Again there is a fairly consistent picture. Brands in the 1 to 3 percent range overinvest in advertising by an average of 5 percentage points, and brands in the 28 to 30 percent range underinvest by an average of 5 percentage points. The size brackets in between follow an approximate continuum but with some discontinuities.

These data can be set out diagrammatically (figure 20–1), and although

Table 20–3
Brands in Balanced Packaged Goods Markets

How Much Share of Voice is Above or Below Share of Market (Percentage Points)

Sample size: 666 brands in 117 markets	
Share of market	
1 to 3%	+5
4 to 6%	+4
7 to 9%	+2
10 to 12%	+4
13 to 15%	+1
16 to 18%	+2
19 to 21%	no difference
22 to 24%	−3
25 to 27%	−5
28 to 30%	−5

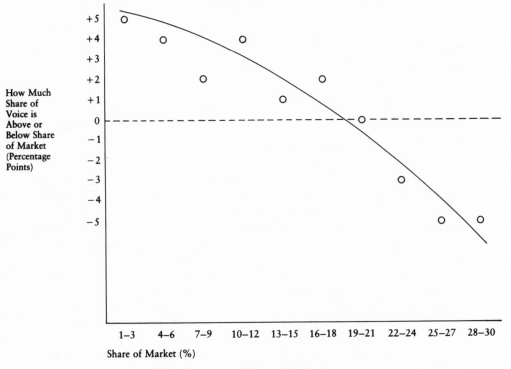

Figure 20–1. Brands in Balanced Packaged Goods Markets (*n* = 666)
Share of Voice and Share of Market

the trend line is not a perfect fit, there is a reasonable-looking curve, which descends in a convex path. This provides a hint that the gap between share of voice and share of market tends to increase as share of market grows.

This curve can be used in a rough-and-ready way for operational purposes. Any brand in a balanced packaged goods market can have its advertising appropriation tested according to the averages embodied in this curve. The brand's market share can be located on the curve, and the advertising share of voice for all brands of that same size can be read off. This figure can be converted without much trouble into an advertising expenditure calculated in dollars or any other currency. And doing so will provide a normal expenditure level against which the brand's actual expenditure can be compared and from which operational conclusions can be drawn.

We have carried out a further analysis that also yields what we believe to be operational conclusions. We have taken all the brands with market shares of 13 percent or more in these balanced packaged goods markets in order to arrive at the average share of voice in comparison with the market share. We have then broken out those brands which are on upward, static, and declining trends (table 20–4).

Table 20–4
Brands in Balanced Packaged Goods Markets

	How Much Share of Voice is Below Share of Market	
13% + brands with rising trends	(*n* = 83)	−1 percentage point
13% + brands with static trends	(*n* = 53)	−3 percentage points
13% + brands with declining trends	(*n* = 64)	−4 percentage points

Allowing for the small sample sizes, we can tentatively conclude that the average larger (13 percent +) brand with a rising sales trend will be profit taking—underinvesting in advertising by 1 percentage point. But there are signs that with a greater underinvestment, the sales increase will be imperiled, and if the underinvestment opens out to 4 percentage points, the sales increase will turn into a decline for the average brand.

We must reiterate that our data demonstrate that profit taking by planned underinvestment in advertising is a normal (and successful) policy *only for large brands*. The others—specifically, those with a market share of less than 13 percent—are on average in an investment situation characterized by a higher share of voice than share of market.

There is not much more to be said about this analysis of shares of market and shares of voice, except the rather obvious point that so long as we accept the sample as reasonably representative, the investigation provides an unambiguous confirmation of our hypothesis that in general, large brands are less advertising intensive than small brands are, and thereby yield scale economies.

Second Hypothesis: A Growing Heterogeneity

Our investigation provides partial and suggestive, but not conclusive, confirmation of the second hypothesis.

In table 20–5 we have analyzed the 1,096 brands according to their size (again grouped in ranges of three percentage points of market share). The total number of brands is also broken down into four categories representing:

1. packaged goods in the United States and Canada
2. packaged goods in the rest of the world
3. other products in the United States and Canada
4. other products in the rest of the world

Table 20–5
Numbers of Brands by Size

	All Brands	U.S.A. and Canada Packaged Goods	Rest of World Packaged Goods	U.S.A. and Canada Other Products	Rest of World Other Products
Sample size	1,096	185	681	164	66
	100%	100%	100%	100%	(100%)
Market share					
1 to 3%	21%	34%	18%	20%	(8%)
4 to 6%	20%	24%	20%	20%	(14%)
7 to 9%	14%	7%	15%	17%	(14%)
10 to 12%	9%	8%	11%	11%	(8%)
13 to 15%	7%	5%	7%	6%	(9%)
16 to 18%	5%	4%	4%	4%	(4%)
19 to 21%	5%	3%	4%	5%	(13%)
22 to 24%	3%	4%	3%	5%	(3%)
25 to 27%	2%	2%	2%	2%	(4%)
28 to 30%	2%	1%	2%	1%	(6%)
31 or more	12%	8%	14%	9%	(17%)

Note: We have covered only advertised brands.

We can draw one important conclusion from the data in table 20–5. This point pertains to the first of the market categories above—packaged goods in the United States and Canada. We believe that this group represents the most developed and mature group of product categories in the most sophisticated geographical region of all those being examined.

In this first group, the proportion of small brands (those with market shares in the 1 to 6 percent range) is significantly above the proportion in all the markets together (58 percent, compared with 41 percent). This finding implies that development, sophistication, and maturity of markets tends to be accompanied by a degree of fragmentation and a consequent reduction in the market shares of many brands.

The sheer size of the American market means that small-share brands account for more substantial dollar volumes than brands with a similar share in smaller markets do. But the difference between the number of small brands in the United States and the number in other countries is greater than can be accounted for by this factor alone. It is the result of development and maturity, and simple observation of the introduction of successful new brands into smaller countries suggests a similar continuous tendency toward fragmentation as these markets mature. Introducing new brands substantially differentiated in functional terms from those already there is about the only effective way of innovating in markets that show little overall growth and have well-entrenched existing brands.[6]

In this book, we have seen a number of specific examples of this type of innovation leading to market fragmentation—in, among others, the markets for mouthwash, petfoods, shampoo, soft drinks, and toilet soap. And although the data are not completely generalizable, we believe that we do have something here that is much more solid than an unsupported hypothesis. We have the strong feeling that as markets develop, they become not more homogeneous but more heterogeneous.

The large brands handled by JWT (table 20–2) merit brief note. The markets investigated generally coincided, as mentioned, with the sources of the agency's business (a fact that did not make for a seriously untypical sample, because of the broad spread of JWT's coverage of markets). In this sample, JWT handles 33 percent of the larger brands—a remarkably high figure and a dramatic illustration of not only the agency's experience in handling large brands but also to some extent its expertise in building them.

Third Hypothesis: Maturity Equals Flatness

There are at least three aspects of flatness, the stationary market conditions that have been referred to so often in this book—(a) a relatively unchanging limit to the size of any market, (b) relative constancy in the shares of individual market segments, and (c) relative stability in individual brand shares. Some useful though not complete data from our investigation suggest that stationary conditions have a wide (but not universal) application.

It is in packaged goods that a large number of markets show little or no overall growth. In this regard, table 20–6 demonstrates a clear difference between packaged goods and other types of goods and services.

The data in table 20–6 can be collapsed into the following simpler statistical distribution (table 20–7).

Although this table shows that 32 percent of packaged goods markets are growing strongly, the statistic calls for two qualifications. First, all the data in the table are unweighted by market size. In fact, the growing markets tend to represent new and often insecurely established subsegments that account for low volumes of consumption (examples of annual per capita consumption taken at random are 0.58 pounds, 143 milliliters, 90 milliliters, 44 milliliters, 1.2 kilograms, and 300 grams). It is the larger, long-established markets that tend to be flat or declining (again, a few random examples of annual per capita consumption levels: 3.55 kilograms, 12.19 packages, 19.2 pounds, 7.2 pounds, 9.1 pounds, and 3.8 rolls). Second, in a small minority of cases, annual increases in unit sales were accompanied by a reduction in the average size per unit, leading to a virtually unchanged total volume of consumption.

Taking into account these two qualifications—in particular, the first one—it is fairly obvious that the 68 percent of packaged goods markets that

Table 20–6
Annual Market Growth

	All Markets	Packaged Goods Markets	Non-Packaged-Goods Markets
Sample size:	215	170	45
	100%	100%	(100%)
+14 p.a. or more	15%	12%	(27%)
+11 to +13% p.a.	3%	2%	(7%)
+8 to 10% p.a.	9%	6%	(23%)
+5 to +7% p.a.	13%	12%	(16%)
+2 to 4% p.a.	21%	23%	(9%)
STABLE	25%	30%	(4%)
(+1 or 0 or −1 p.a.)			
−2 to −4% p.a.	7%	8%	(4%)
−5 to −7% p.a.	3%	3%	(2%)
−8 to −10% p.a.	1%	1%	(2%)
−11 to −13% p.a.	1%	1%	(2%)
−14 p.a. or more	2%	2%	(4%)

Notes: From the total of 242 questionnaires, fully usable data on market growth were available from only 215.

In the majority of cases, the average growth or decline covered the five years 1982–1986. In a minority of cases, we have relied on estimates for four or (rarely) three years.

Table 20–7
Simplified Analysis of Rates of Growth in Markets

	Packaged Goods	Nonpackaged Goods
Total	100%	(100%)
Markets that are:		
Growing strongly	32%	(73%)
Growing weakly	23%	(9%)
Flat	30%	(4%)
Declining	15%	(14%)

are in the lowest categories of growth should receive a heavier emphasis than what is shown in the table. This means that, in general, much the largest majority of *substantial* and *established* markets for packaged goods show little total growth. The situation with other types of goods and services is different, although the strong increase in many of these markets is also accompanied by considerable volatility. It is nevertheless important for clients and agencies to look outside the packaged goods field for the most substantial future sales increases. And agencies in particular—as they have recently discovered to their cost—can expect only sluggish growth in the advertising budgets of their traditional packaged goods clients.[7]

Our investigation does not shed any light on movements in the shares of specific market segments. But the data in table 20–2 regarding sales trends for larger brands indicate a generally small degree of upward and downward movement, hence a further general confirmation of the stability of the market situation of those brands.

21
The Search for General Patterns

> [Bacon] supposed that natural laws would disclose themselves by the accumulation and due arrangement of instances without any need for original speculation on the part of the investigator. . . . [Whewell] saw that science advances only in so far as the mind of the inquirer is able to suggest organizing ideas.
> —Henry Sturt, *Encyclopedia Britannica, 1910*[1]

Lessons That Cut Across the Cases

Readers will remember the twenty points, or signposts, described in Chapter 1: the features we recommended that readers look out for when going through the case studies. In Chapter 20, we examined three of those signposts in more detail, with the help of additional information collected from a narrowly focused but widespread inquiry carried out among JWT offices in many parts of the world.

Although, as we emphasized in Chapter 1, it is not possible to make a statistically sound survey of the marketing field on the basis of a sample of nineteen brands, we believe that we can use the data qualitatively and impressionistically. Indeed, it seems to us that the information in the cases and in chapter 20 provides substantial confirmation of the twenty points with which we began this book. Although it would be superfluous to labor these points by repeating them in detail, the individual cases have presented more than a hundred separate lessons. Two-thirds of these lessons overlap, and a number overlap extensively; some lessons thus have more widespread significance than others.

We have therefore taken a number of the more important points listed in chapter 1 (marked in this chapter with a triangle), and are here re-presenting them in a somewhat different form, in some instances fusing them to supplementary points raised by the cases. In addition, we have added a number of fresh conclusions, and, with a few of them, attempted something more ambitious than a mere tabulation or synthesis of the arguments. Some of these points will be used as a springboard for thoughts that are frankly speculative; the present condition of the advertising business is not so healthy that practitioners can allow themselves to treat as irrelevant all speculation about what might (or should) happen to it in the future.

Some Original Signposts—And Some New Ones

In this chapter we shall confine ourselves to conclusions about advertising rather than about markets or brands; our focus will therefore be more narrow than in chapters 1 and 20. And we shall confine the discussion to the following five topics: advertising strategy, the creative contribution, international campaigns, budgeting and scale economies, and the point of maximum sensitivity. The points we make will (as in chapter 1) be listed in a single sequence.

Advertising Strategy

1. **Demographics and Psychographics.** Although studies of demographics (Smarties, TSB) and psychographics (Campari, Timotei) can be used to find clear market opportunities, it is dangerous to take such studies too far—to hypothesize, for instance, that there are defined market segments of exclusive users of any brand. The danger stems from the fact that in the majority of packaged goods markets, consumers buy clusters of brands, often functionally different from one another. This practice makes it misleading to try to match product segments based on functional differences with consumer segments based on demographics and psychographics. In markets where multibrand buying is the exception and not the rule, however, demographic and psychographic segmentation of the most sophisticated variety becomes possible and can provide a most productive planning tool (Ford Escort).

2. **Finding Opportunities in Flat Markets.▲** This is a real problem for old and new brands in stationary markets. There are, however, at least five strategies that have a track record of success, the last of which appears to have the most widespread application.

a. Ferreting out growing subsegments within stable total markets (Campari, Mumm).

b. Using growth in retail distribution as a dynamic to increase sales (Mumm).[2]

c. Exploiting regional opportunities (Kraft P'tit Québec).[3]

d. Searching for and exploiting functional superiority in a brand (Ford Escort) or major functional differences between it and other brands (Discover, Listerine, Quaker Kibbles 'n Bits, Slice). Remember also the downside of this point—the danger of neglecting functional improvement (Oxo).

e. Gradually changing the focus of marketing activity from penetration growth to usage growth (Campari, Mumm, *Kodak,* Listerine, Quaker Kibbles 'n Bits, TSB). Research is of above-average importance in implementing this strategy.

All these policies are most logically supported by advertising that employs mainly discriminating arguments. It will also occur to the reader that it is certain of the strategies listed here that have contributed most to the growing heterogeneity of markets.

3. Coherence and Continuity. One of the most striking characteristics of many successful brands is the complementarity and integration of their brand values: the rational and nonrational features they communicate (Ford Escort, *Kodak,* Listerine, Lux, Slice, De Beers). In some cases, the brand values have identifiable national associations (Kraft P'tit Québec) or a unique identity that is national in origin (Timotei). The strategy for most of these brands has not changed much over time. But in certain other cases, a carefully planned strategic evolution has achieved success at least temporarily and in some instances in the long term (Oxo, Smarties).

4. Modifying Attitudes. In a number of cases in this book, the advertising has successfully modified public attitudes toward brands. Sometimes this was done to correct communications weaknesses, which in certain instances were concealed and somewhat unexpected (Goodyear, Oxo). At other times, a planned long-term effort served to broaden and enrich people's perceptions of the brand as part of the overall strategy for the company (Ford Escort, TSB). In none of these cases was an attempt made to reverse existing public attitudes; the objective throughout was to add an extra dimension to the brand's existing strengths.

5. The Importance of Advertising.▲ As explained in chapter 1, there are no cases in this book in which advertising represents the sole stimulus to purchase. With the majority of packaged goods, advertising acts primarily as a reinforcement of other stimuli (not least, people's personal satisfaction with the brand). In these circumstances, advertising has an undeniable long-term importance, although the effect of its withdrawal would not be strongly felt in the short term.

In other cases in this collection, advertising has a positive but somewhat polarized role. We are thinking about those campaigns described on the King Continuum as stimulating people to seek information (Orkin, USMC). The business simply could not function without the advertising trigger. Yet the advertising plays a secondary part in the final purchase decision—a decision that is resolved, in the cases we cite, by the consumer as a result of a relatively rational consideration of all the options. The advertising puts the brand on the consumer's shopping list. Having done so, its value lies in the contribution it has made over time to strengthening people's attitudes toward the brand. In this, its role resembles the more indirect part that advertising plays in selling packaged goods. On occasion, this indirect role can be of major, even decisive, importance, although it is a lagged effect.

With De Beers, advertising's role is small in comparison with other influences on sales, yet a fairly clear differential exists between sales in countries where advertising expenditure is comparatively high and in those where it is low. This point suggests an effect real enough to be measurable at the margin. Yet we cannot argue that advertising is the primary or even the secondary stimulus to sales.

With TSB, advertising has had a clear influence on consumers' use of the bank services, despite the extremely low advertising-to-sales ratio. The advertising works synergistically with other parts of the marketing mix, especially the selling efforts of the bank branches.

6. Leadership. In a number of cases in this book, a brand seems to benefit from something above and beyond its battery of rational and nonrational values in the consumer's mind. Such brands have a confidence—a tone of voice—whose value cannot in any way be measured, yet such a quality seems to provide an extra measure of credibility and importance to each of the brand's intrinsic and extrinsic qualities (*Kodak*, Listerine, Lux, Oxo). This benefit is the result not only of long history and secure establishment but also to some extent of the response of competitors (a manifestation of oligopoly). This factor can actually provide a third-part endorsement, itself a most valuable benefit. That Listerine, for instance, is featured in Procter and Gamble's Scope commercials is, we would argue, of considerable advantage to Listerine, since Listerine is set up in such advertisements as a standard of quality against which Scope is being compared.

7. The Future. One of the features of modern business that impinges strongly on marketing and advertising is the general increase in the information load. That the flow of data is rising exponentially has—subject to some qualifications—a great potential influence on how we shall be able to develop advertising strategy in the future. There are many new types of information. The following are important but do not represent an exclusive list:

a. single-source data, measuring individual consumers' day-by-day purchasing in different product fields, related in each case to day-by-day media exposure.

b. an extension of the first source, to provide data that measure the individual components of consumer purchasing: penetration, purchase frequency, frequency distribution, repeat purchasing, and multibrand buying.

c. model building and other econometric techniques, to trace mathematically the discrete effects of advertising.

The problem for agencies (as for all organizations feeling the impact of what is rather imposingly called the communications revolution) is not so much to generate, process, and interpret the data; it is the much more difficult task of inoculating the most critical information into the bloodstream of the organization's working professionals in such a way that it *continuously* influences their intellectual and imaginative contributions to the enterprise. What makes the problem particularly difficult is that the flow of data increases at a geometrical rate while the increase in the supply of material of operational value is arithmetical at best. This means that the job of sifting and discriminating is already considerable and will become more so in the future.

This trend has implications for the future organization of agencies. Marketing analysts claim plausibly that massive increases in the information flow must be met by greater specialization and decentralization within the organization.[4] There is, of course, very little new about the principle of specialization; in the eighteenth century, Adam Smith recognized it as the key to increased productivity. And Stanley Resor confirmed more than three decades ago its relevance to the agency business when he said: "All our progress to date has been by the division of labor."[5] There is also no doubt that the increases in available information should call for a dramatic increase in the lubrication of the organization's inner workings.

All the matters discussed here are related to other aspects of agency work and are considered further at the end of the next section.

The Creative Contribution: "Everything Else is Plumbing"[6]

8. Motivating and Discriminating Arguments. ▲ Some brands have been built by the continuous use of motivating arguments (*Kodak*, Nescafé, Oxo, De Beers). In the marketplace, however, are forces—notably, the trend toward heterogeneity—that gives an increasing importance to discriminating, brand-specific arguments, and the use of such arguments is the most appropriate strategy for both established second brands in a market (USMC) and most new brands (Discover, Quaker Kibbles 'n Bits, Slice, Timotei). (There was a particular problem with Slice, because with the launch of rival juice-based soft drinks, it became necessary to find a brand-specific discriminating argument; this represented the point of maximum sensitivity for both Slice and JWT.)

For well-entrenched brands, the balance of motivators and discriminators is a matter of exceptional importance and nice judgment, particularly since large established brands are inevitably and continuously vulnerable to competitive assault (Nescafé). The creative stance of *Kodak,* Listerine, Lux, and Oxo deserves comment. In each case, the brand is projected as a market leader but one that reminds users that its superiority is based on both general *and specific* excellence.

In exceptional circumstances, smaller brands can be advertised effectively by appropriating motivating arguments (Mumm). But the effectiveness of such a strategy depends on whether the ground has been left clear by larger competitors: those which should be using motivating arguments but which have neglected the opportunity to adopt them as their exclusive property.

9. Rational Strategy and Nonrational Execution. This point highlights the difference between an advertising stimulus and the response it evokes. The strategy may aim to achieve a perfectly serious and rational response, yet the stimulus itself can afford on some occasions to be lighthearted (Goodyear, TSB) and on other occasions to be partly, even substantially, emotional (Discover, Orkin). Nonrational stimuli stand a generally better chance of involving the consumer than rational stimuli do, which means that the technique described here has practical advantages based on consumer psychology. The distinction between an advertising stimulus and the consumer's response to that stimulus has been a central part of JWT's advertising philosophy for more than two decades. It is one of the agency's most important planning disciplines.

10. Production Values. In this collection are a number of cases in which production values, particularly in filmmaking, have made a significant contribution to the selling power of an advertising campaign (De Beers, *Kodak,* Lux, Slice, Smarties, Timotei, USMC). In every case, the production values have represented an extra ingredient contributing to greater consumer involvement and increased persuasiveness. But in no cases have high production values been used to compensate for a deficiency in the creative idea. Our instinct tells us that to do so would be ineffective policy, although there is no empirical evidence to demonstrate this view.

Advertising production is expensive, and the costs are continually rising. Small improvements in the quality of the final execution normally mean a disproportionate increase in total production cost. Such increase is often resisted by agencies (and a fortiori by clients) on substantially emotional grounds. This resistance is not always wise. Screen-time budgets are often ten times or more the size of production budgets, which means that modest improvements in a campaign's execution have an enlarged effect because they are (as it were) magnified by the size of the screen-time investment. This inflated effect provides a return that is often greater than the increase in the basic production cost, despite the fact that the latter is normally quite substantial.

11. Integration. In virtually every product field, expenditure on promotions below-the-line represents a substantial addition to a brand's investments in advertising above-the-line. Indeed, with packaged goods in the United States, money spent on the former normally exceeds what is spent on the latter by a ratio of 2 to 1.[7]

A simple point emerges: There are obvious synergistic advantages if the two types of activities are planned to work in cooperation. Notable examples in this book demonstrate this point (De Beers, Discover and Ford Escort, none of which is a brand of packaged goods). Oddly enough, integration tends to be less in most packaged goods fields, where relative expenditures below-the-line are generally highest, because in these categories the two activities are generally planned separately, to achieve different objectives—advertising to build the consumer franchise and promotions to operate tactically and competitively to help the brand meet short-term sales goals. Evidence from many cases outside this collection indicates that these two activities, as they operate in the marketplace, can pull in opposite directions, with an obviously counterproductive overall outcome.

12. Too Few Ideas—or Too Many? As noted on more than one occasion, the cases in this book are, from one point of view, grossly untypical of the advertising field, in that they all represent demonstrable successes. Outside this collection and across the whole field of new brand launches, failure is the norm; and for ongoing brands, there is suggestive evidence that the quality of the campaign makes a different to sales only in about 30 percent of all cases.[8] With such discouraging odds, it is no exaggeration to say that the production of campaign ideas—something that lies at the heart of all agencies' work—is a highly uncertain business, most commonly characterized by the production of either too few ideas or too many: too few to throw up a selling concept or else too many for the ability of the evaluators at the agency and in the client's organization to distinguish the sheep from the goats. There are not many business enterprises whose output is either so infertile or so erratic. It is often a surprise to professional observers that advertising sometimes actually works: such is the low level of our expectations.

With the pressure on all businesses today, not least the specific pressure to increase progressively the productivity of advertising (common in packaged goods and also in many other fields—witness Orkin and the USMC), we think it might be useful to think about the influence of agency organization on the centrally important process of idea generation.

Agencies in developed markets are organized on a seemingly decentralized matrix principle, built around the multidisciplinary account group. This system has, however, been modified over the years to introduce very pronounced hierarchical and managerial elements. One influence has been the growth of multitier account management, a system originally introduced to reflect the structure of multitier brand management in client organizations. Account management in U.S. agencies currently comprises approximately 15 percent of the total staff—an astonishing figure in comparison with the amount of management in most other businesses.[9] Account managers in agencies are generalists (very few of them have even come out of a specialist background), and although they are only peripherally involved in the general management of the agency, their job is to manipulate its resources on their clients' behalf. This makes it legitimate to classify their function genuinely as management.

A second factor contributing to the growth of hierarchies and tighter managerial control has been the development (sometimes with increasing rigidity) of internal agency procedures—plans boards, review boards, and systematized planning and research methods. These procedures have been set up only partly with the aim of increasing quality and efficiency. An equally strong motivation has been to bring in top agency management to establish a uniform "look" to the agency's work, with the aim (at least partly) of helping to sell the advertising to the client.

We must add at this point that the JWT systems do not fall into this category. The agency's planning procedures (a number of which have been mentioned in this book) have evolved slowly on the basis of feedback and experience, and they have been set up with some delicacy with the explicit objective of not stifling creativity. In this regard, JWT's systems are very much the exception in the industry and if not unique are certainly unusual.

Yet a third influence on the growth of hierarchical management is the increasingly intrusive financial controls imposed on account groups—a side effect of the public ownership of agencies. For many years, senior account managers have been provided with data (admittedly, of a rather crude quality) on the profitability to the agency of the accounts they control. This information has often introduced a tension, a conflict of loyalties, between (a) the account managers' duty to provide the best possible service to their clients, and (b) their duty to their agency's top management (and via them to the stockholders) to maximize the agency's profit. The effect has been a generally more intrusive management of the operation of the account group.

The problem with such a growth is that it is widely believed—by people with a practiced sensitivity to the business—to inhibit originality and unorthodoxy, qualities that are the agency's essential stock-in-trade. Although this point should be readily apparent to men and women in the agency business itself, most such persons are too close to their day-to-day operations to appreciate it, or at least for it to occur to them spontaneously. The point is more strikingly obvious to well-trained but objective outsiders, such as the better management consultants. The following quotation expresses the opinion of Booz, Allen and Hamilton on what that organization deems to be at the heart of the advertising agency business: "[T]he key element is *creativity*. The key to creativity is *collaboration*, not authority."[10]

Judged by the most important criterion—its growth relative to other agencies—JWT made its greatest strides in the marketplace during the four decades from 1920 to 1960. For all this time, the hierarchy was minimal. There were forty people in the New York office who reported to Stanley Resor, and every overseas operation in every part of the world reported directly to Sam Meek. A well-known anecdote, one that has caused continuous amusement over the years, relates how a consultant (*not* Booz, Allen and Hamilton) advised Stanley Resor to establish a more hierarchical structure within JWT and how Resor erased all the lines connecting the boxes on the proposed organization chart.[11]

Admittedly, the agency in the 1950s was a much smaller organization than it is today. But the experience of the past twenty-five years has shown that despite a great deal of organizational innovation, there has been no lasting solution to how a complex multinational agency should be run—with, of course, its central role of full client service in mind. We suspect that some of the trouble has stemmed from the fact that the efforts to rationalize have been *too* intensive, continuous, and restless.

Interestingly enough, the diseconomies of large hierarchical structures are currently being widely debated in professional management circles, and strong sentiment is being expressed in favor of less rather than more management as a general principle. A recent article in *The Economist* states: "A survey by A. T. Kearney, a management consultancy, divided 41 large American companies into winners and losers based on long-term financial performance. It found that the winners had, on average, almost four fewer layers of management than the losers."[12]

Peter Drucker, who, as noted, is deeply concerned with the recent dramatic increase in the information load, believes that businesses generally would benefit from being reorganized in the most radical fashion, to make them operate perhaps as symphony orchestras or hospitals—organizations having a large number of specialists, each of whom has an intimate knowledge of the jobs the others perform, and who work in the closest possible collaboration, but who are subject to the minimum amount of supervisory management—one conductor to a hundred musicians in the case of an orchestra.[13]

To people with a knowledge of the advertising business, the parallel between Drucker's ideas and the way agencies *might* work has a startling appositeness. Agency managements, however, are unlikely to appreciate this parallel fully unless they persuade themselves to step back and become significantly detached from the grind of their day-to-day responsibilities. The agency business does not easily permit the luxuries of isolation and calm—which is itself rather strange, since detachment can produce unorthodox thinking, and (as we pointed out) the essence of the advertising business is, or should be, such unorthodoxy. This point should surely apply as much to how the agency organizes itself as it applies to the creative recommendations the agency presents to its clients.

What we are saying, in summary, is that agencies should not accept their present structure as the ideal, no matter how long it has been in place. Advantages could follow a thinning of the management layers, an increase in specialization and decentralization, and an improvement in the systems of internal intelligence and communications. Such changes call for a reeducation of both transmitters and receivers of information: in effect, everybody in the agency.

International Campaigns

13. The Manufacturer's Point of View. One of the notable features of the long-lasting debate about international campaigns, which itself forms part of a wider debate about global marketing, is that the arguments have for a long time been presented in terms of what is attractive to manufacturers. Much has been made of the scale economies of worldwide or regional manufacture and marketing. Much has also been made of the increasingly captive audience that has supposedly been homogenized by internationally uniform cultural stimuli, foreign travel, and the rapid increase in the flow of information that has been cited more than once in this chapter.[14]

In view of the many plausible arguments put forward in favor of global marketing, it comes as rather a surprise to learn that for every success in the field, history has provided at least one failure. Most commonly, this situation cannot be explained by deficiencies in resolution, resources, or organization; something else has caused the problem. That elusive extra variable is what matters, and it is what we should be searching for. The "globalists" have, regrettably, been not too interested in such a search; indeed, their arguments have generally been characterized by a startling absence of informed and focused empirical support.

14. The Consumer's Point of View. We believe that a useful starting point for considering the merits of international advertising campaigns is to evaluate what attractions they hold for consumers in country A and country B. If we start with consumers in this way (an approach that, after all, is the essential point of distinction between marketing and selling), we can be realistic rather than optimistic about the extent of the scale economies that our globalism will actually yield.[15]

JWT has been running international campaigns since the 1920s. The arguments in this section are derived from this wider experience (which was shared by the author during the fifteen years he personally spent working for JWT in the international field); however, a number of lessons are highlighted by the cases in this collection.

Working, then, from the standpoint of the consumer, there are five general principles that can be supported (with varying degrees of firmness) by the agency's experience of specific successes and failures in running international campaigns.

a. There is evidence from direct response that people in different countries respond in a remarkably similar fashion to the same advertising stimuli.[16] This conclusion, if not generalizable to all types of advertising, is suggestive, and it has been confirmed in a piecemeal way in many packaged goods fields.

b. International campaigns have a better chance of success in growing product categories. Once market maturity has brought a hardening of usage patterns, the difficulties of introducing new brand concepts become much greater (although not necessarily insuperable). The early success of Lux was the result of its introducing the concept of a beauty soap into an expanding product field in many countries. (Esso, Coca-Cola, and Pan American also succeeded internationally by introducing new product concepts.) We suspect that Timotei's lack of uniform success in every market into which it has been introduced is attributable to the fact that the shampoo category in many countries was too developed and crowded before Timotei's entry.

c. International campaigns work best if they are the expression of a strong brand concept (Lux, Timotei). Nevertheless, many strong brand concepts have been unsuccessful internationally—a result of the next factor.

d. International campaigns work best if their symbolism has an intrinsic attraction to the consumer. If this attraction comes from the country with which the symbol is originally associated, it can be a real and often unique strength. (Lux is a good example, and so are Coca-Cola, Pepsi-Cola, McDonald's, Chanel, and British Airways.)

e. Some flexibility in adapting advertising material to specific markets is nearly always necessary. This is a matter of sensitive evaluation, because there is an ever-present danger of what was described in the Timotei case as balkanizing strong concepts.

15. Pragmatism. The principles listed in the preceding section mean that decisions about international campaigns require as much cool judgment as vision and drive. To reduce the risks, many of the most successful campaigns have been exposed gradually by being rolled out from market to market. By this process, the advertiser and the agency have learned as they have gone along. The procedure offers many advantages, but there is also a danger: a loss of time, which can permit competitors to make their own retaliatory plans (Timotei).

Another important lesson from the Timotei case is that a strong concept can employ different media in different countries.

16. Cost Savings. We believe that although there are economic advantages to exposing international campaigns—advantages related to the cost sharing of production budgets—they must be looked at in a special way. With campaigns just like those for De Beers, Lux, and Timotei, initial production costs can be high, but the international syndication of the advertising material means that the greatest possible mileage can be gained from the initial investments. High-quality film material (in particular) can be used in countries that would not otherwise be able to afford it. International campaigns do not provide cheap options; they offer high-quality options at an economic price.

Rather than consider international campaigns in strictly money-saving terms, we believe it more sensible to reason from the starting point that effective advertising campaigns are rarities. If a campaign demonstrates its effectiveness anywhere, it is worth the effort to use it on as wide a scale as possible. In the last analysis, this is the rationale for the Lux campaign that has been run for sixty years, as well as for a number of others that have all proven their worth, although less dramatically.

17. Where International Campaigns Are Difficult to Use. In most countries except the most economically undeveloped ones, the markets that demonstrate the greatest maturity tend to be those for food and drink. Often these markets have a commodity rather than a brand orientation, but with both commodities and brands, consumption patterns tend to be firmly established and in many cases have developed much rigidity. Rather importantly, these patterns differ widely from country to country.

As a general rule, new food brands will be successful only if they are tailored to the consumer in one country (Kraft P'tit Québec). The best prospect for a global brand lies in its ability to create a new product concept, perhaps by exploiting a new and promising subsegment in a market. Although this procedure is difficult, a number of cases demonstrate that it can be done, or at least that it could be done in the past. (Nescafé, as well as Coca-Cola, Kellogg's Corn Flakes, and McDonald's; readers will also remember that the development of Slice in the United States was influenced by Pepsi-Cola's experience of soft drinks with fruit juice in Japan and Latin America).

In our general observation, there is more variation country by country in the advertising campaigns for international food brands than for brands in any other fields, a point confirmed obliquely by Sir David Orr's observation in the Foreword about how uniform product concepts had to be tailored in different countries in the marketing of brands of instant soup and low-fat spreads. This is a de facto recognition by advertisers and agencies that the food field is more idiosyncratic than others and that even global brands must be "massaged"—adapted and presented in some different fashion to take into account local variations in buying habits.

Budgeting and Scale Economies

18. Three Trends.▲ The cases in this book, supplemented by the separate inquiry described in chapter 20, suggest the existence of three market trends that all point in a similar direction and that may indeed be different expressions of a single underlying phenomenon:

a. Large brands are less advertising intensive than small brands are, and advertising intensity tends to decline progressively as brands increase in size. This point is evidence of an advertising-related scale economy of considerable importance.

b. There is pressure in many markets for the effectiveness of advertising campaigns to be progressively increased. Rather surprisingly, brands often demonstrate their ability to deliver with the required extra productivity. This situation is a description of long-term increasing returns that (as described in chapter 1) are a phenomenon separate from but compatible with short-term diminishing returns. With packaged goods, the underlying pressure for increased advertising productivity is caused by continuous reductions in relative investments above-the-line to finance increasing investments below-the-line. In certain other cases (for example, Orkin and the USMC), special forces are at work.

c. In mature markets, brands tend to grow by gradually changing the emphasis of their marketing strategy from building penetration to increasing the frequency and quantity of usage. This change is related to the ability of large brands to generate greater purchase and repurchase frequency than is the case with small brands.[17]

Knowledge of these trends has a considerable *practical* value. In fact it is possible to draw up four guiding principles for operational practice.

19. Four Guiding Principles. a. Since larger brands are relatively more profitable than smaller ones, larger brands require and deserve careful protection. Although it is true that some manufacturers are occasionally able to finance new brand ventures partly from the above-average profitability of their larger brands, great care is always needed to avoid cutting into the muscle of the latter. The danger point of cutting into this muscle can be fairly precisely identified.

b. In specific terms, and subject to the limitations of our research, we suggest that brands of packaged goods with a market share of 13 percent or greater can afford to underinvest on advertising within defined parameters. The average brand can maintain a rising trend by investing a share of voice that is on average 1 percentage point below the brand's market share. It can maintain a static trend with a share of voice 2 or 3 percentage points below market share; however, a share of voice reduced to 4 percentage points below market share is *likely to cause a brand's sales to decline.* (These data are amplified in chapter 20, and there are interesting similarities with the experience of Lux in its major markets.)

c. Although budgeting is generally an imprecise activity, it is possible to arrive at average budget levels for large numbers of ongoing brands, expressed in terms of average shares of voice for brands of different market shares. We believe that this tool is of operational value, and it is detailed in chapter 20.

d. Econometric techniques are capable of adding an extra precision to the budgetary process (TSB). It is rather a striking feature of this collection that econometric analysis is so rare; it has played role in determining the budgets of virtually none of the brands we have described.[18] We have a stubborn belief that because of the pressures of oligopolistic competition, many advertisers could well be spending too much rather than too little money on advertising. Advertisers are reluctant to cut back expenditure for fear of consequential loss of market share. They could therefore be paying a price in wasted investment for their skepticism of the modern, complex, but rapidly developing tools of econometric analysis. We must, however, make the point that the issues here are too important for us to oversimplify them. Even when there is overwhelming evidence that it will pay to reduce advertising investments in the short run, there are other longer-term forces at work that muddy the issues. We have therefore devoted the next chapter, chapter 22, to examining the more salient aspects of this entire matter.

The Point of Maximum Sensitivity

20. Longevity.▲ Despite the persuasive evidence that a brand can have a virtually indefinite life if it is skillfully enough managed and nurtured,[19] the advertising campaigns for such brands clearly do not benefit from quite such longevity. The Lux campaign, by its unusually long life, is probably an exception that proves the general validity of the rule.

Although many campaigns are durable, few last longer than one or two decades, and even that amount of time is rather exceptional (*Kodak,* Oxo, Timotei). Campaigns can dwindle in effectiveness for a number of reasons. The strategy for the brand may have evolved in such a way that the old campaign is now an ineffective (or a less effective) expression of the up-to-date strategy. The competitive situation may have developed in a way that somehow causes the cutting edge of the campaign to be blunted. The most common circumstance, however, is when the campaign itself loses its salience. In Europe, this is sometimes called the wallpaper effect; the campaign, like the wallpaper in a room, remains inconspicuously present, but it has effectively receded into the background so that nobody notices it anymore.

The need to change poses an agonizing dilemma. On the one hand, if the change is premature, there is a substantial opportunity cost in lost sales. On the other hand, if the decision is postponed until sales have begun to turn downward, the brand loses any leadership stance it may have had and becomes essentially responsive, a situation in which mistakes are easily made. Further sales losses can anyway be expected because of the very delay that has already taken place.

21. Two Problems.▲ The first and most urgent problem is obviously how to detect *whether* and *when* a change in campaign is necessary. The second problem is to judge whether a newly developed campaign will solve the problem it was developed to address. These are matters of extreme delicacy. Hence our description "the point of maximum sensitivity" for the nodal point—that which JWT was unable to pass in the cases of certain important advertisers featured in this collection (Discover, Slice), although it is only fair to state that the agency successfully passed it in most of the other cases in this book, and in effect passes the point, often with demonstrable success, with every one of its clients when a campaign is changed.

The successes are the result of good judgment supported by good (although sometimes less good) research. There is no guarantee that better research would have led to a happier outcome with Discover and Slice. But our judgment tells us that the chances of success would have been marginally better.

22. Tracking Studies.▲ Since the latent problems with certain campaigns are hidden from view and even unexpected (Goodyear, Oxo), any research used to detect such problems must be subtle if it is to be really helpful. A full battery of image attributes and user attributes for our brand and its competitors is one research mechanism that has proved its worth. The tracking must be continuous, although the intervals need not be too close (for example, twice a year or even annual readings are normally satisfactory, because changes in images and user attributes tend not to be dramatic in the short term). The same total number of attributes should be measured in period after period, since an increase in the number covered in the research tends to depress the scores (the result of interview fatigue), producing highly misleading results. Data on brand awareness, both "top of mind" and "share of mind," are also useful.

Tracking advertising awareness is a more problematical procedure.[20] Nevertheless, information on the density of the advertising imagery often provides a useful guide to whether the campaign is holding or losing its salience.

There is not much more to be said about what might be considered the rather predictable recommendations in this section, except to remind readers of the specific examples in this book of the eminently *practical* value of such tracking studies—Kraft, TSB, USMC. The preeminent example, however, is Oxo, which from this point of view (and also from at least one other) represents a case study of above-average value and importance.

23. Contingency Planning. This is the second outstanding feature of the Oxo case. The problem addressed is how we can know with reasonable certainty whether it is correct to move from campaign A to campaign B. Consider the following test design.

Run campaign A nationally with the full panoply of image- and sales-tracking research, all of this accompanied by the concurrent exposure in one single area of campaign B, also tracked with a similar barrage of research. After a time, and when campaign B reveals strong signals of success with consumers, move to a second phase in the campaign, exposing campaign B nationally (again with its accompanying research tracking) but now with campaign A in a single geographical area (also with its tracking mechanism).

Readers will readily appreciate the immense (and to some extent disheartening) trouble and expense involved in such an operation. But they surely also cannot deny its subtlety and sheer intellectual elegance. Even more important is the evidence from Oxo of such a plan's effectiveness in the marketplace. It represents marketing of a most elevated level of precision and sophistication. In the United States, area testing is currently being subjected to much criticism, and based on their unhappy experience with it, certain advertisers are frankly disenchanted.[21] Nevertheless, if for no other reason than that good and improving quantitative data are being produced in a greater flow than ever before, we believe unhesitatingly that programs of the Oxo kind are going to expand in number and importance in the future. In fact, they are the strongest images in our crystal ball.

22

Does It Pay to Advertise?

> The fact that advertising cannot reverse a major trend in national consumption or in the consumption of a product group as a whole does not, of course, mean that individual advertisers are wasting their money when they fight a trend. Advertising may add sufficient value to an individual *brand* of a product to enable it to resist the trend.
> —Martin Mayer[1]

A Rhetorical Question

The reader will have noticed that the title of this book is a question, although it is in fact a more complicated one than it appears to be at first glance. Since the question has been posed, the reader has every reason to expect an answer. We shall try to provide one in this concluding chapter, although in view of the complexity of the problem posed by the question, we shall offer not one answer but three.

At the simplest level, the question is merely rhetorical and therefore invites an easy response. The cases in this book demonstrate, without exception, that for the brands described it does pay to advertise, or at least has paid to do so in the past. We hope that readers, having examined the cases—especially the many examples of new campaigns that have triggered immediate increases in sales—will have no doubt in their minds that the facts are strong enough to support this first answer to the question.

From two points of view, however, this is a worrying oversimplification. For one thing, successful brands are the exception, not the rule, in the real world. It is therefore quite impossible to extrapolate the lessons of this book to support the view that it always pays to advertise. In the next section, we shall make an attempt to describe quite specifically when it actually *does* pay.

For another thing—and this point is more subtle and more disturbing— the campaigns described in this book were demonstrably effective when they were supported by certain levels of media pressure, levels described in most of these cases. No proof is provided in any rigorous scientific sense that the budget actually deployed was the correct sum of money to optimize sales and maximize profit. What in fact do we know about the best advertising level at which it pays to advertise with maximum effect?

When Does It Pay to Advertise?

One of the things we know with certainty about advertising is that no matter how strong a campaign may be creatively or how powerfully and extensively it is exposed, advertising will not compensate for major deficiencies in the rest of a brand's marketing mix. For success, the brand must fulfill a real consumer need and the product must offer some functional advantage in a competitive marketplace. The price must be acceptable. And the retail distribution must be reasonably extensive (although advertising can operate as an effective, albeit expensive, engine to force distribution, despite the fact that the process takes time to accomplish and potential sales are sacrificed during the buildup). If the marketing mix has major weaknesses in any of these respects, it is difficult for us to view advertising as anything but a weak force, because of its inability to compensate.

Still, if the brand does fulfill a consumer need, if it is functionally effective in the eyes of at least a substantial minority of people, if its price is acceptable, and if it is reasonably well distributed (four rather large *ifs*), there is a good chance that advertising can increase the brand's sales. (Advertising will not always increase its profit, which depends not only on sales volume but also on other variables that will be discussed in this chapter.) But sales increases are possible even if the brand is competing in a stationary or declining market—the situation faced by most packaged goods. To use a trite but substantially true analogy, the brand is the chicken and the advertising is the egg. As in the original conundrum, the chicken is not independent of the egg, because the advertising helps to create the brand in the first place by providing its psychological added values. But this notion can be accommodated by extending the chicken-egg analogy to include the element of heredity, with the product generating the advertising, which in turn begins to transform the product into the brand, which in turn generates more advertising to continue the process.

Most of the cases in this book demonstrate advertising as working in that way. Brands are substantially created by psychological values added to functional ones—a cumulative process, the advertising building the added values in the minds of people at least slightly familiar with the brand, and in most circumstances existing users. This process has a behavioral outcome, as frequent users are encouraged to buy similar quantities as often as they previously did and infrequent users are encouraged to buy larger quantities more often.

From the processes described so far, it obviously pays to advertise a brand only if the rest of the marketing mix is strong. This point is a thread that runs through every case in this book. It is not, however, true for the majority of new brands, hence their high rate of failure. And even for ongoing brands, a weakening of the nonadvertising elements in the marketing mix (most often, a relative weakening in comparison with competitive brands) can affect sales adversely and in some cases fatally.

It is also true that despite strengths in the rest of the mix, a brand can still fail for reasons directly related to the advertising—if there are creative or budgetary or media deficiencies.

These points all emphasize the fact that the cases in this book represent exceptional rather than normal experience. The brands described here have all beaten the odds. For them, it pays to advertise. But for many others, it does not. In this sense, there is truth in the well-known aphorism uttered originally by Lord Leverhulme and later by John Wanamaker that half his advertising was wasted but he could not tell which half.[2] Indeed, the saying probably makes an exaggerated estimate of the amount of advertising that pays. In such circumstances, practitioners cannot in any way afford to be complacent about the "state of the art".

This is our second answer to the question, "Does it pay to advertise?" Our third answer is more complex, and it is developed in the next section.

What Is the Best Advertising Level at Which It Pays to Advertise with Maximum Effect?

It is theoretically possible to arrive at the optimal advertising level to maximize profit as a result of experimental adjustments to pressure, up and down, and measurement of the resulting sales. In normal circumstances, increases in advertising will, of course, cause sales to go up, and the additional profit can be compared with the cost of the extra advertising. It can also be expected that decreases in advertising will cause sales to go down, and the fall in profit from the sales reduction can be compared with the money saved by the advertising cutback. Although this procedure sounds useful, there are great complications.

The main difficulty stems from the problem of isolating the influence of the advertising from the other parts of the marketing mix in a precise way. Precision is needed if we are to use the procedure operationally, basing action on estimates of *how much* of the extra sales can be firmly attributed to the increased advertising pressure (or how much of the sales reduction is caused by the cutback).

Reasonably exact estimates of how much sales variability can be attributed to changes in advertising pressure can be made as a result of regression analysis. This method can produce a mathematical measure, the coefficient of advertising elasticity, the percentage rise in sales that will follow a 1 percent increase in advertising pressure and vice versa. It is a fairly difficult procedure, but it has in fact been done for hundreds of brands.

The British analyst Simon Broadbent, of Leo Burnett, has published a summary of the advertising elasticities of eighty-four different European brands.[3] The actual measures vary from virtually zero to more than 0.50. The average coefficient is 0.20, which means that for the average brand in these studies, a 1 percent increase in advertising will cause sales to go up by 0.2 percent. A more practicable 10 percent increase in advertising pressure will lift sales by 2 percent.

Nariman Dhalla, formerly of JWT New York, has published elasticities for twenty-one different American brands, with an average coefficient interestingly close to Broadbent's (0.23, compared with 0.20).[4] The particular point of interest in Dhalla's studies is that he makes it quite clear that his elasticities, like Broadbent's, are measures of short-term effect—the immediate change in sales resulting from increases and decreases in advertising pressure. But Dhalla introduces the additional thought that an increase in advertising will have not only a short-term but also a lagged effect, because of the repeat purchase that will follow the first purchase stimulated by the advertising. Dhalla evaluates this additional delayed effect by including a lagged dependent variable as one of the independent variables in his calculation, a procedure that is open to technical criticism. Nevertheless, despite the supposed lack of precision introduced by this technique, the notion of a carryover effect for advertising is valuable and is, incidentally, entirely harmonious with the double effect of advertising discussed in chapter 1's section entitled "Advertising That Works Does So Immediately."

That Dhalla's lagged effect represents extra sales on top of the short-term increase means that his long-term, or cumulative, advertising elasticity is in every case above his short-term coefficient. Dhalla estimates it to be at least twice as high and in many cases higher.

We can now look at how this measure of advertising elasticity can be used in practice. There are three factors we need to isolate if we wish to determine whether upward (or downward) movements in advertising pressure will cause profit to rise or fall:

1. the brand's advertising elasticity coefficient (the cumulative coefficient is a truer measure of sales effect than the short-term one is)

2. the brand's advertising-to-sales (A:S) ratio

3. the brand's net profit ratio (after contribution to overhead)

To arrive at the figures in items 2 and 3, sales should be measured by net sales value (n.s.v.), that is, excluding wholesale and retail margins. These last two ratios (unlike the advertising elasticity) are routinely available for any brand.

The way in which these three measures interact is best illustrated by working out some relatively simple arithmetical tables. Because it is difficult to accommodate clearly three variables in one table, we found it best to select one variable (the brand's A:S ratio, but the others could have been chosen equally well) and examine the interaction of the other two variables as they pertain to a single A:S ratio. We then repeated the procedure for other A:S ratios. We worked out estimates in table 22–1 for A:S ratios of 3 percent, 5 percent and 7 percent. This range is typical of most packaged goods, but it takes little trouble to estimate the figures for any other advertising levels. There is, in fact, a simple formula for working out the tables, but we have relegated this formula to the notes for this chapter because we think it important to devote our argument here to discussing typical levels of the variables described, as well as their operational implications.[5]

In each table, we have plotted a range of advertising-elasticity coefficients, against each of which is a figure for the "Profitability Barrier." This barrier can act as a decision, or trigger, point. If the brand's actual net profit is below the Profitability Barrier, it pays to reduce advertising; if it is above, it pays to increase advertising. The tables can be used as a "ready reckoner." Readers will be able to read off the Profitability Barrier for any brands whose

Table 22–1
Profitability Barriers for Brands in Different Ranges

Advertising Elasticity	Profitability Barrier for Brand with 3 Percent A:S Ratio
+0.10	30.0%
+0.20	15.0%
+0.30	10.0%
+0.40	7.5%
+0.50	6.0%
+0.60	5.0%

Advertising Elasticity	Profitability Barrier for Brand with 5 Percent A:S Ratio
+0.10	50.00%
+0.20	25.00%
+0.30	16.67%
+0.40	12.50%
+0.50	10.00%
+0.60	8.33%

Advertising Elasticity	Profitability Barrier for Brand with 7 Percent A:S Ratio
+0.10	70.0%
+0.20	35.0%
+0.30	23.3%
+0.40	17.5%
+0.50	14.0%
+0.60	11.7%

A:S ratios and advertising elasticities are known and are covered in the tables. And actionable conclusions can be drawn.

We hope that readers will find this a helpful device, if used with qualifications, to guide budgetary strategy. But as we have suggested, there are also some general observations that should be made about the data contained in these tables.

It is obvious from all this information, which certainly pertains in approximate terms to many real-life brands, that there appear to be opportunities for profit improvement via reduction in advertising pressure. Let us take one single but typical example—a brand with an A:S ratio of 5 percent and an advertising elasticity coefficient of 0.40. (Remember that this is the long-term coefficient and might represent the cumulative advertising elasticity for an average brand whose short-term elasticity is 0.20.) For such a brand, it pays in the short term to cut back advertising if its net profit after overhead is below 12.5 percent. Such a situation is common in the real world; indeed, we believe that the majority of brands probably yield net profits below this level.

Long-Term Considerations

If a brand's advertising elasticity can be reliably estimated, the immediate effect of pressure change on profit can be reliably predicted. But is this the whole story? Regrettably, it is not, because on top of the difficulty of calculating the advertising elasticity are a number of additional factors that complicate the issues. We shall briefly describe three separate points that have varying degrees of importance when we consider the long-term implications of changes (especially reductions) in advertising pressure aimed at boosting profit in the short term.

1. Such advertising cutbacks may endanger the brand's market share, despite the fact that the loss of profit on the reduced sales may well be of smaller value than the advertising reduction (thus resulting in a net gain). Such a loss in sales is possible unless other manufacturers follow the same path of budget reduction—something that may or may not happen. If it does, aggregate sales and individual shares in the market may hold with a lower overall advertising level,[6] which has certainly happened in the past on occasions.[7] There have even been cases of advertising reductions associated with *increasing* sales.[8] But the sales outturn is more likely to show a reduction (albeit a predicted one).

This matter can be quite serious; it should be remembered that the absolute volume of sales is sometimes as important as the brand's profit, because volume can represent a "critical mass" with an ability to generate scale economies. By its very size, a brand's sales volume often enables it to make an important contribution to an advertiser's general overhead (to provide the same absolute amount, the brand's *relative* contribution to overhead would need to be larger if its total sales were smaller).

2. A second long-term consideration is the possibility of increases in the consumer price of the brand, justified by the added values built by advertising (generally by advertising increases). Price increases could possibly boost the brand's eventual profit rate to a significant degree. There is a generalized tendency for stronger brands to justify above-average prices (see chapter 20).

3. Another factor complicating the issues stems from the advertising elasticity itself. The possibility of increasing profit by manipulating the advertising budget naturally depends on the elasticity coefficient remaining constant. A different campaign, however, can yield a different elasticity; the elasticity of the brand can in fact vary year by year, although this situation may be untypical.[9]

It is therefore possible, although not probable, that boosting profit by increasing sales through a more productive campaign is as interesting an option as moving the advertising appropriation up and down. In fact, as any practitioner knows, changing the campaign is the main thing advertisers and agencies have always done (and presumably always will do) in order to try to increase the sales of the brands they advertise. But what they have not often done in the past is to use econometric techniques to measure the effects. There are reasons for this reluctance to use econometrics.

Over and beyond the difficulty of developing the econometric tools are two special problems, one concerned with the methodology and the other connected with the likely extent of the effects of the campaign change. The methodological problem is that a new campaign must be exposed for a time in at least one region before its advertising elasticity can be calculated (and thereafter used operationally). There is therefore a lag in the system, and the *existing* elasticity cannot be used as a planning tool, as is the case when we are manipulating media pressure. The other problem is that those campaigns which make a significant quantifiable difference in the sales of a brand are rarities, although the minority of campaigns whose marginal contribution can be thus demonstrated often produce a striking sales effect.

For these reasons, econometric evaluation is generally more helpful when we are increasing and decreasing advertising pressure than when we are changing advertising campaigns.

The question we are left with is whether these long-term complications invalidate the procedure discussed in this chapter—using econometrics to vary advertising expenditures, with the objective of boosting profit in the short term. On balance we think not, but it is clearly important to carry out area tests of the reduced (or increased) advertising pressure, monitoring the results on sales and profits for fairly extended periods; we suggest at least two years. Advertisers and agencies in all events have a strong gut resistance to cutting back advertising for fear of a galloping loss of market share. And although this fear is not always justified, clients and agencies will need evidence before any policies of changing advertising pressure (in particular, reducing it) are implemented on a more than experimental basis. Such a desire to provide objective evidence is not to be distrusted, so long as it is not used as a euphemism for preconception and prejudice.

Indeed, a matter that deserves emphasis is that planning advertising budgets has for too long been an activity controlled by rules of thumb, myth, and (at best) a very fragmentary knowledge of the effects of differential pressure. In all human endeavors—including those which are greatly more important than advertising—the development of the scientific attitude can bring measurable and almost instantaneous increases in operational effectiveness. Such an attitude means developing a mind-set characterized by objectivity, skepticism, and curiosity. All this seems simple, but the practical problems of changing attitudes in this way should not be underestimated.

One of the more difficult yet more important concepts to be grasped is that with advertising investments, as with investments of any kind, the absolute expenditure, whether large or small, is less significant than the return from that investment. Measurable payback (in the long term and still less in the short term) is a concept not in the lexicon of most modern advertisers and advertising agencies (except those in the direct-response field). But it was not always so; the reader will remember that the Listerine business was built essentially on the basis of this principle. It also makes a fitting conclusion to this chapter to remind the reader of the argument of George Washington Hill, an eminently practical advertising man of the old school whose splendid oxymoron follows the title page: ". . . advertising that produced results and increased sales, regardless of its expense, is inexpensive. On the other hand, advertising that does not increase sales, no matter how cheap it may be, is a drag on the business."[10]

Afterword: Some Keys to Understanding Effective Advertising: Speakers, Viewers, Tone of Voice, and Brand Personality

Harold F. Clark, Jr.

Advertisers—clients and their agencies—still talk about getting messages to consumers. "This is what we want to tell them," says the client's brief. "Key message," the agency calls it. Just get the proposition right and all the rest follows.

The case studies in this book demonstrate that it isn't really as simple as all that.

Consider the familiar scene in a supermarket on any Saturday morning in any town . . . anywhere. The five-year-old boy confronts his mother: "I want this." ("This," let us say, is a jar of chocolate-marshmallow dessert topping.) "No," says the mother firmly, already fearful of what she knows lies ahead. "But I want it," insists the five-year-old, slightly more loudly, since he knows the value of volume in public. "We don't need it. It's not good for you," argues his mother, with two vain attempts to provide a rational reason. "Well, I want it anyway. Why can't I?"—this time tinged with an incipient wail. "Because I say so," and the mother moves down the aisle. Retreat is often an effective form of communication. At this point, the boy turns to screaming, and possibly even to tears. Observers turn to watch the mother-child battle of wills in the supermarket arena. The scene plays itself out with the mother finally screaming back, perhaps with a threat, "If you don't put that back on the shelf this minute, I'll. . . . " The child cries. She is embarrassed. And the manufacturer of the chocolate-marshmallow topping has lost another sale.

The mother's "message" is clear. The child's "message" is equally clear. Neither is very successful. Giving someone the message in either rational terms ("It's not good for you") or emotional terms ("Well, I want it anyway") doesn't seem to work in this situation.

Why do we keep assuming it will work in the passive arena of television or magazine advertising?

It seems to me that anyone who still believes in delivering messages to unwilling consumers has never been a parent. Or at least has never been to a supermarket on a Saturday morning.

We all recognize this common household example and know that such communication never works. Why don't we apply that understanding to the advertising we create, place, or pay for?

In 1969, Jeremy Bullmore, then creative director of the London Office of J. Walter Thompson, gave a speech to a group of Kraft executives assembled on the top of a mountain in Switzerland. In this as-yet-unpublished speech (entitled "The Consumer Has a Mind as Well as a Stomach"), Bullmore talked about the way communication works. It is not, he suggested, a four-part process, as traditionally thought in academic circles: sender-receiver-medium-message. It is, rather, a five-part process: sender-receiver-medium-stimulus-response.

Thompson people are still accustomed to citing his most telling example: If you were a comedian and wanted people to believe that you were funny, you would not walk up to the microphone and begin by saying, "Good evening, ladies and gentlemen, I am funny."

The comedian knows that if the audience is to believe he is funny, he must tell a joke that makes them laugh.

The comedian's audience are not passive receivers of his "message." They participate actively. They laugh at his joke and conclude, "He is funny."

No audience simply absorbs messages. People respond to stimuli and draw their own conclusions. They contribute, complete, modify, reject, select, or repudiate—whether we communicators like it or not.

The successful advertising described in these case histories has worked because its creators have understood how communication works. Thompson-created advertising does not "send messages" to consumers; they carefully try to elicit specific responses from a specific target group.

Yet much of the advertising that we see every day is unsuccessful. It elicits a negative response, seeming, as it does, to scream out at us, "Buy my product." That is the same kind of noisy imperative of the child screaming, "Buy me this chocolate-marshmallow dessert topping." The "buy my product" kind of advertising doesn't lead to a successful sale of the client's product either.

In the next few pages, we shall explore some of the reasons that certain kinds of communications seem to work while others fail. First, we shall stand back from the maelstrom of advertising clutter and look once again at the elements of communication. Acknowledging the importance of stimulus and response in the place of messages, what can we learn about senders and receivers? Is it completely clear just who is involved? Whose voices do we hear in any communication and how do we detect them?

Then we shall look at tone of voice, remembering those unhappy voices in the supermarket. What do they tell us? How do they relate to advertising?

Finally, we shall look at the relationship of these elements to the development of a coherent, long-term brand personality. What have we learned that will help us develop more successful and lasting brand personalities?

Manufacturers, Advertisements, Consumers, and Viewers of Advertising

The heading above translates the title of an important essay written by Walker Gibson, "Authors, Speakers, Readers, and Mock Readers."[1] In this essay, Gibson begins with the distinction, familiar to academicians, between the author of a work and the fictitious speaker within that work. This distinction is by no means so well understood or accepted in the world of advertising.

Let us consider a double-page spread for the Guardian Life Insurance Company of America as it appeared in *Business Week:*

Picture: Young boy with a football helmet in a smudged after-the-game football jersey.

Headline: When I Grow Up I Want to Be an Insurance Agent.

Body copy: My Dad's a Guardian agent. And I can't believe how many friends he's made.

        Just yesterday, he showed our new neighbor how Guardian Life Insurance could protect his family while helping to put his kids through college. And last week he showed the president of a big company how to keep his family business in the family.

        My dad says that these are just two examples of the Guardian's commitment to serving clients for a lifetime. A commitment they made when they wrote their first policy in 1860.

        Talk to your local Guardian representative. If you don't know who that is, call the Guardian at 1-800-482-6474.

        Or wait twelve years and talk to me.[2]

This copy is supposedly the real words of that twelve-year-old football player. It is not the Guardian Life Insurance Company. We know that much.

As we start to read, however, we quickly realize that it isn't a twelve-year-old boy's language. They don't talk that way. "Talk to your local Guardian representative," or "a commitment they made when they wrote their first policy in 1860," or "while helping to put his kids through college" are not words this presumed speaker would say. So, someone else is talking. Someone who wants us to believe that this is a twelve-year-old.

Who is talking? The Guardian Life Insurance Company obviously paid for the advertisement, but we've already decided that they aren't the speaker. And it isn't a boy's language. It is the voice of the writer of the advertisement, anonymous and hidden. It seems to me that we reject that voice. It's not a true voice. We reject phony voices in advertising all the time.

Now consider another advertisement. This one, from Hewlett-Packard, has a supposed letter from a Mr. Greg Wallace to me. "Dear reader:" it begins. Well, I'm the reader so it must be to me.

I read on. It's all about the Hewlett-Packard DeskJet Printer and how it cannot be distinguished in quality from a normal laser printer that costs much more. In the body copy (as well as in the headline) I am told that "to see the difference you've got to look at the price."[3]

There are four people involved in this communication:

1. *The writer of the advertisement.* Maybe Mr. Wallace or someone else who isn't identified. Clearly not, however, Hewlett-Packard. We know they don't sit down and write these things.

2. *The speaker in the advertisement.* The voice talking to me personally. He's a pretty clever fellow. He leaves open-ended ideas, allowing me to fill in the missing parts. He never actually says how much more the laser printer is; he assumes I already know that.

3. *The reader.* The real reader. Me.

4. *The presumed reader.* Who isn't me, since Mr. Wallace doesn't know me. The writer of this advertisement picked out a fictitious reader, "Dear reader." This "presumed reader" is not the author of the ad or the actual reader of the ad.

(Indeed, we complicate this process further since you are my reader at this moment. Who are you? I don't know, but I could assume that you are an undergraduate student at a business school laboring through a case study course on effectiveness in advertising. Or you could be an overworked professor of marketing/advertising who is trying, in a limited amount of time, to make a decision on a new textbook. Or you could be an advertising professional at some agency other than JWT, trying to see if you can learn anything about why they keep winning so many Effies. Or you could be my business partner, who isn't any of the above.)

Every piece of communication has these components: author, speaker, real reader, and assumed reader, or, as Gibson calls him, mock reader:

> Closely associated with this distinction between author and speaker, there is another and less familiar distinction to be made, respecting the reader. For if the "real author" is to be regarded as to a great degree distracting and mysterious, lost in history, it seems equally true that the "real reader," lost in today's history, is no less mysterious and sometimes as irrelevant.

The fact is that every time we open the pages of another piece of writing, we are embarked on a new adventure in which we become a new person— a person as controlled and definable and as remote from the chaotic self of daily life as the lover in the sonnet. Subject to the degree of our literary sensibility, we are recreated by the language. We assume, for the sake of the experience, that set of attitudes and qualities which the language asks us to assume, and, if we cannot assume them, we throw the book away.[4]

So, too, is it with advertising. If we, the viewers of advertising, cannot assume the role demanded of us, we reject the advertisement—as we may have rejected the twelve-year-old in the Guardian Life Insurance advertisement. We were not prepared to become someone who believes young, smudgy football players talk that way.

A bad advertisement, then, is one in whose mock reader we discover a person we refuse to become, a mask we refuse to wear, a role we will not play.

When a copywriter distills all the potential readers of an advertisement down to a "target audience," he or she is creating an artifact. The writer defines who that person is, what his or her attitudes are, and what behavior the writer wants to affect through the advertisement. A useful injunction to beginning writers is to write to a person—and not to an amorphous group of people. So, good copywriters instinctively know all about their mock readers.

In understanding how advertising works, it is helpful to keep these distinctions in mind. To return to Bullmore's terminology, the sender is not a single entity: There are both the copywriter and the speaker in the advertising, two separate voices that may or may not be in harmony with each other.

And there is more than the "receiver." There is the real reader/viewer (the person who is actually reading the magazine or watching the TV) and the one who is presumed to be there—the mock reader, or, in the case of commercials, the mock viewer. That is the person created by the language, attitudes, and tone of voice used by the speaker in the advertising.

One more example. One of the more talked-about television campaigns in the United States in 1987–1988 was for Isuzu motors. In it, an on-camera presenter, Joe Isuzu, makes some outrageous, patently false claims about Isuzu. In a series of supers, another voice contradicts him, saying, "He's lying." Here we have a series of voices:

First, the sender voices:

- the on-camera presenter, Joe, making his outrageous claims;

- the voice in the super, contradicting everything that the on-camera presenter is saying;

- the writer—the governing intelligence who has created both voices and who is saying to us something about the nature of all advertising puffery claims;

- the advertiser—that person whose voice really isn't present in this commercial at all but about whom the viewer can infer a great deal.

The real viewer distinguishes easily among these voices. The difference between the first two is clear. The presence of the third is also clear, since we recognize what is happening. We get the joke, just as the nightclub patron gets the joke the comedian tells. We conclude, "This is a funny commercial." It was paid for by a company whom we respect. We like Isuzu for their intelligence and we know they want us to approve of their car as a result. Although not in the commercial, the fourth voice, the advertiser, is very much present in our response to this communication.

Now let's turn to the viewer. We, the real viewers, know who we are. We're sitting at home watching the commercial. Perhaps we watch a bit more attentively, since we are familiar with other spots in this campaign and want to see what's going on with this one.

There is also the mock viewer, the person who supposedly believes the outrageous claims and who somehow needs the clarification of the supers to disavow those claims. We recognize that we are not that person, yet we still do not reject the commercial. That is because we also recognize the voice of the writer, the one who says, in effect, "You and I, dear viewer, know this is all advertising puffery." The writer creates this mock viewer who will understand the joke.

The communication is successful because we elect to become this second mock viewer. We do get the joke and feel rewarded. We identify with the governing intelligence that assumed we would in the first place.

The analysis of this commercial is labored to make the point about real speakers, mock speakers, real viewers, and mock viewers. To understand the commercial, no one really goes through this degree of analysis. The point is valid, nonetheless, since all these voices are present in all communications—even if we don't so clearly recognize and label them.

The success of any communication depends upon these voices and the kinds of attitudes they elicit from us, the real viewers. If we accept the mock-viewer role assigned to us, then the commercial has achieved an initial goal: It has been noticed.

In a thirty-second commercial, there is a short period of time in which to establish contact with the attitudes and assumed experiences of the speaker. Viewers are far more critical and discerning than they are often given credit for. They reject commercials quickly if the mock world of advertising does not agree with their everyday, real-world experience.

The ability of advertising language to affect human behavior in a direct and practical manner is related to its relevance to our real-world values. Viewers know the difference between advertising land and their local neighborhoods. Even as they recognize advertising for what it is—language designed to affect their attitudes—they are still prepared to get involved if they find the mock-viewer role assigned to them acceptable.

The Parent, the Adult, and the Child

Let's now turn to ways in which communication can have a better chance of eliciting the kind of acceptance we are talking about.

In the early 1970s, a book about transactional analysis, Thomas A. Harris's *I'm OK—You're OK*, became a best-seller.[5] Transactional analysis, a popular fad in those days when people were obsessed with "relating" to each other, declined in drawing room acceptability with the "me generation" of the 1980s. It's too bad that we did not hold on to some of the distinctions that Harris drew; they have great relevance in how any kind of successful communication works.

Let's review them briefly. Harris divides speakers into three parts:

1. *The Parent:* that person who told us as children what to do. He gave us laws that we tested—for example, "Don't touch a hot stove," which we decided made sense, or "Don't water flowers with cold water," which we decided made somewhat less sense.

> They range all the way from the earliest parental communications, interpreted nonverbally through tone of voice, facial expression, cuddling, or noncuddling, to the more elaborate verbal rules and regulations espoused by the parents as the little person became able to understand words. . . . The significant point is that whether these rules are good or bad in the light of a responsible ethic, they are recorded *truths* from the source of all securing, the people who are "six feet tall" at a time when it is important to the two-foot-tall child that he please and obey them.[6]

The Parent pretends to be rational. He or she "knows" what was right and wrong and teaches us accordingly. We remember the mother's reason-why directive in the supermarket: "It's not good for you."

2. *The Child:* the recipient of much of this teaching, who initially had no vocabulary with which to respond and who relies on feelings to test the validity of what he is hearing from the Parent. Early on, a child responds by crying, and if it works, he will try it again (as in a supermarket years later).

> As is the case of the Parent, the Child is a state into which a person may be transferred at almost any time in his current transactions. There are many

things that can happen to us today which recreate the situation of childhood and the same feelings we felt then. Frequently we may find ourselves in situations where we are faced with impossible alternatives, where we find ourselves in a corner, either actually, or in the way we see it. These "hook the child," as we say, and cause a replay of the original feelings of frustration, rejection, or abandonment, and we relive a latter-day version of the small child's primary depression.[7]

Particularly in our frustrations with rules we resent or do not understand, we resort to our Child's response to the world. Law enforcement agents depend on our Child's acceptance of their Parent roles. We all recognize the Child in us as we recall our feelings when we are given a speeding ticket or when a customs official rummages through our suitcases of dirty laundry. Teenagers battle their parents, painfully rejecting their directives and curfews. Boot camp in the army works hard to reestablish the parent-child relationship, because military discipline depends upon acceptance of a hierarchy of authority.

Not all of our Child responses are unpleasant. The joy of pure fantasy, the catharsis of spontaneous tears, the gush of emotion at a favorite song— all are unexplored, emotional responses from our Child. Feelings are legitimate witnesses of the world. Our memory stores feelings and a frequent goal of advertisers is to tap into those emotions as a means of affecting our attitudes.

3. *The Adult:* that person who weighs and tests what he or she hears in order to come to an independent conclusion. The Adult tells us whether the emotional response is reliable and true. Through our Adult, we determine the difference between life as it was taught and demonstrated to us (the Parent) and life as we feel it, or wish it, or fantasize about it (Child).

One of the Adult's primary functions, says Harris, is "probability estimating . . . checking out data, validating or invalidating it and refiling it for future use."[8]

It is our Adult who finally accepts or rejects advertisements, who decides whether or not to assume the mock-viewer role the commercial asks for. This process of judgment is often automatic and speedy. The Adult doesn't stop to think and ponder when he recognizes certain signals. A car cuts in front of you and you immediately step on the brake: an Adult reflex. A commercial opens with yet another housewife giving over-the-washing-machine detergent advice and we immediately tune it out: a learned Adult reflex.

In the Parent-Child-Adult voices, we begin to understand the kinds of speakers we hear in advertising:

The Parent = the stand-up presenter, the "talking head," telling us what is right and wrong. A presumably rational argument is given for us to accept. The Child in us rejects this Parental speaker. We don't want to be told what to think, and we tune out the person who tries.

The Child = the one who makes emotional arguments and screams out to get attention. The advertising Child claims, in effect, "My product is bigger, better, lasts longer" in the same tone of voice as a real child might use to make similar claims about his daddy.

In the "Mine Is Better" game, many superlatives originate in the Child. All of us recognize the "Mine Is Better" advertising game. And tune out.

The Adult = the one who gives us enough experience so that we can decide for ourselves what is right or wrong and appropriate or inappropriate. We choose to believe the Adult because that voice seems to match our experience with the world around us.

Harris goes on to describe communications between these various states:

> . . . a language, a stimulus by one person and a response by another, which response in turn becomes a new stimulus for the other person to respond to. The purpose is to discover which part of each person—Parent, Adult, or Child—is originating each stimulus and response. . . . [t]he clues to help identify stimulus and response include not only the words used but also the tone of voice, body gestures, and facial expressions.[9]

Communication works, Harris concludes, when stimulus and response are parallel (that is, Child-to-Child, Parent-to-Parent, or Adult-to-Adult). Communication is open and mutually satisfying. Two youngsters playing together in a fantasy world understand each other perfectly, Child-to-Child. They are equally capable of extending the boundaries of their imaginations far beyond the limits of mere words. And it isn't just young people who communicate Child-to-Child; two employees complaining about their new boss—"We'll quit and then he'll be sorry!"—are highly reminiscent of two four-year-old's planning to run away.

Parent-to-Parent exchanges use judgmental observations, often without any real data to support them. Two businessmen speculating on the on-time possibilities of their commuter train are apt to be in the Parent mode. Together, they find fault and assign blame—a process that makes both of them feel good.

Adult-to-Adult communication uses opinions and provides data so that each person can arrive at a considered conclusion for himself or herself. The goal is some form of mutual understanding and the conversation continues until both parties have reached that level of understanding.

Parallel communication can also occur between two different states. An Adult can talk to a Child and the Child can respond back to the Adult. Both understand where the other "is coming from" and can respond appropriately.

Problems occur when the lines are crossed. Communication breaks down. Our example in the supermarket: Mother begins as Adult, giving out rational information from which her son can make a decision: "It's not good for you." Response from the boy's Child: "I want it anyway." Finally, Mother resorts to Parent as authority: "Because I say so." The boy remains as Child, feeling misunderstood and possibly rejected. Communication dissolves into tears and feelings of frustration.[10]

Communication has a greater chance of succeeding when the lines of communication are parallel, and in the case of advertising, complementary communication is an absolute requisite if the advertising is to work. A successful advertisement is invariably Adult-to-Adult communication, since it is the goal of every persuasive communication to provide information that the respondent will sift and evaluate and ultimately accept as consistent with his or her own view of the world. Since the ultimate response we seek is an Adult one, then we had better be certain that the advertising contains an Adult voice somewhere in it.

Advertising usually fails when it does not provide a recognizable Adult voice with whom we care to identify.

To bring both speakers/viewers and Parent/Adult/Child arguments together at this point, it is fair to say that advertising has a better chance of working when the mock speaker has an Adult voice that the viewer's Adult can identify with and understand. The vehicle through which this is done is the mock reader/viewer, who must also have Adult attitudes that we are willing to adopt.

In the Guardian Life Insurance advertisement, the speaker pretends to be a child but clearly isn't one. Our Adult rejects the attempt, and communication breaks down. In the Hewlett-Packard advertisement, a greater likelihood for success exists The Adult in us accepts the premise of the Adult speaker in the advertisement and we are willing to take on the mock reader role asked of us. The on-camera Isuzu speaker is clearly a Child telling fibs. The speaker in the supers is also a Child, a tattletale, saying, "He's lying." The Adult speaker behind both of them is the one to whom we respond; he appeals to our Adult by saying that we both recognize what is going on here and we understand each other.

In the creative process, then, we are concerned with a series of variables:

1. Who is speaking? The mock speaker creates certain responses. What kinds of responses are they?

2. The persona that this mock speaker assumes. Is the Adult present? Where? How? What clues do we provide for the real viewer?

3. The mock viewer, that person to whom the advertisement is ostensibly addressed and with whose Adult persona the real viewer must be willing to identify.

4. And the real viewer, the person who sees the commercial in his or her living room and whose Adult attitudes we wish to influence.

Advertising That Works: Some Evidence from the Case Histories

The case histories in this book demonstrate many valuable lessons about how brands work. Professor Jones, an intelligent, instructive, and affable speaker, brings a wealth of background and experience to his observations. He has asked you, his "mock reader," to assume the role of student of brands, someone with an open, inquisitive mind, eager to uncover new truths and make fresh connections. He appeals to your Adult with a series of hypotheses for you to explore and validate—or invalidate.

His case studies also illuminate the hypothesis I am developing here: Most successful brands over time adopt a recognizable speaker—whose persona we choose to identify with—because that speaker appeals consistently and reliably to the Adult in us. The executions in these cases vary enormously. What unites all of them is their appeal to an Adult real viewer through a variety of Adult mock viewers. Let's review a few of them.

Ford Escort

In relating the differences in the Escort advertising, Professor Jones says: "A consistent attempt is made to avoid a hectoring, aggressive approach—a style of advertising that is regrettably still rather common in car advertising all over the world." We recognize Jones's description of a Parent voice in automotive advertising—the kind of voice that people reject because it does not give them any Adult information to respond to.

Jones goes on, "The commentary treats the viewer as an intelligent person, someone who brings something to the communication and will not respond to being browbeaten." The "intelligent person" (= Adult) responds as an Adult.

Later on, Jones describes some of the common attitudes that the Adult speaker in the advertising asks the Adult viewer to assume: "[The] tone of voice is, however, very much in harmony with the target group: educated young people with relatively low incomes but on an upward career path." There is a difference between the values being communicated and the means by which they are being communicated. The mock viewer of the "Blue Danube" series is a Child who enjoys games, a person who will detect the humor in using a war-horse piece of music to provide the tempo for a piece of serious communication about a major purchase. Our Child laughs; our Adult recognizes the irony and appreciates the maker of a car who consciously avoids automotive clichés and uses irony to present his case.

Professor Jones refers to earlier automotive campaigns written by Stirling Getchell, David Ogilvy, and Bill Bernbach. The Doyle Dane Bernbach advertising for Volkswagen is a supreme example of carefully crafted advertising that appears to have one mock reader ("what an ugly car") but appeals to a real reader who senses the Adult intention of the advertising. The reader concludes quite the opposite of what the advertising appears to be saying.

Lux

The Lux movie-star campaign is certainly one of the phenomena in the history of advertising. Conceived in 1927, it has run successfully for more than six decades on five continents and has played a vital part in establishing Lux as the world's largest selling toilet soap.

The speaker in this campaign builds a compelling analogy: just as movie stars whose careers depend on their complexions use Lux, so, too, can you enhance your complexion by using Lux. The vehicle is plausible, appropriate, and entertaining. Millions and millions of Adult readers/viewers have accepted the analogy, understood its relevance and developed a strong loyalty to the brand as a result. The analogy has prevailed through numerous relaunchings of the brand, product improvements, and the advent of television stars to augment screen stars.

Throughout, the campaign speaker hasn't changed. The speaker has never been condescending; both the movie stars and their fans have been treated with dignity and respect. As a result, the speaker has become a good friend, someone like us, who appreciates beauty, likes movies, and follows the stars who made them great. Our Adult responds to the speaker's Adult, much as Helen Lansdowne Resor intended we should.

In a few markets, however, alternative Lux campaigns have been tested and in several markets, notably the United States, the movie-star campaign has been abandoned altogether. Unilever has never been able to find a campaign that works so well as the movie-star testimonials. In those markets where Lux has become a price brand, sales and share have fallen off. The speaker of a price brand ("now cheaper than ever!") gets very close to a bragging Child dealing in superlatives. What a difference from our friend, the compatible speaker in the movie-star campaign! We like having that speaker around. By contrast, we tune out the price-brand barker and, feeling a bit betrayed, shift our loyalty to another brand in this category.

Goodyear

Consider, first, the famous McGraw-Hill advertisement that prefaces the Goodyear chapter. The voices are very clear: The publisher selects a speaker who is a difficult, demanding executive, the kind who intimidates every salesman who enters his room. We recognize him. And share the mock reader's anxiety. And who is this mock reader? He's clearly sitting in the chair on the other side of the desk, about to launch into a sales pitch for something that he feels the adversary confronting him has never heard of, doesn't want, and probably won't buy. We empathize with this mock reader; we've all been there. We, at home reading the magazine, feel some relief that this time it's someone else in the catbird seat. And we recognize the Adult warning that is being communicated: A little corporate advertising will help take the pain out of this situation by providing some very necessary information about "your company" before the personal sales call.

In his Goodyear study, Professor Jones describes a very useful form of qualitative research; "Who Is a Company?" This kind of research defines an important link between the speaker in an advertisement and the brand/company for which that speaker speaks. Just as consumers can pick out who is really speaking in an advertisement, so, too, can they determine the human characteristics of the real brand/company behind that speaker. Their information is learned from Adult voices. Adult voices belong to people, and so they are quite prepared to give those voices human other human characteristics. An understanding of speakers allows us to comprehend why this kind of valuable research works so well. And why it provides such a rich resource for a copywriter looking for a consistent voice to adopt in advertising communications.

Kodak

Consistency in speakers over time is an important part of building a consistent brand image. For years, the *Kodak* speaker was a warm, caring, sensitive Adult who reminds our Adult that we ought to take pictures now; if we don't take those pictures now, we will regret it later on. Over time, we have come to trust the wisdom of the avuncular voice of experience who recounts those emotionally true stories about families growing up.

It was an enormous challenge for *Kodak* and its agencies to keep this tone of voice when *Kodak* wanted to enter the arena of high-technology product improvements. The temptation to drop the familiar speaker and adopt a new, more "modern" speaker was difficult to resist. The risk was confusing viewers who had come to expect a specific personality from *Kodak* speakers.

Does this mean that a brand cannot adopt a new voice? Not necessarily. Many companies have been able to change their tone of voice over time. One must be careful, however, since consumers' impressions are deeply embedded and difficult to change. A familiar, trusted speaker can talk about new technology. But changing the persona of the speaker can be extremely disorienting to loyal consumers. If they begin to think they cannot trust the speaker, they may conclude they cannot trust the brand either.

Kraft P'tit Québec

The consistency in speaker is critical in the case of *Kodak*. In the case of Kraft P'tit Québec, the consistency in mock viewer has provided a competitive advantage.

The first commercials designed to introduce P'tit Québec were carefully crafted to imply a specific mock viewer: the French Canadian housewife who understands the symbols, values, and life-styles of French Canada. The commercials have consistently appealed to those values. Some associated the product with the abundant, appetizing produce of the region. The advertising featured local television actors and actresses who personified those values. It all added up to a total communications unity. Product taste, packaging, promotions, and advertising had a single mock viewer in mind—the tradition-minded French Canadian housewife who cherishes the special qualities of her life and home ("just as *we* do," agrees the real French Canadian viewer).

This recognition of the strength of the mock viewer's values in relation to the consumer's values in the real world of the Province of Quebec has given the brand its unity over the past twelve years. Specific executions have changed. The mock viewer has not.

Nescafé

The Nescafé advertising in Spain is another example of building business via a long, successful campaign appealing to a consistent mock viewer. Here the brand was positioned with everyday real people, doing everyday real things that Nescafé was part of.

The real viewer recognized these people, admired them, and was prepared to assume their identity for the duration of the commercial. The writer can use this connection between the real viewer and the mock viewer to make a concrete rational copy point that Nescafé is a real cup of coffee with all the taste and rich smell of ground beans. We have permission to believe this argument because we accept the mock-viewer role assigned to us and are therefore prepared to believe what the speaker in the advertising is saying.

Listerine

The Listerine case brings up the whole issue of slice-of-life advertising—a form of advertising that, many have said, Procter and Gamble perfected. Briefly, it allowed people "like you and me" to observe little real-life mini-dramas in which the value of the product proposition would be demonstrated and communicated.

For many years, the slice-of-life approach was a most effective form of communication. The early slice-of-life commercials worked because the values that the advertising ascribed to the mock viewer were largely in sync with actual values of real viewers. When the speaker began to use language that wasn't the language of the real viewer ("waxy yellow buildup," for instance), slice-of-life commercials seemed to appeal to a mock viewer who wasn't one of us. We quickly saw that the speaker behind the commercial wanted us to believe our values were the same, but since they weren't, we rejected the commercials. They were no longer slices of *our* life: they were slices-of-advertising life . . . one we didn't want to live.

In considering slice-of-life commercials, it is instructive to remind ourselves that the speaker in the commercial is *not* the person or persons who actually appear in the commercial. Those people speak the lines that someone has given them to speak. The person we are interested in is the person who chooses those words and not the actors who actually say them.

Advertisers frequently make the assumption that people in the advertising must be the same people who are in the target group of the advertising. By now, we ought to be able to repudiate this assumption quite convincingly. The target group (or, in our terms, the real viewers) can readily tell the difference between the speaker and the actors; they don't confuse the people appearing in slice-of-life commercials with anyone real whom *they* know. Goodyear isn't really those cartoon folks. One doesn't really play bumper-cars with Ford Escorts. Real viewers are quite prepared to look behind those commercials to determine the values of the real speaker, the person who is using these on-camera actors to say something to them. And if we appeal to the real viewers' Adult—that part of them which makes these kinds of distinctions—they are likely to reward us for the effort.

At one point in its diverse advertising history, Listerine went to a campaign known as Hate/Love. One of the commercials featured a longshoreman on a New York City dock, supposedly being interviewed by an off-camera announcer. "Tell me, what do you think of the taste of Listerine?" the announcer asks. The longshoreman begins to answer and then interrupts himself: "Hey, that wasn't good enough. Let me try again." The camera backs off. The longshoreman begins to feel abandoned: "Oh, I get it, don't call me, I'll call you! Well, let me tell you what I *really* think of the taste of Listerine. I use it but it tastes *crummy.*" The super at the end of the commercial sums it up: "Listerine. The taste you hate twice a day."

Here the mock speaker (the longshoreman) is the skeptic that all advertising testimonials awaken in us: someone paid to say something he doesn't believe. Our Adult responds to the parody of the familiar advertising execution. Then, suddenly, he says what we all do believe ("it tastes crummy"). If it tastes bad, the supposition goes, then it must be effective. Here, the advertiser yields the very ground that his competition (Procter and Gamble's Scope, with its accusations of "medicine breath") was attacking. Our Adult response gives the advertiser full credit for this action. By admitting something we already know, the Listerine speaker gains the trust of our Adult and reinforces the efficacy claim.

Oxo

The Oxo campaigns are also, technically, slice-of-life advertising campaigns. But they are a different kind of campaign. "The direction the campaign took was to depart from the normal, idealized, anodyne 'advertising family,'" Jones says, "and to move toward a family possessing a very special and arrestingly realistic character." The Oxo family is familiar: They fight; they make up; they forget to close the door on a snowy day; they forget to tell their mother that the guest of honor is not coming to dinner. These are scenes we all relate to. "Aha," our Adult says. "I've been there before."

All the while Oxo plays an unassuming, appropriate part in the family life. It is not the hero of the day; a bouillon cube seldom is. It fits in just where it belongs. The speaker behind the Oxo family tells us that families aren't perfect (we know that well enough) and that Oxo is a part of the daily lives of not-so-perfect families like ours. We recognize the truth in the family, and so we are willing to recognize the truth about Oxo. The Adult Oxo communicator has completed the communication to our Adult without ever talking about the product and its versatile uses.

This brief overview is not intended to preempt the many examples of speakers and mock viewers that you have found in these case histories. My intention here is merely to demonstrate how the understanding of speakers and mock viewers and of Parent/Adult/Child tones of voice can help us predict why advertising succeeds or fails.

The Relation among Speakers, Viewers, and Brand Personality

Throughout this discussion of speakers and viewers, we have been focusing on the ultimate goal: communication that is designed to affect consumers' perceptions and actions. That, finally, is the goal of advertising: without some promise of affecting behavior, there is little reason to invest in advertising in the first place.

Consumers see many advertisements. They have learned over the years to discern the various voices in them, and they accept or reject those voices in accord with how well they mesh with their own values. These voices become part of the overall impression that a consumer has of a brand.

A consumer's overall impression of a brand is what J. Walter Thompson calls brand personality. It is an impression based on a combination of all aspects of a brand—product, manufacturer, brand name, packaging, advertising, promotions, and so on. It is this impression that a consumer describes if he or she is asked the question, "Who would this brand be if it came to life?"

Important in the list of attributes affecting brand personality are both the advertising and the users of the brand. The advertising is known by the voices that it assumes—the speakers. Consumers draw conclusions about the users of a brand from the people to whom the advertising appears to appeal—the mock viewers. If they reject bad advertising because they refuse to accept the role of mock viewer that is assumed in the advertising, then it is not difficult to assume that they will reject brands whose implied users they refuse to become.

This discussion of advertising broadens at this point to become a discussion of all aspects of the brand personality. In product design, in packaging, in promotion, in direct-response materials—in short, *in every piece of communication* directed to consumers—there is a speaker, someone who is making assumptions about the reader. And there is a mock reader, the person you and I are supposed to become.

It's relatively easy to distinguish these various roles in advertising. In packaging, product design, and direct response, doing so is more difficult only because we take less time in our professional lives to make such distinctions. Many marketers nonetheless understand and use these principles. Ford picked a highly appropriate tone of voice to create a distinctive personality for Escort, one the company used consistently in advertising, catalogs, and showroom displays.

The De Beers case study demonstrates the validity of these principles for even a commodity we do not immediately recognize as a "brand." De Beers has treated diamonds as a brand throughout all its advertising, promotional, point-of-sale, and publicity materials, and the result has been a remarkable story of communications success. Materials are created in seven markets centrally and then used both in those markets and over twenty more. Everywhere, a diamond has become the ultimate symbol of love, the warm, affectionate expression of the "diamond-is-forever" commitment of the giver. In Anglo-Saxon markets that already had a tradition of diamond jewelry, this personality simply built on existing attitudes. In markets such as Japan, where no such tradition existed, diamonds have come to mean the symbol of love in just twenty years, an amazingly short period of time as traditions go and a very long time as advertising campaigns go. Throughout that period, De Beers has used the same Adult speaker, with a loving, caring, and highly evocative tone of voice, in all its advertising, displays, broadsheets, publicity—in every piece of trade and consumer communication. The consistency of this voice, whom customers now recognize as a trusted and familiar friend, helped give diamonds a common cultural meaning in the world's most diverse cultures.

Consumers look for such consistency. A brand is a friend from whom they expect predictable behavior. All the elements should reflect a single speaker, a mock viewer/reader with whom we can repeatedly identify. The result will be a coherent set of attitudes evoked by a cohesive communications plan. The payoff will be more consistent consumer behavior and a more successful brand in the marketplace.

Appendix

PLEASE RETURN THE QUESTIONNAIRE TO: MR. HAROLD F. CLARK, JR.,
JWT, NEW YORK.

Questionnaire prepared by _____ Office _____

Country _____   Market described (soft drinks, cold breakfast
cereals, etc.) _____

[Fill out this questionnaire in handwriting, if this is easier for you.]

QUESTION 1

What are annual sales in the total market
and what is the trend?

Notes

1. State the sales each year in units per
   capita.

2. Calculate the per capita figures by
   dividing total sales by the total
   population, not just product users.

Units of measurement (grams, gallons,
etc.) _____

Total market sales per capita in:

1982 _____
1983 _____
1984 _____
1985 _____
1986 _____

QUESTION 2

What brands are on the market and what
is their relative importance?

1. Include as many brands as possible:
   go down to brands with a 5% market
   share (or even smaller for new
   introductions).

2. Calculate share of market by volume,
   not value.

3. Under "Share of Total Market
   Advertising," include advertising in all
   media, but exclude promotions.

4. Include figures only for 1986.

Brand Name	1986 Share of Market by Volume	Share Trend (Upward, Static, or Downward)	1986 Share of Total Market Advertising	Consumer Price (Above Average, Average, or Below Average)	Mark X If Handled by JWT

[Add more brands on overleaf, if necessary.]

Notes

Chapter 1. Signposts

1. Bernard Fergusson, Lord Ballantrae, *The Wild Green Earth* (London: Collins, 1946) p. 165.

2. A few additional cases were prepared and written, but it proved impossible to obtain permission to publish them, mainly because of their reliance on confidential or otherwise sensitive material. As expected, the lessons from these unpublished cases tend to underscore the lessons from the cases published in this book.

3. Descriptions of the branding process can be found in John Philip Jones, *What's in a Name? Advertising and the Concept of Brands*, (Lexington, Mass.: Lexington Books, 1986), chapter 1, together with the references in the endnotes.

4. See also Jones, *What's in a Name?* pp. 6–7, 28–32.

5. James Webb Young, *How to Become an Advertising Man* (Chicago: Crain Books, 1963).

6. This controversial matter is discussed in Jones, *What's in a Name?* pp. 232–35.

7. Leo Bogart, B. Stuart Tolley, and Frank Orenstein, "What One Little Ad. Can Do," *Journal of Advertising Research* (August 1970), pp. 3–13.

8. This topic is discussed in general in Jones, *What's in a Name?* chapter 6. The endnotes to that chapter include a number of relevant source references.

9. Ibid.

10. Arthur Koestler, *The Act of Creation* (New York: Macmillan 1964), pp. 35–38.

11. Stephen King, "Practical Progress for a Theory of Advertisements," *Admap* (October 1975), pp. 338–43.

12. The reasons why agencies lose their clients are discussed from a knowledgeable point of view by William M. Weilbacher in *Choosing an Advertising Agency* (Chicago: Crain Books, 1983), chapter 2.

13. See, for instance, Jeremy Elliott, "Kellogg's Corn Flakes: Adding Values to the Brand," commended paper in the 1980 Institute of Practitioners in Advertising *Advertising Effectiveness Awards*; "Kellogg's Rice Krispies: The Effect of a New Creative Execution," in *Advertising Works: Papers from the IPA Advertising Effectiveness Awards*, Simon Broadbent, ed. (London: Holt, Rinehart and Winston, 1981),

pp. 78–88; and "Breaking the Bran Barrier: Kellogg's Bran Flakes, 1982–84," in *Advertising Works 3: Papers from the IPA Advertising Effectiveness Awards,* Charles Channon, ed. (London: Holt, Rinehart and Winston, 1985), pp. 55–69. In the last collection, see also Evelyn Jenkins, "Fulfilling the Potential of St. Ivel Gold," pp. 105–16, and Terry Bullen, "Kraft Dairylea: The Transformation of a Brand's Fortunes," pp. 198–211.

14. A number of cases are described in Jones, *What's in a Name?* chapters 8 and 9.

15. See also Jill Greenop, "Kellogg's Coco Pops: A 'Story Book' Success," in *Advertising Works 3,* pp. 212–26. The published data in this study can be recomputed to demonstrate the Steiner Paradox.

Chapter 2. Campari and Mumm in Germany

1. André L. Simon and S. F. Hallgarten, *The Great Wines of Germany* (New York: McGraw Hill, 1963), p. 14.

2. Alexis Lichine, *Encyclopaedia of Wines and Spirits* (London: Cassell, 1967), p. 168.

3. Hugh Johnson, *The World Atlas of Wine* (London: Mitchell Beazley, 1971), pp. 10–11, 124. The estimate of German wine consumption is from JWT Frankfurt; that of U.S. wine consumption is from Liquid Consumption Trends, *Beverage Industry Annual Manual* Issue (Cleveland: Harcourt Brace Jovanovich, 1987), pp. 12–17. The last full year for which data are available is 1985.

4. Data on consumption trends were provided by JWT Frankfurt.

5. Hugh Johnson, *Wine* (London: The Cookery Book Club, 1966), p. 103.

6. Information on the composition of the market was provided by JWT Frankfurt.

7. Information on the development of the Campari campaign was provided by JWT Frankfurt.

8. This topic is discussed in John Philip Jones, *What's in a Name? Advertising and the Concept of Brands* (Lexington, Mass.: Lexington Books, 1986), pp. 235–36.

9. Ibid., chapter 6.

10. Frances Foster, "An Evaluation of the Effectiveness of the Current Campari Campaign," in *Advertising Works: Papers from the IPA Effectiveness Awards,* Simon Broadbent, ed. (London: Holt, Rinehart and Winston, 1981), pp. 117–24.

11. Simon and Hallgarten, *The Great Wines of Germany,* p. 107.

12. They include Alexis Lichine and André Simon. See Lichine, *Encyclopaedia of Wines and Spirits,* pp. 271, 434, and André Simon, *A Wine Primer* (London: Michael Joseph, 1951), p. 140.

13. According to the German Wine Law of 1971, *sekt* can be used to describe wine based on any mixture of home-produced wine and imports. If the wine is made at least 60 percent from German wine, it can be called *Praedikat Sekt.* Johnson, *The World Atlas of Wine,* p. 125.

14. Simon, *A Wine Primer,* p. 140.

15. Frank Schoonmaker, *Encyclopaedia of Wine,* (London: Nelson, 1967), p. 273.

16. Simon and Hallgarten, *The Great Wines of Germany,* pp. 108–09.

17. These and most of the subsequent market data were provided by JWT Frankfurt.

18. Lichine, *Encyclopaedia of Wines and Spirits,* p. 271.

19. See Jones, *What's in a Name?* chapters 8 and 9.

20. Robert L. Steiner, "Point of View: the Paradox of Increasing Returns to Advertising," *Journal of Advertising Research 27,* no. 1 (February/March 1987), pp. 45–53.

Chapter 3. *Kodak* Cameras and Films

1. Quoted in Hannah Campbell, *Why Did They Name It?* (New York: Ace Books, 1964), p. 190.

2. "Eastman Kodak Co.," *Advertising Age,* September 4, 1986, pp. 92–93.

3. Annual reports on the photographic market by the Target Group Index (Axiom Market Research Bureau) and Simmons Market Research Bureau. The figures relate to individuals, the net figures for household penetration being somewhat larger than those for men or women alone. A trade-press source provides a number of different estimates of net household penetration of still cameras, including a figure as high as 86.2 percent, which was estimated by the Photo Marketing Association in 1984: *Modern Photography Magazine,* the 1985–86 *Wolfman Report* on the Photographic and Imaging Industry in the United States, p. 53.

4. Annual reports on the photographic market by the Target Group Index (Axiom Market Research Bureau) and Simmons Market Research Bureau. Data from the *Wolfman Report* suggest similar overall levels of camera purchasing but a smaller degree of annual fluctuation: *Modern Photography Magazine,* the 1985–86 *Wolfman Report* on the Photographic and Imaging Industry in the United States, p. 28.

5. Annual report on the photographic market by Simmons Market Research Bureau.

6. In one important part of the market, 35-mm autofocus rangefinder cameras, Kodak is in second place behind Canon, and the two brands between them account for 50 percent of total sales. Lisa E. Phillips, "Kodak Ups 4th Quarter Advertising Budget," *Advertising Age,* August 3, 1987, p. 61.

7. "Eastman Kodak Co.," *Advertising Age,* September 10, 1981, pp. 70–72, and *Advertising Age,* September 4, 1986, pp. 92–93.

8. *Modern Photography Magazine,* the 1985–86 *Wolfman Report* on the Photographic and Imaging Industries in the United States, pp. 99, 62.

9. Annual reports on the photographic market by the Target Group Index (Axiom Market Research Bureau) and Simmons Market Research Bureau.

10. Ibid.

11. *Modern Photography Magazine,* the 1985–86 *Wolfman Report* on the Photographic and Imaging Industry in the United States, p. 43.

12. Phillips, "Kodak Ups 4th Quarter Advertising Budget."

13. Annual reports on the photographic market by the Target Group Index (Axiom Market Research Bureau) and Simmons Market Research Bureau. There was also a report about the disc camera on *All Things Considered,* National Public Radio, February 2, 1988.

14. Phillips, "Kodak Ups 4th Quarter Advertising Budget."

15. See, for instance, "Eastman Kodak Co.," *Advertising Age,* September 8, 1983, p. 65.

16. These general points are developed in some detail in John Philip Jones, *What's in a Name? Advertising and the Concept of Brands* (Lexington, Mass.: Lexington Books, 1986), chapter 2.

17. There is a well-documented published example that demonstrates a related point—the effect of a new brand introduction on injecting growth into a market. The market described is the mouthwash market in Canada. Stephen Greyser, *Cases in Advertising and Communications Management,* 2nd ed. (Englewood Cliffs, N.J.: Prentice Hall, 1981), pp. 148–67.

18. See, for instance, the examples quoted in Jones, *What's in a Name?* chapter 11.

19. Ibid.

20. "Eastman Kodak Co.," *Advertising Age,* September 9, 1982, pp. 73–76; September 8, 1983, pp. 64–65; September 14, 1984, p. 76; September 26, 1985, pp. 66–68; and September 4, 1986, pp. 92-93.

21. Jones, *What's in a Name?* chapter 4.

22. Information supplied by JWT New York.

Chapter 4. Kraft P'tit Québec

1. Mrs. Beeton, *Family Cookery* (London: Ward, Lock and Co. Ltd., undated), p. 607.

2. Charles M. Schaninger, Jacques C. Bourgeois, and W. Christian Buss, "French-English Canadian Subcultural Consumption Differences," *Journal of Marketing,* vol. 49 (spring 1985), p. 91.

3. Prosper Montagné, *New Larousse Gastronomique* (London: Hamlyn, 1977), p. 209.

4. "A Mother Culture's Daughter Grows Up," *Economist,* November 28, 1987, pp. 95–96.

5. Information from JWT Montreal. See also "Decade of Change: French Canadian Advertising Industry Blossoms," *Advertising Age,* November 30, 1987, p. 64.

6. Schaninger, Bourgeois, and Buss, "French-English Canadian Subcultural Consumption Differences," p. 84.

7. Ibid., p. 87.

8. Ibid., p. 89.

9. René Pelletier, *Allocution Prononcée à Toronto le Compte de Télémédia,* September 25, 1987, p. 6.

10. Schaninger, Bourgeois, and Buss, "French-English Canadian Subcultural Consumption Differences," p, 90.

11. Montagné, *New Larousse Gastronomique*, p. 207.

12. Saine Marketing, *P'tit Québec Line Extension Qualitative Research*, December 1986.

13. Data on the early history of P'tit Québec were provided by JWT Montreal.

14. Data provided by JWT Montreal.

15. Saine Marketing, *P'tit Québec Line Extension Qualitative Research*.

16. Data provided by JWT Montreal.

17. John Philip Jones, *What's in a Name? Advertising and the Concept of Brands* (Lexington, Mass.: Lexington Books, 1986), pp. 12, 47–49, 107–8.

18. ISL International Surveys Ltd., *Cheddar Cheese Tracking Study*, August 1987.

19. Jones, *What's in a Name?* chapter 6.

20. Ibid., pp. 86–87.

21. Ibid., pp. 45–46.

22. Saine Marketing, *P'tit Québec Line Extension Qualitative Research*.

23. Jones, *What's in a Name?* chapter 6.

Chapter 5. Listerine Antiseptic

1. Annual report on the mouthwash market by Simmons Market Research Bureau, 1985.

2. Warner-Lambert, *Quarterly Tracking Studies on Mouthwash*, 4th quarter 1985.

3. JWT New York, *Report on Listerine Antiseptic Plans Board*, November 6, 1981.

4. A. C. Nielsen, *Food, Drug and Mass Merchandiser Indexes*, 1968–1985.

5. Annual report on the mouthwash market by Simmons Market Research Bureau, 1985.

6. Warner-Lambert, Quarterly Tracking Studies on Mouthwash, 4th quarter, 1985.

7. A. C. Nielsen, *Food, Drug and Mass Merchandiser Indexes*.

8. The information in this section comes in the main from Gerard B. Lambert's autobiography, *All Out of Step* (Garden City, N.Y.: Doubleday and Company, 1956).

9. JWT New York, *Listerine Creative Review*, 1975.

10. A. C. Nielsen, *Food and Drug Indexes*.

11. It is no coincidence that the widespread use of slice-of-life commercials by Procter and Gamble was accompanied by the use of standardized day-after-recall testing. Both are now much less used by that company. (Personal observation and private information.)

12. There is evidence from Canada that the first slice-of-life commercials used for the introduction of Scope pushed advertising awareness for Scope higher than for Listerine. Stephen Greyser, *Cases in Advertising and Communications Management*, 2nd ed. (Englewood Cliffs, N.J.: Prentice Hall, 1981), pp. 150, 157.

13. A. C. Nielsen, *Food and Drink Indexes*.

14. Ibid. Note that data from the Nielsen food and drug indexes slightly un-

derstate Listerine's market share because of the brand's marginally stronger position in mass-merchandiser outlets. Unfortunately, discontinuities in the data prevent us from using information from all three outlet types for the complete period covered by this study.

15. John Philip Jones, *What's in a Name? Advertising and the Concept of Brands* (Lexington, Mass.: Lexington Books, 1986). See especially chapter 11.

16. The facts of this case are are taken from Greyser, *Cases in Advertising and Communications Management,* "The FTC and Listerine Antiseptic."

17. *Advertising Age,* November 2, 1981.

18. Jones, *What's in a Name?* chapter 5, especially p. 126.

19. JWT New York, *Report on Listerine Antiseptic Plans Board,* November 6, 1981.

20. Jones, *What's in a Name?* chapter 4.

21. Ibid., chapter 11.

22. JWT New York, *Listerine Antiseptic Historical Reel,* 1968–86.

23. Annual reports on the mouthwash market by the Target Group Index (Axiom Market Research Bureau) and Simmons Market Research Bureau, 1976 through 1985. Note a statistical problem in these data: As more brands were included in the Simmons surveys (the number went up from nine in 1976 to nineteen in 1985), the figures for each individual brand tended to weaken. (This is connected with interview fatigue.) The result is an exaggeration of any real reduction in individual brand penetration figures.

24. Greyser, *Cases in Advertising and Communications Management,* pp. 162–63.

25. JWT New York, *Listerine Creative Review,* 1975.

26. Warner-Lambert, *Quarterly Tracking Studies on Mouthwash,* 4th quarter, 1985.

27. Greyser, *Cases in Advertising and Communications Management,* pp. 150–51.

28. Jones, *What's in a Name?* chapter 6.

Chapter 6. Lux Toilet Soap

1. Neil Hopper Borden, *The Economic Effects of Advertising* (Chicago: Richard D. Irwin, 1942) p. 425.

2. Frank Spencer Presbrey, *The History and Development of Advertising* (Garden City, N.Y.: Doubleday, Doran, 1929), p. 338.

3. The early story of Ivory is told in Oscar Schisgall, *Eyes on Tomorrow, the Evolution of Procter & Gamble* (Chicago: J. G. Ferguson, 1981), pp. 25–42.

4. Ibid., pp. 102–3.

5. "Toilet Soaps," from "The Centennial of the J. Walter Thompson Company," *Advertising Age,* December 7, 1964, p. 127.

6. Martin Mayer, *Madison Avenue, U.S.A.* (New York: Harper and Brothers, 1958), p. 71.

7. Early testimonial campaigns developed by JWT are described in "The Cen-

tennial of the J. Walter Thompson Company," *Advertising Age,* December 7, 1964, pp. 56–58.

8. This statement is not intended to imply that impact, or noticeability, is something that can easily be evaluated by research. This controversial matter is discussed in John Philip Jones, *What's in a Name? Advertising and the Concept of Brands* (Lexington, Mass.: Lexington Books, 1986), chapter 6.

9. Most of the data on the early history of Lux advertising come from "The Centennial of the J. Walter Thompson Company," *Advertising Age,* December 7, 1964, pp. 58, 126.

10. Sales data come from a private JWT document, *Lux Toilet Soap Advertising Review,* July 6, 1984. The source of the brand penetration data is the various reports on the toilet soap market by the Simmons Market Research Bureau.

11. Sam Meek, formerly head of international operations at JWT, quoted in Mayer, *Madison Avenue, U.S.A.,* p. 90.

12. The sales data cover all world markets. The remaining market information is based on the thirty-two markets in which JWT handles the Lux advertising. These include almost without exception the most important countries measured by the brand's sales, but they also include a number of smaller markets.

13. The data on the films and their usage come from the private JWT document *Lux Toilet Soap Advertising Review,* July 6, 1984.

14. This is a generalized tendency that is examined and illustrated in Jones, *What's in a Name?* chapter 4. In chapter 10 of this book, the greater productivity of the advertising for large (as opposed to small) brands is related to another phenomenon of large brands: their greater endemic purchase and repurchase frequency, something for which the author has coined the phrase *penetration supercharge.*

15. See the examples discussed in Jones, *What's in a Name?* chapter 4.

Chapter 7. Nescafé in Spain

1. *Encyclopedia Britannica,* 11th ed. (New York: The Encyclopedia Britannica Company, 1910), vol. 6, p. 649.

2. Jan Heer, *World Events 1866–1966: The First Hundred Years of Nestlé* (Vevey, Switzerland: Nestlé Alimentana S.A., 1966), p. 164.

3. Ibid., pp. 28–35.

4. Nestlé had a worldwide sales value of $21.9 billion in 1986, a figure more than twice the worldwide sales value of Philip Morris's General Foods. "The Hundred Leading National Advertisers," *Advertising Age,* September 24, 1987, pp. 131, 139.

5. Heer, *World Events 1866-1966,* pp. 164–66.

6. Ibid., pp. 180–83.

7. "Coffee Consumption Continues to Decline," *Advertising Age,* April 27, 1987, p. 54.

8. Kevin Cote, "Nestlé Hatches Strategic Brands," *Advertising Age: Focus,* December 1986, pp. 11–15.

9. Jan Morris, *Spain* (New York: Oxford University Press, 1979), p. 140.

10. Heer, *World Events 1866-1966,* pp. 166, 187, 219.

11. Stephen Greyser, *Cases in Advertising and Communications Management,* 2nd ed. (Englewood Cliffs, N.J.: Prentice Hall, 1981), p. 526. In 1986, the per capita consumption of coffee in the United States was 2.3 percent below that in 1985. "Coffee Consumption Continues to Decline," *Advertising Age,* April 27, 1987, p. 54.

12. Data provided by JWT Madrid, May 1, 1987.

13. This phenomenon is discussed in John Philip Jones, *What's in a Name? Advertising and the Concept of Brands* (Lexington, Mass.: Lexington Books, 1986), pp. 12–13, 47–49, 107–8.

14. Camillo Pagano, "Pushing the Parent Around," *Advertising Age: Focus,* December 1986, pp. 14–15.

15. Vance Packard, *The Hidden Persuaders* (Harmondsworth, Middlesex, U.K.: Penguin Books, 1979), pp. 120–21.

16. This brings to mind the aphorism attributed to Bismarck that it is the foolish man who learns from his own mistakes; the wise man learns from other people's.

17. This point is amplified chapter 20, as well as in Jones, *What's in a Name?,* pp. 83–92.

18. This matter is discussed in Jones, *What's in a Name?,* pp. 83–92, 235–36.

19. Jones, *What's in a Name?,* pp. 56–59.

20. Nestlé's strengths are, of course, widely recognized in the worldwide business community. See Ralph Z. Sorenson II, "U.S. Marketers Can Learn from European Innovators," *Harvard Business Review,* September-October 1972, pp. 89–99.

Chapter 8. Oxo

1. Data in this section come mainly from a document prepared by JWT London, *Oxo: Past, Present and Future,* September 27, 1985.

2. On October 17, 1914, during the crisis days of the First Battle of Ypres, General Sir Douglas Haig recounts having given some Belgian refugees "2 doz. 'Oxo' soup squares for which they seemed most grateful." Quoted in Robert Blake, ed., *The Private Papers of Douglas Haig, 1914–19* (London: Eyre and Spottiswoode, 1952), p. 74.

3. This phenomenon is described in microeconomics as negative income elasticity. The best known example is enshrined in the so-called Giffen Paradox, which relates to demand for bread. As incomes go down, the demand for bread increases, because people can no longer afford more interesting and varied types of food; the opposite happens when incomes increase. This apparently also operates with cornflakes—people with reduced incomes tend to eat them twice, not once, a day.

4. Stephen King, *Developing New Brands* (London: J. Walter Thompson Company, 1984), p. 4.

5. This possibility is discussed in John Philip Jones, *What's in a Name? Advertising and the Concept of Brands* (Lexington, Mass.: Lexington Books, 1986), pp. 171–73, 227.

6. Data in this section come mainly from the JWT document, *Oxo: Past, Present and Future,* September 27, 1985.

7. According to Nielsen evidence, this is the minimum preference level if a new brand is to succeed. Jones, *What's in a Name?* pp. 5, 15.

8. Carys Bowen-Jones, "Oxo's Popularity Boosts 'Realistic' Ads," *Marketing*, March 5, 1987.

9. "Oxo's 'Real Lives' Is Winning Campaign," *London Daily News*, March 4, 1987.

10. Bowen-Jones, "Oxo's Popularity Boosts 'Realistic' Ads."

11. This matter is discussed in Jones, *What's in a Name?* chapter 6, especially pp. 149–50.

12. Ibid., pp. 83–92.

13. Thomas J. Peters and Robert H. Waterman, Jr., *In Search of Excellence, Lessons from America's Best-Run Companies* (New York: Harper and Row, 1982), note, p. 223.

14. See, for instance, the example quoted in Jones, *What's in a Name?* p. 4, last paragraph.

15. That is, in the rather rare cases when advertising has a demonstrable effect that can be isolated.

Chapter 9. Quaker Oats Kibbles 'n Bits

1. Quoted in Arthur F. Marquette, *Brands, Trademarks and Good Will: The Story of the Quaker Oats Company* (New York: McGraw-Hill, 1967), p. 265.

2. Hannah Campbell, *Whey Did They Name It?* (New york: Ace Books, 1964), pp. 37–40.

3. This historical development is discussed in general terms in John Philip Jones, *What's in a Name? Advertising and the Concept of Brands* (Lexington, Mass.: Lexington Books, 1986), chapter 2.

4. Marquette, *Brands, Trademarks and Good Will*, chapters 7–8.

5. The data on the size and composition of the market are based on estimates made by John C. Maxwell of Lehman Bros., Kuhn, Loeb Research and are published in four *Advertising Age Yearbooks* (Chicago: Crain Books, 1981–1984). Some of the figures differ marginally from those we have derived from other sources.

6. The initial growth cycle for new brands is discussed in Jones, *What's in a Name?* pp. 72–76.

7. Ibid., chapter 6, especially pp. 145–49.

8. Marketing features in the *Wall Street Journal*, March 7, 1985, and March 13, 1986.

9. The long-term ongoing market shares of virtually all successful brands of packaged goods settle at a lower level (on average, 20 percent lower) than the initial sales peak. See Jones, *What's in a Name?* pp. 72–76.

10. Penetration and purchasing data come from the Quaker Oats *Dry Dogfood Brand Performance Review* (MID no. N 8604), February 6, 1986. Value market share data come from *Advertising Age Yearbook* (Chicago: Crain Books, 1984).

11. This is normal for a new brand. See Jones, *What's in a Name?*, p. 84.

12. "Pet Foods Collar Modest Gains," *Advertising Age,* October 5, 1987, p. 40.

13. JWT Chicago, *Puppy Kibbles 'n Bits Case History,* August 1985, p. 1.

14. Ibid.

15. Jones, *What's in a Name?* pp. 56–59.

16. This matter is discussed in Stephen King, *Developing New Brands* (London: J. Walter Thompson Company, 1984), pp. 22–27, 92–94.

17. See, for instance, Rosser Reeves, *Reality in Advertising* (New York: Alfred A. Knopf, 1961), pp. 114–19.

18. This matter is discussed in Jones, *What's in a Name?* pp. 177–78.

19. Interestingly, the long-established British campaign for Andrex Toilet Tissue, which also features puppies, has some similarity with the Kibbles 'n Bits campaign. There is ironclad evidence not only that the Andrex campaign is widely popular with the public but also that it sells the brand.

Chapter 10. Slice

1. Roger Enrico and Jesse Kornbluth, *The Other Guy Blinked* (New York: Bantam Books, 1986), p. 260.

2. The success rate of new brands is discussed in John Philip Jones, *What's in a Name? Advertising and the Concept of Brands* (Lexington, Mass.: Lexington Books, 1986), pp. 64–66.

3. *Beverage Industry Annual Manual* Issue (Cleveland, OH: Harcourt Brace Jovanovich, 1987), p. 16. The last full year for which data are available is 1985.

4. "*Beverage Digest* Report," *All Things Considered,* National Public Radio, December 1, 1987; also "Bubbles at Breakfast," *New York Times,* July 12, 1987.

5. Information provided by Pepsi-Cola U.S.A.

6. "*Beverage Digest* Report," *All Things Considered;* also Enrico and Kornbluth, *The Other Guy Blinked,* p. 64.

7. However, taking account of "fountain" (on-premise) sales, Coca-Cola is larger than Pepsi-Cola.

8. A. C. Nielsen food store index, twelve months ending March 1988.

9. These processes are described with the greatest understanding of the real world by Friedrich von Hayek in "The Meaning of Competition," *Individualism and Economic Order* (Chicago: University of Chicago Press, 1980), pp. 92–106.

10. This is the normal pattern for first and second brands in any market. See Jones, *What's in a Name?* pp. 45–46.

11. It has been estimated that 352 new light/lite brands were introduced into supermarkets between 1982 and 1988. Lewis H. Lapham, *Money and Class in America* (New York: Weidenfeld and Nicolson, 1988), note, p. 181. From observation and press comment, however, it seems that consumers are at the moment rather less manic about eating healthy foods than they were in the early 1980s.

12. Jim Risley, "The Quality, Convenience, Health-Conscious Consumer," speech to the Merchandising Executives Club, 1985, pp. 7–9.

13. Strategic Services Department, JWT U.S.A., *Portraits of the CSD Family,*

May 1987. (This analysis is based on data provided by the Simmons Market Research Bureau.)

14. Enrico and Kornbluth, *The Other Guy Blinked,* pp. 64–65.

15. Ibid., pp. 65–66.

16. Ibid., p. 151.

17. The problems are illustrated even more dramatically by Coca-Cola's experience with New Coke, which, in blind test, outperformed Old (now Classic) Coke. In the marketplace, where consumers were aware of the identify of the two varieties of Coke, they responded quite differently.

18. Enrico and Kornbluth, *The Other Guy Blinked,* pp. 156–57.

19. Ibid., pp. 66–72.

20. Ibid., pp. 155–57.

21. Jennifer Lawrence, "Testing Juices Up Slice's Performance," *Advertising Age,* August 24, 1987, pp. S2–S5.

22. Jones, *What's in a Name?,* pp. 59–60.

23. Lawrence, "Testing Juices Up Slice's Performance," p. S4.

24. This matter is discussed in Jones, *What's in a Name?* pp. 56–59.

25. Data on the growth of Mandarin Orange Slice come from JWT U.S.A., *The Effie '87 Brief of Effectiveness.*

26. Jones, *What's in a Name?* pp. 72–76.

27. Data in this section were provided by Pepsi-Cola U.S.A.

28. Lawrence, "Testing Juices Up Slice's Performance," p. S5.

29. Jones, *What's in a Name?* p. 84.

30. Patricia Winters, "Pepsi Slices JWT," *Advertising Age,* November 30, 1987, pp. 3, 93.

31. Ibid.

32. Ibid.

33. Ibid.

34. Data were provided by Pepsi-Cola U.S.A.

35. Ibid.

36. Arthur Koestler, *The Act of Creation* (New York: Macmillan, 1969), p. 108.

37. Ibid., p. 109.

38. See note 10.

39. This conclusion is based on the author's personal experience of international markets, which is reasonably extensive.

Chapter 11. Smarties

1. Arthur Koestler, *The Act of Creation* (New York: Macmillan, 1969), p. 322.

2. British Market Research Bureau, *Target Group Index, Sweets in Tubes and Sweets for Children,* 1987, p. 72.

3. JWT London, *Information Pack for "Campaign,"* 1987.

4. Data in this section were provided by JWT London.

5. Ibid.

6. Ibid.

7. BJM Qualitative Research, *Smarties Advertising Research* (BJM 4228), 1987.

8. Ibid.

9. Ibid.

10. Ibid.

11. Ibid.

12. Data from JWT London, based on information provided by Gordon Simmonds Research.

13. Data from Pope Trevains, 1985.

14. Data from Pope Trevains, 1987.

15. Data from JWT London.

16. James O. Peckham, Sr., *The Wheel of Marketing* (privately published but available from A. C. Nielsen, 1978), p. 73.

17. Ibid., p. 54.

18. Ibid., pp. 55–56, 64; also John Davis, *The Sales Curve of New Products* (London: J. Walter Thompson, 1965).

19. Peckham, *The Wheel of Marketing,* p. 67.

20. Davis, *The Sales Curve of New Products.*

Chapter 12. Timotei Shampoo

1. American writer Marya Mannes, quoted in Donald S. Connery, *The Scandinavians* (London: Eyre and Spottiswoode, 1966), p. 22.

2. Interestingly, in recent years a number of "mildness" brands have been successful on the American market—for example, Johnson and Johnson Baby Shampoo (used widely by adults), Neutrogena, Ivory Shampoo, and Revlon Clean and Clear.

3. Most of the information about the formulation and development of Timotei is taken from a JWT document, *Timotei: The Story of an International Success* (JWT London International Unilever Unit, April 1985).

4. The low success rate of new brands is discussed in John Philip Jones, *What's in a Name? Advertising and the Concept of Brands* (Lexington, Mass.: Lexington Books, 1986), chapter 3.

5. James O. Peckham, Sr., *The Wheel of Marketing* (privately published but available from A. C. Nielsen, 1978), p. 54.

6. This is the normal pattern for the initial growth of brands; however, Timotei sales show a cyclical pattern of rather longer duration than the average. Jones, *What's in a Name?* pp. 74–76.

7. It must be remembered that it is impossible to achieve a buildup of coverage much more quickly than this without the use of commercial television. In the United States, a large-budget program can cover virtually all households within a month of the start of an advertising campaign, although it cannot, of course, build up much frequency within that time.

8. In a limited number of markets, a large pack size was subsequently intro-

duced, because of the special importance of large sizes in these markets. In a number of cases, the large sizes made a significant contribution to the Timotei business.

9. To the best of our knowledge, there has been no formal empirical study of this commonplace phenomenon. Some of the aggregated data described in chapter 20 have a bearing on it.

10. Sweden, Norway, and Denmark are closely similar markets. That Timotei was launched in Denmark nine years after the successful introduction in Sweden and seven years after that in Norway is practical evidence of the independence of local Unilever operating companies.

11. David Kilburn, "Timotei Rises to the Top," *Advertising Age*, November 16, 1987, p. 74.

12. The data in this section come in the main from the analysis made by the JWT International Unilever Unit.

Chapter 13. Diamond Gemstones (De Beers)

1. Thorstein Veblen, *The Theory of the Leisure Class* (Harmondsworth, Middlesex, U.K.: Penguin Books, 1899 and 1979), p. 91.

2. Part of the copy of a De Beers advertisement written by N. W. Ayer in the United States in 1948. Julian Lewis Watkins, *The 100 Greatest Advertisements* (Toronto, Canada: Coles Publishing Company, 1980), p. 176.

3. The only important market where diamonds are sometimes branded is Japan. *Advertising Age Yearbook, 1984* (Chicago: Crain Communications, 1984), pp. 227–28.

4. Godehard Lenzen, *The History of Diamond Production and the Diamond Trade* (New York: Praeger, 1970), p. 12.

5. Communication Research Ltd., *Diamond Advertising Penetration Study in France, Germany and Italy,* February 1987. The growth in the ownership of diamonds in the United States and certain other countries was influenced by the growth in the mail-order engagement-ring business, which was strong in the 1960s.

6. "Even Iran Cannot Spoil Wall Street's Birthday Party," *The Economist*, August 8, 1987, pp. 65–73.

7. De Beers, *International Survey of the Diamond Market*, 1987.

8. Theodore Gregory, *Ernest Oppenheimer and the Economic Development of Southern Africa* (New York: Arno Press, 1977), p. 39.

9. Information in this section comes mainly from Lenzen, *The History of Diamond Production and the Diamond Trade*, chapters 4–7.

10. Ibid., p. 155.

11. Ibid.

12. The information in this section comes from Gregory, *Ernest Oppenheimer and the Economic Development of Southern Africa*, chapters 2–6.

13. Ibid., p. 380.

14. Watkins, *The 100 Greatest Advertisements*, p. 177.

15. Lenzen, *The History of Diamond Production and the Diamond Trade*, p. 196.

16. De Beers, *International Survey of the Diamond Market*, 1987.

17. "The World's 50 Biggest Industrial Corporations," *Fortune*, August 3, 1987, pp. 24–25.

18. Advertising Age Yearbook, 1984, p. 227.

19. "Diamonds Still Dazzle," *New York Times*, November 29, 1987, business section, p. 1.

20. See, for instance, Communication Research Ltd., *Diamond Advertising Penetration Study in France, Germany and Italy*, February 1987.

21. Watkins, *The 100 Greatest Advertisements*, p. 177.

22. Communication Research Ltd., *Diamond Advertising Penetration Study in France, Germany and Italy*, February 1987.

23. De Beers, *International Survey of the Diamond Market*, 1987.

24. *Advertising Age Yearbook*, 1984, pp. 227–28.

Chapter 14. The Discover Card

1. Gordon L. Weil, *Sears, Roebuck, U.S.A.* (New York: Harcourt Brace Jovanovich, 1979), p. 215. This is a comprehensive secondary source. Although Sears cooperated with the author, the book is not an "official history" of the company.

2. The others were Richard Sears (one of the two founders), Julius Rosenwald, and Lessing Rosenwald. Robert E. Wood was not a bogus general. He was educated at West Point but left the U.S. Army as a major. Recalled during the First World War, Wood was eventually promoted to general rank as acting quartermaster-general in Washington—a job that has considerable similarities to running a large retailing organization. Ibid., pp. 112–32.

3. Ibid., p. 115; see also pp. 118, 134–42, 280–83.

4. Ibid., p. 156.

5. Data provided by Sears, Roebuck and Company (speech by Randolph Aires, June 24, 1987).

6. The data are based on *Advertising Age* estimates. The trends in retail advertising are discussed in John Philip Jones, *What's in a Name? Advertising and the Concept of Brands* (Lexington, Mass.: Lexington Books, 1986), chapter 11.

7. Interest paid was fully deductible from federal and state taxes until the end of 1986 but only partially deductible during and after 1987. The eventual total removal of such deductibility as a result of President Reagan's tax reforms may have a serious negative effect on the credit card industry.

8. In March 1987, American Express announced the launch of its Optima card, which offers extended credit and is therefore directly competitive with Discover, MasterCard, and Visa. Significantly, Optima offers lower rates of interest than its competitors—a strong reliance on a discriminating benefit.

9. "Credit-Card War Looms," *Advertising Age*, March 16, 1987, pp. 1, 84.

10. This matter is discussed in detail in Jones, *What's in a Name?*, chapter 6.

11. "Credit-Card War Looms," pp. 1, 84.

12. Laurie Freeman, "JWT, Discover Face Uphill Fight," *Advertising Age*, November 23, 1987, p. 1. Data also provided by Dean Witter Reynolds Inc.

13. This matter is discussed in Jones, *What's in a Name?*, chapter 6.

14. Laurie Freeman and Kate Fitzgerald, "Sears May Hold Winning Card," *Advertising Age*, January 18, 1988, p. 12. Data on dollars per transaction for the Discover Card supplied by Dean Witter Reynolds Inc.

15. Freeman and Fitzgerald, "Sears May Hold Winning Card."

16. Lisabeth Weiner, "Sears Reveals Card Volume for Discover," *American Banker*, March 31, 1988, pp. 1, 14. Data on volume of usage of the Discover Card supplied by Dean Witter Reynolds Inc.

17. Matthew Lewis, "Dusk for Discover at JWT? A Tale of Two Cities Confounds Review for $42 Million Card Account," *Adweek* (August 24, 1987), pp. 1, 8.

18. Stephen King, *Developing New Brands* (London: J. Walter Thompson Company, 1984), p. 25.

19. Freeman and Fitzgerald, "Sears May Hold Winning Card."

Chapter 15. The Ford Escort

1. Theodore Levitt, "Marketing Myopia," *Harvard Business Review* 38 (July-August 1960), p. 51.

2. Ibid.

3. John Kenneth Galbraith, *The New Industrial State* (Harmondsworth, Middlesex, U.K.: Penguin Books, 1978), p. 212.

4. David Halberstam, *The Reckoning* (New York: William Morrow, 1986), p. 528.

5. Ibid., p. 533.

6. Ibid., chapters 32–33.

7. Ibid., pp. 534–35. The Ford Escort is, incidentally, widely thought to resemble the Honda Civic. Brock Yates, *The Decline and Fall of the American Automobile Industry* (New York: Empire Books, 1983), p. 42.

8. Halberstam, *The Reckoning*, p. 513.

9. Lee Iacocca and William Novak, *Iacocca* (New York: Bantam Books, 1984), p. 118. As further evidence of the investment costs in front-wheel drive, it has been reported that the Escort, despite its sales success, was barely profitable in 1985. Robert Lacey, *Ford, the Men and the Machine* (Boston: Little, Brown and Company, 1986), p. 477.

10. "The World's Fifty Biggest Industrial CEOs," *Fortune*, August 3, 1987, p. 24–25.

11. Halberstam, *The Reckoning*, pp. 646–47.

12. Ibid., p. 643.

13. This matter is discussed in John Philip Jones, *What's in a Name? Advertising and the Concept of Brands* (Lexington, Mass.: Lexington Books, 1986), pp. 3–6.

14. Ibid., p. 5.

15. Headline from the launch advertisement for the Ford Escort. *Advertising Age Yearbook, 1982* (Chicago: Crain Books, 1982), p. 147.

16. Yates, *The Decline and Fall of the American Automobile Industry*, p. 274.

17. Ibid., p. 141.

18. Ibid., p. 73.

19. Imports offer generally better resale value than domestically produced cars do. Nevertheless, the Escort has been commended for its good resale value (also for its safety in crashes). Jack Gillis (Director of Public Affairs, Consumer Federation of America), statement on *All Things Considered,* National Public Radio, December 22, 1987.

20. *Advertising Age Yearbook, 1981* (Chicago: Crain Books, 1981), p. 130.

21. Andrew Hacker, ed., *U/S: A Statistical Portrait of the American People* (New York: Viking Press, 1983), pp. 268-69.

22. Alex Taylor III, "Who's Ahead in the World Auto War?" *Fortune,* November 9, 1987, p. 75.

23. Data provided by JWT Detroit.

24. "Special Report on Automotive Marketing," *Advertising Age,* August 10, 1987, p. S-2.

25. This matter is discussed in Jones, *What's in a Name?,* pp. 53–54, 119–20.

26. Ibid., p. 116.

27. Data on this section were supplied by JWT Detroit.

28. Ibid.

29. Yates, *The Decline and Fall of the American Automobile Industry,* page 73.

30. Leon Festinger, "Cognitive Dissonance," *Scientific American,* October 1962, pp. 93–102.

31. Data in this section were provided by JWT Detroit.

32. Ibid.

33. *Advertising Age Yearbook, 1982,* p. 150.

34. According to data published annually by *Advertising Age.*

35. Data supplied by JWT Detroit.

36. See note 9.

37. Taylor, "Who's Ahead in the World Auto War?", pp. 76–77.

38. *Advertising Age Yearbook, 1981,* p. 131.

39. Yates, *The Decline and Fall of the American Automobile Industry,* p. 241.

Chapter 16. Goodyear Corporate

1. Kenneth E. Runyon, *Advertising,* 2nd ed. (Columbus, Ohio: Charles E. Merrill, 1984), p. 579.

2. James Webb Young, *How to Become an Advertising Man* (Chicago: Crain Books, 1963; 1979), p. 54.

3. "The Hundred Leading National Advertisers," *Advertising Age,* September 24, 1987, pp. 110–11.

4. Information in this section comes from *Winning! Brouillard Communications Study of Corporate Reputations and Rewards* (New York: Brouillard Communications, 1986).

5. Ibid., p. 9.

6. Ibid., p. 11.

7. This quotation, together with most of the information in this section, came from a speech by W. L. Newkirk, "On Being Both David and Goliath," given at a *Fortune* seminar in Tucson, Arizona, on March 4, 1986, p. 8.

8. The dangers of using advertising recall are discussed in John Philip Jones, *What's in a Name? Advertising and the Concept of Brands* (Lexington, Mass.: Lexington Books, 1986), chapter 6.

9. "CEO 1,000: A Directory of America's Corporate Elite," *Business Week,* October 23, 1987, p. 195.

10. Newkirk, "On Being Both David and Goliath," p. 17.

11. Ibid., p. 25.

12. Ibid.

13. There is a well-documented published case in which an improvement in public perceptions of a company, the result of effective corporate communications, was accompanied by an increase in the amount of trade in the company's shares and a rise in the stock price. The company in question was the Abex Corporation, formerly the American Brake Shoe Company. See Stephen A. Greyser, *Cases in Advertising and Communications Management,* 2nd ed. (Englewood Cliffs, N.J.: Prentice Hall, 1981), p. 415–46.

14. This matter is discussed in Jones, *What's in a Name?*, p. 177.

Chapter 17. Orkin

1. *Encyclopedia Britannica,* 11th ed. (New York: The Encyclopedia Britannica Publishing Company, 1910), vol. 6, p. 628, and vol. 26, p. 643.

2. Subheading in Orkin brochure, *Subterranean Termite Control Proposal,* 1986.

3. Orkin brochure, *America's Number One Termite Control Program,* 1988, and *Your Orkin Customized Pest Control Program,* 1983.

4. Data in this section come from the standardized survey of professional exterminators by Mediamark Research Inc., spring 1987. It is important to note that the data on usage of professional exterminators are based on responses from individual adults, not households. This fact accounts for the discrepancy between the 2.6 million adults estimated by Mediamark and Orkin's own stated customer base of 1 million households.

5. Copy from Orkin brochure, *Subterranean Termite Control Proposal.*

6. Data from JWT Atlanta.

7. Kenny and Associates Inc., *Research into Creative Strategy Statements, 1986,* pp. 7, 10.

8. Ibid., p. 7.

9. Data in this section were provided by JWT Atlanta.

10. Ibid.

11. This matter is discussed in John Philip Jones, *What's in a Name? Advertising and the Concept of Brands* (Lexington, Mass.: Lexington Books, 1986), chapters 8–9. In the endnotes are extensive references to other published studies.

Chapter 18. The Trustee Savings Banks

1. Quoted in *Aberdeen Savings Bank: Its History from 1815 to 1965* (Aberdeen, Scotland: Aberdeen University Press, 1967), p. 3.

2. Ibid., p. 10.

3. Ibid., p. 3.

4. Their situation was different from that of savings and loan banks in the United States, whose assets have been largely invested in private real estate mortgages, many at low fixed interest rates. The illiquidity of these mortgages, in addition to their low or negative profitability, has contributed to the desperate problems that are currently assailing the American "thrifts." See "Thrifts: America's Own Minefield," *The Economist,* August 15–21, 1987, pp. 60–62.

5. George Pitcher, "TSB Steps Back from Investors," *The Observer,* April 26, 1987.

6. Financial Research Services (a Division of NOP Market Research Ltd.), *Bank Account Report, Great Britain,* October 1986–March 1987, p. 19.

7. Data in this paragraph come in the main from Millward Brown, *Bank Advertising Tracking Study,* March to May 1987.

8. Data from Media Expenditure Analysis Ltd.

9. John Philip Jones, "New TSB Advertising," *TSB Management Magazine,* January 1979, p. 203.

10. Ian W. Lindsey and John Philip Jones, "Finding a Growth Sector in Hard Times: The TSB Trustcard," *Admap,* December 1980, pp. 616–622.

11. Data provided by TSB.

12. In the spring of 1987, 42 percent of the public as a whole (47 percent of TSB customers) could spontaneously recall the slogan "We like to say yes." This was a very high level in comparison with the campaigns for other banks. Millward Brown, *Bank Advertising Tracking Study,* March to May 1987. The reader should, however, remember the problems with the use of recall as a measure of advertising effectiveness. See John Philip Jones, *What's in a Name? Advertising and the Concept of Brands,* (Lexington, Mass.: Lexington Books, 1986), chapter 6.

13. The data in this section come from Jeremy Elliott, *TSB's School Leaver Campaign, 1984–85,* submission for the IPA Advertising Effectiveness Awards, June 1986.

Chapter 19. The United States Marine Corps

1. Samuel W. Meek (former first lieutenant, USMC), "The Yalie at Soissons," in Henry Berry, *Make the Kaiser Dance* (New York: Arbor House, 1978), p. 95.

2. In World War II, *Semper Fidelis* was contracted into *Semper Fi* by the marines in the Pacific Theater and used as a catchphrase to say, "Take care of yourself out there" or, "Protect your hindquarters." Henry Berry, *Semper Fi, Mac* (New York: Arbor House, 1984), p. 13.

3. Data on the history of the USMC come from *Funk and Wagnalls New Encyclopedia* (New York: Funk and Wagnalls, 1979), vol. 24, pp. 17–18.

4. Slogan from USMC advertising during the 1970s and 1980s.

5. Burke Market Research, *Marine Recruiting Study*, August 1985 (BMR no. 52-856), pp. 8, 13.

6. Burke Market Research, *Marine Recruiting Study*, p. 11.

7. Nancy M. Ostrove, Robert M. Bray, Henrick J. Harwood, Sara C. Wheeless, and Elizabeth R. Cavanaugh, *Youth Attitude Tracking Study, Fall 1986* (RTI/ 3624/06-02FR, June 1987).

8. Ibid., p. 1–10.

9. Burke Market Research, *Marine Recruiting Study*, pp. 1, 19.

10. Ibid., p. 2.

11. Ostrove et al., *Youth Attitude Tracking Study*, p. 5–2.

12. Ibid., p. 6–7.

13. Ibid., p. 7–2.

14. Burke Market Research, *Marine Recruiting Study*, p. 22.

15. Ostrove et al., *Youth Attitude Tracking Study*, p. 1–2. Data on advertising budgets provided by JWT Atlanta.

16. Slogan from USMC advertising during the 1970s and 1980s.

17. Burke Market Research, *Marine Recruiting Study*, p. 14.

18. Data provided by JWT Atlanta.

19. Ostrove et al., *Youth Attitude Tracking Study*, p. 4–9.

20. Ibid., especially pp. 1–8, 4–10, 4–17, and 5–2.

21. Discussed in John Philip Jones, *What's in a Name? Advertising and the Concept of Brands* (Lexington, Mass.: Lexington Books, 1986), chapter 6.

22. Burke Market Research, *Marine Recruiting Study*, pp. 37, 43.

23. See also Jones, *What's in a Name?* chapter 11.

Chapter 20. A Bird's-Eye View of a Thousand Brands

1. John Maynard Keynes, *The General Theory of Employment, Interest and Money* (New York: Harcourt Brace Jovanovich, 1964), p. 40.

2. John Philip Jones, *What's in a Name? Advertising and the Concept of Brands* (Lexington, Mass.: Lexington Books, 1986), pp. 8, 247, 263.

3. James O. Peckham, Sr., *The Wheel of Marketing* (privately published but available through A. C. Nielsen, 1978), p. 73.

4. See, for instance, Nariman K. Dhalla and Sonia Yuspeh, "Forget the Product Life Cycle Concept," *Harvard Business Review* 54 (January-February 1976), p. 102.

5. Jones, *What's in a Name?* pp. 86, 114, 126.

6. A classic analysis of this tendency can be found in the essay by Friedrich August von Hayek, "The Meaning of Competition," in *Individualism and Economic Order* (Chicago: University of Chicago Press, 1948), pp. 92–106.

7. Jones, *What's in a Name?* chapter 11.

Chapter 21. The Search for General Patterns

1. *The Encyclopedia Britannica,* 11th ed. (New York: The Encyclopedia Britannica Company, 1910), vol. 14, p. 502.

2. This phenomenon is also demonstrated with Kellogg's Coco Pops in Britain. See Jill Greenop, "Kellogg's Coco Pops: a 'Story Book' Success," in *Advertising Works 3: Papers from the IPA Advertising Effectiveness Awards,* Charles Channon, ed. (London: Holt, Rinehart and Winston, 1985) pp. 212–26.

3. Campbell's Soup in the United States provides another excellent example of this strategy. Christine Dugas, Mark N. Vamos, Jonathan B. Levine, and Mark Rothman, "Marketing's New Look," *Business Week,* January 26, 1987, pp. 64–69.

4. See, for instance, Peter F. Drucker, "The Coming of the New Organization," *Harvard Business Review 66,* (January-February 1988), pp. 45–53.

5. Martin Mayer, *Madison Avenue, U.S.A.* (New York: Harper and Brothers, 1958), p. 71.

6. Famous observation attributed to Stanley Resor.

7. Simon Broadbent, "American Practice and Lessons for Brits," *Admap,* June 1988, pp. 25–28.

8. James O. Peckham, Sr., *The Wheel of Marketing* (privately published but available from A. C. Nielsen, 1978), pp. 80–91.

9. William M. Weilbacher, *Advertising,* 2nd ed., (New York: Macmillan, 1984), p. 69.

10. Booz, Allen and Hamilton, quoted by William M. Weilbacher in *Auditing Productivity* (New York: Association of National Advertisers, 1981), p. 14.

11. Mayer, *Madison Avenue, U.S.A.,* p. 77.

12. "Middle Managers Face Extinction," *Economist,* January 23, 1988, p. 59.

13. Drucker, "The Coming of the New Organization," pp. 47–48.

14. A widely-read and by no means extreme expression of the value of global marketing from the manufacturer's viewpoint can be found in Theodore Levitt, "The Globalization of Markets," *The Marketing Imagination* (New York: Free Press, 1983), pp. 20–49.

15. The importance of the consumer is demonstrated with considerable force by Harold F. Clark, Jr., in "Consumer and Corporate Values: Yet Another View on Global Marketing," *International Journal of Advertising,* vol. 6, no. 1, 1987, pp. 29–42. Another enlightening contribution to the debate is made by Greg Harris in "The Globalization of Advertising," *International Journal of Advertising,* vol. 3, no. 3, 1984, pp. 223–34.

16. See John Philip Jones, *What's in a Name? Advertising and the Concept of Brands* (Lexington, Mass.: Lexington Books, 1986), p. 104.

17. First described by Andrew Ehrenberg; discussed in Jones, *What's in a Name?,* chapter 5.

18. However, there are published cases, including those which feature the work of JWT, to demonstrate a most sophisticated use of econometric techniques. See, for instance, Jeremy Elliott, "Kellogg's Corn Flakes: Adding Values to the Brand," commended paper in the 1980 IPA *Advertising Effectiveness Awards;* "Kellogg's Rice Krispies: The Effect of a New Creative Execution," in *Advertising Works: Papers*

from the IPA *Advertising Effectiveness Awards,* Simon Broadbent, ed. (London: Holt, Rinehart and Winston, 1981), pp. 78–88; and "Breaking the Bran Barrier: Kellogg's Bran Flakes, 1982–84," in *Advertising Works 3: Papers from the IPA Advertising Effectiveness Awards,* Charles Channon, ed. (London: Holt, Rinehart and Winston, 1985), pp. 55–69. In the last collection, see also Evelyn Jenkins, "Fulfilling the Potential of St. Ivel Gold," pp. 105–16, and Terry Bullen, "Kraft Dairylea: The Transformation of a Brand's Fortunes," pp. 198–211.

19. Interesting data on brands that have maintained brand leadership in the United States (over a sixty-year period) and the United Kingdom (over a fifty-year period) are in Steve Winram, "The Opportunity for World Brands," *International Journal of Advertising,* vol. 3, no. 1, 1984, pp. 17–26.

20. Discussed in Jones, *What's in a Name?,* pp. 149–50.

21. Broadbent, "American Practice and Lessons for Brits."

Chapter 22. Does It Pay to Advertise?

1. Martin Mayer, *Madison Avenue, U.S.A.* (New York: Harper and Brothers, 1958), p. 312.

2. David Ogilvy, *Confessions of an Advertising Man* (New York: Atheneum, 1984), p. 59.

3. Simon Broadbent, "Price and Advertising: Volume and Profit," *Admap,* November 1980, p. 536.

4. Nariman K. Dhalla, "Assessing the Long Term Value of Advertising," *Harvard Business Review* 56 (January-February 1978), pp. 87–95.

5. The formula for determining the Profitability Barrier is as follows:

$$\text{Profitability Barrier} = \frac{\text{A:S Ratio}}{\text{Advertising Elasticity.}}$$

If the A:S ratio is 5 percent and the advertising elasticity is 0.40, the Profitability Barrier is 12.5 percent. The validity of this measure can be tested by the following arithmetical example.

a. Assume an arbitrary sales level, for example, $100,000,000.

b. Assume an A:S ratio, for example, 5 percent, which yields a basic advertising budget of $5,000,000.

c. Take a typical advertising-elasticity coefficient, for example, 0.40.

d. If advertising is reduced by 10 percent ($500,000), sales will be reduced by 4 percent ($4,000,000).

e. In these circumstances, if the brand's net profit ratio is 12.5 percent, the loss of profit will be $500,000, equaling the advertising saving—leading to a break-even situation.

f. If the brand's net profit ratio is 10 percent, the loss of profit will be $400,000, which is less than the advertising saving, demonstrating that it pays to reduce advertising.

g. If, by contrast, the brand's net profit ratio is 15 percent, the loss of profit will be $600,000, demonstrating that the advertising should not be cut back. If we now increase the advertising by 10 percent ($500,000), sales will go up by 4 percent ($4,000,000). With a 15 percent net profit ratio, the increase in net profit will be $600,000, which is higher than the cost of the extra advertising, demonstrating that it pays to increase advertising.

6. This complex and controversial matter is discussed in John Philip Jones, *What's in a Name? Advertising and the Concept of Brands* (Lexington, Mass.: Lexington Books, 1986), p. 261.

7. This more or less describes the situation in the U.S. tobacco industry when cigarette advertising was removed from the television screen in early 1971.

8. Russell L. Ackoff and James R. Emshoff, "Advertising Research at Anheuser-Busch," *Sloane Management Review*, winter 1975, pp. 1–15.

9. A published case demonstrates this situation, the brand in question being Kellogg's Bran Flakes in Britain. Jeremy Elliott, "Breaking the Bran Barrier: Kellogg's Bran Flakes 1982–84," in *Advertising Works 3: Papers from the IPA Advertising Effectiveness Awards*, Charles Channon, ed. (London: Holt, Rinehart and Winston, 1985) pp. 212–26.

10. Mayer, *Madison Avenue U.S.A.*, p. 309.

Afterword

1. Walker Gibson, "Authors, Speakers, Readers, and Mock Readers," in *Reader-Response Criticism: From Formalism to Post-Structuralism*, ed. Jane P. Tompkins (Baltimore and London: Johns Hopkins University Press, 1986). This is a vitally important collection of essays that chart the thinking of literary critics on the whole process of reading and response.

2. *Business Week*, May 23, 1988, pp. 172–73.

3. Ibid., p. 63.

4. Gibson, "Authors, Speakers, Readers, and Mock Readers," p. 1.

5. Thomas A. Harris, *I'm OK—You're OK* (London: Pan Books, 1973).

6. Ibid., p. 20.

7. Ibid., p. 26.

8. Ibid., p. 34.

9. Ibid., p. 63.

10. A much-expanded description of these kinds of communication patterns can be found in Harris, *I'm OK—You're OK*, pp. 62–83. My summary highlights the principles; the text is filled with rich examples.

Index

About the Author

Born in Wales in 1930, **John Philip Jones** graduated in economics from Cambridge University (B.A. with Honors 1953; M.A. 1957).

From 1953 to 1980, he worked in the advertising agency field. This experience included twenty-five years with J. Walter Thompson as a market research executive in London (1953–55); advertising account executive in London (1957–65); account supervisor and head of television in Amsterdam (1965–67); account director and head of account service in Scandinavia (1967–72); and account director in London (1972–80). He worked on a wide variety of accounts, *inter alia* Lux Toilet Soap (as international account director).

From 1980 Mr. Jones has been a tenured full professor of the Newhouse School of Public Communications, Syracuse University, New York. He is also a member of the Mellon Foundation project team, which for two years explored the interconnections between liberal and professional education. (A book describing the project, *Contesting the Boundaries of Liberal and Professional Education,* was published by the Syracuse University Press in 1988.) He is a member of the Chancellor's Panel on the Future of Syracuse University and an editor of the *Syracuse Scholar,* an interdisciplinary journal of ideas.

Mr. Jones has published in a variety of business and professional publications, including *Admap,* and the *International Journal of Advertising* (Guest Editor of a United States issue, 1987). He wrote *What's in a Name? Advertising and the Concept of Brands* published by Lexington Books in 1986.